Time Out

Vienna

www.timeout.com

D1296067

Guides

Time Out Digital Ltd
4th Floor
125 Shaftesbury Avenue
London WC2H 8AD
United Kingdom
Tel: +44 (0)20 7813 3000
Fax: +44 (0)20 7813 6001
Email: guides@timeout.com
www.timeout.com

Published by Time Out Digital Ltd, a wholly owned subsidiary
of Time Out Group Ltd. Time Out and the Time Out logo are
trademarks of Time Out Group Ltd.

© Time Out Group Ltd 2015
Previous editions 2000, 2003, 2005, 2007, 2011.

10 9 8 7 6 5 4 3 2 1

This edition first published in Great Britain in 2015 by Ebury Publishing.
20 Vauxhall Bridge Road, London SW1V 2SA

Ebury Publishing is part of the Penguin Random House group of companies
whose addresses can be found at global.penguinrandomhouse.com

Distributed in the US and Latin America by Publishers Group West
(1-510-809-3700)

For further distribution details, see www.timeout.com.

ISBN: 978-1-84670-358-4

A CIP catalogue record for this book is available from the British Library.

Printed and bound in China by Leo Paper Products Ltd.

MIX
Paper from
responsible sources
FSC
www.fsc.org   FSC® C018179

Contents

11

154

181

Essential Information 208

Maps 238

217

Time Out Vienna

Editorial
Editor Peterjon Cresswell
Consultant Editor Geraint Williams
Copy Editor Dominic Earle
Listings Editor Maite Bachero
Indexer Patrick Davis
Proofreader Jo Willacy

Editorial Director Sarah Guy
Group Finance Manager Margaret Wright

Design
Art Editor Christie Webster
Designer Alaa Alsaraji
Group Commercial Senior Designer Jason Tansley

Production
Production Controller Katie Mulhern-Bhudia

Picture Desk
Picture Editor Jael Marschner
Deputy Picture Editor Ben Rowe
Picture Researcher Lizzy Owen

Advertising
Managing Director St John Betteridge

Marketing
Senior Publishing Brand Manager Luthfa Begum
Head of Circulation Dan Collins

Time Out Group
Founder Tony Elliott
President Noel Penzer
Publisher Alex Batho

Contributors
Peterjon Cresswell, Geraint Williams, Christopher Green (Gay & Lesbian), Rob Jessup (Nightlife) and Matthew Marth (Classical Music, Itineraries: Musical Vienna).

The editor would like to thank Cormac Doyle for mapping assistance and all contributors to previous editions of *Time Out Vienna*, whose work forms the basis for parts of this book.

Maps JS Graphics Ltd (john@jsgraphics.co.uk)

Cover and pull-out map photography © imageimage/Alamy

Back cover photography Clockwise from top left: Phillip Horak, PHB.cz (Richard Semik)/Shutterstock.com, Burgtheater/Georg Soulek, Javier Martin/Shutterstock.com, Adsy Bernart

Photography pages 5 (top), 63, 145, 148, 149, 152, 154, 155 Adsy Bernart; 10/11 Seth Weiner; 13 © Belvedere, Vienna; 16 Studio Huger; 17 Roman Bönsch/ÖBB/aerial Redl; 20 Tatiana Volgutova/Shutterstock.com; 21 (top), 68/69 Radiokafka/Shutterstock.com; 21 (bottom), 151 Philip Martin Rusch; 23 (bottom) Brendan Howard/ Shutterstock.com; 24 (top) Javier Martin/Shutterstock.com; 25 (top) David Peters; 25 (bottom) Eva Kelety; 26/27 Nataliya Nazarova/Shutterstock.com; 27 Jeroen Komen/Wikimedia Commons; 28 (top) Michael Poehn; 28 (bottom) Monika Rittershaus; 29, 144, 146 Life Ball/© Harald Klemm; 30 (top) Robert Newald; 30 (bottom) Christian Husar; 32/33 (top) APA-Fotodienst/Picturedesk/Ian Ehm; 34, 115 Shane Mulhall; 35, 132/133, 162, 164, 165 Wiener Staatsoper/Michael Poehn; 36/37 Dafinka/Shutterstock.com; 38 © Lee Miller Archives England 2015; 41 Philip Bird LRPS CPAGB/Shutterstock.com; 44 © Weite Welt/Rudi Froese; 54 Arnold Poeschl; 57 (left) © Albertina, Vienna - Batliner Collection © VBK, Wien 2009; 57 (right) Albertina, Vienna - Batliner Collection; 64, 65 © Christoph Panzer; 66 © Birgit und Peter Kainz; 67 Exhibition Insight Leopold Museum, Vienna © Leopold Museum/Bildit; 74 Peterjon Cresswell; 77, 78 dinkaspell/Shutterstock.com; 84 Stefan Joham; 88 © Margherita Spiluttini; 88/89 Igor Plotnikov/Shutterstock.com; 99 (bottom) graphia/Shutterstock.com; 106, 108 Gerhard Berthold; 116 Sigmund Freud Foundation/Florian Lierzer; 116/117, 124/125 Jorg Hackemann/Shutterstock.com; 123 Halberstadt; 135 Alexandra Eizinger; 137 Copyright Schmetterlinghaus; 139 Jutta Kirchner; 142 © OeFM/Hertha Hurnaus; 143 Snap Stills/REX Shutterstock; 156, 157 Alexander Biedermann; 163 Lukas Beck/Wiener Konzerthaus; 167 (top) © Lukas Beck; 167 (bottom) © Judith Schlosser; 168 Franz Zwickl; 170, 171 Burgtheater/Georg Soulek; 176 Creativemarc/ Shutterstock.com; 186/187 badahos/Shutterstock.com; 188/189 Popperfoto/Getty Images; 190 Hans Part/ Wikimedia Commons; 195 Wikimedia Commons; 196 Coyau/Wikimedia Commons; 198 IMAGNO/Austrian Archives/ Getty Images; 199 Ferdinand Schmutzer/Wikimedia Commons; 201 Bundesarchiv/Wikimedia Commons; 202 Buchhändler/Wikimedia Commons; 206 (left) Helmut Baar/Getty Images; 206 (right) Schleyer/ullstein bild/ Getty Images; 210, 216 © Meliá Hotels; 213 Gerald Berghammer; 214 AnnABlaU; 218, 219 Franz Pfluegl; 220 © Caritas Vienna

The following images were supplied by the featured establishments: pages 5 (bottom), 12 (top), 14, 15, 22, 45, 46/47, 48, 51, 59, 60, 73, 80, 81, 87, 91, 95, 113, 131, 134, 140, 141, 158, 160, 161, 169, 172, 173, 204, 207, 208/209, 211, 212, 217

About the Guide

GETTING AROUND
Each sightseeing chapter contains a street map of the area marked with the locations of sights and museums (❶), restaurants and coffeehouses (❶), cafés, pubs and bars (❶) and shops (❶). There are also street maps of Vienna at the back of the book, along with an overview map of the city. In addition, there is a detachable fold-out street map.

THE ESSENTIALS
For practical information, including visas, disabled access, emergency numbers, lost property, websites and local transport, see the Essential Information section. It begins on page 208.

THE LISTINGS
Addresses, phone numbers, websites, transport information, hours and prices are all included in our listings, as are selected other facilities. All were checked and correct at press time. However, business owners can alter their arrangements at any time, and fluctuating economic conditions can cause prices to change rapidly.

The very best venues in the city, the must-sees and must-dos in every category, have been marked with a red star (★). In the sightseeing chapters, we've also marked venues with free admission with a FREE symbol.

THE LANGUAGE
Many Viennese, especially younger people, speak good English, but learning a few basic Austrian German phrases will go a long way. You'll find a primer on page 231 to get you started, along with some help with restaurant ordering.

PHONE NUMBERS
The area code for Vienna is 01. You don't need to use the code when calling from within Vienna; simply dial the number as listed in this guide. From outside Austria, dial your country's international access code (00 from the UK, 011 from the US) or a plus symbol, followed by the Austrian country code (43), then 1 and the number as listed in this guide. So, to reach the Schloss Schönbrunn, dial + 431 811 13-239. For more on phones, see p229.

FEEDBACK
We welcome feedback on this guide, both on the venues we've included and on any other locations that you'd like to see featured in future editions. Please email us at guides@timeout.com.

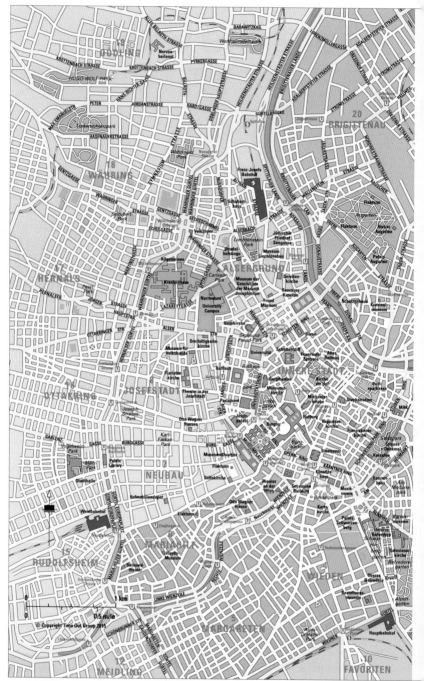

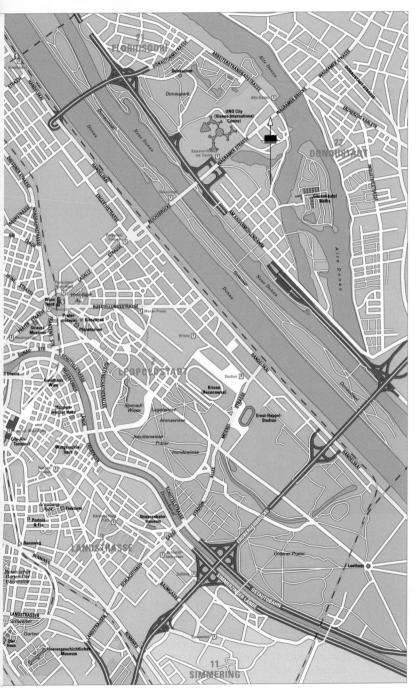

Vienna's
Top 20

From big wheels to Baroque palaces, we count down the capital's finest.

1 Wiener Riesenrad
(page 85)

Vienna's giant wheel will forever be known as the one that rotates behind Orson Welles and Joseph Cotten in *The Third Man*. Amazingly, for nearly 40 years after that black-and-white Cold War drama, the Riesenrad remained the world's tallest Ferris wheel. Today, you can hire luxury cabins by the hour – and it stays operational and illuminated until late.

2 MAK
(page 77)

One of the first of its kind in the world, the Museum of Applied Arts (Museum für Angewandte Kunst/Gegenswartskunst or simply MAK for short) is akin to a mini Viennese equivalent of London's V&A Museum. There's contemporary art, architecture and design aplenty – plus fascinating temporary exhibitions that have recently ranged from the creative impulses of 20th-century Bucharest to the works of German graphic designer Christoph Niemann.

③

3 Hofburg
(page 53)

The grounds of this former imperial palace are open to the public 24 hours a day. Individual attractions, such as the Spanish Riding School and the Secular & Sacred Treasury, charge a separate (and pricey) admission. It's still the workplace and residence of the Austrian president, and has been the seat of government since the late 13th century. Other attractions include the Museum of Art History and the Sisi Museum.

4 Leopold Museum
(page 73)

One of the largest collections of modern Austrian art in the world – and, in the case of Egon Schiele, the largest bar none – is housed in this landmark gallery. Admire works by the likes of Klimt and Kokoschka, as well as temporary exhibitions. In 2015, works by Tracey Emin and the German Expressionists brought in the crowds.

5 Wien Museum
(page 98)

The history of the city told in entertaining detail, starting with a room full of the medieval statues that once embellished Stephansdom, taking in the Turkish Siege of 1683, and outlining Vienna's modern urban development during the 18th and 19th centuries. There are even a handful of paintings by Klimt, plenty of artefacts from the Biedermeier period and furniture that belonged to modernist architect Adolf Loos.

6 Stephansdom
(page 41)

'Steffl' survived the Turkish sieges, Napoleon's assaults and the Allied bombing of World War II. First created in early medieval times, the cathedral gained its signature steep, multi-coloured roof centuries later. Stephansdom is also characterised by its four towers. The tallest, the south tower, provides commanding views of the Vienna skyline; while the north holds the huge Pummerin bell that ushers in the New Year. Among the relics in the catacombs are the remains of Prince Eugène of Savoy, hero of the 1683 Siege, and Duke Rudolf IV, who extended the church in the 1300s.

7 Kaisergruft
(page 46)

Eerie and always extremely popular,
the Kaisergruft is where nearly all of
the Habsburgs were laid to rest after 1633.
Ranged in chronological order around the
dark and extensive crypt of the Church
of the Capuchins, the dusty tomb of
each royal bears a name and a date, with
tourists dutifully trooping past in silence
and at a respectful distance. Franz Josef
dominates the room dedicated to him,
flanked by his wife and only son.

8 Secession
(page 98)

'To each time its art, to art its freedom'
runs the famous legend above the
entrance of this monument to the
Secessionist era, built to house the
exhibitions to be staged by those artists
who seceded from the conservative
Künstlerhaus in 1896. Its most stunning
exhibit is the famous *Beethoven Frieze* by
Gustav Klimt, who himself seceded from
the Secessionists shortly after creating it.
Some 34 metres (111 feet) long, it occupies
its own climate-controlled room in the
basement, with long benches in front
for visitors to sit and work out Klimt's
interpretation of the 'Ninth Symphony'.

9 Belvedere
(page 94)

Vast, sumptuous and still with a glorious
view across to Vienna, the Baroque
Belvedere was built as the summer
residence of Prince Eugène of Savoy
by Johann Lukas von Hildebrandt. It
comprises two main palaces, the Lower
Belvedere and Upper Belvedere. Today,
the latter houses the most comprehensive
collection of works by Gustav Klimt.
There's loads more to see apart from
The Kiss, with pieces by contemporary
artists such as Jeff Koons and Marina
Abramović scattered between sections
dedicated to medieval, impressionist
and romantic art.

10 MUMOK
(page 75)

MUMOK houses Vienna's most
important collection of contemporary
art. There are 10,000 pieces in all, with a
particular focus on American pop art by
the likes of Jasper Johns, Andy Warhol
and Roy Lichtenstein. There are also
expressionist works by Richard Gerstl
and Oskar Kokoschka, surrealist works
by Max Ernst and René Magritte, and an
overview of the simply bizarre movement
known as Viennese Actionism, whose
creations led to arrests in some cases.

11 Schönbrunn
(page 126)

Vienna's most popular tourist
destination was the summer residence
of the Habsburg royals for nearly
200 years – Franz Josef was born and
died there. Although no architectural
masterpiece, Schönbrunn's sheer scale
can't fail to impress, with its 1,400 rooms
set among vast, free-to-enter parkland
and gardens, former hunting and
recreation grounds. The Imperial Tour
provides access to the private rooms

here that Mozart composed *The Marriage of Figaro* during the 1780s. On display are an assortment of instruments, original sheet music, paintings of Mozart and his family, as well as all kinds of interactive audiovisual exhibits that tell the story of Wolfgang Amadeus, his work and his influence.

14 Jüdisches Museum
(page 50)

This excellent museum in Dorotheergasse tells the story of Vienna's Jewish community. At its centre is a compelling permanent exhibition, 'Our City!', unveiled in 2013. It tells the little-known story of Jews in Vienna from 1945 until the setting-up of modern-day Austria ten years later, and the terrible struggles they faced even after the end of Nazism. A visit can be combined with the nearby Museum Judenplatz, which is set around the ruins of Vienna's medieval synagogue, with Rachel Whiteread's austere monument to the Holocaust above ground.

of Franz Josef and his wife, Elisabeth of Bavaria, and the bed in which the old emperor died.

12 Zentralfriedhof
(page 129)

Some of the most illustrious figures in classical music lie here for eternity, including Beethoven, Brahms, Schubert and the Strauss clan. All in all, there are more than two million graves, with areas dedicated to Soviet soldiers who died in the Liberation of Vienna in 1945 and Austrians who fell fighting the Nazis. There's also an old Jewish section, with members of the Rothschilds, but parts are sadly overgrown and desecrated.

13 Mozarthaus Wien
(page 40)

The only remaining residence of Mozart's many Viennese addresses, the Mozarthaus reopened as a museum in 2006, exactly 250 years after the day of his birth. Locals also know the building as the Figarohaus, as it was

15 Kunsthalle Wien
(page 73)

Another MuseumsQuartier heavyweight, the Kunsthalle Wien has no permanent collection and so deals only in temporary exhibitions. With the MUMOK and the Leopold Museum set on either side, it has to pull out a few stops to bring in the punters. Challenging, thought-provoking contemporary shows fill the agenda, complemented by regular curator's tours and Sunday visits guided by experts. It's also central to the monthly MQ art night around the big hitters of the MuseumsQuartier.

16 Albertina
(page 56)

The Albertina museum was originally built on the city's historic fortifications, and housed the graphic and print collection of Duke Albert of Teschen in the late 1700s, one of the largest and finest of its kind in the world. Expanded by his various successors, the collection passed to the Republic of Austria after World War I. Heavily bombed during World War II, the collection was eventually rehoused under a controversial roof created by Hans Hollein in 2008. Drawings by Rembrandt, Dürer and Raphael are among the highlights. You can also visit the 21 Habsburg state rooms in the same complex, ranged around the magnificent Hall of the Muses.

17 Spanische Reitschule
(page 56)

The Spanish Riding School is a pricey but popular tourist attraction, set in Fischer von Erlach's Baroque winter riding hall in the Hofburg. The morning training session allows you to see the magnificent Lipizzaner horses on their rounds – admission to the shows later in the day can run to well over €100. This is classical dressage at its most rigorous and disciplined, so don't expect anything too showy or spectacular.

18 Parlament
(page 69)

Facing the Imperial Palace, the Austrian Parliament was opened when Vienna was at the height of its pomp. Designed in Greek Revival style by Theophil Hansen, who had studied Byzantine architecture in Athens, it was heavily damaged in World War II and later restored to its original

splendour. A visitors' centre allows you to enter the building at the front at street level and admire the magnificent stucco work and statuary.

19 Sigmund Freud Museum
(page 122)

Set in the apartment where the father of psychoanalysis, Sigmund Freud, lived and worked for 40 years before leaving Nazi-ruled Vienna, this museum is filled with all manner of artefacts: the tins of cocaine Freud would use, his travel rug, a dateline map of his many jaunts, and scores of photographs, letters and diplomas, all clearly documented and put into the context of Freud's life and career.

20 Staatsoper
(page 165)

The Vienna State Opera was the first major building on the new Ringstrasse in the 1860s. Czech architect Josef Hlávka built what was first called the Vienna Court Opera in neo-renaissance style according to plans by August Sicard von Sicardsburg and Eduard van der Null, neither of whom lived to attend the opening in the presence of Franz Josef. Rebuilt in the same style after Allied bombardment, today the State Opera has one of the largest repertoires in the world.

Vienna Today

Friday in mid July and the temperature is over the 30-degree mark. In Vienna's city centre, tourists clutch their bottles of Alpine-quality tap water and the locals check their watches to see when they can legitimately down tools. Soon they'll be heading for one of the city's 30-odd public swimming pools, the beaches of the Danube or out of town completely, as 38 per cent of the population do on an average weekend. The remaining 62 per cent spend the evenings at the bars along the Danube Canal or the Gürtel, catch a film at an alfresco screening or sup a few spritzers at the *heurigen* (wine taverns) among the vineyards overlooking the city. Indeed, before World War II and the austerity of reconstruction put it on hold, Vienna's culture, especially in summer, was one of the bucolic, wine-drinking, music-making variety, albeit with an unhealthy dose of melancholy thrown in. Today, despite the trials of modern life, the easternmost city of the West is as attached as ever to its earthly pleasures and leisurely pace of life. And this in itself is one of the best reasons to visit.

Since the fall of the Berlin Wall in 1989 and Austria's entry into the European Union in 1994, Vienna has become increasingly more vibrant and varied than the stodgy imperial capital of old, in whose magnificent carcass it's forced to live and face the future. As a grand city bereft of many of its former citizens, Vienna is fortunate to have space at its disposal to accommodate the growth it has experienced during the last 15 years. Some 250,000 extra people have moved into the city since 2000 – equal to the entire population of Austria's second city, Graz.

By the start of 2015, Vienna was home to 1.8 million citizens – a figure last attained in 1934 – making it the second largest German-speaking city after Berlin. Indeed, this is a place that can comfortably accommodate a much larger population, as it did before

World War I when, as the capital of a vast, multinational empire, more than two million people called it home. Away from the tourist hotspots of the Innere Stadt or the shopping enclave of Mariahilfer Strasse, today's latest growth spurt is barely noticeable. The trams and underground are busier these days, sure, but outside the centre Vienna's beautifully appointed streets remain strangely empty, often devoid of activity but brimming with allusions to the past.

COSMOPOLITAN CONUNDRUM
Having ridden the worst of the financial crises so far, Austria's economy is in comparatively good health and its universities are virtually cost-free. For these two reasons, Vienna is attracting EU citizens in droves, particularly from Germany, but also from Hungary,

Slovakia and the former Yugoslavia, adding to the city's established Turkish population. This is perceptible in the babble of languages on the streets, in the range of national speciality restaurants and, inevitably, in the increasingly large numbers of Eastern European beggars. What many commentators celebrate as the city's rekindling of its former cosmopolitan status as Europe's original multicultural capital, others of a more nostalgic bent view as a sign of decline.

For many, however, Vienna can do no wrong. In 2015, Mercer Consulting put it at the top of its list of the world's most liveable cities for the sixth year in a row. It's easy to be cynical about such executive-lifestyle studies, with their emphasis on the availability of international schools and high-end properties to rent, but Mercer's findings point to tangible advantages that benefit the population as a whole. Thanks to the Greens, a year's pass for the whole public transport network works out at just a euro a day, and the sight of unaccompanied primary school kids on the underground indicates a level of safety that few other cities can boast. As the

Financial Times put it recently: 'The standard of living Vienna offers is exceptional – and not just for Russian oligarchs.'

SOCIAL SUCCESS

The responsibility for Vienna's equitable standard of living lies fairly and squarely on the shoulders of 70 years of municipal government led by the Social Democrats, the SPÖ. The outstanding provision of public services – social housing and rent control, public transport, leisure facilities and education – has long ensured the SPÖ's hegemony in Vienna. However, in the 2010 municipal elections, they failed to achieve an overall majority and were forced into a coalition with the fourth-placed Green Party.

This occasionally acrimonious administration reaches its end in autumn 2015 but has made considerable progress, especially in the field of transport and infrastructure, another of Mercer's criteria. One of the Greens' flagship causes – to pedestrianise the Mariahilfer Strasse shopping drag – was completed in summer 2015 in the face of considerable opposition

Hauptbahnhof. See p18.

(taxi drivers call it the 'Great Wall of China'). On top of this, successful car-sharing projects are up and running, cycle lanes have been expanded and the Hauptbahnhof, the new main railway station, went into operation in 2015. Extensions to the underground network, including an entirely new line, are also underway, one of the measures that convinced climate strategist Boyd Cohen to place Vienna third worldwide in his 2014 Smart Cities Index.

Naturally, environmental issues figure highly in these rankings. With the Greens supplying the ideas and the SPÖ administering the cash, Vienna has gradually built on its historic environmental record. In the 1870s, the city had already ensured the supply of Alpine drinking water, and in the 1970s a district heating system powered by the incineration of household waste began to heat homes all over the city. Strict zoning laws have long protected the Vienna Woods green belt from the attention of developers. More recently, important investments have been made in carbon-neutral buses, an advanced sewage treatment system and solar power stations.

The SPÖ's role has focused on the provision of public housing – a cornerstone of Vienna's enduringly high standard of living and the party's principal vote-catcher. Now nearing completion, the most ambitious project is the Urban Lakeside (Seestadt) project, a whole new district in the north-east housing 20,000 people. It's built around an artificial lake and has its own U-Bahn station.

TAXES AND REFUGEES

Another successful project is the St Marx eco-cluster in the 3rd district where more than 15,000 people will be living and working by 2016. The real bonus of these projects is that private developers must, by law, make substantial contributions to the public infrastructure and amenities that such developments require.

Critics point to the SPÖ's appetite for collecting taxes and profligate use of public funds. *The Economist* has pinpointed a trend among multinationals to eschew Vienna for less costly Central European capitals such as Prague or Warsaw. On the subject of taxation, the *Financial Times* quoted the Head of Research for Austria's Raiffeisen Bank International: 'We are among the top five highest in Europe, even surpassing Sweden in terms of tax and social security contributions. At 43.5 per cent, these are roughly ten per cent higher than the European average'.

Vienna's thrice-elected mayor, Michael Häupl, has more pressing problems than the whims of penny-pinching corporations, though. Despite the return to its multicultural roots, all is not well in Red Vienna. The right-wing, foreigner-baiting Freedom Party (FPÖ) came a strong second in the 2010 municipal elections with more than 25 per cent of the vote, and its perma-tanned leader HC Strache is proving to be an able manipulator of traditional disaffected SPÖ voters. Tapping into legitimate concerns over rising unemployment and channelling resentment against asylum seekers, Strache's tactic of playing on fears of loss of identity and the vilification of Muslims is likely to score highly in the coming elections.

In the wake of the Syrian refugee crisis, the FPÖ's rhetoric has intensified: a regional FPÖ chief described refugees as 'cavemen', while party supporters in Vienna greeted newly arrived families with placards telling them they're not welcome. Despite occasional calls from party leaders for a softening of this blatantly xenophobic rhetoric, opinions aired on FPÖ social media sites are so brutal that it would be in bad taste to quote them here.

While Vienna has recently seen great structural and demographic changes, its slow-moving character remains intact – for example, after years of procrastination, the much-touted smoking ban has finally been earmarked for 2018. No one here knows how to address the endemic culture of complaint that colours life in the city. Many of its citizens are extraordinarily sceptical folk, doubting the virtues of any modification to the city's urban fabric; the forthcoming revamp of public space along the Ringstrasse will inevitably face huge resistance (*see p74* **The Ringstrasse at 150**).

The Viennese continue to show a lack of spontaneity, manifested in their reluctance to strike up conversation with strangers, even to acknowledge the existence of others as they gruffly push their way past others to descend from the tram or the bus, or hurtle round the Ringstrasse on their bicycles. It's a tough call for them to coexist with the past, but they should count themselves lucky to have the fortune to live in such a magnificent setting.

TURNING PINK

It's going to take more than same-sex traffic lights to change a staid city.

In 2014, when cross-dressing bearded singer Conchita Wurst won the Eurovision Song Contest, the world's media were rapt. The eloquent, softly spoken Conchita was catapulted to global fame – and briefly became Google's seventh most popular search item – eliciting both adoration and scorn. 'We are unity, we are unstoppable,' she announced defiantly in faultless English.

As a poster girl for Austria, Conchita was hardly a popular nationwide choice. Within days, an anti-Wurst Facebook page had racked up 31,000 'likes' across the country. In Russia, politicians referred to her as the 'Austrian pervert', accusing her of 'blatant propaganda of homosexuality'.

Her triumph also thrust Vienna into the limelight as the venue for the following, 60th anniversary edition of the contest – scheduled the week after the Life Ball, the city's long-established glamorous AIDS fundraiser. The PR team for the city had no choice but to put LGBT issues to the fore as tolerance became central to the preparations. This included the idea to replace the green and red figures on traffic crossings with pictograms of same-sex couples. The initiative was lapped up by the world's media in a further PR coup for the city.

The contest went like a dream, with Conchita's hirsute face appearing on everything from advertising for a bank to a Life Ball commemorative gold coin struck by the Austrian Mint, depicting her as Gustav Klimt's Golden Lady, Adele Bloch-Bauer. However, by the time the festivities were over, many here were already questioning the motives behind Vienna's tolerance campaign.

On the subject of LGBT rights, Austria still falls short of its neighbours: a limited same-sex union is all that's currently available. The major stumbling block is the veto of the conservative Austrian People's Party (ÖVP), the eternal parliamentary coalition partners of the Social Democrats and the political voice of the Catholic Church in Austria. As for public opinion, a recent poll conducted by the Mauthausen Committee of Austria found that 22 per cent of Austrians would reject an openly homosexual family member. Conchita has definitely done her bit, but there's still a long way to go.

Itineraries

Plot your perfect trip to Vienna with our step-by-step planner.

9AM

12.30PM

Day 1

9AM Start the day surrounded by grandeur at **Café Central** (*see p53*), former haunt of Sigmund Freud, Vladimir Lenin and Adolf Hitler, who all came through the doors here in 1913. If the tourist chatter gets too much, there's a little pavement terrace.

From Café Central, it's just a short walk down Herrengasse to Michaelerplatz, and to the imposing façade of the **Hofburg** (*see p53*), the Imperial Palace. This complex, which is patrolled by horses

towing their tourist carriages, contains a dozen or more key sights and attractions. To get a real sense of how the Habsburgs lived and entertained, first visit the **Kaiserappartements**, **Silberkammer** and **Sisi Museum** (*see p54*), a lavish introduction to royal Vienna.

The glittering wealth the Habsburgs garnered is on display at the unmissable **Kaiserliche Schatzkammer** (*see p54*), the Secular and Sacred Treasury. Highlights include the Byzantine crown of the Holy Roman Empire.

Strolling around the buildings, between Alte Burg and Neue Burg, is a pleasure in itself.

12.30PM You'll want to find a spot to relax post-sightseeing in the Burggarten. The **Palmenhaus** (*see p75*) would be an ideal choice for lunch, a Jugendstil greenhouse and terrace now converted into an excellent restaurant.

Afterwards, ease yourself into the afternoon with a visit to the **Schmetterlinghaus** (*see p135*), the Butterfly House attached to a wing in the same building as the

1.30PM

8PM

From left: **Hofburg**; **Schmetterlinghaus**; **Kunsthistorisches Museum**; **American Bar**.

restaurant. Huge, brightly coloured creatures fly around your head as you stroll through the verdant interior in tropical heat.

1.30PM By now, it's time for some art. Across Burggarten, the **Kunsthistorisches Museum** (see p69), the Museum of Fine Arts, is one of the finest of its kind in the world. It's too much to take in at once, so perhaps spend a couple of hours around the Caravaggios, Canalettos and Tintorettos in the east wing, but also stop to admire the

murals by Klimt and Makart in the grand entrance.

Just across the road is the **MuseumsQuartier** (see 72), the major arts complex that contains the **Kunsthalle Wien** (see p73), **MUMOK** (see p75) and the stand-out **Leopold Museum** (see p73), with its unrivalled collection of works by Egon Schiele. There's also plenty of Klimt and Kokoschka on show.

6.30PM Stroll back past the Hofburg to the heart of town and the iconic **Stephansdom** (see p41), which dominates

the skyline. St Stephen's Cathedral is open until the late evening, allowing you to cram in another Vienna sightseeing essential. Reward your endeavours with an aperitif at the **American Bar** nearby (see p48), designed by Adolf Loos.

8PM It's time for dinner. **Figlmüller** (see p44) is by no means contemporary but it's known for its huge wiener schnitzel. If you're up for a drink afterwards, the **Roberto American Bar** (see p151) is a classy spot.

9AM

Day 2

9AM Begin proceedings at the sunny café terrace in the **Augarten** (see p80), the Baroque gardens within easy reach of Leopoldstadt and the Prater. Walk along Obere Augartenstrasse that runs along the edge of the gardens, then over to Praterstrasse, where you'll find the **Johann Strauss Wohnung** (see p85). This was the home of the King of the Waltz and houses, among other things, his piano.

10AM Stroll along Praterstrasse to the transport hub of Praterstern, behind which you'll be able to see the familiar red cabins of the **Wiener Riesenrad** (see p85) going round; it's a gentle 20-minute ride. In the near distance are the colourful new buildings of the Economic University and the Danube beyond. All around are the 60 square kilometres (23 square miles) of the **Prater** park (see p84), formerly hunting grounds.

From Praterstern, walk down Franzensbrückenstrasse then over the bridge of the same name – nearby is the **Museum Hundertwasser** at the **Kunsthaus Wien** (see p90), dedicated to the life and works of the unusual artist-architect Friedensreich Hundertwasser. Its courtyard café is a lovely spot for a mid-morning break.

11.30AM Head towards town, over the narrow Wien river, and you'll come to the **Museum für Angewandte Kunst** (see p77), or **MAK**. This Museum of Applied Arts is similar to London's V&A Museum, only it's full of Jugendstil furniture and the odd work by Klimt. You're close to the **Stadtpark** (see p75) here, with its statue of Strauss and bust of Schubert. At its southern end stands one of Otto Wagner's beautiful U-Bahn stations. See p105 **Rail Revival**.

1PM For lunch, you'll find Viennese classics at the **Gmoakeller** (see p91), a short walk from the Stadtpark. From here, it's not too much

1PM

Clockwise
from far left:
Augarten;
Belvedere;
Karlskirche.

6PM

of a stretch to the leafy expanses of the **Belvedere** (*see p94*). Built for military strategist Prince Eugène of Savoy, these exquisite palaces and gardens include the **Oberes Belvedere** (*see p94*), with the world's largest Klimt collection. You'll need

a good couple of hours inside – and another half an hour to stroll around the gardens.

6PM Wind up your day's sightseeing by admiring the beautiful Baroque exterior of **Karlskirche** (*see p98*), built after the 1713 plague.

Cross Resselpark to Karlsplatz, then head over to the **Staatsoper** (*see p165*) and an early-evening drink at **Café Mozart** (*see p76*). Stroll up Kärntnerstrasse to Stephansplatz, and finish the day with dinner at **Do&Co Restaurant** (*see p44*).

Musikverein.

Musical Vienna

Thanks to its remarkable legacy of classical music superstars, Vienna is a virtual open-air hall of fame. The Viennese are reverent about their home-grown and adopted classical icons, with Mozart, Beethoven, Brahms, Schubert, Johann Strauss the Younger and Mahler among the leading lights. The care taken in preserving and presenting Vienna's illustrious musical past is both an expression of pride and an example of good business acumen.

Back when the greats were penning their masterpieces, the city of Vienna was more or less contained by the Ringstrasse. The 1st district or 'City' was – and still is – the heart of the action, where they lived, premiered their symphonies and drank their wine. This relatively compact area offers a pedestrian pilgrimage through its dense constellation of historical sites and monuments. The walk described here connects the dots of this constellation, leading you on a journey through the homes, museums, concert halls and coffeehouses of Vienna's most noteworthy musical geniuses.

This stroll of around six kilometres (three-and-a-half miles) can be done in one full day, though some may prefer to stretch it out over two in order to take it all in at *tempo moderato*.

Start out further afield, in the 2nd district. **St Johann Nepomuk Church** (Nepomukgasse 1, www.pfarre-nepomuk.at), by Nestroyplatz U-Bahn, provides a handy landmark. It's located diagonally opposite the **Johann Strauss Wohnung** (*see p85*), which is now a museum to the King of Waltz.

Heading across the water towards the city centre, the route now takes you over Schwedenbrücke to Schwedenplatz. From there, your next port of call is **Brahms' former home** at 1, Postgasse 6. This is one of six lodgings around the city where Brahms stayed, and the only one still standing. The composer lived here around 1866-1867.

The following stop, close by, is an absolute must: **Mozarthaus Wien** (see p40), directly behind Stephansdom. The only one of Mozart's apartments in Vienna to survive, it was also the most expansive and luxurious. Many of the objects are of the same era rather than directly related to Mozart – though he would have composed *Le Nozze di Figaro* here. Since 2010, the museum has also contained the 70-person **Bösendorfer Hall** (see p166) in its vaulted cellar, with excellent acoustics.

From there, the route sends you to the Stadtpark for a welcome breath of fresh air. Among the immaculately tended flowers you'll find statues of Schubert, and the much-photographed, gilded Johann Strauss the Younger; it's a pleasant spot for a rest.

Pilgrims not content with merely walking in the footsteps of the great composers can also sit in their seats at **Café Frauenhuber** (see p47), Vienna's oldest, and a favourite hangout of both Mozart and Beethoven.

Next on the walk is the **Haus der Musik** (see p46). The **Vienna Philharmonic** (see p167) got its start here, but nowadays it's an interactive sound museum providing edutainment about the great Viennese masters, including a chance to conduct the Vienna Philharmonic yourself – only virtually, of course.

From there, heading out just beyond the Ring on Schwarzenbergstrasse, the route takes you to the **Musikverein** (see p164), where Brahms was once concert director and where the Vienna Philharmonic performs today. If you time it right, you can catch a concert, or at least buy tickets for a show later in the evening.

The next stop is the **Staatsoper** (see p165), where Gustav Mahler once wielded his baton. The best thing to do here is to bask in the rarefied air of an evening performance, but you can also book a daytime tour (usually 2pm and 3pm) that includes a look at Mahler's piano and Rodin's bust of the composer.

Moving back around the Ring clockwise, stroll through the Burggarten and see the famous Mozart statue. Close to the Burggarten, the **Collection of Historical Musical Instruments** in Neue Burg (see p55) houses the most important selection of renaissance and Baroque instruments worldwide, including many that were owned and played by the great masters.

The last star in the constellation is the **Beethoven Pasqualatihaus** (see p57), where the great man lived for eight years and wrote his fourth, fifth, seventh and eighth symphonies, as well as his opera *Fidelio*. Original personal items and numerous documents help to illustrate the life and work of the composer.

Mozarthaus.

Diary

*When and where to join
Vienna's social whirl.*

It's hardly surprising that Vienna has such a packed cultural calendar – although its remit is broader than you might imagine. Devotional music, acclaimed ensembles and serious theatre all feature, but the city also embraces virtuoso accordionists, quirky performance artists and a joyous Pride parade. There are plenty of seasonal shindigs, too, from summer outdoor screenings to Christmas markets. Fasching is Vienna's carnival season, running from mid November to Ash Wednesday. It famously brings a series of grand balls to the city, most of which take place from February to March; if you're planning on attending, bring your ballgown and dancing shoes. Meanwhile, in late May, Torgom Petrosian and Gery Keszler have literally picked up the ball and run with it. In Europe's biggest charity event, the Life Ball raises millions of euros for AIDS charities and brings the biggest names from the worlds of fashion, film and music to Vienna.

Spring

Easter Market

*1, Freyung (www.altwiener-markt.at). U2
Schottentor.* **Date** 2wks up to Easter. **Map** p250 E6.
A traditional Easter market, selling hand-painted
eggs, plus food and drink. There are puppet shows
and craft workshops for children too.
▶ *Another Easter market (www.ostermarkt.co.at)
is held at Schönbrunn Palace; see p127.*

OsterKlang

*Theater an der Wien, 6, Linke Wienzelle 6
(58885, www.theater-wien.at).* **Date** Easter.
Map p250 D8.
The 'Sound of Easter' festival brings a week of
performances of devotional works to Theater an der
Wien. The Wiener Philharmoniker opens the festival.

Vienna Blues Spring

*Main venue: Reigen, 14, Hadikgasse 62
(www.reigen.at; www.viennabluesspring.org).
U4 Hietzing.* **Date** late Mar-late Apr.
Claiming to be the world's longest-running blues
festival, this six-week event attracts some big names.
Among the acts for 2015 were Bernard Allison, Steve
Guyger and Zakiya Hooker, daughter of John Lee.

★ Donaufestival

*Various venues (02732 908030, www.
donaufestival.at).* **Date** late Apr-May.
Held in the Danube Valley town of Krems (*see p181*),
this cutting-edge festival takes in performance art
and film as well as music. Battles and Godspeed You!
Black Emperor featured on the 2015 line-up, alongside theatre installations, lectures and workshops.
Shuttle buses run from Vienna.

Left to right: **Easter
Market; Donaufestival**.

EVERYBODY WALTZ!

Ball season is big business.

Fasching, the German-speaking world's version of Carnival, runs until Ash Wednesday. Far from being a hidebound tradition, designed to lure the tourist euro, ball season remains an important part of Viennese life. Locals generally learn how to waltz in their teens, and more traditional balls are opened by a line of debutantes in white dresses and bashful-looking boys. After they've danced, the dancemaster cries '*Alles Walzer!*' ('Everybody waltz!'), and festivities begin in earnest. Anyone's welcome to buy tickets and attend, so long as you stick to the dress code.

The biggest events of the season are, quite literally, front-page news. Held on the Thursday before Ash Wednesday at the Staatsoper and dating back to 1935, the **Opernball** (www. wiener-staatsoper.at) remains a monument to tradition, complete with debutantes in virginal white and insignia-decorated politicians. The glittering climax of the ball season, it still commands an entire evening of live coverage on state television, laden with saccharine smiles. The Ringstrasse is closed to traffic, security forces patrol the cordoned-off streets around the opera house and a box will set you back a five-figure sum.

Other balls come in all stripes. LGBT balls include the **Regenenbogenball** or Rainbow Ball (www.hosiwien.at/regenbogenball). The flamboyant **Rosenball** (www.heaven.at) is another option, with drag queens, gents in close-fitting lederhosen and a lot of big frocks. In March, the **Flüchtlingsball** or Refugee Ball (www.integrationshaus.at) at the Rathaus raises money to help asylum seekers. Finally, May's **Life Ball** (see p29) is Europe's biggest HIV/AIDS fundraising event, with the likes of Sharon Stone, Bill Clinton and the Scissor Sisters in attendance.

Vienna City Marathon
606 9510, www.vienna-marathon.com.
Date Apr/May.
The marathon route passes plenty of the city's landmarks; if the full course seems too much, there's a half marathon on the same day.

SOHO in Ottakring
Various venues (524 0909, www.sohoin ottakring.at). **Date** May-June. **Map** p246 A/B6.
This annual cultural shindig aims to promote communication between the Austrian and (mainly Turkish) immigrant populations in the 16th district. Exhibitions, gigs and films are put on in bars, restaurants and shops in the Brunnenmarkt area.

Stadtfest
Various venues (51543-964, www.stadtfest-wien.at). **Date** May.
A Saturday of music, circus-style acts and children's activities, staged throughout the 1st district as the People's Party's answer to the Donauinselfest (*see p29*). It's not quite the same extravaganza, but it's entertaining nonetheless.

★ Wiener Festwochen
Various venues (589 22-0, www.festwochen.at).
Date May-June.
Taking a different theme each year, the Vienna Festival is the city's premier performance arts showdown. Internationally acclaimed theatre groups, dance companies and orchestras descend on Vienna for six heady weeks; proceedings kick off with a free musical extravaganza. Rendered in English simply as the Vienna Festival, this event established in 1951 extends over five weeks and occasionally dovetails with other festivals. In 2015, it involved nearly 40 productions, some event-specific, from 20 countries.

Above: **Life Ball**. Below left:
Wiener Festwochen.

SUMMER

★ Donauinselfest

*22, Donauinsel (www.donauinselfest.at). U1
Donauinsel or U6 Neue Donau.* **Date** June.
Map p244 J3.
Organised by the Social Democrats, this three-day
festival on the Danube island is a gigantic knees-up
attracting some three million revellers. Its stages
feature a huge variety of orchestras, bands and acts;
the FM4 stage generally has some interesting indie
and dance action. There's a special section for kids.

Identities – Queer Film Festival

Various venues (524 6274, www.identities.at).
Date June.
This biennial ten-day gay and lesbian film festival
takes place at several venues across town, usually
including the atmospheric Filmcasino *(see p141).*

JazzFest Wien

Various venues (712 4224, www.viennajazz.org).
Date June-July.
Famous names of jazz, soul and blues perform in
all kinds of venues – including the grounds of the
Spittelau power station. Highlights of the 2015

edition included David Sanborn, Rufus Wainwright
and the Jason Marsalis Vibes Quartet. Venues include
Porgy & Bess and Jazzland (for both, *see p161).*

Life Ball

www.lifeball.org. **Date** May/early June.
This annual AIDS fundraiser is awash with glitz and
celebrities. *See p146* **You Shall Go to the Ball.**

Rainbow Parade

www.regenbogenparade.at. **Date** late June.
Vienna's wild and wonderful Pride event has been
marching round the Ringstrasse since 1996.

★ ImPulsTanz

Various venues (523 5558, www.impulstanz.com).
Date July-Aug.
This month-long contemporary dance festival
attracts companies and artists from around the
world, and runs dance workshops for all levels.

Above: **Viennale**. Right:
ViennAfair. Opposite:
Christkindlmärkte.

Musikfilm-Festival
*1, Rathausplatz (319 8200-0,
www.filmfestival-rathausplatz.
at). U2 Rathaus or tram 1,
2, D.* **Date** July-early Sept.
Map p250 D6.
Every evening at twilight
during the annual Musikfilm-
Festival, a range of opera,
classical rock and jazz music
films are projected on to a giant
screen in front of the Rathaus (City Hall) for free.
The surrounding food stands stay open all day.

Popfest Wien
*4, Karlsplatz (www.popfest.at). U1, U2, U4
Karlsplatz or tram 1, 2, D.* **Date** late July.
Map p250 E8.
Held over the space of three days around Karlsplatz,
with two main stages and several smaller ones,
the Vienna Pop Festival isn't afraid to stretch its
remit – guests for 2015 included the likes of Lee
Scratch Perry and Fijuka.

AUTUMN

ViennAfair
*2, Messe Platz 1 (72720-0, www.viennafair.at).
U1 Praterstern.* **Date** early Oct. **Map** p244 J5.
Vienna's international contemporary art fair focuses
on artists and galleries from central and eastern

Europe, and features the displays of more than 100
galleries from 20 different countries.

Viennale
*7, Siebensterngasse 2 (526 5947, www.viennale.at).
U3 Neubaugasse.* **Date** late Oct-early Nov.
Austria's biggest global film festival features home-
grown and international premieres. In all, some 300
screenings attract 100,000 visitors. *See also p140.*

Wien Modern
*Konzerthaus, 3, Lothringerstrasse 20 (242 002,
www.wienmodern.at). U4 Stadtpark or tram D.*
Date Nov. **Map** p251 F8.
Founded by Claudio Abbado in 1988, Wien Modern
is devoted to contemporary composition, fearlessly
combining re-runs of pioneering work by the likes
of György Ligeti or Luigi Nono, with excursions into
electronica and the constant presence of Vienna's
leading new music ensemble, Klangforum Wien.

WINTER

Christkindlmärkte

www.christkindlmaerkte.at. **Date** Nov-Dec.
Christmas for the Viennese is a social affair, where people meet up at the markets for *punsch* or *glühwein* (mulled wine), chestnuts and spicy Christmas cookies. Venues include the Kunsthandwerksmarkt on Karlsplatz; the Weihnachtsmarkt on Am Hof; and the Wiener Christkindlmarkt on Rathausplatz.

Silvester (New Year's Eve)

www.wien.info. **Date** 31 Dec.
The city centre becomes party central. Children's events start on Rathausplatz around 2pm, the streets of the old town are lined with food and drink stalls, and there's music in the squares. Festivities end in Stephansplatz for the cathedral chimes and fireworks.

New Year's Day Concert

1, Rathausplatz. U2 Rathaus or tram 1, 2, D.
Date 1 Jan. **Map** p250 D6.
Those without the political clout or luck to be selected in the internet draw to secure a pricey ticket for the famous concert by the Wiener Philharmoniker in the Golden Hall of the Musikverein (*see p164*) can watch it live on a huge screen in front of the Rathaus.

Wiener Eistraum

1, Rathausplatz. U2 Rathaus (www.wienereistraum. com). **Date** Jan-Mar. **Map** p250 D6.
Ice-skating outside City Hall to the accompaniment of disco lights and hackneyed tunes.

Vienna International Accordion Festival

Various venues (www.akkordeonfestival.at).
Date Feb-Mar.
This month-long squeezebox celebration features the finest accordion practitioners from the Balkans to the Basque country, at various unusual venues.

PUBLIC HOLIDAYS

New Year's Day
1 Jan

Epiphany
6 Jan

Easter Monday

May Day
1 May

Ascension Day

Whit Monday

Corpus Christi

Assumption Day
15 Aug

Austrian National Holiday
26 Oct

All Saints' Day
1 Nov

Immaculate Conception
8 Dec

Christmas Day
25 Dec

St Stephen's Day
26 Dec

Vienna's
Best

*There's something
for everyone with our
hand-picked highlights.*

Belvedere.

Sightseeing

VIEWS

Leopoldsberg p130
Where Beethoven wandered
for inspiration.

Wiener Riesenrad p85
The city spread out from
Vienna's iconic big wheel.

Donauturm p86
Austria's tallest structure,
revolving restaurant and all.

Belvedere p94
Not just a brilliant view but a
Baroque wonder too.

Krapfenwaldbad p139
Soak up the views from these
public baths.

Bellevuewiese p130
Gorgeous spot where Freud
had his eureka moment.

Stephansdom p41
Follow in the footsteps of
the city's nightwatchman
and climb the south tower.

ART

Leopold Museum p73
More Schiele than anywhere
else in the world.

**Kunsthistorisches
Museum** p69
Caravaggios, Canalettos,
Rembrandts, van Dycks,
Vermeers and more.

Albertina p56
How Raphael, Rembrandt
and Dürer draw – plus the
Batliner Collection.

Kunsthalle Wien p98
Blockbuster shows with
plenty of edge.

Volksgarten.

MAK p77
Furniture, design and Klimt.
TBA21 – Augarten p81
Site-specific art.
Österreichische Galerie p94
Klimt's *The Kiss*, plus
Kokoschka and Schiele.
Secession p96
Where Klimt painted his
Beethoven Frieze.
MUMOK p75
Austria's premier collection
of modern art.

HISTORY
**Heeresgeschichtlichtes
Museum** p95
1914 and all that.
Wien Museum p98
How the city came to be.
Kaisergruft p46
Franz Josef and the Habsburg
clan at rest.
Jüdisches Museum p50
Great new exhibition on
post-1945 Vienna through
Jewish eyes.
**Kaiserliche
Schatzkammer** p54
Treasures of the Holy
Roman Empire.
**Kaiserappartements/
Silberkammer/
Sisi Museum** p54
How the Habsburgs lived.

OUTDOORS
Prater park p84
Great expanse of green just
over the Danube Canal.
Volksgarten p75
The People's Garden,
festooned with roses.
Stadtpark p75
Verdant backdrop for
Strauss waltzes.
Grinzing p130
Green space galore and
vineyards aplenty.

CHILDREN
Haus des Meeres p135
Watery wonders plus a new
Amazon Jungle Passage.

Bogi Park p138
Climb, slide, bounce
and run amok.
Wiener Eislaufverein p138
Open-air skate.
Tiergarten p127
The world's oldest zoo
with giant pandas and a
Rhino Park.
Wurstelprater p136
The city's venerable funfair.

Eating & Drinking

Charlie P's.

BLOW-OUTS

Steirereck im Stadtpark p91
With produce from the chef-
owner's farm in Styria.
Tian p48
Michelin-starred vegetarian
in Innere Stadt.
**Restaurant Konstantin
Filippou** p65
Basque-trained chef goes
it alone.
Do&Co Restaurant p44
Vienna's most expensive
doner kebab.
Bank p58
Recently opened and part
of a five-star hotel.
Fabios p58
Designer Italian treats.

GLOBAL

Okra p81
Top-notch Japanese.
L'Ase p85
Homage to Catalonia.
Café Ansari p86
Gorgeous Georgian.
Mochi p86
Hipster sushi spot.
ON Market p102
Creative Chinese.
Konoba p119
Dalmatian right down
to its *blitva*.
Schuppich p84
Dishes from formerly
Habsburg Friuli and Trieste.

Gasthaus am Nordpol p81
Bare Bohemian *beisl*.
Expedit p62
All the joys of Liguria.

CREATIVE VIENNESE

Gasthaus Wild p90
Neo-*beisl* overlooking
Radetzkyplatz.
Skopik & Lohn p84
Visual and culinary triumph
in Leopoldstadt.
Österreicher im MAK p77
TV chef mixes Asia
and Vienna.

CLASSIC COFFEEHOUSES

Café Hawelka p50
Timewarp fave.
Café Bräunerhof p50
Literary landmark with
Vienna's best selection
of newspapers.
Café Prückel p77
Where the 1950s meet
fin-de-siècle.
Café Landtmann p72
Freud's favourite, still
guglhupffing after all
these years.
Café Central p53
Trotsky and Hitler were
regulars.

Café Frauenhuber p48
Where Beethoven tickled
the ivories.

PUBS & BARS

Bockshorn p51
Authentic hideaway for
chat and ale.
Charlie P's p123
Savvy, no-nonsense
gastropub.
Ungar Grill p156
Great bar in an old
Magyar eaterie.
American Bar (Loos Bar) p48
Over a century old and still
looking sassy.
Bonbonnière Bar p48
Chocoholics' delight.
Roberto American Bar p151
Pukka cocktails for a
chic clientele.
1516 p48
Own-brewed beer and
plenty of TV football.
Espresso p109
Retro to the nth degree and
all the better for it.
Phil p104
Informal concept store and
chatty drinkerie.
Lutz p104
Sip until you drop on Vienna's
main retail drag.

Shopping

GIFTS & SOUVENIRS
Viennastore p53
Tasteful souvenirs with a local theme.

BOOKS & MUSIC
Shakespeare & Co p65
English-language fiction and academic tomes.
Audio Center p60
Improv, bebop and jazz.
Market Vinyl p114
House, techno and disco.
Teuchtler Alt&Neu p105
Aladdin's cave of vinyl and CDs, nicely priced.
Comic-Treff Steiner p105
Marvel, manga and quirky US mags.

FASHION
Unikatessen p102
Pick of the off-beat and up-and-coming.
Park p114
Concept store with the latest designer pieces.
Arnold's p112
Hip streetwear, footwear and shades.
Ludwig Reiter p61
Bespoke shoes.
Camille Boyer p112
Sought-after labels from Berlin, Finland and beyond.
Vintage in Vienna p105
Mint-condition clothes from the 1920s onwards.
Nachbarin p105
Europe's coolest designers, all in one place.
Kauf dich glücklich p113
Buy yourself happy with cool Danish brands.
Freitag p112
Laptop bags for the urban hipster.
Burggasse 24 p112
All manner of retro garments on display.
Flo Nostalgische Mode p103
Retro cocktail party togs.

FOOD & DRINK
Altmann & Kuhne p52
Exquisite, hand-made chocs since the 1930s.
Naschmarkt p103
Fresh, ethnic eats.
Xocolat p61
The sweet flavours of Catalonia.

Nightlife

CLUBS
Flex p150
Ever-popular spot by the Danube Canal.
Grelle Forelle p156
Welcome waterside addition to local club culture.
Volksgarten p152
Mainstream, pricey but sumptuous surroundings.
Pratersauna p153
On its night, the top spot in town.

MUSIC
((szene)) Wien p160
Heavy rock and cool oddities.
Arena p159
Big names in an old slaughterhouse.
WUK p160
Eclectic sounds in an ivy-clad courtyard.
Jazzland p161
Sax sounds in a cosy cellar.

Chelsea p159
Led the trend of Gürtel live dives.
Porgy & Bess p161
Best place in town for jazz and blues.

Arts

FILM
Haydn English Cinema p141
UK and US films shown on four screens.
Filmcasino p141
Cool 1950s landmark, neon and all.
Schikaneder p142
Alternative cinema with a bar to match.
Metro Kino p142
Belle époque beauty.

OPERA & BALLET
Staatsoper p165
Home to Gustav Mahler, Richard Strauss and Herbert von Karajan.
Theater an der Wien p166
Hosted premieres by Strauss and Beethoven.
Musikverein p164
Beamed from here to the rest of the world on New Year's Day.
Konzerthaus p163
Grand, gorgeous temple to classical music.

Staatsoper.

Explore

Innere Stadt

Bounded by the encircling Ringstrasse, the Innere Stadt – the 1st district – forms Vienna's historic core. This is where the Viennese come to shop, stroll, eat, drink and work – and unlike many other capitals, a fair few of them actually live here too. Occupying an area slightly smaller than New York's Central Park, the Innere Stadt is crammed to the gunnels with heavyweight cultural institutions, museums and churches, along with myriad top-flight restaurants and hotels, venerable old-school coffeehouses and a Mediterranean-style pavement café vibe. Vienna's city walls stood standing into the 1850s, a Habsburg fear of Ottoman invasion putting paid to any growth for centuries. Bisected by the north–south axis of Kärntnerstrasse and Rotenturmstrasse, the Innere Stadt district centres around Stephansdom, Vienna's magnificent Gothic cathedral. From Stephansplatz, the elegant thoroughfare of Graben eventually leads to the vast, rambling Hofburg, the Imperial Palace, which was the headquarters of the Habsburg Empire until its demise in 1918.

EXPLORE

Albertina.

Don't Miss

1 Albertina Big-hitting exhibitions in modern surroundings (p56).

2 Kaiserliche Schatzkammer The glittering treasures of the Holy Roman Empire (p54).

3 Kaisergruft Resting place for generations of Habsburgs (p46).

4 Haus der Musik Conduct your own orchestra (p46).

5 Stephansdom Imposing city symbol, topped by a panoramic tower (p41).

EXPLORE

STEPHANSPLATZ & AROUND

Situated at the junction of two of Vienna's most famous pedestrian streets, Kärntner Strasse and Graben, Stephansplatz and the imposing **Stephansdom** cathedral are useful landmarks when exploring the Innere Stadt. The buildings that surround Stephansdom are a mixture of Baroque and 19th-century, apart from the post-war block facing the main entrance.

On the north side of Stephansplatz is the **Dom- und Diözesanmuseum** (Cathedral & Diocesan Museum; 1, Stephansplatz 6, www.dommuseum.at). Currently undergoing renovation and due to reopen in 2016, its artistic treasures include a 1360 portrait of Rudolf IV and works by Austrian masters such as Anton Kraus and Franz Maulbertsch. Facing the main entrance to the cathedral, the buildings are nondescript post-war edifices. One such was demolished to make way for Hans Hollein's curvaceous Haas Haus, back in 1990 the city's most controversial newbuild thanks to its proximity to the cathedral. Having started life as a shopping arcade, it now houses the **Do&Co Hotel** (*see p210*), whose superb fifth-floor bar offers superb views of the cathedral.

At the Kärntner Strasse end of Stephansplatz, the square's name changes to Stock-im-Eisenplatz ('Iron in Wood'). Here, journeymen would hammer a nail into a log to ensure their safe passage home after a trip to Vienna. A glass case protecting a stump of larch studded with nails can be found on the side of the neo-Baroque, 19th-century Palais Equitable building.

The two principal streets to the east of Stephansdom, Singerstrasse and Domgasse, lead towards Vienna's only remaining medieval quarter. This small but charming labyrinth of streets directly behind the cathedral is known as the Blutviertel (Blood Quarter), which supposedly derives from a massacre of renegade Templar Knights in 1312 on Blutgasse, which connects Singerstrasse and Domgasse.

At Blutgasse 3, there is a so-called *pawlatschenhaus* ('gallery house', derived from the Czech *pavlac*), while Singerstrasse is home to several 17th-century palaces. The Neupauer-Breuner at no.16 houses the church and treasury of the Teutonic Knights: the **Schatzkammer des Deutschen Ritterordens**.

Sights & Museums

Mozarthaus Wien

1, Domgasse 5 (512 1791, www.mozarthaus vienna.at). U1, U3 Stephansplatz. **Open** 10am-7pm daily. **Admission** €10; €3-€8 reductions; €18 family. **No credit cards. Map** p43 E4 ❶
Mozart's only remaining Vienna residence reopened as a museum on 27 January 2006, the day of his 250th

Stephansdom.

birthday, and is known locally as the Figarohaus (he wrote *The Marriage of Figaro* here). Mozart lived on the first floor from 1784 to 1787, reputedly his happiest (and most prosperous) years in the city. The museum offers a thoroughly documented portrait of Mozart's years in Vienna, with numerous drawings and paintings of the clan, original sheet music, letters, musical instruments and a host of interactive audio-visuals; most of his personal effects are in his home town of Salzburg.
▶ *The Bösendorfer concert venue now occupies the house's vaulted cellar; see p166.*

Schatzkammer des Deutschen Ritterordens

1, Singerstrasse 7/1 (512 1065, www.deutscher-orden.at). U1, U3 Stephansplatz. **Open** 10am-2pm Tue, Thur, Sat; 3-5pm Wed, Fri. **Admission** €5. **No credit cards. Map** p43 E4 ❷
The Teutonic Knights (Deutscher Ritterorden) were one of the most powerful orders to emerge from the Crusades. They had the Schatzkammer (Treasury) constructed in the 14th century as a shelter for the needy – good works that began during the Crusades and continue to this day. The Treasury has a varied collection of bric-a-brac picked up during the Crusades. Note also a Papal Bull from 1235, sundry coins, insignia and maps, and the sporadic use on

EXPLORE

various gowns and weaponry of the Teutonic Black Cross, later adapted for the Iron Cross for the German military. The Treasury is set on an upper floor of the Deutsches Haus, with a church in the main entrance. Documentation is in English. Mozart lived in the building in the spring of 1781.

★ FREE Stephansdom

1, Stephansplatz 3 (51552-3526, www.stephans kirche.at). U1, U3 Stephansplatz. **Open** 6am-10pm Mon-Sat; 7am-10pm Sun. **Tours** *All areas* (with audio guide) 9am-11.30am, 1-4.30pm Mon-Sat; 1-4.30pm Sun. *Cathedral* (English) 10.30am Mon-Sat. **Admission** free. *Tours* All areas €17.90. Cathedral €5.50; €2-€3 reductions. **No credit cards. Map** p43 E4 ❸

St Stephen's Cathedral lies at the centre of Innere Stadt and dominates the city's skyline. No other building is so unanimously revered by the Viennese as the Steffl ('Little Stephen'). It's a real symbol of endurance, having undergone numerous phases of building and repair due to the ravages of the Turks, the French and the Allies. The last thorough restoration was completed in 1948 after fire destroyed the roof of the nave, though efforts are ongoing.

On a sunny day, the geometrically designed tiled roof of the nave, depicting the Habsburg crown protected by chevrons, is magnificent. The cathedral's main entrance, the Romanesque Riesentor (Giants' Gate), is it oldest extant feature, dating from the late 13th century. The origin of the name is unclear, but the most attractive explanation is that mammoth bones dug up during building work were taken by the good burghers of Vienna to be the remains of a race of giants killed in the Biblical flood. The entrance is flanked by the impressive Heidentürme (Pagan Towers), so called because of their tenuous resemblance to minarets.

Look out for the circular recess to the left of the entrance, which enabled citizens to check that their local bakers weren't peddling undersized loaves, and on the other side the inscription O5 – the capital O and the fifth letter (E), representing the first two letters of Oesterreich – a symbol of Austrian resistance during World War II. Now protected by Plexiglas, it used to be regularly highlighted in chalk whenever the alleged war criminal and ex-Austrian president Kurt Waldheim attended Mass. The icing on the cake is the 137m (450ft) south tower, a magnificently hoary Gothic finger completed in 1433 after 74 years of work. Unfortunately, it is almost permanently obscured by scaffolding. A north tower of similar dimensions was projected in the early 16th century, but austerity measures imposed during the first Turkish siege of 1529 put paid to the idea.

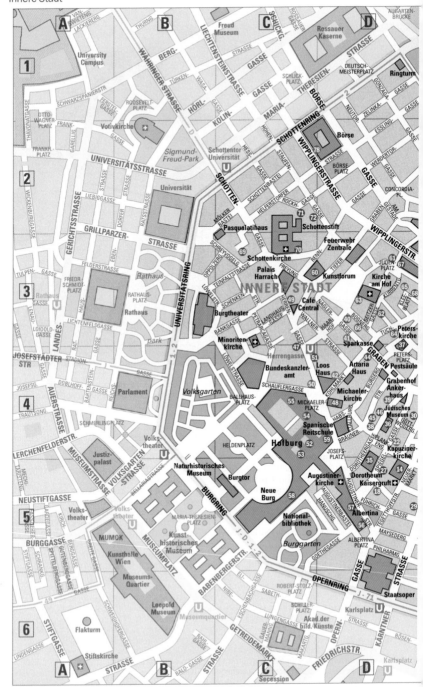

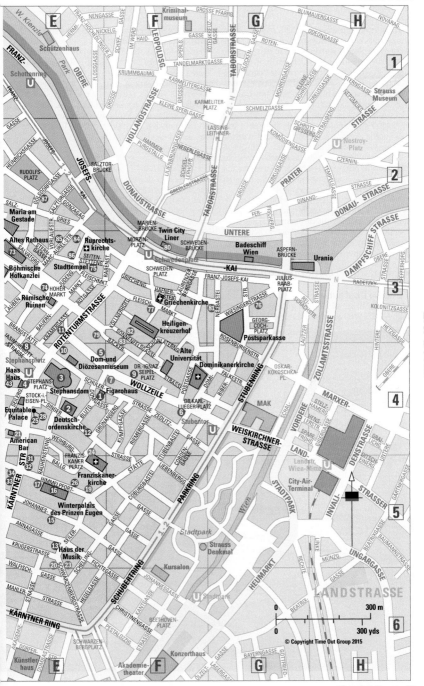

The interior, with its beautiful high vaulting, is surprisingly gloomy and always packed. Still, it remains very much a place of worship, and access is denied to most of the nave during Mass. It is worth going inside to see the extraordinary carving of the Pilgram pulpit at the top of the nave, where the sculptor, contravening the usual stonemasons' code of practice, has depicted himself looking out of a window to admire his own work. This motif is repeated under the organ loft. Other highlights include the tomb of war hero Eugène of Savoy in the Tirna Chapel, north of the nave, just inside the main entrance. In an ancestral tradition, the cathedral's catacombs house the entrails of the principal Habsburgs; their hearts and corpses dwell in Augustinerkirche and the Imperial Crypt, respectively.

A lift operates from the north side of the nave to the top of the north tower, where the cathedral's enormous bell, the Pummerin ('Boomer'), hangs. For a sense of achievement, another option is to climb part of the way up the south tower: be warned, it's a punishing 343-step slog, up a narrow spiral staircase.

Restaurants & Coffeehouses

★ Do&Co Restaurant

1, Stephansplatz 12 (535 3969, www.doco. com). U1, U3 Stephansplatz. **Open** noon-3pm, 6pm-midnight daily. **Main courses** €26-€29.50. **Map** p43 E4 ❹ International

There's no finer location for a splurge than Do&Co's elegant premises, overlooking Stephansdom. There's something for all tastes on the wide-ranging menu – Mediterranean, pan-Asian and Austrian classics, all equally reliable. Choose from superb ingredients at the open kitchen for a wok feast or sample Vienna's most expensive doner kebab (€26). Otherwise there's sensational sushi, Uruguayan beef and excellent desserts.

Figlmüller

1, Wollzeile 5 (512 6177, www.figlmueller.at). U1, U3 Stephansplatz or bus 1A. **Open** *Jan-July, Sept-Dec* 11am-10.30pm daily. **Main courses** *Schnitzel* €13.90. **Map** p43 E4 ❺ Viennese

Ask a hotel porter where to eat wiener schnitzel and you'll almost certainly be directed towards Figlmüller. Tucked into a lane between Wollzeile and Bäckerstrasse, this busy, cramped restaurant certainly fries up fine schnitzels of alarming dimensions, but the tourist trade and pseudo-rustic bonhomie can be slightly irritating. All wines come from the owner's vineyards in Grinzing; no beer is served. This simple concept has been so successful that the Figlmüller clan have now opened Lugeck, a vast temple of Viennese dining, in the imposing

Regensburgerhof, once home to Vienna's ill-fated Buddha Bar. No schnitzel, but you can choose from a selection of 25 craft beers.

Other locations 1, Bäckerstrasse 6 (512 1760); 1, Lugeck 4 (512 5060); 19, Grinzinger Strasse 55 (320 4257).

Plachutta

1, Wollzeile 38 (512 1577, www.plachutta.at). U3 Stubentor or tram 1, 2 or bus 1A. **Open** 11.30am-11.15pm daily. **Main courses** €16-€23. **Map** p43 F4 ⑥ Austrian

Stately Plachutta is the Viennese temple of beef eating, and rightly famed for one dish: *tafelspitz.* The boiled beef tenderloin, Emperor Franz Josef's favourite Sunday lunch, is served with rösti, puréed spinach and an apple and horseradish sauce. Its elaborate preparation (the meal begins with bowls of the tremendous beef broth left over after cooking the meat) has prevented it from becoming well known internationally, so a meal here should be a priority for carnivores. Plachutta has branches throughout Vienna but the latest, on Wahlfischgasse, is a centrally located spot with a great bistro feel.

Other locations: Grünspan 16, Ottakringer Strasse 266 (480 5730); 13, Auhofstrasse 1 (877 7087-0); 19, Heiligenstädter Strasse 179 (370 4125). 1, Walfischgasse 5-7 (512 2251).

Haus der Musik. *See p46.*

Cafés, Bars & Pubs

Diglas

1, Wollzeile 10 (512 5765, www.diglas.at). U1, U3 Stephansplatz or bus 1A. **Open** 8am-10.30pm daily. **Map** p43 F4 ⑦

Plush red velvet booths give this Biedermeier café an air of intimacy. No surprise, then, that Viennese grandes dames reputedly come here to discuss their infidelities. Renowned for its coffee menu and good selection of teas served in bird-bath cups, Diglas offers some of the best cakes in town and possibly the best *apfelstrudel* going. German speakers may be able to fathom the *Wiener schmäh* (ironic, occasionally biting, always charming humour); the waiters here ooze it.

Shops & Services

Hartmann

1, Jasomirgottstrasse 6 (533 1584, www.textil pflege-hartmann.at). U1, U3 Stephansplatz. **Open** 9am-6pm Mon-Fri. **Map** p43 E4 ⑧ Dry cleaners

A reliable, centrally located dry cleaners.

Other location 6, Linke Wienzeile 164 (597 0208).

Herzilein Wien

1, Wollzeile 17 (0676 657 7106, www.herzilein-wien.at). U1, U3 Stephansplatz. **Open** 10am-7pm Mon-Fri; 10am-6pm Sat. **Map** p43 F4 ⑨ Children's fashion

Herzilein's clothes for babies and toddlers have been wowing Vienna's comfortably off for more than a decade. Excellent finishing, attractive designs and hard-wearing materials are the key to its success. The unmistakable bright red frontages of their stores have also put them on the map. The one in the 6th district also sells jolly textiles by the metre.

Other locations 6, Amerlingstrasse 8 (0676 657 7107); 8, Josefstädter Strasse 29 (0676 616 3188).

Manner

1, Rotenturmstrasse 2 & Stephansplatz 7 (513 7018, www.manner.at). U1, U3 Stephansplatz. **Open** 10am-9pm daily. **Map** p43 E4 ⑩ Food & drink

Austria's most popular chocolate snack is Manner Neapolitaner Schnitten: hazelnut-flavoured wafer biscuits in a distinctive pink wrapper. The flagship store by Stephansdom sells them in packs, along with T-shirts, souvenirs and retro pink ski helmets.

Schau Schau Brillen

1, Rotenturmstrasse 11 (533 4584, www.schau-schau.at). U1, U3 Stephansplatz. **Open** 10am-6pm Mon-Sat. **Map** p43 E3 ⑪ Accessories

If horn rims are your bag, this bespoke shop is the real thing. If not, there's a wide range of handmade frames, and they're even happy to rebuild broken favourites for you.

EXPLORE

Woka

1, Singerstrasse 16 (513 2912, www.woka.com).
U1, U3 Stephansplatz. **Open** 10am-6pm Mon-Fri;
10am-5pm Sat. **Map** p43 E4 ⓬ **Homewares**
Since 1978, Wolfgang Karolinsky and his firm
have been making superb reproductions of Wiener
Werkstätte lamps and lights. As Karolinsky has
acquired many of the original moulds and presses,
they're as close to the real thing as you're likely to get.

KÄRNTNER STRASSE & AROUND

Pedestrianised since the 1970s, Kärntner Strasse
connects Stephansplatz with one of Vienna's
great institutions, the **Staatsoper** (Opera House;
see p165). Luxury shops used to trade here,
but the street is now a cacophony of illuminated
signs announcing chain stores and takeaways.
An occasional glimpse of former glories is offered
by such places as **Lobmeyer** at no.26, a famous
glass-maker with a museum containing original
items by the Wiener Werkstätte design firm.

Near the corner of Stock-im-Eisenplatz is the
Kärntner Durchgang, with its fabulous, Adolf
Loos-designed **American Bar**. Meanwhile,
Weihburggasse leads down towards one of
Vienna's most pleasant squares, the Italianate
Franziskanerplatz – best known locally for
the **Kleines Café**. Sit here during the summer
and admire the Baroque houses, the delightful
18th-century Moses Fountain and, of course,
Franziskanekirche (1, Franziskanerplatz 4,
512 4578, open 6.30am-6pm daily), which
dates from 1611.

The other streets to the east of Kärntner
Strasse – Himmelpfortgasse, Johannesgasse
and Annagasse – all have a number of splendid
Baroque houses and a sprinkling of sights. The
most notable are the **Literaturmuseum** and
the **Winter Palace of Prince Eugène of
Savoy**, both recently opened to the public.

Directly west of Kärntner Strasse lies Neuer
Markt, a congested rectangular square that used
to be the medieval flour market. Architecturally,
the square is a dreadful hotch-potch of styles that
don't so much contrast as clash; however, amid
the parked cars is a copy of Donner's glorious
Providentia Fountain (1739). The naked figures
of the original – allegories of Austria's four main
rivers – proved too much for Maria Theresa's
Chastity Commission and were removed in 1773,
but returned intact in 1801. To the south, behind
an unassuming façade, the **Kaisergruft** crypt
holds the tombs of the Habsburgs.

Sights & Museums

Haus der Musik

1, Seilerstätte 30 (513 4850, www.hdm.at).
U1, U2, U4 Karlsplatz or tram 1, 2, D. **Open**

Literaturmuseum.

10am-10pm daily. **Admission** €13; €5.50-
€9 reductions; €28 family. **Map** p43 E5 ⓭
Housed in the former residence of Otto Nicolai,
founder of the Wiener Philharmoniker, this interactive sound museum is a bold attempt to illustrate the
listening experience. Appropriately, the show begins
with a history of Vienna's most celebrated orchestra
and a large screen showing the previous year's New
Year's concert. The Sonosphere floor traces elemen-
tary aural experiences: the Prenatal Listening Room
(sounds of the womb), the Polyphonium (the perfect
surround sound experience) and various natural
and environmental sounds that can be combined at
will and burned on to a CD to take away. Interactivity
also abounds in Futuresphere, where you can tinkle
on 'hyperinstruments' and sensors. The best simu-
lation, though, is the 'virtual conductor' on the Great
Composers floor where you can wield an electronic
baton and conduct the Philharmoniker yourself.
When it's full the place is a veritable cacophony,
so make use of the late opening hours. *Photos p44.*

Kaisergruft

*1, Tegetthoffstrasse 2 (512 6853-16, www.
kaisergruft.at).* U1, U2, U4 Karlsplatz or U1, U3
Stephansdom or tram 1, 2, D. **Open** 10am-6pm
daily. **Admission** €5.50; €2.50-€4.50 reductions.
No credit cards. Map p42 D5 ⓮

are Archduke Franz Ferdinand and his beloved wife Sophie, whose remains were taken from Sarajevo in 1914 to the seat of the Hohenburg family, Artstetten Castle in Lower Austria. A plaque in the Kaisergruft commemorates the 'first victims of World War I'.

Literaturmuseum

1, Johannesgasse 6 (53410, www.onb.ac.at/ literaturmuseum.htm). U1, U2, U4 Karlsplatz or U1, U3 Stephansdom or tram 1, 2, D. **Open** 10am-6pm Tue-Wed, Fri-Sun; 10am-9pm Thur (also 10am-6pm Mon June-Sept). **Admission** €7; free under-19s. **Map** p43 E5 **15**

The Literature Museum of the Austrian National Library opened in 2015, in the former Royal & Imperial Court Chamber Archive where leading dramatist Franz Grillparzer was director in the mid 1800s. His office, in its original condition, forms part of the exhibition, which attempts to illustrate the history of Austrian literature from the 1700s to the present day. English speakers are provided with a tablet to help them make sense of a somewhat confusing and cluttered collection. TV screens on bookshelves show interviews with modern-day writers and abstract works such as Peter Handke's 'The Line-Up of 1.FC Nuremberg on 27.1.68', while themes such as calligraphy and literary censorship in Grillparzer's day are touched upon but not explored in any great depth. All in all, it's a very mixed bag, but with ample scope for special exhibitions on another floor.

Winter Palace of Prince Eugène of Savoy

1, Himmelpfortgasse 8 (795 57-0, www.belvedere. at). U1, U3 Stephansplatz. **Open** 10am-6pm daily. **Admission** €9; €7 reductions; free under-18s. **Map** p43 E5 **16**

Conceived by perhaps the most important architect of the day, JB Fischer von Erlach, and completed by his great rival Lukas von Hildebrandt in 1709, this fine Baroque palace was the chief residence of the great military commander and patron of the arts, Prince Eugène of Savoy. Office for the Ministry of Finance from 1848 to modern times, the Winter Palace was extensively renovated from 2007 to 2013. It was then opened to the public as an exhibition hall in the city centre for the Belvedere (*see p94*), the summer residence of Prince Eugène, with its outstanding permanent collection of Austrian art. The Winter Palace hosts heavyweight temporary exhibitions, such as the Rembrandt Titian Bellotto show that brought in the crowds during 2015.

From 1633 onwards, the Habsburgs were laid to rest in the crypt of the Church of the Capuchins. Each funeral was preceded by a belittling ritual consisting of the reigning emperor announcing his various titles to the waiting prior, who then refused him entry. Finally, the emperor was forced to identify himself as 'a humble sinner who begs God's mercy' and the cortège would be granted permission to enter. Today, an admission fee and silence ('Silentium!' reads the inscription over the entrance) are all they ask. Many of the early tombs are decorated with skull-and-crossbones, weapons and bats' wings, progressively increasing in size until you reach the gigantic iron double tomb of Empress Maria Theresa and her husband, Franz Stefan. Above the tomb the couple appear to be sitting up in bed embroiled in a marital tiff. Further along is the New Vault, where Maximilian I of Mexico and Napoleon's second wife, Marie Louise, are to be found. People tend to dwell a little longer in the Franz-Josef Vault, where Franz Josef I is flanked by his eternally popular wife Empress Elisabeth (invariably with freshly laid offerings from Hungary) and their son, the unhappy Prince Rudolf. The last room contains the remains of Empress Zita, who was buried with full pomp and ceremony in 1989, and a bust of her husband, Emperor Karl I, who died in exile in Madeira and preferred to remain there. Also missing

Restaurants & Coffeehouses

Café Frauenhuber

1, Himmelpfortgasse 6 (512 53 53, www. cafe-frauenhuber.at). U1, U3 Stephansplatz. **Open** 8am-11pm Mon-Sat; 10am-10pm Sun. **Map** p43 E5 **17** Coffeehouse

EXPLORE

The Baroque façade of Vienna's oldest café and the neighbouring Winter Palace of Prince Eugène (*see p47*) are both the work of Johann Lukas von Hildebrandt. In business since 1824, Frauenhuber is steeped in musical mythology and history of the highest order, since Mozart lived in the building for a time and Beethoven occasionally performed his piano sonatas in the café. Today, its plush interior is filled with shoppers and tourists from nearby Kärntner Strasse, but thankfully it still retains the essential coffeehouse attributes. Prices are on the steep side, unsurprisingly.

Reinthaler

1, Gluckgasse 5 (512 3366). U1, U2, U4 Karlsplatz. **Open** 9am-11pm Mon-Fri. **Main courses** €5.70-€10.50. **Map** p42 D5 ⓲ Viennese

This is a rare example of an authentic, low-priced Innere Stadt *beisl*. Its wood-panelled rooms and green Formica tables are nearly always packed with pensioners, students, workers in overalls and suits – all hunched together at companionable tables over beers and newspapers. You'll find the usual dishes, including great *schweinsbraten* (roast pork), a stinging goulash and much offal.

Other location 1, Dorotheergasse 2-4 (513 1249).

★ Tian

1, Himmelpfortgasse 23 (890 4665, www.tian-vienna.com). U1, U3 Stephansplatz. **Open** noon-midnight Tue-Sat. **Set menus** €89, €104, €120. **Map** p43 E5 ⓳ Vegetarian

Vienna's only address for vegetarian fine dining sports a Michelin star and the kind of extravagant decor and prices that go hand-in-hand with such accolades. At Tian, vegetarians can spend the same kind of money as carnivores and receive all the corresponding indulgences: detailed descriptions from highly attentive waiters, birchwood and moss chandeliers, fresh flowers in abundance, and immaculate ingredients from Tian's own market garden in Carinthia. Most diners opt for one of the three set menus; the eight-course version comes with two other surprise dishes. The basement houses a dimly lit cocktail/wine bar.

Cafés, Bars & Pubs

1516 Brewing Company

1, Schwarzenbergstrasse 2 (961 1516, www.1516brewingcompany.com). U1, U3 Stephansplatz or U1, U2, U4 Karlsplatz. **Open** 10am-2am daily. **Map** p43 E5 ⓴

See p115 **Going Gastro**.

★ American Bar (Loos Bar)

1, Kärntner Durchgang 10 (512 3283, www.loosbar.at). U1, U3 Stephansplatz. **Open** noon-4am Mon-Wed, Sun; noon-5am Thur-Sat. **Map** p43 E4 ㉑

Known locally as the Loos Bar after the architect Adolf Loos, who designed it in 1908, this tiny, modernist gem makes ingenious use of mirrors to create an illusion of space. Onyx, marble and headily potent cocktails ooze the glamour of a bygone age; scoring a table (no mean feat) is the icing on the cake. Drinks prices are on the high side, but it's not every day you get to sip in an architectural masterpiece.

Bonbonnière Bar

1, Spiegelgasse 15 (512 6886). U1, U3 Stephansplatz. **Open** 6pm-2am Mon-Sat. **Map** p42 D4 ㉒

Calling itself 'the oldest bar in Vienna', this known-only-to-locals piano bar is wonderfully charming and authentic. Tiny and bordello-like, it charges an extra few schilling for its well-mixed cocktails, but for that you get romantic standards tickled on the ivories and can gawp at how eccentric old Viennese spin out their days.

Flanagans Irish Pub Vienna

1, Schwarzenbergstrasse 1-3 (513 7378, www.flanagans.at). U1, U3 Stephansplatz or U1, U2, U4 Karlsplatz. **Open** 10am-2am Mon-Thur, Sun; 10am-4am Fri, Sat. **Map** p43 E5 ㉓

Lobmeyr.

EXPLORE

Now approaching its 20th anniversary of providing Guinness, pub grub and TV sports in this southwest corner of Innere Stadt, Flanagan's has recently been superseded by the trend for craft beers – such as at 1516 (*see p48*) diagonally opposite. But its popular combination of authentic Irish atmosphere and traditional cooking (Sunday roasts for €9.80) is so long established, it needn't worry. The interior was transported lock, stock and barstool from Flannery's in Churchtown, County Cork in 1996. There's also a busy terrace in summer.

Kleines Café

1, Franziskanerplatz 3 (no phone). U1, U3 Stephansplatz. **Open** 10am-2am Mon-Sat; 1pm-2am Sun. **Map** p43 E4 ㉔

As the name suggests, this place is tiny, though architect Hermann Czech's design makes great use of mirrors. Customers, and indeed staff, are an eccentric mix of arty intellectuals, actors and proto-bohemian types; in summer, sitting out on the square is a delight. It's perhaps more of a boozer than a coffeehouse, though there is a wall of newspapers and a light menu, with excellent open sandwiches and omelettes.

Shops & Services

Bipa

1, Kärntner Strasse 1-3 (512 2210, www.bipa.at). U1, U3 Stephansplatz. **Open** 8am-8pm Mon-Fri; 8am-6pm Sat. **Map** p43 E4 ㉕ **Beauty**

Bipa, Billa's cosmetics and cleaning products outlet, is present on every major shopping street. It also offers cheap photo developing.

Other locations throughout the city.

Galerie Slavik

1, Himmelpfortgasse 17 (513 4812, www.galerie-slavik.com). U1, U3 Stephansplatz. **Open** 10am-1pm, 2-6pm Wed-Fri; 11am-5pm Sat. **Map** p43 E5 ㉖ **Accessories**

Galerie Slavik shows off the work of international jewellery designers, displayed in sleek glass vitrines that hang from the ceiling. Prices range from around €100 for young designers up to stratospheric sums.

★ Gragger & Cie

1, Spiegelgasse 23 (513 0555, www.gragger-cie.at). U1, U2, U4 Karlsplatz or U1 U3 Stephansplatz. **Open** 8am-7pm Mon-Fri; 8am-6pm Sat. **Map** p42 D5 ㉗ **Food & drink**

This outlet bakes its organic, naturally leavened sourdough bread in a wood-fired oven. From noon, while stocks last, lunch is served, running from soup and bread to wholesome stews and light lunches.

Humanic

1, Kärntner Strasse 1 (513 89220, www.humanic.at). U1, U3 Stephansplatz. **Open** 10am-7pm Mon-Fri; 10am-6pm Sat. **Map** p43 E4 ㉘ **Footwear**

The flagship store of Austria's leading shoe chain stocks a wide range of brands, including Bronx, Buffalo, Adidas and Walter Bauer.

Other locations throughout the city.

Lobmeyr

1, Kärntnerstrasse 26 (512 0508, www.lobmeyr.at). U1, U2, U4 Karlsplatz or tram 1, 2, 71, D. **Open** 10am-7pm Mon-Fri; 10am-6pm Sat. **Map** p42 D5 ㉙ **Homewares**

Lobmeyr is a class act that has produced chandeliers for such lofty interiors as the Hall of the Supreme Soviet and the Metropolitan Opera. It also reproduces Josef Hoffmann's iconic Serie B drinks set. The second floor houses a small museum.

Mühlbauer

1, Seilergasse 10 (512 2241, www.muehlbauer.at). U1, U3 Stephansplatz. **Open** 10am-6.30pm Mon-Fri; 10am-6pm Sat. **Map** p42 D4 ㉚ **Accessories**

Klaus Mühlbauer has carried the family millinery business forward with this stylish, contemporary shop, stocking beautiful hats of every description. There are merino wool hats, leopard-print bowlers, understated cloche hats, trilbies and plenty more.

Rositta

1, Kärntner Strasse 17 (512 4604, www.rositta.at). U1, U3 Stephansplatz. **Open** 10am-6.30pm Mon-Fri; 10am-5.30pm Sat. **Map** p43 E5 ㉛ **Fashion**

Vienna is full of little designer lingerie boutiques, and Rositta is one of the loveliest, selling nighties, slips, bras and knickers; brands include La Perla.

Steffl

1, Kärtner Strasse 19 (930 560, www.steffl-vienna.at). U1, U3 Stephansplatz. **Open** 10am-8pm Mon-Fri; 9.30am-6pm Sat. **Map** p43 E5 ㉜ **Department store**

Vienna's most prominent department store, the eight-floor Steffl is crowned by its Skybar; there's a great view of the Stephansdom.

Swarovski

1, Kärntner Strasse 24 (512 9032, www.swarovski.com). U1, U3 Stephansplatz. **Open** 9am-9pm Mon-Fri; 9am-6pm Sat. **Map** p43 E5 ㉝ **Jewellery & accessories**

Tyrolean crystal glass specialist Swarovski is one of Austria's biggest exporters. The Vienna flagship store has a glittering array of crystal animals, jewellery and bags.

Wolford

1, Kärntner Strasse 22 (512 8731, www.wolford.com). U1 U3 Stephansplatz. **Open** 9.30am-6.30pm Mon-Fri; 9.30am-6pm Sat. **Map** p43 E5 ㉞ **Fashion**

Its superior quality tights and stockings have a worldwide reputation, but Wolford from Bregenz also carries a range of underwear and some clothes. **Other locations** throughout the city.

EXPLORE

EXPLORE

GRABEN & KOHLMARKT

The area bounded by Neuermarkt to the east, Graben to the north and Kohlmarkt to the west consists of a network of narrow streets. It's dotted with restaurants, antiques shops, galleries and landmark coffeehouses such as the **Hawelka** and **Bräunerhof**. The other big attractions are the **Jüdisches Museum**, with its new permanent exhibition, and **Dorotheum** auction house.

Graben and Kohlmarkt are Vienna's most majestic thoroughfares, entirely composed of Baroque, 19th-century and belle époque buildings. Today Graben ('ditch') is a broad pedestrian causeway built along what was the southern moat that defended the Roman camp established on Hoher Markt a few streets to the north. Commerce harks back to imperial times with innumerable shops bearing the 'k.u.k.' – kaiserlich und königlich – royal warrant.

Graben's most exuberant flourish is the resoundingly Baroque Pestsäule (Plague Monument), a feature common to all Austrian cities. Vienna's was built in 1692, its Baroque stone carving created primarily by Fischer von Erlach of Schönbrunn fame. Nearby, on Petersplatz, is **Peterskirche**, while on the corner of Tuchlauben is the fine neoclassical Erste Österreichisches Sparkasse (First Austrian Savings Bank), built in 1836 and emblazoned with an enormous gilded bee symbolising thrift and hard work. At nos.14-15 is the monumental Grabenhof (1876) built by Otto Wagner to another architect's plans. This early Wagner work has hints of the Jugendstil he would later champion – a style more clearly visible in the Ankerhaus at no.10, which Wagner designed, built and for a time used as his studio.

Graben grinds to an abrupt halt with the imposing façade of the **Meinl am Graben** store, all that remains of the chain of coffee roasters and grocery stores that once fed the bourgeoisie of much of Central and Eastern Europe. This flagship store is Vienna's Fortnum & Mason, and well worth a visit.

Sights & Museums

FREE Dorotheum

1, Dorotheergasse 17 (515 60-0, www.dorotheum. com). U1, U3 Stephansplatz. **Open** 10am-6pm Mon-Fri; 9am-5pm Sat. **Admission** free. **Map** p42 D5 ❸
In the past, a 'visit to Auntie Dorothy's' was a popular euphemism for falling on hard times. Set up in 1707 by Emperor Josef I as a pawn shop for the wealthy, the Dorotheum is now Vienna's foremost auction house. The present building is a slice of neo-Baroque bombast from the 1890s that provides a thoroughfare between Dorotheergasse and Habsburgergasse. Auctions are held daily, with regular specialised

sales; otherwise, the Glashof on the ground floor has an ever-changing selection of reasonably affordable bric-a-brac on display.

★ Jüdisches Museum

1, Dorotheergasse 11 (535 0431, www.jmw.at). U1, U3 Stephansplatz. **Open** 10am-6pm Mon-Thur, Sun; 10am-2pm Fri. **Admission** *With Museum Judenplatz* €10; €8 reductions; under-18s free. **Map** p42 D4 ❸
See p59 **Jewish Vienna.**

FREE Peterskirche

1, Petersplatz (533 6433, www.peterskirche.at). U1, U3 Stephansplatz. **Open** 7am-8pm Mon-Fri; 9am-9pm Sat, Sun. **Admission** free. **Map** p42 D4 ❸
Erected on the site of what was probably Vienna's oldest Christian church (dating from the late fourth century), Peterskirche was built by Lukas von Hildebrandt and completed in 1733. The finest Baroque church in Innere Stadt, Peterskirche has a green copper dome that echoes the nearby Michaelertor entrance to the Hofburg. The dome's fresco has faded, but the interior remains spectacular thanks to a wealth of trompe-l'oeil effects around the choir and altar.

Restaurants & Coffeehouses

Café Bräunerhof

1, Stallburggasse 2 (512 3893). U3 Herrengasse or bus 2A, 3A. **Open** 8am-8.30pm Mon-Fri; 8am-6.30pm Sat; 10am-6.30pm Sun. **Map** p42 D4 ❸ **Coffeehouse**
The ironically named Café Sans Souci was one of many cafés to be 'aryanised' – expropriated from its Jewish owners – during the Nazi era, and it was renamed Café Bräunerhof. Its reputation as a literary café owes much to the patronage of former regular Thomas Bernhard, the irascible novelist and playwright, and philosopher Paul Wittgenstein. A touch more austere than the other classic coffeehouses, with its dim lights and mottled brown and beige upholstery, the Bräunerhof still attracts colourful characters such as blood 'n' guts performance artist Hermann Nitsch. Along with one of the best selections of international newspapers in the city, it has a fine array of cakes and strudels. A string trio plays on Saturday and Sunday afternoons (3.30-6pm).

Café Hawelka

1, Dorotheergasse 6 (512 8230, www.hawelka.at). U1, U3 Stephansplatz. **Open** 8am-midnight Mon-Wed; 8am-1am Thur-Sat; 10am-midnight Sun. **Map** p42 D4 ❸ **Coffeehouse**
Hawelka seems to exist in a twilit timewarp. The striped sofas are charmingly threadbare, with the clientele favours newspaper-thumbing over laptop-tapping. Nonetheless, there have been changes over the decades. It's no longer the intellectual hangout it was between the 1950s and '70s, when it was a

favourite of the Viennese Actionists, and Canetti, Warhol and Millers Henry and Arthur all used to drop by. Part of its charm lay in the husband-and-wife duo of Leopold and Josefine Hawelka; since Josefine's death in 2005, there has been nobody to seat single clients next to lonely members of the opposite sex. Hawelka was one of the first Viennese cafés to institute a no-smoking policy.

Esterhazykeller

1, Haarhof 1, off Naglergasse (533 3482, www.esterhazykeller.at). U3 Herrengasse. **Open** 4-11pm daily. **Buffet menus** €6.50-€14. **Map** p42 D3 ⑩ **Austrian**
Located in the bowels of the Palais owned by the Hungarian nobles of the same name, this conspiratorial cellar became the first outlet for Hungarian wine and food in Vienna in the late 18th century. Apart from a few refrigerated cabinets for the cold cuts and dips, little has changed since. (Descend the steep stone steps with care.) Today, the reasonably priced *heuriger*-style food and rough-and-ready wines attract mostly local custom in spite of its location on touristy Haarhof.

Cafés, Bars & Pubs

★ Bockshorn

1, Körblergasse, off Naglergasse 7 (532 9438, 0676 420 1342, www.bockshorn.at). U3 Herrengasse or U1, U3 Stephansplatz. **Open** 4pm-2am daily. **Map** p42 D3 ⑪
Opened in April 1991, this chummy cubbyhole of a pub has kept its authenticity while scores of faux Irish venues have set up across Vienna. It's certainly intimate, and if you're looking for space to spread out and open up the laptop while an overpriced all-day breakfast is brought to your table, this is not for you. If you're looking for lashings of Guinness, Kilkenny, Stiegl or Magners, backdropped by a well chosen indie/rock soundtrack and interspersed with the interactive, international conversation that pings around the busiest of the city's bar counters from 4pm onwards – well, walk right in, squeeze up close and get involved. There's no food, no Wi-Fi, no TV and no pool table. You're here to drink and chat – and maybe rub shoulders with a post-gig passing musician or two. Their hotel receptionist will have directed them to a tiny cul-de-sac, signposted off Naglergasse, just off the far end of Graben.

Esterhazykeller.

Demel

1, Kohlmarkt 14 (535 1717, www.demel.at). U3 Herrengasse or bus 2A, 3A. **Open** 9am-7pm daily. **Map** p42 D4 ⑫
This 200-year-old former imperial bakery has a magnificent choice of cakes and steep prices to match. More a *konditorei* (pâtisserie) than a *kaffeehaus*, its grandiose interior is sickly sweet, with a more modern glassed-over patio at the back. A hot chocolate here is a must, as is the *sachertorte*.

A great place to pick up some Viennese confectionery in gorgeous period-piece boxes, many of them with Jugendstil designs, Demel also has the most wonderful window displays.

Shops & Services

Altmann & Kuhne

1, Graben 30 (533 0927, www.altmann-kuehne.at). U1, U3 Stephansplatz. **Open** 9am-6.30pm Mon-Fri; 10am-5pm Sat. **Map** p43 E4 ❹ **Food & drink**

This famous confectioner's premises on Am Graben dates back to the early 1930s. The handmade chocolates are exquisite, as are the Wiener Werkstätte-designed boxes in which they are presented. Chocolates are also available in minature versions.

Meinl am Graben

1, Graben 19 (532 3334, www.meinl.com). U1, U3 Stephansplatz or U3 Herrengasse or bus 2A, 3A. **Open** 8am-7.30pm Mon-Fri; 9am-6pm Sat. **Map** p42 D4 ❹ **Food & drink**

Vienna's most elegant grocery store sells food from all over the world, from ready meals to exotic condiments, plus fresh meat, fish and fine cheeses. The city's great and good also patronise the wine bar, sushi stand, coffee shop and restaurant.

R Horn

1, Bräunerstrasse 7 (513 8294, www.rhorns.com). U1, U3 Stephansplatz. **Open** 10am-6.30pm Mon-Fri; 10am-5pm Sat. **Map** p42 D4 ❹ **Accessories**

The city's foremost leather goods emporium does a fine line in handbags, briefcases and purses in Italian-sourced nubuck, calf and cowhide leather. The outstanding quality and variety of the grain, as well as a dangerously tempting palette of colours, can be a threat to your finances. Local legal eagles love to sport Horn's Samuel Beckett portfolio case, a snip at €425. As it says on the website: 'What are you waiting for? Godot?'

Other locations 1, Stephansplatz (512 2507); 1, Mahlerstrasse 5 (513 6507).

Wiener Interieur

1, Dorotheergasse 14 (512 2898). U1, U3 Stephansplatz. **Open** 10am-1pm, 2.30-6pm Mon-Fri; 10am-1pm Sat. **Map** p42 D4 ❹ **Accessories**

Dorotheergasse and its environs are full of antique jewellery shops. This small establishment deals in art nouveau, art deco and 1950s costume jewellery.

MICHAELERPLATZ & HERRENGASSE

Kohlmarkt discharges the crowds into circular Michaelerplatz, a carousel of ministerial limos, horse-drawn carriages, cyclists and jay-walking tourists circumventing some nondescript Roman ruins. Lying in a nifty recess designed

by architect Hans Hollein, this is all that remains of the Roman *canabae*, which was the residential and whoring district.

Although dwarfed by the entrance to the Hofburg, the Kohlmarkt side of the square is the site of one of modernism's seminal edifices: the so-called Loos House, now a bank. Built between 1909 and 1911, it was known as the 'house without eyebrows' until Loos added ten window boxes. Franz Josef was so appalled by the façade that he ordered the curtains to be drawn on all palace windows overlooking it.

Across the street is **Michaelerkirche**, whose neoclassical façade hides the church's early Gothic origins. These can be seen from a pretty courtyard by entering Kohlmarkt 11; notice, too, the well-preserved Baroque carriage houses.

West of Michaelerplatz, Herrengasse (Lords' Lane) is lined with innumerable palaces that today house government agencies, newspapers and corporate galleries. At no.13, the Landhaus witnessed the outbreak of the 1848 Revolution, when troops fired on a crowd demanding the resignation of Prince Metternich. Just opposite, the neo-Renaissance Palais Ferstel, built by and named after architect Heinrich Ferstel, is the home of **Café Central**. It has an elegant Italian-style shopping arcade that leads into Freyung.

Further along Herrengasse are two other fine, accessible aristocratic mansions: Palais Harrach, which was rebuilt in 1690 after it burned down during the Turkish siege, and the high Baroque Palais Kinski, built by von Hildebrandt (1713-19). Both have airy courtyards, and upmarket shops and galleries.

The streets heading south off Herrengasse lead to the impressive but lifeless ministerial quarter around Minoritenplatz. The cobbled square is dominated by the brooding, Gothic Minoritenkirche and its octagonal tower. From here, it's a short walk to the lawns and benches of the **Volksgarten** (*see p75*), one of Vienna's historic inner city parks.

Sights & Museums

Esperantomuseum/Globenmuseum

Palais Mollard, 1, Herrengasse 9 (534 10-464, www.onb.ac.at). U3 Herrengasse. **Open** 10am-6pm Tue, Wed, Fri-Sun; 10am-9pm Thur. **Admission** €4; €3 reductions; free under-19s. **Map** p42 C4 ❹

Set in the Baroque, 17th-century Palais Mollard, where enlightened despot Josef II held his round tables in the late 1700s, this branch of the Austrian National Library contains two quirky attractions: an Esperanto Museum on the ground floor and a Globe Museum above. The former tells the story of the doomed but fascinating attempt to create a universal language, the lingua franca for POWs from across the Habsburg Empire when imprisoned in Siberia during World War I. Gorgeous posters advertise world Esperanto congresses from Zamenhof's day – sadly there's no gift shop to buy replicas or postcards. The Globe Museum displays a vast array of globes, mostly pre-1850.

▶ *Also included in the combined ticket is a visit to the Papyrus Museum (1, Heldenplatz, same number, website and opening hours), with one of the largest collections in the world.*

FREE Michaelerkirche

1, Michaelerplatz 5 (533 8000, www. michaelerkirche.at). U3 Herrengasse. **Open** 7am-10pm daily. **Tours** (in German & English) 1pm, 3pm Wed. **Admission** free. *Crypt* €5; €3 reductions. **No credit cards. Map** p42 D4 ⑬
With its origins in the late Romanesque, the Church of St Michael mutated via the Baroque to the neoclassical look that it sports today. Recitals played on Vienna's largest Baroque organ, with a backdrop of falling angels above the main altar, can move even the most sceptical. The crypt and its collection of decrepit coffins, many of which reveal still-clothed corpses, are accessible by regular tours. See the website for details.

Restaurants & Coffeehouses

Café Central

1, Herrengasse 14 (533 37 64-26, www.ferstel.at). U3 Herrengasse or bus 1A, 2A, 3A. **Open** 7.30am-10pm Mon-Sat; 10am-10pm Sun. **Map** p42 C3 ⑬ **Coffeehouse**
When the original Café Griensteidl was demolished at the turn of the 19th century, the literary set moved to the Central, making it Vienna's main intellectual hangout. Trotsky – or Bronstein, as he was known in his clandestine years before World War I – was such an assiduous regular that an Austrian minister, on being informed of imminent revolution in Russia, supposedly remarked, 'And who on earth is going to make a revolution in Russia? I suppose you're going to tell me it's that Bronstein who sits all day at the Café Central!' These days, the clientele is almost exclusively tourists. Pop in, though, to admire the pseudo-Gothic vaulting and pay your respects to the dummy of the penniless poet Peter Altenberg that sits reading the paper.

▶ *Over the road, the konditerei at no.17 stocks irresistible chocolate truffles.*

Café Griensteidl

1, Michaelerplatz 2 (535 2692, www.cafegriensteidl. at). U3 Herrengasse or bus 2A, 3A. **Open** 8am-11.30pm daily. **Map** p42 C4 ⑭ **Coffeehouse**
The present Café Griensteidl remains in the shadow of the Hofburg, on the site of the original café – a hangout of such late 19th-century literary giants as Karl Kraus, Arthur Schnitzler, Hermann Bahr and Hugo von Hofmannstahl, before they all decamped to Café Central (*see above*). Theodor Herzl is said to have drafted *The Jewish State*, his blueprint for

Zionism, here. Reopened in 1990, the café attracts a mixture of civil servants from the adjoining ministries and tourists recovering from their visit to the Hofburg. Its spacious interior and windows overlooking Michaelerplatz are the principal attractions; unusually, it's child-friendly, smoke-free and has several high chairs.

Shops & Services

Viennastore

1, Herrengasse 6 (535 0141, www.thevienna store.at). U3 Herrengasse. **Open** 10am-7pm Mon-Sat. **Map** p42 C4 ⑭ **Gifts & souvenirs**
Searching for a souvenir that isn't utter tat? The Viennastore may have that elusive keepsake. A porcelain version of the typical Würstelstand cardboard plates? Heurigen wine glasses? A copy in English of the Adolf Loos guide to homemaking? All a cut above average. *Photos p54.*
Other location 1, Hohe Markt 5 (535 0565).

HOFBURG

The vast Imperial Palace and its parks and gardens occupy most of the south-eastern part of the Innere Stadt. Within its confines are two of Vienna's iconic institutions: the **Spanische Reitschule** (Spanish Riding School) and the **Burgkapelle**, where the Vienna Boys' Choir sings Sunday Mass. Rewarding museums include the **Kaiserliche Schatzkammer** (Secular & Sacred Treasuries) and the collections of the **Kunsthistorisches Museum** in the Neue Burg. The Baroque splendour of the National Library's **Prunksaal** should also be seen.

A public thoroughfare runs right through the Hofburg, connecting the Ringstrasse to Kohlmarkt and Graben, so the whole ensemble is open 24 hours a day and is particularly atmospheric after dark. Built over a period of seven centuries until 1918, the palace owes its size to the reluctance of successive royal families to occupy their predecessors' quarters.

The sprawling seat of the Habsburgs can be divided into four parts: the Alte Burg, the oldest section containing the Schatzkammer (Treasury) and the Burgkapelle (Chapel); In der Burg, where Franz Josef and Elisabeth's apartments are located; Josefsplatz, access point to the Spanish Riding School, the National Library and numerous minor museums; and finally the Neue Burg on Heldenplatz.

Alte Burg

The core of the palace is the Alte Burg, constructed around the original fortress of 1275, built by King Ottokar II of Bohemia. The oldest part is the portion of moat running beside the Schweizertor, the entrance to this section.

EXPLORE

FREE Burgkapelle

1, Schweizerhof (533 9927, www.hofmusikkapelle. gv.at). U3 Herrengasse or U3 Volkstheater or tram 1, 2, D. **Open** 10am-2pm Mon, Tue; 11am-1pm Fri. **Admission** free. **Map** p42 C4 ❷

Dating from the late 1440s, the original Gothic features of the Palace Chapel have been considerably tampered with over the years, but the vaulting and wooden statuary are still intact and visible. Concerts take place at 9.15am on Sunday – tickets are sold on the website, which also has a seating plan.

★ Kaiserliche Schatzkammer

1, Schweizerhof (525 24-0, www.kaiserliche-schatzkammer.at). U3 Herrengasse or U3 Volkstheater or tram 1, 2, D. **Open** 10am-5.30pm Mon, Wed-Sun. **Admission** €12; €9 reductions; free under-19s. **Map** p42 C4 ❸

Undoubtedly the most important of the Hofburg's museums, the Secular & Sacred Treasury contains wonders of the Holy Roman Empire, gold and precious stones aplenty, and a number of totemic artefacts. Most of the exhibits were amassed by Ferdinand I (1521-64) but assembled in the Hofburg under the reign of Karl VI in 1712. There are 20 smallish rooms, with labelling in German; an audio guide (€4) gives English commentary. Notable exhibits include the crown of Rudolf II, festooned with diamonds, rubies, pearls and topped with a huge sapphire; the ornate silver cot of Napoleon's son, the Duc de Reichstadt; and an agate bowl once thought to be the Holy Grail, though more likely stolen from Constantinople in 1204. Here, too, is the 'horn of the unicorn', a 2.5m (8ft) narwhal's horn. In the dimly lit rooms, don't miss the star attraction: the Byzantine octagonal crown of the Holy Roman Empire. Finally, there are a number of relics (Karl VI was an inveterate collector of these), including splinters of wood that supposedly came from the True Cross, a shred of the tablecloth from the Last Supper and one of John the Baptist's teeth.

In der Burg

This section comprises the buildings around the large square of the same name, opposite the Schweizertor. The buildings are uniformly Baroque, and the square itself is empty save for the lone statue of Emperor Franz, the first Austrian emperor and the last of the Holy Roman Empire. To the south is the Leopoldinischer Trakt, where Maria Theresa and Josef II resided, now the offices of the Austrian President. Opposite is the Reichskanzleitrakt, housing Franz Josef and his wife Sisi's apartments.

Kaiserappartements/Silberkammer/Sisi Museum

1, Innerer Burghof Kaisertor (533 7570, www.hofburg-wien.at). U3 Herrengasse or U3 Volkstheater or tram 1, 2, D. **Open** Sept-June

EXPLORE

Viennastore. *See p53.*

9am-5.30pm daily. *July, Aug* 9am-6pm daily.
Admission with audio guide €12.50; €7.50-
€11.50 reductions; free under-6s. **Map** p42 C4 ⑳
To see how the Habsburgs liked to entertain, the
Silver and Porcelain Collection, with its 290-piece
Sèvres dinner service given to Maria Theresa by
Louis XV, says it all. By contrast, the Imperial Rooms
are surprisingly austere; then again, Franz Josef was
a frugal old dog whose daily routine consisted of a
cold wash at 4am, a spartan breakfast of a bread roll
and coffee, then down to affairs of state while 'his
cities snored from the Swiss to the Turkish border'.
The Sisi Museum (named after Franz Josef's wife,
Empress Elisabeth) forms the prelude to the Imperial
Rooms and, with its portraits, photos of various foreign residences, personal railway carriage and the
file used to assassinate Sisi, it's not a bad show.

The museum leads directly to the Imperial
Apartments. The first is the waiting room for
petitioners, with a display of wooden dummies
dressed in the national costumes of the Habsburgs'
subject nations. The Audience Chamber has the
raised desk where Franz Josef stood to receive
petitions, one of his favourite pastimes. In his study
hangs a portrait of Sisi by Franz Winterhalter.
In the Grand Salon there's a bust of Field Marshal
Radetzky, and Winterhalter's larger, oft-reproduced
portrait of Sisi, exuding a glamour that is difficult
to detect in her chambers, which come next. In Sisi's
bedroom and boudoir the fittings are almost as
spartan as Franz Josef's – simple iron bed, copper
bathtub – although a quirky note is struck by the
set of wooden exercise bars. After the bathroom
come the two chambers known as the Bergl rooms,
after the painter who created these exotic murals in
tropical fauna and flora. Beyond, four rooms form
the Alexander apartments, where Alexander I, Czar
of Russia, stayed during the Congress of Vienna in
1815; sadly, there is no memento of his stay. The last
room is the dining room, with a lavishly decorated
banqueting table. Improvements in 2009 hardly
helped congestion in the narrow, poorly lit corridors
– expect a squeeze.

Neue Burg

Monumental Neue Burg overlooks vast
Heldenplatz (Heroes' Square), laid out at the
end of the Napoleonic Wars. Its original features
include Anton Fernkorn's two fine equestrian
statues: Prince Eugène of Savoy and Karl IV,
vanquisher of Napoleon at Aspern in 1809.
Beneath the square is a network of tunnels that
once served as the emperor's larder and wine
cellar. Today, they contain the moulds of all the
sculptures and reliefs that adorn the Ringstrasse,
covered in drapes; sadly, this ghostly labyrinth
is closed to the general public.

Not completed until 1926, eight years after
the demise of the Habsburgs, Neue Burg's
monumental neoclassicism gives Vienna a

Washington DC-style 'seat of power' look. Today,
Neue Burg houses the main reading room of the
National Library and four museums. There is no
access to the balcony where Hitler stood in 1938,
but a reasonable view can be had from inside. The
whole panorama can be viewed in comfort from
the gorgeous **Volksgarten Pavillon** (*see p152*).

In 1934, the triumphal Burgtor on the
Ringstrasse side was transformed by the Austro-
Fascists into a monument to the Austrian dead
of World War I. They also built two entrances to
the square on either side of the Burgtor, whose
stylised eagles represent one of Vienna's rare
examples of truly fascistic architecture. It's
instructive that Thomas Bernhard, the great
dramatist and enfant terrible of post-war Austria,
should have entitled his most scathing attack
on his country's past '*Heldenplatz*'. The flags
fluttering on the north side of the square mark
the headquarters of the Organisation for Security
and Cooperation in Europe (OSCE).

The **Völkerkundemuseum**, or Ethnological
Museum (525 24-0, www.ethno-museum.ac.at),
is closed for renovation until autumn 2017.

Sammlungen des Kunsthistorisches Museums in der Hofburg

*1, Neue Burg (525 240, www.khm.at). U3
Herrengasse or U3 Volkstheater or tram 1, 2, D.*
Open *Sept-May* 10am-6pm Tue, Wed, Fri-Sun;
10am-9pm Thur. *June-Aug* 10am-6pm Mon-
Wed, Fri-Sun; 10am-9pm Thur. **Admission** €14;
€11-€13 reductions; free under-19s. **Map** p42 C4 ⑳
The three collections of the fine arts museums in
the Hofburg are an excuse to enter the imposing
edifice of Neue Burg. The museums are located
on either side of its monumental central staircase.
The Ephesus Museum displays the spoils from
19th-century archaeological digs in Ephesus and
Samothrace, while the Collection of Arms and
Armour was originally made up of ceremonial
weapons acquired by two Habsburgs (Archdukes
Ernst of Styria and Ferdinand of Tyrol). It's now one
of the world's most extensive displays of arms and
armour from the 15th to the 17th centuries. Another
collection started by Ferdinand of Tyrol is that of
Ancient Musical Instruments – a chronologically
arranged exhibition containing the world's greatest
assembly of Renaissance instruments.

Albertina & Josefsplatz

From the old Hofburg ramparts directly behind
the magnificent **Palmenhaus** (*see p75*), the
Albertina hoves into view. These former imperial
apartments take their name from their former
residents – Maria Theresa's favourite daughter
Maria Christina and her husband, Duke Albert
of Sachsen-Teschen. Childless, the couple poured
their energies into founding one of the world's
finest collections of drawings and graphic art.

EXPLORE

Access to the **Albertina** museum is via triangular Albertinaplatz, a space formerly occupied by the Philliphof apartment building, in whose cellar 400 people were buried alive during a 1945 bombing raid. The tragedy is marked by Austrian sculptor Alfred Hrdlicka's controversial *Monument Against War and Fascism*. It consists of four separate elements – two marble blocks symbolising the Gate of Violence; a representation of Orpheus entering Hades; the Stone of the Republic engraved with fragments of an Austrian Declaration of Independence published in 1945; and, in the middle, the origin of the outrage, a small bronze statue of a kneeling Jewish man, scrubbing the street clean.

Skirting the eastern limits of the Hofburg, Augustinergasse leads to Josefsplatz. It's named after Josef II, who in 1783 ordered the demolition of the wall that encased the square within the Hofburg, thus converting it into a public thoroughfare. His equestrian statue stands in the middle of the square, which affords access to **Augustinerkirche**, the **Nationalbibliothek**, the **Spanish Riding School** and the attractions of Alte Burg.

The square featured in *The Third Man*, as the setting for Harry Lime's staged death in a motor accident in front of the Palais Pallavicini – his rather sumptuous place of residence. Both the Pallavicini (1784) and the nearby Palais Pálffy are fine examples of the aristocratic Baroque palaces that surround the Hofburg. Another, the Lobkowitz Palace, houses the **Austrian Theatre Museum** (1, Lobkowitzplatz 2, www.theatermuseum.at; closed Tue), which now includes artefacts from the Opera House Museum.

★ **Albertina**

1, Albertinaplatz 3 (534 83, www.albertina.at). U1, U2, U4 Karlsplatz or tram 1, 2, D. **Open** 10am-6pm Mon, Tue, Thur-Sun; 10am-9pm Wed. **Admission** €11.90; €7-€9.70 reductions; free under-19s. **Map** p42 D5 ⑯

Looking down on the Burggarten and Staatsoper, the Albertina takes in a series of plush state rooms and impressive, modern exhibition spaces, which were opened in 2003. This overhaul also added an emblematic yet controversial canopy by Hans Hollein. It runs up to three temporary shows of international, crowd-pleasing names at any one time, bolstered with items from the Albertina collection. This consists of some 1.5 million prints and 50,000 drawings, watercolours and etchings, including 145 Dürer drawings, 43 by Raphael, 70 by Rembrandt, a large number by Schiele and many more by Leonardo da Vinci, Michelangelo, Rubens, Cézanne, Picasso, Matisse and Klimt.

In 2007, these were bolstered by the long-term loan of the Batliner Collection, with works by Monet, Renoir, Cézanne, Modigliani, Giacometti, Bacon and

many more. Selected examples are generally to be found on the first floor, the theme changing two to three times a year. Admission includes access to the Habsburg state rooms, while entry to the lovely café, with sublime views from its terrace, only costs the price of a coffee.

▶ *At street level, the Albertina is also home to the Österreichisches Filmmuseum; see p142.*

FREE **Augustinerkirche**

1, Josefsplatz (533 7099, www.facebook.com/augustinerkirche). U1, U2, U4 Karlsplatz or U3 Herrengasse or tram 1, 2, D. **Open** 7.30am-5.30pm Mon; 7.30am-7.30pm Tue, Thur; 7.30am-6pm Wed, Fri; 8am-7.30pm Sat, Sun. **Admission** free. **Map** p42 D5 ⑰

The Gothic, early 14th-century church of St Augustin is where you'll find the Herzgrüftel (Little Heart Crypt), containing the hearts of generations of Habsburgs (viewing by appointment only). Free for all to see is Canova's impressive marble memorial to Maria Theresa's daughter Maria Christina and the rococo organ on which Brückner composed his memorable *Mass No.3 in F minor*. Sunday morning Mass is celebrated with a full orchestra.

Nationalbibliothek

1, Josefsplatz 1 (53410, www.onb.ac.at). U1, U2, U4 Karlsplatz or U3 Herrengasse or tram 1, 2, D. **Open** 10am-6pm Mon-Wed, Fri-Sun; 10am-9pm Thur. **Admission** €7; €4.50 reductions; €12.50 family; free under-19s. **Map** p42 C5 ㊳

Entrance to Austria's largest library is through the western side of Josefsplatz. Created by Fischer von Erlach, the Prunksaal is considered 'one of the finest Baroque interiors north of the Alps'. Completed by his son in 1735, the immense space is adorned with marble pillars, an enormous frescoed dome showing the *Apotheosis of Karl IV* by Daniel Gran, and gilded wood-panelled bookcases containing over 200,000 works. They include a 15th-century Gutenberg Bible and the 15,000 volumes of Prince Eugène of Savoy's impressive collection, which his spendthrift niece sold to the Habsburgs.

Spanische Reitschule (Spanish Riding School)

1, Michaelerplatz 1 (533 9031, www.srs.at). U1, U3 Stephansplatz or U3 Herrengasse. **Open** *Visitor centre* 9am-4pm Mon-Thur, Sat, Sun; 9am-7pm performance Fri. *Box office* (Josefsplatz) 9am-noon Tue-Fri. **Tours** (German & English) 2pm, 3pm, 4pm daily. **Morning training** 10am-noon Tue-Sat. Closed Jan, Feb. **Performances** check website for details. **Admission** *Tours* €16; €8-€13 reductions. *Morning training* €14; €7-€10 reductions. *Shows* €23-€210. Free under-6s; under-3s not admitted. **Map** p42 D4 ㊴

The Spanish Riding School, with its Lipizzaner horses, is one of Vienna's top tourist attractions. The full show is pretty costly and morning training,

Albertina.

though allowing you to admire these magnificent creatures and Fischer von Erlach's Baroque winter riding hall, lose their interest quite quickly into the two-hour session.

FREYUNG & AROUND

To the west, Herrengasse narrows down into Schottengasse, leading eventually to the Ringstrasse at Schottentor, a busy junction overlooked by the neo-Gothic Votivkirche. To the south are a few remaining chunks of the old city walls, in the form of the minuscule but picturesque Mölker Bastei. Take the Mölkerstieg steps that lead into Schreyvogelgasse. It's here that Harry Lime makes his first shadowy appearance in *The Third Man*, in the doorway of no.8.

At no.10, the Dreimäderlhaus, it is purported that Schubert had a carnal interest in all three of the daughters who lived there. Today, it is the premises of fashionable shoemaker **Ludwig Reiter**. Follow the cobbled street round and you are now on the Mölker Bastei, the old rampart. Beethoven lived for a period at no.8, the **Pasqualatihaus** (1798), where there's a small museum (535 8905, closed Mon).

The name Schottentor (Scots' Gate) refers to the Scottish Benedictine monks invited by

the Babenbergs to run the church and monastery they had founded in 1155. The monks in fact came from Scotia Major, the medieval name for Ireland. The Schottenstift (Monastery of the Scots) offered asylum to fugitives in the Middle Ages, hence the name of the broad tract that runs past the monastery: Freyung or sanctuary. On one side is the **Museum im Schottenstift** (1, Freyung 6, www.schottenstift.at; closed Mon), with its collection of 17th- and 18th-century Dutch, Flemish and Austrian paintings, as well as the 15th-century winged Schottenaltar.

Freyung itself, its broad cobbled pavements flanked by the palaces of Harrach and Ferstel to the south and the so-called Schubladlkastenhaus (Chest of Drawers House, 1774), is transformed on Fridays, when it hosts a market of organic farmers, apiarists, schnapps distillers and craftsmen. Further along on the north side is the **Bank Austria Kunstforum**, hosting prestigious itinerant exhibitions of modern art.

Freyung slopes gently upwards to Am Hof. Formerly the power centre of the Babenberg dynasty and the scene of jousts and executions, the biggest square in the Innere Stadt has recently been transformed by the opening of the **Park Hyatt** hotel (*see p211*), which not only contains quality European cuisine at the **Bank** but

forms part of the Golden Quarter (www.
goldenesquartier.at). This upscale retail hub
between Am Hof, Bognergasse, Seitzergasse,
Tuchlaubenhof and Tuchlauben contains
brands such as Prada, Armani and Roberto
Cavalli, with more surely to follow.

Previously, the most impressive building
on Am Hof was the Kirche am Hof, from whose
balcony the end of the Holy Roman Empire was
announced in 1806. Today, it's the spiritual home
of Vienna's Croatian community. At no.10 is the
18th-century Bürgerliches Zeughaus or Citizens'
Armoury, topped with a double-headed eagle
and gilded globe. For a time it housed Vienna's
fire brigade before it moved next door to the
Feuerwehr Zentrale. Nos.7-9 now house the
Firefighting Museum (9am-noon Sun, 53199).
At no.15 in the Palais Collalto, Mozart made his
public debut, performing at the ripe old age of six.

As you leave Am Hof to the north, an attractive
network of ancient lanes and alleyways leads to
what was once Vienna's medieval Jewish ghetto.
Schulhof, a pretty cobbled lane beside the Kirche
am Hof, is home to one of Vienna's many small
museums – the **Uhrenmuseum** (Clock Museum).
Behind, the magnificently Baroque Kurrentgasse
leads north into Judenplatz, the historic centre of
the ghetto, centrepieced by Rachel Whiteread's
austere monument to the Austrian victims of
the Shoah. The **Museum Judenplatz** provides
a permanent home for parts of the synagogue
that once stood here.

Facing Whiteread's monument is a statue of
Gotthold Ephraim Lessing, a major figure of the
German Enlightenment, who wrote *Nathan the
Wise*, a paean to tolerance towards the Jews. The
original was destroyed by the Nazis; sculptor
Siegfried Charoux made a new cast after the
war, not erected until 1982.

At no.2 is Zum Grossen Jordan (The Great
Jordan), the oldest house in the square. The relief
on its façade dates from the 16th century and
couldn't be further from the spirit of Lessing,
in that it actually celebrates the events of 1421.
Its Latin inscription reads: 'The flame rising
furiously through the whole city in 1421 purged
the terrible crimes of the Hebrew dogs.'

Apart from the fine apartment buildings,
the square's most spectacular edifice is the
Böhmische Hofkanzlei (Bohemian Chancery),
from which the Habsburgs ruled over the Czech
lands for almost 300 years.

Sights & Museums

Bank Austria Kunstforum

*1, Freyung 8 (537 3326, www.bankaustria-
kunstforum.at). U3 Herrengasse.* **Open** 10am-
7pm Mon-Thur, Sat, Sun; 10am-9pm Fri. **Tours**
6.30pm Fri; 3.30pm Sat; 11am Sun. **Admission**
€10; €4-€8.50 reductions. **Map** p42 C3 ⑩

Owned by Austria's biggest high-street bank, the
popular Kunstforum proffers a changing menu
of blockbuster exhibitions: Chagall, Van Gogh or
Kandinsky, perhaps, or themed shows (Art and
Delusion, Futurism). Work by younger contemporary
artists is relegated to a former strong room in the
basement called Tresor.

Museum Judenplatz

*1, Judenplatz 8 (535 0431, www.jmw.at).
U3 Herrengasse.* **Open** 10am-6pm Mon-Thur,
Sun; 10am-2pm Fri. **Admission** *Combined
with Jüdisches Museum* €10; €8 reductions;
under-18s free. **Map** p42 D3 ㉛
See p59 **Jewish Vienna**.

Uhrenmuseum

*1, Schulhof 2 (533 2265, www.wienmuseum.at).
U3 Herrengasse, U1, U3 Stephansplatz.* **Open**
10am-6pm Tue-Sun. **Admission** €6; €4 reductions;
free under-19s & all 1st Sun of mth. **Map** p42 D3 ㉜
Covering three floors of the Baroque Obizzi
Palace, the Clock Museum houses timepieces and
chronometers from the 15th to the 20th centuries, all
kept to time. The stellar exhibit is David Cajetano's
finely detailed 18th-century astronomical clock.
Spare a thought for Franz Zajíček, whose astro clock
telling the time in Vienna, Paris and London, the
days of the week, months of the year and phases of
the moon, cost him ten years of his life and 10,000
gulden. He later sold it to Vienna's Museum of Arts
& Industry for far less.

Restaurants & Coffeehouses

★ Bank

*Park Hyatt Vienna, 1, Am Hof 2 (22740-1236,
www.vienna.park.hyatt.com). U1, U3 Stephansplatz
or U3 Herrengasse.* **Open** noon-2.30pm; 6-10.30pm
Mon-Sat. **Main courses** €21-€92. **Map** p42 D3
㊳ International

A century-old bank was converted by Park Hyatt
into a five-star hotel (*see p211*) in 2015, thus transforming this oldest but most neglected of Innere
Stadt squares (the Bank has its own entrance on
Bognergasse). Beneath huge, high ceilings, guests
and non-guests alike tuck into European regional
cuisine created from as much locally sourced produce as possible: pike-perch from Lake Neusiedl in
Burgenland, T-bone steak and organic bison from
Manfred Höllerschmid's farm in Walkersdorf, and
trout from the streams of Radlberg. Sundays are
given over to *gabelfrühstück*, the Viennese equivalent of brunch (noon-3pm).

Fabios

*1, Tuchlauben 6 (532 2222, www.fabios.at).
U1, U3 Stephansplatz or U3 Herrengasse.*
Open *Bar* 10am-1am Mon-Sat. *Restaurant*
noon-11.30pm Mon-Sat. **Main courses**
€28.50-€38. **Map** p42 D3 ㉞ Italian

EXPLORE

JEWISH VIENNA

A new exhibition explores the struggles of Vienna's post-Holocaust survivors.

When a memorial was planned to the Austrian victims of the Holocaust, in the heart of what was Vienna's Jewish quarter, Judenplatz, it was deemed fitting that the proposed piece by British sculptor Rachel Whitehead should be unveiled in 1998, on the 60th anniversary of Kristallnacht. Instead, the unexpected discovery of the remains of the medieval synagogue that once stood here, burnt down in another ferocious pogrom in 1421, caused the opening to be delayed until 2002.

Along with Whitehead's austere work – a concrete cast of a library with the spines of the books facing inward, set on a low plinth engraved with the names of concentration camps – a **Museum Judenplatz** (*see p58*) was opened, a permanent home for those parts of the synagogue that were salvaged. It also recreates the medieval ghetto that thrived here. Meanwhile on Dorotheergasse, another victim of the horrific scenes of 1938, the **Jüdisches Museum** (*see p50*) has recently gained a permanent exhibition of stark power, strong on detail and sweeping in context. A single ticket covers both museums and visitors are given a simple map for the short walk between them.

The Jewish Museum on Dorotheergasse was the world's first when it opened in 1895. Closed down in 1938, it reopened here, at the Palais Esekeles, in 1993. The new permanent show 'Unsere Stadt!' – which opened in 2013, 75 years after Kristallnacht – tells a lesser-known story, that of the terrible struggle of the last remnants of the Jewish community in Vienna in the decade from the end of World War II to the declaration of the Austrian Republic, 1945 to 1955.

The 1421 pogrom described at the Museum Judenplatz, led by Duke Albert ('The Magnanimous'), sounds utterly horrific, with 92 men and 120 women burned to an agonising death. But, as 'Unsere Stadt!' explains, the hardships suffered by the pitifully few of Vienna's Holocaust survivors were, in their own way, almost as bitter. Offered no citizenship, no rights and no assistance, a few thousand struggled to eke out a living. Meanwhile, hundreds of thousands remained in displaced persons camps across Austria.

Although many headed to Israel, 'Unsere Stadt!' also illustrates another strand of post-war social history: the waves of Soviet Jews who were unable to return to the USSR after emigrating to Ben-Gurion's new state and became disillusioned. Austria was their next port of call.

These stories slowly came into the public arena in the 1950s through Vienna's young cabaret scene, also outlined in the new exhibition. The State Treaty of 1955, a new beginning for a new Austria, did nothing to admit responsibility for the terrible events here in the 1930s and 1940s. There was no sense of shared responsibility and no mention of compensation.

'Unsere Stadt!' goes on to describe the slow rise of a local klezmer music scene during the 1950s and '60s, the Movement of Young Jews in 1968, and the seminal cabaret, 'For Ghetto's Sake!', in 1985. The conflict between controversial post-war Chancellor Bruno Kreisky and Nazi hunter Simon Wiesenthal is also covered in fascinating detail.

In 1991, the Austrian government finally recognised the crimes of the Third Reich before sending out compensation letters to nearly 20,000 survivors of the Holocaust more than a decade later.

EXPLORE

Fabios is an *elegantissimo* designer Italian, clad in acres of dark wood and black leather. Local celebs adore the theatrical summer terrace on pedestrianised Tuchlauben, where they don their shades and pick at the superb fish. The downsides are that the tables are rather crammed in, and the wine list is an expensive affair. Otherwise, if you have the cash, you can eat the best tuna in land-locked Vienna.

Fabios. See p58.

Zum Finsteren Stern

1, Schulhof 8 (535 2100, www.zumfinsteren stern.at). U3 Herrengasse. **Open** 6pm-midnight Tue-Sat. **Main courses** €16-€24. **Map** p42 D3 ⑤ **Austrian**
Ella da Silva's creative Italian-inspired dishes feature plenty of locally sourced, slow-cooked meat and veg served up in relaxed surroundings. Desserts are great, too, and the panna cotta is a local legend. The fairly priced wines are mostly Austrian and excellent, and the summer terrace, in one of Innere Stadt's most charming corners, is simply gorgeous.

Zum Schwarzen Kameel

1, Bognergasse 5 (533 81 25-11, www.kameel.at). U1, U3 Stephansplatz or bus 1A, 2A, 3A. **Open** *Restaurant* noon-11pm daily. *Delicatessen buffet* 8am-midnight daily. **Main courses** €23-€36. **Map** p42 D3 ⑥ **Viennese/Haute cuisine**
This classic Viennese address opened as a grocer's in 1618 and was reputedly patronised by Beethoven. Today, it still sells wine and cold cuts, but most of the expensively dressed clientele come for the vast assortment of delicate open sandwiches and canapés served in the wood-panelled main bar. The restaurant itself has possibly the most beautiful dining room in Vienna, full of gorgeous Jugendstil ceramic reliefs and lamps (avoid the sterile-looking inner sanctum, though). The menu offers good things in and around the Viennese pantheon, but you can't beat the cooked ham with freshly grated horseradish on brown bread from the bar.

Shops & Services

Audio Center

1, Judenplatz 9 (533 6849, www.audiocenter.at). U1, U3 Stephansplatz or U3 Herrengasse. **Open** 10am-7pm Mon-Fri; 10am-5pm Sat. **Map** p42 D3 ⑦ **Books & music**
An excellent jazz store offering CDs and vinyl. It has a good selection of world music, too, and isn't afraid to stock crazier improv and crossover jazz.

Grimm

1, Kurrentgasse 10A (533 1384, www.grimm.at). U1, U3 Stephansplatz. **Open** 7am-6.30pm Mon-Fri; 8am-1pm Sat. **Map** p42 D3 ⑧ **Organic**
Bread is invariably excellent in Austria, and a quite bewildering range of cereals, seeds and spices is employed in its manufacture. This organic establishment offers a splendid array.

EXPLORE

Ludwig Reiter

1, Mölkersteig 1 (533 420 422, www.ludwig-reiter. com). U2 Schottentor. **Open** 10am-6pm Mon-Fri; 10am-5pm Sat. **Map** p42 C3 ➏➒ **Footwear**

One of Vienna's finest bespoke shoemakers, Ludwig Reiter has made an international name for himself. The superbly finished trainers are based on regulation Austrian army issue.

Other locations 1, Führichgasse 6 (512 6146); 4, Wiedner Hauptstrasse 41 (505 8258).

Mag Kottas

1, Freyung 7 (533 9532, www.kottas.at). U2 Schottenring. **Open** 8.30am-6pm Mon-Fri; 9am-12.30pm Sat. **Map** p42 C3 ➐➐ **Health & beauty**

Kottas has been the most reliable herbalist in the city since 1795. Its trademark infusions are available at all Viennese chemists, but for the full range of over 600 herbs, and to admire the magnificent Baroque premises, call in at this branch.

Organic Market Freyung

1, Freyung (www.biobauernmarkt-freyung.at). U2 Schottentor. **Open** 9am-6pm Fri, Sat. **Map** p42 C2 ➐➊ **Organic**

This market sells exclusively organic products directly from the growers. Some stalls also display non-edible wares, such as candles and wooden toys. Check the website for the upcoming schedule.

Xocolat

Palais Ferstel, 1, Freyung 2 (535 4363, www. xocolat.at). U3 Herrengasse. **Open** 10am-6pm Mon-Fri; 10am-5pm Sat. **Map** p42 C2 ➐➋ **Food & drink**

Come to this chocolate emporium, in the stone arches of the Ferstel passage, for the creations of Catalan chocolatier Enric Rovira, Californian Scharffen Berger and Austrian brand Zotter. The outlet in the 9th district, Xocolat-Manufaktur, is a boutique and workshop where you can watch chocolatiers at work and inhale the heady aromas. Workshops (€75) are offered by appointment, led by chef Christian Petz or pastry chef Thomas Scheiblhofer.

Other location 9, Servitengasse 5 (310 0020).

TOWARDS THE DANUBE CANAL

Cobbled Jordangasse leads into Wipplingerstrasse and the Altes Rathaus, the Baroque Old Town Hall, home to various municipal agencies and the **Austrian Resistance Archive**. Its courtyard encloses a beautiful fountain by Donner, the Andromeda Brunnen (1745), and the Gothic Salvatorkapelle, the town hall chapel, with a fine renaissance portal on Salvatorgasse.

Wipplingerstrasse heads north-west towards the Ringstrasse, past an enormous sign showing a chimney sweep (a much-loved figure in Viennese mythology) and over the Jugendstil bridge spanning Tiefer Graben, once the course of the Alserbach Danube tributary.

More atmospheric is the walk to the left of the Altes Rathaus and along cobbled Salvatorgasse to where Maria am Gestade (Our Lady of the Riverbank) looks over a flight of steps leading down into Concordiaplatz. One of Vienna's finest Gothic churches, it used to have strong ties to the Danube fishermen; today, it attracts worshippers from Vienna's Czech community.

Vienna's oldest square, Hoher Markt, is an ungainly ensemble of historicist apartment buildings and shabby post-1945 warrens. At midday tourists congregate around the Jugendstil Ankeruhr, an elaborate mechanical clock set between the two monumental edifices belonging to the Anker insurance company. The figures that trundle out on the hour include Marcus Aurelius, Roman governor of Vindobona, and composer Joseph Haydn; a full list of those honoured and a history of the clock are given on a plaque.

Inside the bridge beneath the clock, look out for the stone brackets depicting Adam, Eve, an angel and a devil with a pig's snout. Running below is Bauernmarkt, a swish shopping street.

The centrepiece of Hoher Markt is Fischer von Erlach the Younger's flamboyant Vermählungsbrunnen (Marriage Fountain). It dramatises Mary's marriage to Joseph, presided over by a high priest. In the shopping arcade on the south side is access to the **Römer Museum**.

North of Hoher Markt, further traces of medieval Jewish Vienna are visible along Judengasse and Seitenstettengasse, where the **Stadttempel**, the main synagogue, is located. Its architect Josef Kornhäusel (1782-1860) built the so-called Kornhäusel-Turm at no.2 as a studio and, according to local legend, a refuge from his nagging wife. Its sheer size can best be appreciated from behind, in Judengasse. Nineteenth-century photos of Judengasse depict it as a bustling street, full of second-hand clothes dealers; today, the rag trade operates in the form of small boutiques.

In the early 1980s, the area became the hub of Vienna's nightlife scene, the 'Bermuda Triangle'. Today, it's naff, but the many bars and restaurants provide a buzz. At the end of Judengasse is a railed balcony overlooking busy Franz-Josefs-Kai and the Donaukanal. Alongside the cityscape stands ivy-clad Ruprechtskirche to the right. The oldest church in the city, squat and Romanesque, its existence is documented from 1137. The steps here take you down to a broad concourse leading east to Schwedenplatz. It's all 1970s cement, but the human traffic makes it one of Vienna's few bustling zones. The ice-cream parlour at no.17 is a local legend. *See p63* **Ice Queens**.

To the west on Morzinplatz stands the Monument to the Victims of Fascism (1985) on the site of the former Hotel Metropole, Gestapo headquarters during the war and bombed to bits in 1945. The monument is emblazoned with the yellow Star of David, the pink triangle and other symbols of Nazi victims. Further west are the streets of the 19th-century textile quarter. If the weather's fine, the wooded parks in Rudolfsplatz and further west on Börseplatz are ideal for a rest.

Named after the red tower that stood on the city wall at today's Schwedenplatz, Rotenturmstrasse cuts through the northern section of the Innere Stadt. At its most northerly end, it divides the Bermuda Triangle area from the medieval streets around Fleischmarkt, the old meat market. Look out for the plaque at no.7 marking film director Billy Wilder's home when he was a schoolboy in Vienna. The building is the original HQ of the Julius Meinl grocery firm and the façade is emblazoned with the coats of arms of the ports of London, Hamburg and Trieste, and symbolic reliefs showing harvesting, transport and roasting of coffee. Further east, the street widens and the gilt and decorative brickwork of Theophil Hansen's Griechische Kirche (1861) comes into view. In the Middle Ages, Greek and Levantine traders made Fleischmarkt their home. Adjoining the church at no.11 is the Griechenbeisl, with rooms dedicated to past patrons such as Beethoven, Brahms, Schubert and Mark Twain.

Fleischmarkt runs directly on into Postgasse and winds round into beautiful Schönlaterngasse, with Baroque façades, such as the Basilikenhaus at no.7. Schönlaterngasse, the 'Street of Beautiful Lanterns' (particularly one at no.6), emerges on to Sonnenfelsgasse. Inside the massive Baroque Hildebrandthaus at no.3 is labyrinthine **Zwölf-Apostelkeller** (Twelve Apostles Cellar), Vienna's largest and best-loved *bierkeller*.

Bäckerstrasse contains the marvellous renaissance Hof at no.7, the premises of violin and piano manufacturers. At no.19, **Café Alt Wien** has long been a bohemian late-night drinking haunt. Note also the bizarre patch of mural unearthed at no.12 during restoration work, showing a bespectacled cow playing backgammon with a wolf – supposedly a parody of the religious tensions of 17th-century Vienna.

To the east, Bäckerstrasse opens out into Dr-Ignaz-Seipel-Platz and the buildings of the Alte Universität, the Akademie der Wissenschaft (Academy of Sciences) and Jesuitenkirche, a gorgeously preserved establishment of the pope's vanguard. The church was built by an unknown architect in 1627, but both the façade and interior were substantially altered in 1703-05 by trompe-l'oeil master Andrea Pozzo, who introduced a painted false 'dome'. This illusion works best from the spot in the nave marked with a white stone.

Sights & Museums

🆓 Archiv des Österreichischen Widerstands

1, Altes Rathaus (Stairway 3), Wipplingerstrasse 6-8 (22 89469-319, www.doew.at). U1, U3 Stephansplatz or U1, U4 Schwedenplatz or tram 1, 2. **Open** *Exhibition* 9am-5pm Mon-Wed, Fri; 9am-7pm Thur. *Archive & Library* 9am-5pm Mon-Thur. **Admission** free. **Map** p43 E3 ⑰
The Austrian Resistance Archive was founded in 1963 by ex-resistance fighters and anti-fascist historians to chronicle the fate of the 2,700 Austrian resistance fighters executed by the Nazis (and the thousands more who died in the camps). The events pre- and post-1938, leading to Austria's disastrous pact with the Third Reich, are also portrayed. The wealth of fascinating material detailing the horror includes photos, personal effects and propaganda.

Römer Museum

1, Hoher Markt 3 (535 5606, www.wienmuseum. at). U1, U3 Stephansplatz or U1, U4 Schwedenplatz or tram 1,2. **Open** 9am-6pm Tue-Sun. **Admission** €6; €4 reductions; free under-19s & all 1st Sun of mth. **Map** p43 E3 ⑭
Hoher Markt was the core of Roman Vindobona, but all that remains is this site of officers' quarters with baths and underground heating, dating from AD 1 to AD 4. Aficionados will enjoy the informative display on what life was like in the Roman garrison.

★ Stadttempel

1, Seitenstettengasse 2-4 (535 0431-130, www. ikg-wien.at). U1, U4 Schwedenplatz or tram 1, 2. **Guided tours** (ID required) 11.30am, 2pm Mon-Thur (except Jewish holidays). **Admission** €3; €1 reductions. **No credit cards. Map** p43 E3 ⑮
Built in neoclassical style by Josef Kornhäusel in 1826, the synagogue is one of the few that escaped destruction in the Nazi years, probably due to its discreet façade or because setting it on fire would have endangered neighbouring houses. On entering, you're confronted by a monument to the 65,000 Austrian victims of the Shoah. Their names are engraved on slate tablets that rotate around a central truncated column. The interior of the synagogue has an elegant simplicity – a blue oval dome strewn with stars and supported by classical pillars.

Restaurants & Coffeehouses

★ Expedit

1, Wiesingerstrasse 6 (512 3313-0, www.expedit. at). U3 Stubentor/tram 1, 2. **Open** noon-midnight Mon-Fri; 6pm-midnight Sat. **Main courses** €10.50-€19.50. **Map** p43 G3 ⑯ Italian
This former textile warehouse now contains one of Vienna's most original restaurants. Instead of rolls of Crimplene, the metal shelves are replete with the joys of Liguria – jars of tiny olives, artichokes in oil and pesto, cases of oil and wine. A no-nonsense communal *cantina*, complete with blaring TV, Expedit serves a young, clubby clientele with exquisitely prepared, if a touch pricey, antipasti and a choice of five main courses, all with a distinctive Ligurian touch. Wines are reliable and fairly priced.

ICE QUEENS

The Viennese are spoilt for choice when it comes to the cold stuff.

Vienna is rightly lauded as a town of cake- and pastry-makers. But it also has some great ice-cream parlours to rival those of Austria's southern neighbour.

Since the dawn of paid holidays, ordinary Viennese have flocked to Lignano, Bibioni and the other beach resorts of northern Italy, and discovered the sweet side of life. Fortunately for Vienna, many enterprising Italians have also made the opposite journey, establishing the kind of ice-cream parlours that would stand proud in their homeland.

The oldest one still in operation is thought to be the ever-popular **Eissalon am Schwedenplatz** (1, Franz-Josefs-Kai 17, www.gelato.at), dating back to 1886. The Innere Stadt has a high density of long-established parlours such as **Eis Tuchlauben** (1, Tuchlauben 15, www.eissalon-tuchlauben. at) and **Gelateria Hohe Markt** (1, Hohe Markt 4, www.gelateria-hohermarkt.at), a favourite with expat Italians.

In the last few years, Vienna has undergone an ice-cream boom, with the arrival of new salons such as the celebrated **Eisgreissler** (1, Rotenturmstrasse 14, www.eis-greissler. at), known for its long queues, vegan varieties and kooky flavours such as pumpkinseed oil;

and **Ferrari** (1, Krugerstrasse 9, www. facebook.com/ferrarigelato), purveyors of Vienna's best lemon sorbet and *gianduja*.

The other ice-cream hotspot in Vienna is in and around the 7th and 8th districts, where the tone was first set by **Veganista** (7, Neustiftgasse 23/3, www.veganista.at) – as the militant-sounding name suggests, it's 100 per cent vegan, using rice, soy, coconut or oat milk, or a combination thereof. All flavours are made from scratch daily and the parlour itself is a real beauty.

The self-styled 'flavour nerds' behind nearby **Schelato** (8, Lerchenfelderstrasse 34, www.facebook.com/schelato), its name a play on the German pronunciation of *gelato*, are the new wild men of Vienna's ice-cream scene. This duo are churning out flavours such as beetroot with poppyseed, pomegranate with basil, and avocado with black sesame in their chic little shop. Great coffee and drinks are also available. More bizarre flavours are on offer at the **Ice Dream Factory** (7, Burggasse 68, www. icedreamfactory.com), where you can slurp a Thai Cotta (coconut milk, lemongrass and lemon zest) in its charmingly distressed interior or outside on the cobblestones.

EXPLORE

Labstelle.

Griechenbeisl

*1, Fleischmarkt 11 (533 1977, www.griechenbeisl.
at). U1, U4 Schwedenplatz or tram 1, 2, 21.* **Open**
11.30am-1am daily. **Main courses** €17.30-€24.90.
Map p43 F3 ⑰ **Austrian**

Originally an inn patronised by Greek and Levantine
merchants visiting Vienna to trade, and mentioned
in chronicles under a variety of names as far back as
1500, the quaint Griechenbeisl suffers from an excess
of historical connections. Due to its association with
illustrious regulars such as Beethoven, Schubert
and (briefly) Mark Twain, as well as its role in the
Viennese legend of street musician Liebe Augustin,
its maze of panelled rooms is generally occupied by
visitors from Omaha or Osaka. All the traditional
Austrian dishes are on the menu, but you pay a
supplement for the history.

Hansen

*1, Wipplingerstrasse 34 (532 0542, www.hansen.
co.at). U2 Schottentor or tram 1, 2, D or bus 1A,
3A.* **Open** 9am-11pm Mon-Fri; 9am-5pm Sat. **Main
courses** €12-€24. **Map** p42 C2 ⑱ **International**

Housed beneath the Stock Exchange yet bathed in
natural light, Hansen takes its name from the building's architect. It's a fragrant combination of restaurant and fine florist – make sure you use the entrance
on the corner of the Ring to see the floral display.
Hansen also runs Vestibül, in the marble-clad
ground floor of the Burgtheater.
Other location Vestibül, 1, Universitätsring 2
(532 4999).

Labstelle

*1, Lugeck 6 (236 2122, www.labstelle.at) U1, U3
Stephansplatz or U1, U4 Schwedenplatz.* **Open**
11.30am-2am Mon-Fri; 10am-2am Sat. **Main
courses** €11.90-€26.90. **Map** p43 E3 ⑲ **Austrian**

It's easy to overlook the entrance to this chic new
eaterie. Obscured by the terraces of touristy establishments on busy Lugeck, Labstelle is located in a
vaulted space where you can choose between open
tables, booths and courtyard seating. Here the accent
is on locally sourced, high-quality produce whose
suppliers' addresses are extensively annotated
on the menu. Of the two lunch deals, a seasonal
salad followed by orecchiette with seared salmon
trout might be an option. In the evening, original
starters include nettle soup and pig's trotters with
snails, while mains range from an excellent rib-eye
with grilled green asparagus to braised rabbit and
pan-fried char. For a quick mid-afternoon snack,
Labstelle serves a variety of open sandwiches on its
superb home-baked bread.

Motto am Fluss

*1, Franz-Josefs-Kai (252 5510, www.motto.at/
mottoamfluss). U2, U4 Schwedenplatz or tram 1, 2.*
Open 11.30am-2.30pm, 6pm-2am daily. **Main
courses** €19.50-€29.50. **Map** p43 F3 ⑳ **Austrian**

Celebrity gastronome Bernd Schlachter has sold his
original Motto restaurant and now concentrates on
this nautical star, located above the new moorings
of the Vienna-Bratislava catamaran service (*see
p223*). Take in views of the Danube Canal and

EXPLORE

Stacked beneath one of von Hildebrandt's most spectacular Baroque houses, this cellar on three subterranean levels is touristy but good fun. A vast quantity of typical Austrian grub, beer and wine is accompanied by traditional music (7-11pm daily), in a labyrinth of vaulted gothic and early Baroque cellars. (It's a long walk up to the toilets from the lower ground floor.) Ordering is made easier by a choice of buffets.

Cafés, Bars & Pubs

Café Alt Wien

1, Bäckerstrasse 9 (512 5222). U1, U3 Stephansplatz. **Open** 10am-2am daily. **No credit cards. Map** p43 F3 ⓖ
A good café during the day and an excellent drinking establishment after dark, with nicotine-stained ceilings, poster-covered walls and a general air of Paris circa 1968. The clientele is a mixture of students and gregarious elderly Bohemians. If you can get a table, order the legendary goulash.

Shops & Services

Pickwicks

1, Marc-Aurel-Strasse 10-12 (533 0182, www. pickwicks.at). U1, U4 Schwedenplatz or tram 1, 2, 21 or bus 2A. **Open** noon-10pm Mon-Sat; 2-9pm Sun. **Map** p43 E3 ⓖ **Film**
Vienna's oldest English-language video/DVD rental store is also the largest. On the ground floor is a cosy café and bookstore.

Satyr Filmwelt

1, Marc-Aurel-Strasse 5 (535 5326). U1, U4 Schwedenplatz. **Open** 10am-7.30pm Mon-Fri; 9am-5pm Sat. **Map** p43 E3 ⓖ **Books & music**
This bookshop specialises in film and stocks a good variety of biographies, posters and scripts, plus DVDs and soundtracks.

Shakespeare & Co

1, Sterngasse 2 (535 5053-11, www.shakespeare. co.at). U1, U4 Schwedenplatz. **Open** 9am-9pm Mon-Sat. **Map** p43 E3 ⓖ **Books & music**
This tiny shop is Vienna's most reliable for literature and academic titles in English. Shakespeare & Co is great on contemporary and classic literature, with a good selection of fine arts and music, sociology and Vienna-related themes on ceiling-high shelves.

Unger und Klein

1, Gölsdorfgasse 2 (532 1323, www.ungerund klein.at). U2, U4 Schottenring. **Open** 3pm-midnight Mon-Fri; 5pm-midnight Sat. **Map** p43 E2 ⓖ **Food & drink**
A magnificent 'theatre of drinking', Unger und Klein's premises were designed by Eichinger oder Knechtl in 1992. Wine bar and store under one roof, Unger und Klein is a favourite with media types – but don't let that put you off.

the Leopoldstadt skyline as you tuck into Motto's expertly cooked tuna steaks and delicious vegetable purées. With a schnitzel retailing at €21.90, a night at Motto is no bargain, but it adds a touch of glamour to the city's sometimes rather utilitarian dining scene. There's also a cheaper café with alfresco seating, serving breakfast, snacks, salads and cakes.

★ Restaurant Konstantin Filippou

1, Dominikanerbastei 17 (512 2229, www. konstantinfilippou.com). U2, U4 Schwedenplatz or tram 1, 2. **Open** noon-3pm, 6.30pm-midnight Mon-Fri. **Dinner** €47-€109. **Business lunch** €22-€33. **Map** p43 G3 ⓖ **Austrian**
Graz-born, Michelin-starred chef Konstantin Filippou worked in San Sebastián and at Le Gavroche before setting up his own restaurant close to the Danube Canal. In a neat, light, 35-seat space, diners can opt for one of two evening menus, four to six courses with wine pairings. Fresh seafood (mackerel, lobster, langoustine) features prominently, along with pigeon, veal and liver. Seasonal produce, meticulously sourced, is the key here, as well as the experience Filippou brings to bear from the Basque lands, London and other top kitchens in Vienna. Weekdays only.

Zwölf Apostelkeller

1, Sonnenfelsgasse 3 (512 6777, www.zwoelf-apostelkeller.at). U1, U3 Stephansplatz. **Open** 11am-midnight daily. **Main courses** €8.50-€19.90. **Map** p43 F3 ⓖ **Austrian**

EXPLORE

Ringstrasse & Around

In 1857, Emperor Franz Josef I ordered the construction of the Ringstrasse – a magnificent new boulevard that would reflect the glory and achievements of the Habsburg Empire, and also help to alleviate the city's acute housing shortage. Tracing the line of the medieval city walls and defensive ditch, the Ringstrasse replaced the area of greenbelt known as the Glacis – a military parade ground that separated the old city from the suburbs. The broad, horseshoe-shaped avenue was built over the next three decades, at astronomical expense. Lined with palaces, parks and imposing civic edifices, it oozes pomp and ostentation. As Bill Bryson observed: 'A Martian coming to earth would unhesitatingly land at Vienna, thinking it to be the capital of the planet.' The 150th anniversary celebrations of the boulevard during 2015 brought into focus its history and splendour.

EXPLORE

MAK.

Don't Miss

1 Leopold Museum Unmissable Egon Schiele collection (p73).

2 Kunsthistorisches Museum From Egyptian artefacts to Venetian and Flemish art (p69).

3 Volksgarten Take a break in Franz Josef's former private garden (p75).

4 MAK Vienna's version of the V&A (p77).

5 Naturhistorisches Museum Dinosaurs and skulls galore (p72).

Kunsthistorisches Museum.

AROUND THE RINGSTRASSE

Although heralding a new age, the buildings of the Ringstrasse – with the exception of Otto Wagner's Postsparkasse – were models of the past, expressing the aspirations of the burgeoning Viennese middle classes, a style baptised as historicism. A day out along the Ringstrasse allows you to admire the principal European architectural styles.

Lined with shady maples, sycamores, lime trees and horse chestnuts, each section of the road has its own name, such as the Burgring for the stretch that passes the Hofburg. The world-famous **Staatsoper** (State Opera House; *see p165*) was the first public building to be opened on the Ring, in May 1869. Vienna's wealthiest citizens, many of them Jews unable to buy property in the Innere Stadt, constructed palatial homes and apartment buildings on the hallowed street.

Along with the opera, other imposing public buildings around the Ring include the Rathaus (city hall), Parlament, the Burgtheater and assorted museums. Most of Vienna's temples to high art are on the Ringstrasse or a stone's throw away. There are many parks and gardens,

too, including the Burggarten, Volksgarten, Stadtpark and Rathauspark.

Today, the Ringstrasse is no longer the address of choice it once was – traffic has put paid to that. Buildings now tend to be used as offices, with shops and restaurants on the ground floors. This commercial activity is also on the decline as high rents dissuade retailers and parking restrictions make access difficult.

DONAUKANAL TO OPER

Named after the Benedictine monks who established a church and monastery just inside the city walls in the late 12th century, the Schottenring ('Scots' Ring') is the most dowdy stretch of the Ringstrasse. Vienna's only inner-city high-rise, the Ringturm (1955), looms over the Donaukanal here and is illuminated at night. The finest public building along here, at Schottenring 20, is the Börse (stock exchange), built by one of the major Ringstrasse architects, Theophil Hansen. The subdued red of the brickwork (Hansenrot, as it is often referred to) and the white stone of the cornices make this one of the Ringstrasse's most elegant edifices.

EXPLORE

would link them to the Neue Burg and its planned mirror image on the other side of Heldenplatz by means of two triumphal arches across the Ringstrasse. Alas, the development of this so-called Kaiserforum was ditched after the fall of the House of Habsburg.

Sights & Museums

★ Kunsthistorisches Museum

1, Maria-Theresien-Platz (52524-0, www.khm.at). U2 Museumsquartier or U2, U3 Volkstheater or tram 1, 2, D. **Open** *Sept-May* 10am-6pm Tue, Wed, Fri-Sun; 10am-9pm Thur. *June-Aug* 10am-6pm Mon-Wed, Fri-Sun; 10am-9pm Thur. **Admission** €14; €11 reductions; free under-19s. **Map** p70 C5 ❶

The Museum of Fine Arts is one of the best of its kind in Europe, showcasing the artistic treasures amassed by the Habsburgs. The opulent architecture and decoration – granite, marble and stucco, interspersed with murals by Makart, Matsch, Gustav Klimt and his brother Ernst – produce an overwhelming effect.

In the west wing, the ground-floor galleries house Greek and Roman antiquities and the superb Egyptian and Near Eastern collections, with their wall paintings, sarcophagi, remains of mummified crocodiles and cats, and intricately inscribed papyri. Meanwhile, the east wing accommodates the Kunstkammer; a chamber of curiosities and exotica, with ornaments, clocks, automatons and astrolabes. The prize exhibit is Benvenuto Cellini's *Saliera*, a priceless gold and enamel salt cellar (1540) stolen from here in 2003 by a window-smashing thief but recovered three years later.

The first-floor galleries are arranged in a horseshoe with Flemish, German and Dutch paintings in the east wing, and Italian, Spanish and French works in the west. A roll-call of the greats here features Caravaggio, Canaletto, Rembrandt, Vermeer, van Dyck and Titian. Room X is perhaps the busiest, with its almost unrivalled collection of work by Pieter Bruegel the Elder, acquired by Rudolf II, which includes *Hunters in the Snow* (1565) and *Peasant Wedding* (1567). Elsewhere, you might find yourself in front of Holbein's crisply objective *Jane Seymour* (1536), his first portrait as Henry VIII's court painter. Note also the last completed work by Velázquez, *Portrait of the Infanta Margarita Theresa* (1659). *The Little Fur* (room XIII) is the name Rubens gave to the portrait of his second wife Hélène Fourment; Hélène was only 16 when she married the 53-year-old Rubens.

In recent years, director Sabine Haag has breathed new life into this slightly musty institution, instigating a number of challenging temporary exhibitions, including a first-ever Lucian Freud show in 2014. Velvet stools and sofas are provided at regular intervals, while the café is in the cupola hall at the top of the grand staircase.

From here, it's a straight run past the Votivkirche, Universität and Rathaus, before a rest in the Volksgarten, and then on to Parlament. Built opposite the spot where Franz Josef survived an assassination attempt by a Hungarian nationalist in 1853, the **Votivkirche** (Rooseveltplatz, www.votivkirche.at) wasn't completed until 25 years later by the meticulous Heinrich Ferstel. He was also responsible for the **University** (1, Karl-Lueger-Ring, www.univie.ac.at), with ceiling frescoes by Klimt in the Grosser Festsaal – you're free to wander round the grounds. The **City Hall**, the most imposing building on the Ringstrasse, is also accessible but to explore inside you'll have to join a free guided tour (www.wien.gv.at/english/cityhall/tours.htm). These are given in German with an English audio guide at 1pm on Mondays, Wednesdays and Fridays unless there's an event or meeting taking place. Regular daily tours (€5; €2.50 reductions) are also given of Theophil Hansen's Hellenistic **Parlament** building (www.parlament.gv.at).

Further on come the **Kunsthistorisches Museum** and **Naturhistorisches Museum**. Designed by Gottfried Semper, these last two were conceived as part of a grandiose plan that

EXPLORE

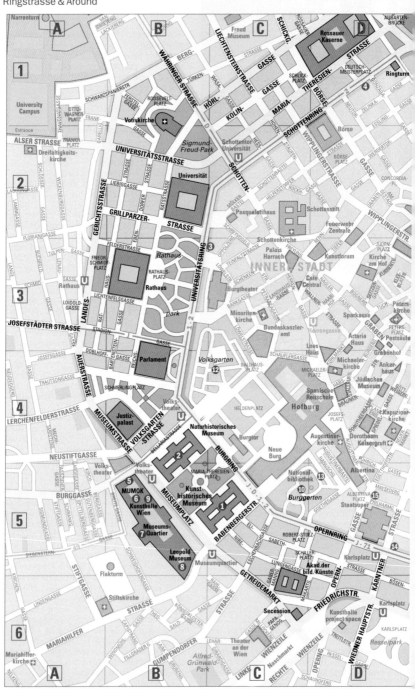

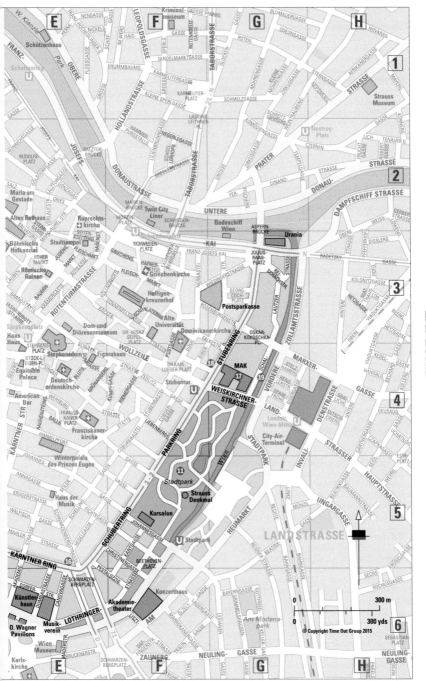

Naturhistorisches Museum

*1, Burgring 7 (52 177, www.nhm-wien.ac.at).
U2 Museumsquartier or U2, U3 Volkstheater or
tram 1, 2, D.* **Open** 9am-6.30pm Mon, Thur-Sun;
9am-9pm Wed. **Admission** €10; €5-€8 reductions;
free under-19s. **Map** p70 B4 ❷

One of the world's largest and most celebrated natural
history museums, the scientific counterpart to the
Kunsthistorisches Museum across the square opened
in 1889. Some of the display cases are magnificent
century-old affairs, the labelling is in German and
there's still a wonderfully studious air about the place.
Explanations of major concepts – how earthquakes
happen, the origin of the Moon – are also given in
English. The basis of the collection was assembled
by Emperor Franz Stefan, Maria Theresa's husband,
an amateur scientist who collected skulls, fossils,
precious stones, meteorites and rare stuffed animals.

Displayed in a dark cubicle, the most valuable piece
is the Venus of Willendorf. Found in the Wachau,
this curvaceous 11cm limestone fertility symbol is
believed to be over 25,000 years old. The museum has
minerals, zoological exhibits and the world's largest
collection of human skulls (some 43,000, dating
from 40,000 BC to the present). Amid the old-school
cabinets and display cases, you can spin a wheel and
see how the continents formed and will reassemble in
millennia to come, look inside a meteorite and watch
how a giant asteroid put paid to the dinosaurs. It's all
delightfully antiquated and often fascinating.

Restaurants & Coffeehouses

Café Landtmann

*1, Universitätsring 4 (24100-120, www.
landtmann.at). U2 Schottentor or tram 1, D.*
Open 7.30am-midnight daily. **Map** p70 C3
❸ Coffeehouse

This elegant coffeehouse was a favourite of Sigmund
Freud, who particularly relished a slice of *guglhupf*,
the sponge cake with a hole. It's a traditional
kaffeehaus where hats and coats are surrendered
to a frowning cloakroom dame and liveried waiters
refuse to smile. Subjected to some serious renovation,
Café Landtmann has lost much of its authenticity
but remains popular with academics, Burgtheater
regulars, businessmen and political powerbrokers.

★ Edvard

*Palais Hansen Kempinski Vienna, 1, Schottenring
24 (236 1000-8070, www.kempinski.com/en/
vienna/palais-hansen/dining/restaurants/edvard).
U2 Schottentor or tram 1, D.* **Open** 6-10pm Tue-
Sat. **Main courses** €35.50-€37. **Map** p70 D1
❹ Contemporary Mediterranean

Opened in 2013, Edvard deals in sophisticated Med
cuisine, working from a concise menu of four mains
(Alpine char, perhaps, or veal belly), which may
follow a scallop starter. In spring 2015, former sous-
chef Anton Pozeg took over from Philipp Vogel, who
led Edvard from its opening to a Michelin star.

MUSEUMSQUARTIER

Beyond Maria-Theresien-Platz lie the former
imperial stables, designed by Fischer von Erlach
and completed by his son in the 18th century.
In 2001, this charmingly dilapidated network of
buildings became the site for the MuseumsQuartier
(MQ; www.mqw.at), one of the most ambitious
building projects undertaken in Vienna in the
20th century. It's now one of the ten largest
cultural complexes in the world.

There was considerable opposition to architects
Ortner & Ortner's original design, particularly
their projected emblematic 'reading tower', which
never materialised. Today's ensemble fits so neatly
and discreetly behind the original Baroque
frontage that the only clue to the wonders within
is the circular orange-and-white MQ logo.

Entering via the vaulted central portal, a piazza
stretches out to reveal the white limestone of the
Leopold Museum to the left and monolithic
**Museum Moderner Kunst Stiftung Ludwig
Wien (MUMOK)** to the right. Between the two,
the former winter riding hall has been modified to
hold the **Kunsthalle Wien** contemporary art
gallery, a concert/performance space and a
restaurant. Several original sculpted horses' heads
serve as a reminder of the building's equine past.

Far more so than the Pompidou Centre or the
Tate Modern, the MQ functions as an attractive
social space, as well as a multiplex of the arts. In
summer, people spend hours lying around on its
colourful, geometrically shaped loungers, chatting,
reading and enjoying DJ sounds. In winter, the beds
can be stacked to form igloo-like constructions
where mulled wine and punch are served.

The MQ includes spaces dedicated to disciplines
as diverse as architecture (**Architekturzentrum
Wien**) and modern dance (**Tanzquartier Wien**,
see p173). Other tenants include the interactive
Zoom Kindermuseum (*see p136*) and the
children's theatre space **Dschungel Wien** (*see
p135*). Meanwhile, the front of the complex is given
over to the Quartier 21 project, which involves the
rental of spaces to peripheral cultural initiatives
such as electronic music, net activism and video
art. Although it has never really fulfilled its
promise as an art lab, its cafés do a roaring trade.

Sights & Museums

Architekturzentrum Wien

*7, Museumsplatz 1 (522 3115, www.azw.at).
U2 Museumsquartier or U2, U3 Volkstheater.*
Open 10am-7pm daily. **Admission** €8;
€6 reductions. **Map** p70 B5 ❺

Architecture in Austria during the last 150 years
is the focus here. The Az W space has a low-key
permanent exhibition of photographs, plans and
information on the people, movements and events
that have shaped the country and the capital, while a

EXPLORE

Edvard.

second gallery across the courtyard hosts temporary exhibitions. Architecture buffs can also visit the small circular library where the Habsburgs' ponies once trotted and thumb a fine array of international architectural periodicals. The centre also gives excellent architecture-themed guided tours and day trips (from €16), although sadly the regular Sunday tours folded in 2012. The former AZ West branch in Flachgasse has also closed its doors.

designforumMQ

7, Museumsplatz 1 (524 4949, www.designforum. at). U2 Museumsquartier or U2, U3 Volkstheater. **Open** 10am-6pm Mon-Fri; 11am-6pm Sat, Sun. **Admission** varies. **Map** p70 B5 ❻
Diagonally opposite Az W, this centre for design features temporary exhibitions on graphics, product design and advertising.

Kunsthalle Wien

7, Museumsplatz 1 (52189-0, www.kunsthallewien. at). U2 Museumsquartier. **Open** 10am-7pm Mon-Wed, Fri-Sun; 10am-9pm Thur. **Admission** €8; €6 reductions; free under-10s. **Map** p70 B5 ❼
Since 2001, the Kunsthalle has been based in the MQ, sandwiched between MUMOK and the Leopold Museum – competition for visitors is fierce. The gallery tends to opt for thematic blockbuster shows – ranging from Salvador Dalí to female pop artists – to pull in the crowds, as well as cultivating its reputation among a more informed art audience with less mainstream fare: Bruce Conner's avant-garde work in the 1970s, perhaps, or the often eerie collages and installations of Georgian artist Andro Wekua.
► *Visits may be combined with the Kunsthalle's smaller branch at Karlsplatz (4, Treitlstrasse 2).*

★ Leopold Museum

7, Museumsplatz 1 (525 70-0, www.leopold museum.org). U2 Museumsquartier or U2, U3 Volkstheater. **Open** 10am-6pm Mon, Wed, Fri-Sun; 10am-9pm Thur. **Admission** €12; €7-€9 reductions; under-7s free. **Map** p70 B5 ❽
The Leopold Museum owes its existence to a Viennese ophthalmologist's lifelong obsession with the great Austrian expressionist Egon Schiele. In the 1950s, Rudolf Leopold acquired his first Schieles for a song. The museum's full catalogue now numbers 44 Schiele paintings and 180 watercolours and drawings. The complete collection takes in over 5,000 works, and embraces many other crucial figures and movements of 19th-century and modernist Austrian painting – from the engrossing peasant art of Albin Egger-Lienz to Richard Gerstl's painfully expressive self-portraits. Kokoschka, Klimt and the Wien Werkstätte makers are also well represented amid the permanent collection, while the third floor showcases long-term loans from the hugely impressive Thyssen-Bornemisza Collection. All is beautifully lit and nicely spaced – if you're going to visit just one museum in town, it should be this one. And as

EXPLORE

THE RINGSTRASSE AT 150
Anniversary celebrations show the Ring in a new light.

Throughout 2015, a fanfare of exhibitions and commemorative events heralded the 150th anniversary of the opening by Emperor Franz Josef of the first completed stretch of the Ringstrasse in 1865. Encircling Vienna's historic centre, the 'Ring', as locals call it, was the result of an epoch-defining urban project that modernised the capital with a planned grandeur that makes it one of the world's great thoroughfares.

Today, the Ringstrasse serves as the visitor's ultimate orientation aid. Main tram and U-Bahn lines converge at the hubs of Karlsplatz and Schottentor. It's also one of Vienna's greatest tourist attractions, with an array of buildings so finely executed that unsuspecting newcomers assume the neo-Gothic Rathaus (see p68) or Votivkirche (see p69) to be the genuine medieval McCoy.

The Ringstrasse is also residential, lined with palatial apartment buildings. The anniversary 'Ringstrasse: A Jewish Boulevard' at the Jüdisches Museum (see p50) showed how, in the wake of the 1860 decree that permitted Jews to own property along it, the Epsteins, Rothschilds and Ephrussis could finally build their mansions on the Ring. It became known as Der Boulevard der Befreiung ('Liberation Boulevard'). The story of the Ephrussis of Odessa, whose family seat is now home to Casinos Austria at Schottentor, is told in Edmund de Waal's *The Hare with the Amber Eyes*, with its vivid descriptions of decades of urban upheaval.

Early photographs displayed in magazine features through 2015 showed a street full of crowded pavement cafés, passers-by in awe of their surroundings. In 1906, the young Adolf Hitler could barely believe his eyes: 'The whole Ring-Boulevard seemed like an enchantment from *1001 Nights*'. Back then, 27 traditional coffeehouses lined the Ring. Now there are barely half a dozen, the others mostly converted into car showrooms and furniture stores. Today's most prominent tenants are five-star hotels, the latest being the Kempinski, housed in a palace designed by Theophil Hansen.

The advent of the car was the turning point for the Ring, converting it into a three-lane traffic funnel, hemmed in by tramlines. The remainder is a tangle of pavements, cycle lanes and parallel access roads. Despite four beautiful parks, the Ring is not the most inviting of streets for pedestrians, who need to be alert at intersections. Enter the Green Party, flushed from its success in making retail showcase Mariahilfer Strasse car-free. The Greens commissioned a study from Danish planning guru Jan Gehl to free up quality space in and around the monuments.

In his report, Gehl railed against the lack of 'points of encounter'. The first remodelling project will see an access road removed from outside the university to create a new square – appropriately on the 650th anniversary of its foundation. However, further modifications will depend on the outcome of the 2015 municipal elections.

if that wasn't enough, there are excellent temporary exhibitions on the three lower floors. Tracey Emin had her first major Vienna show here in 2015.

★ Museum Moderner Kunst Stiftung Ludwig Wien (MUMOK)

7, Museumsplatz 1 (525 00, www.mumok.at). U2 Museumsquartier or U2, U3 Volkstheater. **Open** 2-7pm Mon; 10am-7pm Tue, Wed, Fri-Sun; 10am-9pm Thur. **Admission** €10; €7-€8 reductions; free under-19s. **Map** p70 B5 ❾

MUMOK owns Vienna's premier contemporary art collection, including a fine selection of American pop art by Jasper Johns, Warhol, Lichtenstein and Rauschenberg, plus examples of parallel European movements such as radical realism, arte povera, abstract impressionism and land art. Selected pieces are displayed in regularly changing exhibitions, held over six floors, with four or five shows at any one time. It's a shame that the space itself is so claustrophobic, a feeling accentuated by the absence of natural light.

Lurking deep in the depths of the bunker are exhibitions devoted to Viennese actionism – an unholy brew of animal innards, action painting, and public masturbation and defecation concocted by figures such as Herman Nitsch, Arnulf Rainer and Günther Brus.

RINGSTRASSE PARKS

On the south side of the Ringstrasse are three major parks; the **Burggarten**, **Volksgarten** and **Stadtpark**. They offer a range of curiosities, from statues to hothouses, and a good selection of refreshment outlets.

Burggarten

Main entrance: Burgring. U1, U2, U4 Karlsplatz or tram 1, 2, D. **Open** *Apr-Oct* 6am-10pm daily. *Nov-Mar* 6.30am-7pm daily. **Map** p70 C5 ❿

The Palace Gardens are leafy and informal, with large expanses of lawn. The park is a favourite with sun-seekers, spliffers and frisbee enthusiasts, along with tourists who come to photograph the marble Mozart statue. The musical boy wonder, set on a plinth depicting scenes from *Don Giovanni*, was moved here in 1953 from Albertinaplatz.

▶ *The Burggarten is home to the Schmetterlinghaus butterfly house (see p135) and the adjoining Palmenhaus (see right), now a restaurant.*

Stadtpark

Main entrance: Johannesgasse (beside Stadtpark U-Bahn station). U4 Stadtpark or U3 Stubentor or tram 2. **Open** 24hrs daily. **Map** p70 F5 ⓫

The largest of the Ringstrasse parks, the Stadtpark stretches from just east of Schwarzenbergplatz to Stubentor, either side of the Wien river. Located beside Otto Wagner's Stadtpark U-Bahn station, the main entrance is flanked by superb stone-carved Jugendstil colonnades. The park's most emblematic

building is the neo-renaissance Kursalon, a venue for rather tacky Strauss concerts. Scattered around the park, you'll find busts of Schubert, Bruckner and Lehár.

▶ *Across Hermann Czech's footbridge are the riverside premises of Vienna's most prestigious restaurant, Steiereck (see p91).*

★ Volksgarten

Main entrance: Heldenplatz (opposite Neue Burg). U2, U3 Volkstheater or U3 Herrengasse or tram 1, 2, D. **Open** *Apr-Oct* 6am-10pm daily. *Nov-Mar* 6.30am-7pm daily. **Map** p70 C4 ⓬

Despite its egalitarian-sounding name, the People's Garden was a playground for Vienna's beau monde at the turn of the 19th century. It was built after Napoleon's troops demolished the southern section of the city walls. The centrepiece is the Doric Theseus-Tempel, commissioned by Napoleon as a replica of the Thission in Athens. Between the temple and the Ringstrasse is a lavish rose garden. Dear to many Austrians is the statue of Empress Elisabeth (1837-98) at the northern corner. Today, the name Volksgarten is synonymous with the large semi-alfresco nightspot (*see p152*) over the Ringstrasse from the museums, and the superb Pavillon next door: Oswald Haerdtl's sleek 1950s construction where the tuned-in and turned-on of Vienna drink caipirinhas.

Restaurants & Coffeehouses

Palmenhaus

1, Burggarten (533 1033, www.palmenhaus.at). U1, U2, U4 Karlsplatz or tram 1, 2, D. **Open** 10am-midnight Mon-Thur; 10am-1am Fri, Sat; 10am-11pm Sun. **Main courses** €16.40-€31.20. **Map** p70 D5 ⓭ **Mediterranean**

One of Vienna's most spectacular restaurants, Palmenhaus is located in Friedrich Ohmann's 1901 Jugendstil hothouse at the Hofburg end of the Burggarten, full of tall palms and succulents, and with a fine view from its terrace over the gardens. The kitchen delivers a good variety of fresh fish, steaks and vegetarian mains, as well as crunchy seasonal salads and grilled antipasti. The high glass ceilings mean that acoustics are its main drawback. In the afternoons, Vienna's beau monde shows up for cakes and pastries on the terrace.

SCHWARZENBERGPLATZ & AROUND

South-east of the Staatsoper, the Ringstrasse takes the name Kärntnerring, acknowledging the route south to Kärnten (Carinthia) that bisects it at this point. This is the Ringstrasse at its most bustling, with limos pulling up outside Vienna's big-name hotels, scurrying shoppers and commuters, and tourists snapping the mighty **Staatsoper** (*see p165*). Down a side street stands Vienna's foremost

EXPLORE

concert hall, the **Musikverein** (*see p164*), Theophil Hansen's most extravagant work.

Where Kärntnerring turns into Schubertring, the Ringstrasse opens out into a vast rectangular concourse named after Karl von Schwarzenberg, hero of the Battle of Leipzig (1813). His equestrian statue stands amid the stream of traffic that makes the place a nightmare to cross on foot. Vast and windswept, the square is lined with monumental buildings such as the **Kasino am Schwarzenbergplatz** (*see p171*). At the far end stands the Russen Heldendenkmal (Russian Heroes' Monument), a gift from the Soviet people celebrating their liberation of Vienna. In front of this column is the Hochstrahlbrunnen, a fountain blasting water high into the air, built in 1873 to commemorate Vienna's first mains water supply.

On the west side is the elegant art nouveau French embassy (1912), with its vaguely oriental façade. Nearby on Zaunergasse is the **Arnold Schönberg Center** (*see p166*).

Restaurants & Coffeehouses

Bristol Lounge

Hotel Bristol, 1, Kärntner Ring 1 (515 16 553, www.bristol-lounge.at). Tram 1, 2, D. **Open** noon-midnight daily. **Main courses** €18.50-€38. **Set meals** *Lunch* €17-€24. *Dinner* €49-€74. **Map** p70 D5 ⑭ **Austrian/international**
Raised and trained in Styria and executive chef at the most prestigious address in Vienna since 2013, Dominik Stolzer knows how to source top-notch regional produce – and, judging by the numerous Gault Millau awards here, how to put them to good

use. An evening may start with a Bristol bouilla-baisse, preferably the smaller measure as you'll need to leave room for a main of langoustine, chicory, cucumber and mint, or a 21st-century take on wiener schnitzel or *tafelspitz*. If you can't splash too much cash, there's a weekly-changing lunch deal.

Café Mozart

1, Albertinaplatz 2 (241 0200, www.cafe-mozart.at). U1, U2, U4 Karlsplatz or tram 1, 2, D. **Open** 8am-midnight daily. **Map** p70 D5 ⑮ **Coffeehouse**
Located behind the Staatsoper, the Mozart has become a victim of the tourist trade. Its splendid 19th-century interior made a strong impression on Graham Greene during the shooting of *The Third Man* and it became the film's Café Alt Wien. Anton Karas, composer of the immortal 'Harry Lime Theme', even wrote a 'Café Mozart' waltz in its honour. Probably unbeknown to Greene, the Mozart was confiscated from its Jewish proprietors after the *Anschluss* and handed over to a card-carrying Nazi.

Café Schwarzenberg

1, Kärntner Ring 17 (512 89 98, www.cafe-schwarzenberg.at). Tram 1, 2, D. **Open** 7am-midnight Mon-Fri, Sun; 8.30am-midnight Sat. **Map** p71 E5 ⑯ **Coffeehouse**
This is the oldest coffeehouse on the Ringstrasse, although it has been greatly renovated over the years. Its pseudo-belle époque interior has mirrors gleaming from every wall, while the waiters sport smart tuxedos; from Thursday to Sunday, a pianist plays in the evening. The hot chocolate is famous: try the whipped cream-topped Alt Wiener Art, laced with vanilla and cinnamon.

Volksgarten.

PARKRING & STUBENRING

Beyond Schwarzenbergplatz, the north side of the Ringstrasse is lined with more top-notch hotels overlooking the Stadtpark to the south. It's more enjoyable to cut through the park, check out the Strauss memorial and walk along the riverbank.

At Stubentor, things pick up a little and on this last stretch of the Ringstrasse there are a couple of top-class sights. If you're in need of refreshment, call in at elegant 1950s coffeehouse **Café Prückel** or **Österreicher im MAK**, a funky café and restaurant attached to Vienna's **Museum für Angewandte Kunst (MAK)**.

Further along, the former Kriegsministerium (Ministry of War) today houses less bellicose sections of the civil service. This neo-Baroque monster was completed as late as 1912, demonstrating just how little had changed since the start of the Ringstrasse project in the 1850s. Directly opposite stands Otto Wagner's **Postsparkasse** (1, Georg-Coch-Platz 2, www.ottowagner.com; open 10am-5pm Mon-Fri; admission €6, €4 reductions). Vienna's most monumental of modernist buildings, it's clad in slabs of grey marble, crowned by its name in unmistakable Jugendstil lettering. It still functions as a bank – entry is free to customers.

Walk east and you reach the Donaukanal with its characteristic green railings. Overlooking the canal is the Urania, an observatory built in 1910 by Max Fabiani. Renovated in 2004, it functions as a cinema and puppet theatre, and has a cool café attached on the canal side. Historic local football club Austria Wien were founded here in 1911.

Sights & Museums

★ Museum für Angewandte Kunst/ Gegenwartskunst (MAK)

1, Stubenring 5 (711 36-0, www.mak.at). U3 Stubentor or U4 Landstrasse or tram 2. **Open** 10am-10pm Tue; 10am-6pm Wed-Sun. **Admission** €9.90; €7.50-€8 reductions; free under-19s & all 6-10pm Tue. **Map** p71 G4 ⑰

The Museum of Applied Arts is to Vienna what the V&A is to London. The building dates from 1872 and is yet another neo-Renaissance work by Ferstel, while the permanent exhibition features splendid displays of Jugendstil furniture and design, as well as Klimt's *Stoclet Frieze*. On the ground floor, individual rooms are laid out according to concepts designed by different artists, some of which are superb: Barbara Bloom's presentation of the chair collection in silhouette is particularly inspired. Other participants seemed less sure about the idea: don't miss the late Donald Judd's unexpectedly honest critique in the Baroque and Rococo room. Meanwhile, an excellent restaurant, Österreicher im MAK (*see below*), and stylish shop add to the museum's considerable appeal.

Restaurants & Coffeehouses

Café Prückel

1, Stubenring 24 (512 61 15, www.prueckel.at). U3 Stubentor or tram 2. **Open** 8.30am-10pm daily. **Map** p71 G4 ⑮ **Coffeehouse**

This classic Ringstrasse coffeehouse was given its present 1950s-style look in 1989 by Viennese architect Oswald Haerdtel. The understated furnishings and high ceilings, adorned with magnificent Venetian chandeliers, form a spacious, light-flooded interior loved by everyone from bridge players and elderly ladies to students and arty types. Despite the social mix, the Prückel hit the headlines in 2015 when a lesbian couple were ejected for kissing in public, leading to kiss-ins and a demonstration of around 7,000 people that blocked the Ring.

Österreicher im MAK

1, Stubenring 5 (714 0121, www.oesterreicher immak.at). U3 Stubentor or tram 1, 2. **Open** 11.30am-3pm; 6-11pm daily. **Main courses** €8.50-€25.50. **Map** p71 G4 ⑯ **Viennese**

Since 2013, the restaurant of the MAK has been run by chef Bernie Rieder, a familiar figure on Austrian TV. Diners can choose between the airy main room with a vast wine-bottle chandelier over the central bar or the pastel booths of the winter garden; in summer, there's outdoor seating. Rieder has given the menu a faintly oriental touch with highly popular dim sum sets featuring Austrian ingredients such as wild garlic and roast pork. He's also introduced Stuffed Chicken Mondays when Upper Austrian birds are filled with such things as black pudding, apple and marjoram. But, as a rule, the menu is divided between classic and modern Viennese dishes. Book ahead.

EXPLORE

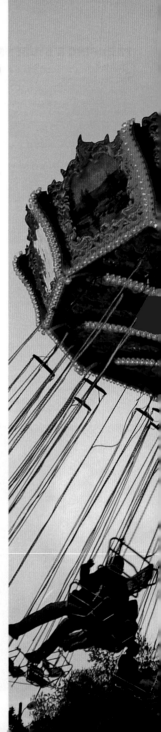

Leopoldstadt & the Danube

Over the bridges of the Donaukanal lies the sprawling 2nd district of Leopoldstadt. Together with neighbouring Brigittenau, the 20th district, it forms an elongated island between the canal and the river. Although some historic buildings remain, it's a somewhat grey area where the Red Army and Wehrmacht fought in 1945. Leopoldstadt does have its charms – and two of Vienna's finest parks, the Augarten and the Prater. Gentrification is well under way, particularly around Karmelitermarkt, one of four small open-air local markets, also including Volkertmarkt, Vorgartenmarkt and Hannovermarkt. Between the canal and the river, a dynamic hub is developing around the recently opened Campus WU University of Economics and major trade-fair centre Messe Wien. Beyond lies the Danube proper, the towering heights of Donau City, and a string of family-friendly beaches and cosy wine taverns.

EXPLORE

Augarten.

Don't Miss

1 **Wiener Riesenrad** No trip would be complete without a spin (p85).

2 **Augarten** Smaller than the Prater but full of curious attractions (p80).

3 **Gasthaus zum Friedensrichter** 100 years of schnitzel (p81).

4 **Johann Strauss Wohnung** Where 'The Blue Danube' was composed (p85).

5 **Prater funfair** Rides galore (p85).

TABORSTRASSE & AROUND

Leopoldstadt is just a short stroll from Innere Stadt, across the Schwedenbrücke bridge from Schwedenplatz. This section of Leopoldstadt, bordering the Donaukanal, is clearly ripe for redevelopment – and there's no missing the 18-storey **Sofitel** hotel (*see p218*). Heading away from the canal, Taborstrasse is a main commercial artery. Among its unremarkable shops, look out for the 19th-century Corn Exchange, home to the **Odeon** theatre (*see p166*). In the streets to the east of Taborstrasse and south of Augarten are the **Kriminalmuseum** and Karmelitermarkt. Among the latter's stripey awning-shaded kiosks and vegetable stalls, there are plenty of signs of renewal. Nonetheless, the market retains its character, and beer and local gossip still prevail.

The **Augarten** is flanked by Obere Augartenstrasse and the upper reaches of Taborstrasse, whose U-Bahn station is near the junction of the two. Far smaller than the Prater, the park has two wartime flak towers standing guard over its venerable tree-lined avenues and formal flowerbeds. It's also home to the **TBA21-Augarten** contemporary art gallery and the **Augarten Porzellan Manufaktur**.

Sights & Museums

★ FREE Augarten

Main entrance: 2, Obere Augartenstrasse (www. kultur.park.augarten.org). Tram 21. **Open** *Apr-Oct* 6am-dusk daily. *Nov-Mar* 6.30am-dusk daily. **Admission** free. **Map** p82 A3 ❶

Laid out in its present form in 1712 and opened to the public in 1775, the Augarten is the oldest Baroque garden in Vienna. Visitors sunbathe on the lawns to the south beside one of the park's two flak towers and enjoy spritzers around an old World War II bunker. The park also houses the Augarten and the new concert hall of the Vienna Boys' Choir, MuTh (www.muth.at), beside the Palais Augarten. A café-restaurant with terrace has also opened at one end of the Porzellan Manufaktur.

Augarten Porzellan Manufaktur

2, Schloss Augarten, Obere Augartenstrasse 1 (21 124 200, www.augarten.at/experience-augarten/museum). Tram 21. **Open** 10am-6pm Mon-Sat. **Admission** €7; €5 reductions. **Tours** €14; €12 reductions. **Map** p82 B3 ❷

Originally Leopold I's summer palace, the Palais Augarten was razed during the 1683 Turkish siege. After rebuilding, it hosted concerts by Mozart, Beethoven and Schubert. The Wiener Porzellan Manufaktur is also based here, its museum containing 150 pieces. The first Viennese factory was opened in 1718, and was reopened in 1923 – items from the 20th century are ranged around the ground floor. The museum also hosts two major exhibitions a year.

Kriminalmuseum

2, Grosse Sperlgasse 24 (0664 300 5677, www.kriminalmuseum.at). Tram 21. **Open** 10am-5pm Thur-Sun. **Admission** €6; €3 reductions. **No credit cards. Map** p82 B4 ❸

Exhibits at the Criminal Museum are mostly photos and press clippings, so a good understanding of German is needed. The show oscillates between

Augarten.

EXPLORE

lionising villains such as Breitwieser (Vienna's greatest safecracker) and offering interesting social background to cases such as that of Josephine Luner, who tortured her maid to death.

FREE TBA21-Augarten

2, Scherzergasse 1A (513 9856-24, www.tba21. org). U2 Taborstrasse or tram 2, 5. **Open** noon-5pm Wed, Thur; noon-7pm Fri-Sun. **Admission** free. **Map** p82 B3 ❹

Based at the Augarten since 2012, ten years after it was founded across town by Francesca von Habsburg, TBA21 is run in collaboration with the Belvedere (*see p94*), for its first four years at least. Experimental, pioneering and sometimes site-specific arts projects are its stock in trade.

Restaurants & Coffeehouses

Gasthaus am Nordpol 3

2, Nordpolgasse 3 (333 5854, www.amnordpol3. at). Tram 5. **Open** 5pm-midnight Mon-Fri; noon-midnight Sat, Sun. **Main courses** €8-€17.80. **Map** p82 B3 ❺ Bohemian

On the northern side of the Augarten, the 'North Pole' is a minimally renovated *beisl* specialising in everything Bohemian – from dishes and beer (Velkopopovicky) to absinthe and attitude. In its gorgeous ageing interior, cluttered with paintings of questionable merit, you can work your way through tripe soup, cured pork with horseradish or own-made *wurst*, as well as typical Bohemian poppyseed desserts. The owners also bake their own bread, welcome children with open arms and provide a great summer terrace.

★ Gasthaus zum Friedensrichter

2, Obere Donaustrasse 57 (214 4875, www. zum-friedensrichter.at). U2 Schottenring. **Open** 11am-10pm Mon-Fri. **Main courses** €10-€24. **Map** p82 A4 ❻ Viennese

Occupying a whole corner on the busy canal front, the 'Justice of the Peace' has been serving sturdy Viennese dishes for more than 100 years. The present crew took over a year ago and have done a fine job of maintaining the splendid, wood-panelled, Formica-topped interior of this classic *gasthaus*, as well as adding interesting salads and vegetable dishes to the traditional menu. All produce is locally sourced, so your €11.50 schnitzel hails from straw-fed pigs in the northerly Waldviertel. Ten quality wines are on offer, including Wieninger's Gemischter Satz – probably the finest white grown in Vienna – and there's regular and organic Weitra beer on tap. Its proximity to IBM makes for a lively midday trade.

Okra

2, Kleine Pfarrgasse 1 (0699 1752 7190, www. okra1020.com). U2 Taborstrasse or tram 2. **Open** 6-11pm Tue-Sat. **Main courses** €8-€21. **Map** p82 B4 ❼ Japanese

The Leopoldsgasse area acquired another fine address in 2014 with this great Japanese-themed eaterie. Influenced by stints in Singapore and Thailand and the recipes of his Japanese wife, globetrotting owner Wolfgang Krivanec serves up a lively mix of raw fish, noodle soups and meats cooked on the robata grill. Highlights include his tuna *tataki* and the grilled skewers of *kushiyaki* heart. As well as reasonably priced Austrian wines, Okra also offers Weitra beer and an impressive selection of sake.

EXPLORE

IN THE KNOW GHETTO HISTORY

In 1624, Ferdinand II sanctioned the creation of a walled Jewish ghetto – and the 2nd and 20th districts became Vienna's main Jewish quarter. Then, during the late 19th and early 20th centuries, Jews fleeing Russian and Polish pogroms flooded into Leopoldstadt's crowded tenements. The **Stones of Remembrance** project (www. steinedererinnerung.net) commemorates Jewish life in the district before the Holocaust, when roughly every second resident was Jewish. Small plaques mark where synagogues, theatres and schools once stood, and points from which Jews were deported to the camps; others bear the names of those who were murdered. After the fall of the Wall, immigrants from ex-Soviet republics and Iran arrived to live alongside a sizeable Turkish and Yugoslav population, as well as more recent arrivals from Africa.

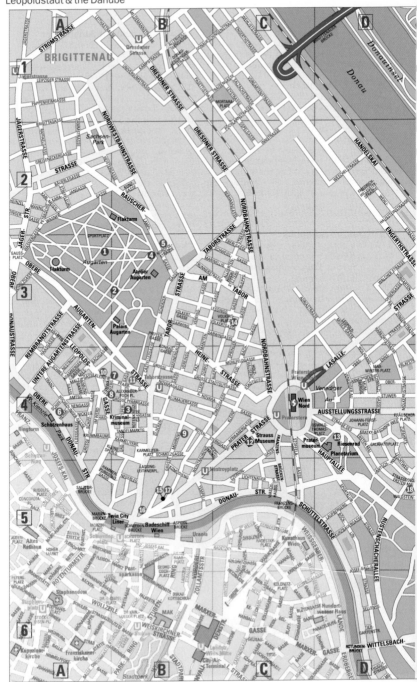

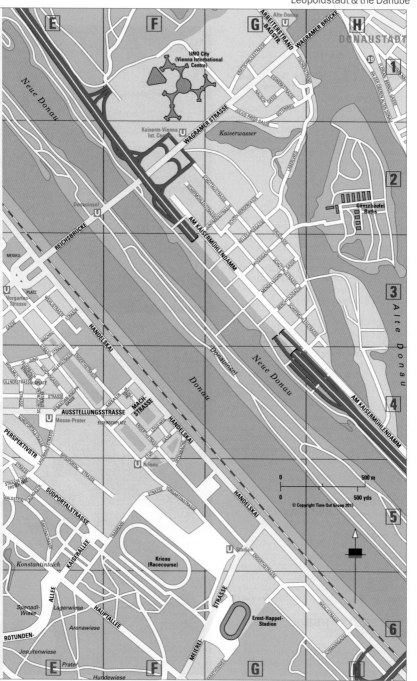

EXPLORE

Schöne Perle

*2, Leopoldsgasse & Grosse Pfarrgasse (0664 243
3593, www.schoene-perle.at). Tram 21.* **Open**
11am-midnight Mon-Fri; 10pm-midnight Sat, Sun.
Main courses €5-€16. **Map** p82 A4 **❽ Viennese**
Conserving the name of its predecessor, a Chinese
restaurant, the 'Beautiful Pearl' is a typical example
of a neo-*beisl*. Besides the schnitzel and *tafelspitz*,
there's always grilled fish and a couple of meat-free
dishes, served in an environment that's informal,
well designed and wearing well over the years. The
larder is stocked exclusively with organic produce.

Schuppich

*2, Rotensterngasse 18 (212 4340, www.
schuppich.at). U1 Nestroyplatz or tram 21.*
Open 6pm-midnight Wed-Sat; noon-4pm Sun.
Main courses €10-€23. **Map** p82 B4 **❾ Italian**
Lurking in the backstreets off Taborstrasse, this
is the address for the hybrid Austro-Italian food of
Friuli and Trieste. Try the €27 four-course set menu
or the seasonal specialities for a good introduction
to a cuisine rarely seen outside Italy. The *beisl*-style
interior oscillates between gloomy emptiness and
packed-to-the-gills chaos, but the food and wines are
reliable and children are welcome.

★ Skopik & Lohn

*2, Leopoldsgasse 17 (219 8977, www.skopik
undlohn.at). U2 Taborstrasse.* **Open** 6pm-1am
Tue-Sat. **Main courses** €14-€26. **Map** p82 A4
❿ Viennese
Since it opened in 2006, Skopik & Lohn has been a
visual and culinary triumph. Its traditional caramel
wood-panelled interior, offset with an impressive
black maze scrawled over the white vaulted ceilings
by artist Otto Živko, seats 100 diners. Food has a
French bistro bent – reflecting owner Horst Scheuer's
Paris sojourn – with a few finely executed Viennese
classics thrown in too. It can be pretty noisy when full.
In summer there's a large terrace seating 80.

Cafés, Bars & Pubs

★ Café Sperlhof

*2, Grosse Sperlgasse 41 (214 5864). U2
Taborstrasse or tram 21.* **Open** 4pm-1.30am
daily. **Map** p82 B4 **⓫**
In operation since 1923, the Sperlhof is a brilliant mix
of fading coffeehouse and an Aladdin's cave piled
high with board games, books, an aquarium and
a display cabinet full of sweets and chocolate bars.
Regulars of all ages play billiards on the three fine
tables in the alcove or hunch over their chessboards.

PRATERSTRASSE & THE PRATER

Once the main boulevard of Jewish Leopoldstadt,
today Praterstrasse contains clothing boutiques
and delicatessens. The fine Jugendstil façade of

EXPLORE

Skopik & Lohn.

no.34 was the work of architect Oskar Marmorek, a close associate of Theodor Herzl. Inside the courtyard is the Nestroyhof: seized and closed down by the Nazis, and used as a supermarket until 1975, it reopened as the **Theater Nestroyhof** (890 8836, www.hamakom.at) in 2009. Johann Strauss Wohnung is at no.54.

Praterstrasse eventually broadens out to Praterstern, a busy traffic junction with Wien Praterstern station at its centre. With constant human traffic heading to and from the nearby Prater funfair, this is Vienna at its earthiest and most bustling, with the iconic Prater Ferris wheel, the **Wiener Riesenrad**, in the background.

Formerly a royal hunting ground, the Prater covers a huge expanse – the funfair only takes up a fraction of it. Attractions range from old-fashioned merry-go-rounds to the latest in fairground technology, while an outpost of **Madame Tussauds** (www.madametussauds.com/wien) is a pricier attraction. The funfair is open from mid March until late October and entrance is free as the booths, rides and restaurants are run by different operators. More leisurely pursuits might include floating through overgrown tracts of the old Danube in a rowing boat, snoozing beneath the hundreds of magnificent oaks and chestnuts, or tucking into roast pork and Budweiser at beer gardens such as the **Schweizerhaus** (*see p86*).

The chestnut-bordered central artery, the Hauptallee, has been synonymous with a Sunday stroll since it was opened to the public in 1766. May Day celebrations attract more than 500,000 people, and the Viennese come in droves year-round for fresh air, jogging, cycling and in-line skating. Amid the greenery, at the end of the Hauptallee, stands the **Lusthaus** (2, Freudenau 254, 728 9565, www.lusthaus-wien.at). Once an imperial hunting lodge, the octagonal pavilion is now a romantic-looking restaurant.

In summer, splashes from the Olympic-sized Stadionbad pool can be heard on the Hauptallee. Locals flock in for football at the **Ernst-Happel-Stadion**, revamped for Euro 2008 and currently staging the home matches of Rapid Vienna (www.skrapid.at) during their stadium rebuild at Hütteldorf. Nearby are trap racing at the **Krieau** course (www.krieau.at) and flat racing at **Freudenau** (www.freudenau.at).

The once-neglected area between the Prater park and the Danube has been transformed by the Campus WU, the seat of Vienna's University of Economics. It breaks convention with the bright, varied architectural work of six renowned firms, most notably Zaha Hadid's, responsible for the Library & Learning Centre and its cantilevered roof. Alongside is the gleaming Messe Wien, Austria's biggest congress centre. All is linked by the extension of the U2 U-Bahn line, which was opened for Euro 2008.

Sights & Museums

Johann Strauss Wohnung

2, Praterstrasse 54 (214 0121, www.wien museum.at). U1 Nestroyplatz. **Open** 10am-1pm, 2-6pm Tue-Sun. **Admission** €4; €3 reductions; free under-19s & all 1st Sun of mth. **No credit cards. Map** p82 C4 ⑫

The King of the Waltz composed 'The Blue Danube' here in 1867. His grand piano, organ and stand-up composing desk are on view, as well as various ball-related memorabilia.

Wiener Riesenrad

2, Riesenradplatz 1 (729 5430, www.wiener riesenrad.com). U1, U2 Praterstern. **Open** times vary. **Admission** €9.50; €4 reductions; free under-3s. **Map** p82 D4 ⑬

No trip to Vienna is complete without a ride on the 19th-century Riesenrad, the iconic giant Ferris wheel created by British engineer Walter Basset for Franz Josef's golden jubilee in 1897. A full circle in one of the 15 wooden gondolas takes a gentle 20 minutes; at its highest point you're 65m (215ft) up.

Restaurants & Coffeehouses

★ L'Ase

2, Rueppgasse 24 (0660 364 9885, www.l-ase.at). U1, U2 Praterstern or tram 2. **Open** 5pm-midnight Tue-Fri; noon-midnight Sat. **Tapas** €2.50-€12.50. **Map** p82 C3 ⑭ Catalan

This Catalan wine-and-tapas bar has pioneered the growing scene around the Völkertmarkt area of Leopoldstadt. L'Ase ('The Donkey') is a laid-back joint with a large terrace. Pau Argemi and his

IN THE KNOW
VINTAGE HEURIGEN

A better quality of *heuriger* (wine tavern) is found in the 21st district. **Göbel** (21, Stammersdorfer Kellergasse 131, 294 8420, 0664 243 9835, www.weinbau goebel.at) is named after prize-winning winemaker and architect Hans-Peter Göbel. He designed this chic *heuriger* himself and it operates more like a restaurant with table service. Also up towards the city's northern outskirts, **Wieninger** (21, Stammersdorfer Strasse 78, 292 4106, www.heuriger-wieninger.at) features the celebrated Stammersdorf wines by Fritz Wieninger, with a sophisticated seasonal kitchen. **Weingut-Heuriger Schilling** (21, Langenzersdorferstrasse 54, 292 4189, www.weingut-schilling.at), at the foot of Bisamberg Hill, offers cuvée Camilla and specialities such as grilled pork knuckle.

EXPLORE

partner Sandrine change the selection of Catalan tapas monthly. Beyond regulars such as *pa amb tomaquet* with anchovies or ham, you might find stuffed calamari on grilled asparagus. To round things off, there's an impeccable crema catalana. L'Ase has a handful of wines from celebrated Catalan denominations, plus the magnificent Schnaitl beer.

Cafe Ansari

2, Praterstrasse 15 (276 5102, www.cafeansari.at) U1 Nestroyplatz. **Open** 8am-11.30pm Mon-Sat; 9am-3pm Sun. **Main courses** €10.70-€26. **Map** p82 B5 ⑮ Georgian
Located on the ground floor of an imposing 19th-century apartment building, Ansari is a beautifully designed café-restaurant hybrid serving Georgian-inspired breakfasts, lunches and dinners. Its spacious, magnificently lit interior was conceived by Gregor Eichinger, Vienna's go-to architect for gastro remakes. Diners sit at communal tables and tuck into *kinkhali*, aubergine rolls, *khachapuri* and the like.

★ Le Loft

2, Praterstrasse 1 (906 6160, www.sofitel-vienna.com). U1, U4 Schwedenplatz. **Open** 6.30-10.30pm daily. **Main courses** €20-€58. **Map** p82 B5 ⑯ Haute cuisine
Le Loft is a popular spot. This is mainly due to the views from the 18th floor of Jean Nouvel's Sofitel hotel (*see p218*), intensified at night by the multicoloured shadow cast over the city by Swiss artist Pipilotti Rist's fabulous illuminated ceiling. Although previously overseen by Antoine Westermann, Le Loft has yet to achieve a Michelin ranking. With the arrival of Florian Günzel in May 2015, this fusion of French dining with Austrian ingredients may reach higher places. Reservations are essential, even for the bar.

Mochi

2, Praterstrasse 15 (925 13 80, www.mochi.at). U1 Nestroyplatz. **Open** 11am-10pm Mon-Sat. **Main courses** €12-€22. **Map** p82 B5 ⑰ Japanese
Seating only 25, it's tough to get a table at this Californian-style Japanese – in summer, tables are set outside on this charming stretch of Praterstrasse. On offer is some of the very best sushi in town, inside-out rolls, and grilled steaks and seafood. Mochi operates a first-come-first-served policy on weekday lunchtimes, but takes reservations in the evenings and on Saturdays. All dishes can be taken away from the small outlet on the other side of the street.

Schweizerhaus

2, Strasse des 1 Mai 116 (728 0152, www.schweizerhaus.at). U1, U2 Praterstern, then tram 21. **Open** *Mid Mar-Oct* 11am-11pm Mon-Fri; 10am-11pm Sat, Sun. **Main courses** €6.60-€16.30. **Map** p82 D5 ⑱ Austrian
This bustling place is loud, beery and housed in and around what was the Swiss Pavilion at the 1870 Expo, on the edge of the Prater funfair. Run since 1920 by the

Kolarik family, it's famous for serving huge portions of *gegrillte steltzen* (grilled pork knuckle studded with caraway seeds – 600 consumed every day) and rivers of Czech Budweiser. Popular with football fans before a match at the Ernst-Happel-Stadion.

THE DANUBE & BEYOND

'The Blue Danube' waltz may be Vienna's signature tune, but it's perfectly possible to visit the city and never set eyes on Europe's longest river. While the Donaukanal snakes through the city centre, the river itself is further east, on the other side of Leopoldstadt and Brigittenau.

Alongside, man-made Donauinsel island was created when a new channel, the Neue Donau, was dug out in the 1970s. Its space and clean water make it ideal for cycling, bathing, in-line skating and picnics. Known as Copa Cagrana after the nearby Kagran district, the environs of the Donauinsel U-Bahn are a nightlife hub in summer, with assorted waterside bars. In June, the island also hosts the **Donauinselfest** (*see p29*).

Beyond the Neue Donau, glassy skyscrapers and housing complexes signal Donau City, Vienna's sequestered ghetto of modern architecture. It includes the **Vienna International Centre** (22, Wagramer Strasse 5, 26060-3328, www.unvienna. org), the Vienna seat of the United Nations. Hour-long guided tours (11am, 2pm, 3.30pm Mon-Fri; €10, €4-€7 reductions) are given – bring photo ID. Nearby rises the 252-metre (825-foot) **Donauturm** (Danube Tower; www.donauturm.at), topped by a revolving restaurant, and the newly unveiled **Meliá** hotel (*see p218*). Below lie the attractive modern gardens of Donaupark.

One tube stop on is the picturesque Alte Donau (Old Danube), lined with chestnuts and willows. You can stroll along these remnants of the river's side arms, rent a boat or have drinks or dinner at the water's edge (take mosquito repellent). The Bundesbad comprises a pebble beach and a 1950s kiosk selling ice-creams, hot dogs and cold beer. On the southern side is the popular Gänsehäufel bathing area. Opposite is a riverside walk with another bathing zone, Angelibad, facing the classic summer schnitzel joint **Birners Strandgasthaus** (www.gasthausbirner.at).

Restaurants & Coffeehouses

Strandcafé

22, Florian-Berndl-Gasse 20 (203 6747, www.strandcafe-wien.at). U1 Alte Donau. **Open** 10am-midnight daily. **Main courses** €7.40-€22.90. **Map** p83 H1 ⑲ Austrian
On a fine summer afternoon, Strandcafé is a great antidote to the rigours of the city. It's situated on the banks of the old arm of the river. The big draw here is the racks of barbecued pork ribs, served with roast potatoes. Tables are laid out on a floating pontoon.

EXPLORE

CAPITAL LETTERS
Vienna's vintage signs.

Keen-eyed visitors will soon find themselves snapping photos of Vienna's commercial signage – one of its unsung visual delights. The city has retained an inordinate number of classy shop signs, evoking a pre-branding era when generic names conveyed all the information the customer required. Simple signs denoting trades such as 'plumber' or 'grocer' or shops ('flowers', 'gloves' or 'sauerkraut') were often rendered in magnificent joined-up lettering or sleek italic scripts. The embossed metal upper-case characters used on the 1920s council housing complexes, such as Karl-Marx-Hof, also became a shopfront favourite. From the 1960s onwards, neon signs brought some badly needed cheer to a dour nocturnal Vienna (such as Kärntner Strasse, visible at http://vintagevienna.at).

As more historic independent shops fall victim to global chains, these elegant, artisan-made signs are fast disappearing. Fortunately, though, enthusiasts are doing their bit to draw attention to these visual treasures. In 2012, Roland Hörmann and Birgit Ecker founded Stadtschrift, an association for the collection, preservation and documentation of historical façade signs. They regard old signs as emblems, landmarks even, of local cultural identity and work with the municipality, property managers and building firms to collect old signs and, where possible, preserve them in their original locations. Now Stadtschrift has amassed a substantial collection of signs and has mounted them on the end of a house at Kleine Sperlgasse 2C in Leopoldstadt (*pictured*) to create an open-air museum of commercial typography.

In similar vein, Achim Gauger's Instagram page ViennaCityTypeFace has more than 800 images of existing or now defunct signs, and also sells prints of many of them. In 2015, Gauger teamed up with LA type guru Steven Spiegel to put on an exhibition of signs from both cities.

Sign geeks should also acquire a copy of Martin Ulrich Kehrer's *Stadt Alphabet Wien*, a splendid illustrated catalogue of Vienna's signage highlights, complete with addresses.

EXPLORE

Landstrasse & Belvedere

Vienna's largest inner-city district is the 3rd, bordered to the east by the Donaukanal and lined with opulent 19th-century apartment buildings. Its southern reaches are markedly more working-class, dotted with Red Vienna housing from the 1920s. Sights here include the Hundertwasser Haus and the Kunsthaus Wien, both linked to artist and eco-activist Friedensreich Hundertwasser. Also on the must-see list is the sumptuous Belvedere with its unparalleled collection of works by Gustav Klimt. The district takes its name from Landstrasse-Hauptstrasse, the busy road heading south-east from the Stadtpark and Wien Mitte station. The station, which was unveiled in 2013 after a multi-million euro redevelopment, is the terminus of the CAT train from Vienna International Airport. Running alongside the Belvedere, Prinz-Eugen-Strasse leads to Vienna's new main train station, Hauptbahnhof.

EXPLORE

Belvedere.

Don't Miss

1 Belvedere Secular Baroque – and Klimt – at their very finest (p94).

2 Kunsthaus Wien Wacky world of Friedensreich Hundertwasser (p90).

3 Heeresgeschichtliches Museum World War I in fascinating detail (p95).

4 St Marxer Friedhof Bucolic final resting place of Mozart (p91).

5 Steierereck im Stadtpark Top table in town (p91).

BY THE DONAUKANAL

The area of the 3rd district bordering the Danube Canal is quiet and residential, with easy access to the lower reaches of the Prater. A steady stream of visitors troops to the **Hundertwasser Haus**, a surreal municipal housing project dreamed up by Friedensreich Hundertwasser (1928-2000), artist, ecologist and amateur architect. If his Gaudi-esque swirls appeal, head for nearby **Kunsthaus Wien**, a similarly extravagant gallery space housing a permanent collection of his work. Meanwhile, the **Wittgenstein-Haus** (3, Parkgasse 18, www.haus-wittgenstein. at, open 10am-4.30pm Mon-Fri) is now the Bulgarian cultural institute, created as a series of grey concrete cubes by Paul Engelmann.

Sights & Museums

Hundertwasser Haus

3, corner of Löwengasse & Kegelgasse (www.das-hundertwasser-haus.at). Tram N. **Map** p92 B4 ❶
Hundertwasser's first of many forays into architecture, finished in 1985, was a commission to jazz up this existing council block. He added all manner of colourful facings, protruberances, onion domes and undulating floors, in a distillation of his 'war on the straight line'. None of it is open to the public, though there's a themed café attached to the premises one floor up. Later on, he used his not inconsiderable business acumen to fashion an adjacent shopping complex in a similar style. The end result feels like a duty-free shop at an airport. Much to the chagrin of local intellectuals, the building is now on virtually every tour-bus itinerary.

Kunsthaus Wien

3, Untere Weissgerberstrasse 13 (712 0491, www. kunsthauswien.com). Tram 1, O. **Open** 10am-7pm daily. **Admission** €10; €5 reductions; free under-10s. *With temporary exhibition* €12; €6 reductions; free under-10s. **Map** p92 A3 ❷
Hundertwasser designed the former Thonet furniture factory as a repository for his dubious eco-art, applying his trademark spirals, splashes of mosaic and undulating brick floors. From the first paintings onwards – a self-portrait by earnest, young Viennese Friedrich Stowasser in 1947 facing his self-portrait four years later as a fiery icon in Marrakech – you can see how the later-named Friedrich Hundertwasser reinvented himself as some global eco-warrior and notable contemporary artist. Hundertwasser skirted the Holocaust to become a figure of world renown, fêted by states and governments. He died aboard the QE2 and was buried beneath a tree he planted for himself in New Zealand. Much of his incredible journey took place at sea, on a boat he adapted himself, the *Regentag*, skipping from country to country, designing stamps for Cape Verde, flags for the Holy Land, a drinking fountain in Linz or a heating plant in Spittelau. A former member of the Hitler Youth who wanted Austria to revert to a constitutional monarchy, Hundertwasser is best seen in one of the biographical films shown here on a loop, as a hippy artist chasing women and enjoying a life of unbounded freedom. His work, in painting, model, plant and postage-stamp form, takes up two floors, while the upper two floors are given over to shows by celebrity photographers and big-name artists. The ground-floor terrace café, set amid exuberant vegetation, is an agreeable spot for a drink.

Restaurants & Coffeehouses

★ Gasthaus Wild

3, Radetzkyplatz 1 (920 9477, gasthaus-wild.at). Tram N. **Open** 9am-1am daily. **Main courses** €6.20-€26.50. **Map** p92 A3 ❸ Viennese
Weinhaus Wild was once one of Vienna's most charming *gasthäuser*, despite appalling food and service. Now, these spacious premises have been given a new lease of life. By conserving original features such as the beautiful wooden *schank* (bar counter) and ditching the net curtains, Wild has become an atmospheric neo-*beisl* without scaring away its original clientele. The menu always has an authentic Viennese meat or offal dish, but the more ambitious dishes can be a lottery. Service is excellent, as are the wines and beers, and the terrace overlooking Radetzkyplatz is a magnet for locals during the summer.

Room

Sofiensäle, 3, Marxergasse 17 (710 5577, www. sofiensaele.com). U3 Landstrasse-Wien Mitte. **Open** 8am-midnight daily. **Main courses** €7.50-€28.50. **Brunch** €18-€20. **Map** p92 B3 ❹ Austrian/international
This lounge bar-restaurant is set in historic Sofiensäle, named after the mother of Franz Josef, Princess Sophie of Bavaria. Originally a steam baths, it was converted into a concert hall and hosted many a waltz conducted by the elder Strauss. Later it became a renowned recording studio for classical music. After a fire in 2001 ('The Death of a Princess', as *Gramophone* reported), its future hung in the balance until a long-term renovation saw it reopen as a hotel, restaurant and events hall in 2013. The surroundings lend themselves to haute cuisine – instead, though, simple, fresh, affordable dishes are the order of the day, for breakfast, lunch, brunch and dinner. The house burger (with cheddar cheese and thousand-island dressing) and vegetarian yellow curry typify the fare on offer.

RENNWEG & BEYOND

Rennweg slopes up the eastern side of the Belvedere from Schwarzenbergplatz, its lower reaches lined with fine buildings such as the early Otto Wagner houses at no.3 and no.5 (where

Gustav Mahler lived from 1898 to 1909). Take a detour down Metternichgasse and along Jaurèsgasse, the heart of Vienna's diplomatic quarter, to see the onion-domed Russian Orthodox church at no.2.

Further north off Neulinggasse, two of the city's war-time *flaktürme* (anti-aircraft towers) stand in Arenberg Park. One of them, the Contemporary Art Tower (CAT), is occupied by the **Museum of Applied Arts** (MAK; *see p77*); it's currently under renovation. One tram stop further lies **St Marxer Friedhof**, Vienna's most bucolic cemetery, hemmed in by busy roads and a motorway flyover. Just across Rennweg is an expanding hub for eco-technology (*see p95* **Back to the Future**).

Sights & Museums

FREE St Marxer Friedhof

3, Leberstrasse 6-8 (4000 8042). Tram 71. **Open** *Apr, Oct* 7am-5pm daily. *May, Sept* 7am-6pm daily. *June-Aug* 7am-7pm daily; *Nov-Mar* 7am-dusk daily. **Admission** free. **Map** p93 H5 ❺

St Marxer was built on the orders of Josef II, who ordained the closure of all the Innere Stadt cemeteries for reasons of hygiene in the 1780s. No burials have been held here since 1874, and crumbling tombs and headstones peep through a mass of vegetation. St Marxer's most illustrious corpse was Mozart's, given a pauper's burial in a mass grave in 1791; his death coincided with the monarch's diktat for mass burial. His wife Constanze's attempts to pinpoint the exact place of burial led to the erection of the so-called Mozartgrab, featuring an angel in mourning and a truncated pillar representing his early death. With the lack of a nearby U-Bahn station, the no.71 tram has been diverted and allows visitors to see St Marxer then trundle on to the Zentralfriedhof (*see p129*), the city's other main cemetery on the same line.

Strassenbahnmuseum

3, Ludwig-Koessler-Platz (7909 468-03, www. remise.wien). U3 Schlachthausgasse or tram 18. **Open** 9am-6pm Wed; 10am-6pm Sat, Sun. **Admission** €6; €4-€5 reductions; free under-15s. **Map** p93 E5 ❻

Modernised with interactive exhibits and reopened in September 2014, Vienna's tram museum is housed in a former tramshed. Some 40 examples include horse-drawn, steam and the classic red-and-white version known as the Bim, after the sound of its bell.

Restaurants & Coffeehouses

Gmoa Keller

3, Heumarkt 25 (712 5310, www.gmoakeller.at). U4 Stadtpark or tram D. **Open** 11am-midnight Mon-Sat. **Main courses** €7.90-€15.80. **Map** p92 D1 ❼ Viennese

Dinner reservations are advisable at this tremendous old vaulted *beisl*, as it's often stormed by crowds from the nearby Akademietheater and Konzerthaus. Owner Sebastian Lakowski has done a fine job of preserving the joint's best aspects – his sole addition being a large Hermann Nitsch 'blood painting' – and bringing in a menu of perfectly executed, affordable Viennese classics.

★ Steierereck im Stadtpark

3, Am Heumarkt 2 (Stadtpark) (713 3168, www. steirereck.at). U4 Stadtpark. **Open** 11.30am-3pm; 6.30pm-1am Mon-Fri. **Main courses** €29-€49. **Set menus** €132, €142. **Map** p92 D1 ❽ Haute cuisine

Luxury restaurants come and go in Vienna, but only the Steierereck maintains the standards in this gruelling category. It currently sports two Michelin stars, and was rated 15th in the San Pellegrino World's 50 Best Restaurants list in 2015. Chef and owner Heinz Reitbauer offers a six- or seven-course menu featuring locally sourced ingredients, many of

EXPLORE

O'Connor's Old Oak.
See p94.

EXPLORE

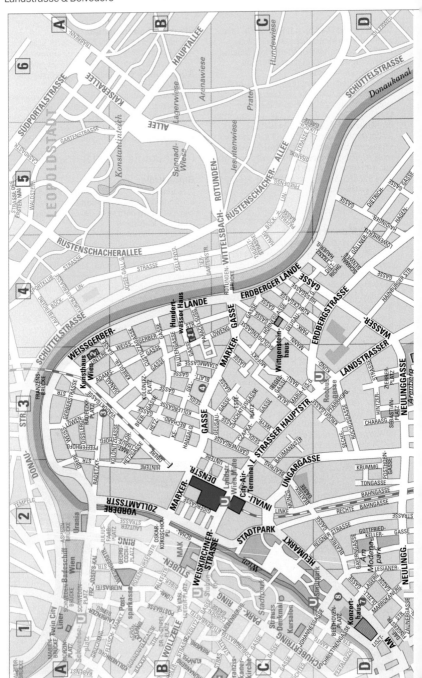

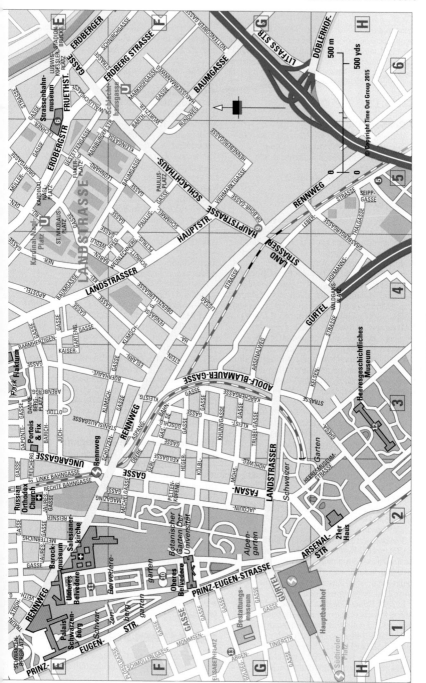

which come from Pogusch, Reitbauer's own Styrian farm, where he cooks at weekends. The wine cellar has more than 35,000 bottles and 120 cheeses from 13 countries. For an affordable taste of the Steierereck, try the river-front Meierei or 'Milk Bar' that serves light lunches, cheeses and great milky puds.

Cafés, Bars & Pubs

O'Connor's Old Oak
3, Rennweg 95/2/1 (236 6721, www.oconnors.at)
U3 Schlachhausgasse then tram 18. **Open**
11am-1am Mon-Fri; noon-midnight Sat, Sun.
Map p93 G5 ❾
See p115 **Going Gastro**. *Photo p91.*

BELVEDERE

Occupying a vast sweep of land that gently rises from Schwarzenbergplatz to the Gürtel, the Belvedere palaces and gardens are both a tourist hotspot and a local amenity. The Belvedere gets its name from the view of the city and the distant Vienna Woods from the terrace of the **Oberes (Upper) Belvedere**, one of the finest secular Baroque buildings in Europe. Military strategist Prince Eugène of Savoy had architect Lukas von Hildebrandt first build the **Unteres (Lower) Belvedere**, then the Upper, as his summer residence. He used the monumental Oberes Belvedere for receptions, negotiations and feasts. The gardens on the eastern side of the grounds contained his menagerie – home to the first giraffe to survive in captivity in central Europe. To the south, botanists will enjoy the Alpine Garden and the University Botanical Gardens. After the Prince's death the Belvedere passed to Viktoria, Eugène's extravagant niece, who sold the contents of his library to the Habsburgs and the picture collection all over Europe.

In 1752, Maria Theresa bought the Belvedere. In 1776, Josef II opened the gardens to the public and had the imperial picture collection moved there. Today, the Upper Belvedere houses the **Oesterreichische Galerie**, the Austrian National Gallery, famed for its collection of Klimts, Schieles and Kokoschkas. The last Habsburg to reside there was Archduke Franz Ferdinand.

The Belvedere returned to the political limelight in 1934 when Schuschnigg, chancellor of the Austro-Fascist government, briefly lived there; and again in 1955, when the Austrian State Treaty that re-established Austria as an independent neutral state was signed in the palace.

In 2013, Prince Eugène's **Winter Palace** (*see p47*) in town was also opened to the public and operates as a gallery for temporary exhibitions under the Belvedere umbrella. Another exhibition space, the **21er Haus** (Schweizergarten, Arsenalstrasse 1, 795 57-770, www.21erhaus.at), shows contemporary Austrian art in Karl

Schwanzer's glass-and-steel pavilion, which was built for the 1958 Brussels Expo. Set a short walk from the Belvedere, it also features a sculpture garden and the Blickle cinema. Various tickets allow access to all four Belvedere attractions.

★ Oberes Belvedere & Österreichische Galerie
3, Prinz-Eugen-Strasse 27 (795 57-134, www. belvedere.at). Tram 18, D or bus 69A. **Open**
10am-6pm daily. **Admission** €14; €11.50 reductions; free under-19s. **Map** p93 F1 ❿

The façade of the Upper Belvedere is one of the city's great sights and the contents of the Austrian Gallery are no less impressive. The big draw is Vienna's modernist triumvirate of Klimt, Schiele and Kokoschka. Klimt's *The Kiss* (1907-08) is given its own wall with a black backdrop to offset the sparkling gold of the painting. The 24 works housed here, eight in this room alone, represent the world's largest collection of Klimt – *Judith* (1901) is another must-see. Nearby you can admire the draughtsmanship of Egon Schiele's emaciated human forms and Oskar Kokoschka's animated, twisted brushstrokes.

Less familiar 19th-century Austrian realism works – Carl Moll's *Naschmarkt in Wien* (1894), *Steamer at Kaisermühlen* (1872) by Emil Jakob Schindler, and Hans Makart's sensual historicism – are another of the gallery's strong points. Meanwhile, a rather chaotic mix of European romanticism, realism and Impressionism includes works by Degas, Delacroix, Monet, Renoir and Van Gogh. Greeting you as you arrive is *Hulk* by Jeff Koons – elsewhere, a DVD of a Marina Abramović piece adds contemporary verve.

There are also empty rooms to sit in and take in the views of the exquisite gardens and beyond. There's a café on the ground floor, decorated with paintings of Franz Josef and Empress Elisabeth.

★ Unteres Belvedere & Orangerie
3, Rennweg 6 (795 57-134, www.belvedere.at). Tram 71, D. **Open** 10am-6pm Mon, Tue, Thur-Sun; 10am-9pm Wed. **Admission** €11; €8.50-€9.50 reductions; free under-19s. **Map** p93 E1 ⓫

The flamboyant interiors of Prince Eugène's summer quarters make the upper palace chambers pale in comparison. The Marmorsaal, with its trompe l'oeil effects and stucco work, celebrates Eugène's military career in a fresco by Martino Altamonte, shamelessly transforming him into the god Apollo. After the Marmorgalerie comes the Goldkabinett – a Baroque extravaganza of 23-carat gold panelling and mirrors. The beautifully renovated Orangerie provides a space for temporary exhibitions.
▶ *Next to the Orangerie, in the stables, is a treasure trove of sacred medieval art (10am-noon daily).*

PRINZ-EUGEN-STRASSE

Running parallel to the Belvedere on the western side, Prinz-Eugen-Strasse divides the 3rd and 4th districts, and is lined with imposing edifices, many of them now embassies. Beside the Soviet memorial on Schwarzenbergplatz is the discreet entrance to the Palais Schwarzenberg (1720), built by Fischer von Erlach and son for Adam Franz von Schwarzenberg, equerry to Emperor Karl VI; it's gradually being converted into a five-star hotel. Nearby, at Prinz-Eugen-Strasse 20-22, Adolf Eichmann ran the Central Office for Jewish Emigration from the former Rothschild palace, where in 1938 fleeing Jews (the lucky ones) were fleeced of their property in return for a passport. The building was destroyed in the war and is now the seat of the Chamber of Labour.

The **Heeresgeschichtliches Museum** (Museum of Military History) is a ten-minute walk from here. You can stroll through the leafy Schweizergarten, taking in its duckponds and new monument to Chopin, *La Note Bleue*. Here, too, is the **21er Haus** art museum (www.21erhaus.at).

Sights & Museums

Heeresgeschichtliches Museum

3, Hauptgebäude, Arsenal Objekt 1 (79 561-0, www.hgm.or.at). U1 Südtirolerplatz-Hauptbahnhof or tram 18, D, O or bus 13A, 69A. **Open** 9am-5pm daily. **Admission** €6; €2.50-€4 reductions; free under-19s. **Map** p93 H3 ⑫
The Museum of Military History was Vienna's first purpose-built museum, one of four large barracks built at Franz Josef's order to quell popular unrest after the 1848 uprising. What appears like another dreary, old-school Vienna museum, as you traipse past tired artefacts from the Napoleonic Wars or the siege of 1683, suddenly springs to life when you stand face-to-face with the car in which Archduke Franz Ferdinand was assassinated in Sarajevo on 28 June 1914. There it stands, the 28/32 Double-Phaeton 32hp, number AIII 118, its paintwork still sleek black with the exception of a small impact shape of grey around the fatal bullethole clearly visible – touchable, in fact – in the back door. Alongside is Franz Ferdinand's blood-stained tunic. These provide an opener to what is a meticulous and gripping multi-room World War I timeline display through Habsburg eyes. Note the huge ear trumpets used to detect enemy airplanes before the invention of radar. World War II is also covered elsewhere, and a collection of armoured vehicles stands outside.

Restaurants & Coffeehouses

Café Goldegg

4, Argentinierstrasse 49 (505 9162, www.cafe goldegg.at). Tram D. **Open** 8am-8pm Mon-Sat; 9am-7pm Sun. **Map** p93 G1 ⑬ **Coffeehouse**
Located in a sleepy corner of the 4th, the Goldegg is a classic Viennese establishment, with plush seating, marble tables, billiards and mirrors aplenty. It does a fine daily menu and good *goulaschsuppe* too.

BACK TO THE FUTURE
Vienna's gleaming eco-tech hub.

With a degree in biology and zoology, Mayor Michael Häupl is hell-bent on resurrecting Vienna's status as a centre of scientific excellence. A cornerstone of his ambition has been the designation of the St Marx area as an enterprise eco-tech zone.

St Marx takes its name from the chapel of St Marcus, which was built by the Order of Saint Lazarus as part of the leprosarium founded in the 13th century to quarantine disease-carrying travellers. The hospital stood near the corner of Rennweg and Landstrassse, home of today's Vienna Biocenter (www.viennabiocenter.org). It's fitting that an institution that oversees postgraduate and research facilities, as well as housing spin-off firms working on cancer treatments and vaccines, should be located on the site of one of Vienna's earliest public-health initiatives.

In the 18th century, St Marx became Vienna's main cattle market and abattoir, until issues of public health forced its closure in 1852. In 2014, it started to be used as a mid-sized gig venue (*pictured*), hosting sell-out gigs by the likes of Pharrell Williams. It also now hosts the Vienna Globe (www.globe.wien), which performs German versions of Shakespeare.

The vast area around the old cattle market is also home to numerous media and TV companies, initially attracted by rumours that national broadcaster ÖRF was intending to relocate here. In the end, though, Deutsche Telekom moved into the colossal T-Center, a spectacular semi-horizontal structure alongside Rennweg designed by maverick Austrian architect Günther Domenig.

EXPLORE

Karlsplatz to Mariahilfer Strasse

With its stellar sights, Karlsplatz should be one of Vienna's great showpieces. In reality, it's a mass of busy streets, tramlines and green spaces that does no justice to the buildings that surround it. Emerging from Karlsplatz U-Bahn, Resselpark gives access to Otto Wagner's Stadtbahn pavilions, Karlskirche and the Wien Museum. Back along the dual carriageway are the Künstlerhaus, the stand-out Secession and the Akademie der Bildenden Künste. Further west is the Naschmarkt, Vienna's main market, lined with lively ethnic eateries and surrounded by funky boutiques. Wienzeile runs parallel to Gumpendorfer Strasse and the city's main shopping strip of Mariahilfer Strasse.

EXPLORE

Karlskirche.

Don't Miss

1 Secession The famous *Beethoven Frieze* (p98).

2 Wien Museum Karlsplatz From medieval backwater to imperial hub (p98).

3 Karlskirche Baroque masterpiece (p98).

4 Otto Wagner Pavillon Karlsplatz Art nouveau gem (p98).

5 Third Man Private Collection One man's obsession with a cult classic (p102).

KARLSPLATZ & AROUND

Originally, a bridge stood where Karlsplatz now stretches, named after the Empress Elisabeth. Sisi would hardly recognise the place today, built over in the early 1900s, site of Vienna's first stretch of U-Bahn in 1978 and now home to a chaotic warren of underpasses frequented by drug addicts.

Above ground, however, is a clutch of worthy sights, headed by the **Secession**, and cultural landmarks, headed by **Musikverein** (*see p164*).

Sights & Museums

Akademie der Bildenden Künste

1, Schillerplatz 3, 1st Floor (588 16-1818, www. akbild.ac.at). U1, U2, U4 Karlsplatz or tram 1, 2, D. **Open** 10am-6pm Tue-Sun. **Admission** €5 reductions; free under-19s. **Map** p101 E2 ❶

The Academy of Fine Arts famously rejected the young Adolf Hitler twice. Theophil Hansen's building houses a fine, if largely forgotten, picture gallery. The star of the show is Hieronymus Bosch's *The Last Judgement* (1504-06). The collection also includes *Tarquin and Lucretia* by Titian and Rembrandt's early *Unknown Young Woman*.

★ Karlskirche

4, Kreuzherrengasse 1 (504 6187, www.karlskirche. at). U1, U2, U4 Karlsplatz. **Open** 9am-6pm Mon-Sat; noon-7pm Sun. **Admission** €8; €4 reductions; free under-10s. **No credit cards. Map** p101 G3 ❷

This Baroque masterpiece has more than a hint of Rome and even a touch of Byzantium about it. Emperor Karl VI commissioned Fischer von Erlach to build a church to mark the end of the 1713 plague, dedicating it to the memory of St Carlo Borromeo, renowned for his role in tending victims of the 1576 plague in Milan. The exterior is a hard act to follow, but inside it is all light and airiness, showing off Rottmayr's immense fresco and Fischer's sunburst above the altar to great effect. In front of the church is an ornamental pond with a Henry Moore sculpture, *Hill Arches* (1978).

Kunsthalle Wien Karlsplatz

4, Treitlstrasse 2 (521 89-0, www.kunsthalle wien.at). U1, U2, U4 Karlsplatz or tram 1, 2, D. **Open** 10am-7pm Mon-Wed, Fri-Sun; 10am-9pm Thur. **Admission** €4; €2 reductions. **Map** p101 F2 ❸

Attached to the Kunsthalle, this glass pavilion replaces a much-criticised temporary building erected in the early 1990s. Emerging artists are given exhibition space, accessible for a modest admission fee. With its busy terrace, the café is a lovely spot.

Künstlerhaus

1, Karlsplatz 5 (587 9663, www.k-haus.at). U1, U2, U4 Karlsplatz or tram 1, 2, D. **Open** 10am-6pm Wed, Fri-Sun; 10am-9pm Thur. **Admission** €8.50; €6.50 reductions; free under-19s. **Map** p101 G2 ❹

Founded in 1861, this institution is the public face of the Künstlervereinigung (Society of Artists), whose members exhibit in the *hausgalerie*. The main space hosts an eclectic array of exhibitions, whose subjects range from landscape design to contemporary sculpture, while the passage gallery provides a platform for young artists. The building also incorporates a theatre and a cinema.

Otto Wagner Pavillon Karlsplatz

1, Karlsplatz (505 8747-85177, www.wien museum.at). U1, U2, U4 Karlsplatz. **Open** *Apr-Oct* 10am-6pm Tue-Sun. **Admission** €4; €3 reductions; free under-19s & all 1st Sun of mth. **No credit cards. Map** p101 F2 ❺

See p105 **Rail Revival**.

★ Secession

1, Friedrichstrasse 12 (587 5307, www.secession. at). U1, U2, U4 Karlsplatz. **Open** 10am-6pm Tue-Sun. *Tours* (in English) 11am Sat. **Admission** €9; €5.50 reductions. *Tours* €3. **No credit cards. Map** p101 E2 ❻

Bankrolled by Karl Wittgenstein, father of Ludwig, and completed in 1898 to a design by architect Josef Olbrich, this building was the focal point of the Secession movement, formed by a group of artists in 1897 who rejected the stultifying historicism of Vienna's leading artists' association, the Künstlerhaus. A line above the entrance clarifies their aims: 'To each age its art; to each art its freedom'.

Crowned with a gilded globe of laurel leaves, the exterior's delicate stucco work is interspersed with sculpted salamanders, ceramic turtles and snake-shaped door handles. The reason you're here, however, and paying a cash-only €9 for one piece of art, is Klimt's astonishing *Beethoven Frieze*. It's wrapped around three walls of an otherwise stark white basement space equipped with benches for ease of admiration. The work, inspired by Beethoven's *Ninth Symphony*, follows the need for happiness in a world of temptation and weakness, by means of willowy maidens, a python-bodied beast and a golden knight. It was painted straight on to these very walls for the 14th Secessionist exhibition in 1901, but not shown again until 1986 – by which time it had been sold by its pre-World War II owners, the Lederer family, to the Austrian State for half its then market price.

In March 2015, a panel declared that the sale in 1972 had been above board – even though the Austrian State had forced the family's hand by not granting them any export licences for their other artworks were they not to sell. Erich Lederer, meanwhile, is honoured with having the air-conditioning unit named after him in memory of his act of kindness.

★ Wien Museum Karlsplatz

4, Karlsplatz 8 (505 8747, www.wienmuseum.at). U1, U2, U4 Karlsplatz or tram 1, 2, D or bus 3A. **Open** 10am-6pm Tue-Sun. **Admission** €8; €6 reductions; free under-19s & all 1st Sun of mth. **Map** p101 G3 ❼

EXPLORE

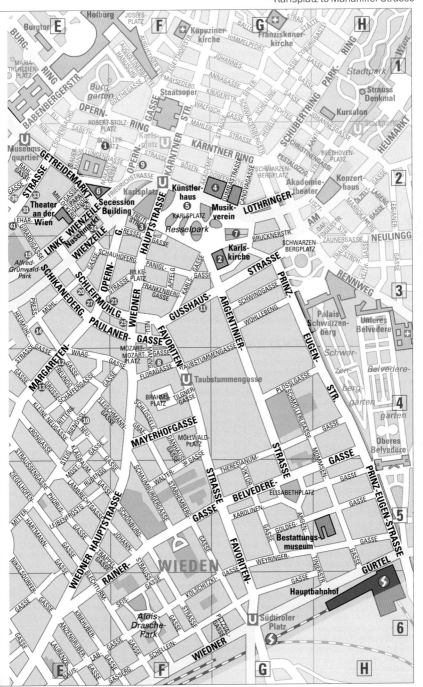

EXPLORE

he earned a Michelin star, chef Christian Petz has turned his back on luxury dining and opened his own restaurant. Petz made a name for himself by bringing offal into the high-dining arena. Among the dishes that pull in the punters is his *vitello dorschato*, with cod-liver mayonnaise. On the down side, the restaurant's interior hasn't been touched in decades.

Shops & Services

Feine Dinge
4, Margaretenstrasse 35 (0699 1010 0177, www.feinedinge.at). U1, U2, U4 Karlsplatz or tram 1, 2, D. **Open** 10am-6pm Mon-Thur, Sat; 10am-7.30pm Fri. **Map** p101 E4 **⓬ Homewares**
It's well worth taking a detour from the Naschmarkt to visit Sandra Heischberger's spacious shop. Having graced the pages of *Elle Decoration*, her porcelain shows that fine things are still being made in Vienna.

★ Unikatessen
4, Margaretenstrasse 45/11-12 (943 0996, www.unikatessen.at). U1 Taubstummengasse or U4 Kettenbrückengasse. **Open** noon-7.30pm Mon-Fri; noon-6pm Sat. **Map** p101 E4 **⓭ Concept store**
Opened in 2013, Dani Cismigiu's Unikatessen brings offbeat and unique pieces by up-and-coming fashion, jewellery and furniture designers under one roof.

NASCHMARKT & WIENZEILE

Ever more tourist-friendly, the Naschmarkt is a major attraction and frequented by bohemian locals for its lively, late-night ethnic eats. Works by Otto Wagner (*see p105* **Rail Revival**) stand either side of the market, along with the **Theater an der Wien** (*see p166*), which opened in 1801 under the directorship of Emanuel Schikaneder, author of the libretto for Mozart's *Magic Flute*. He's depicted as Papageno, the bird-catcher in the opera, in a statue above the main portico.

Off Rechte Wienzeile, Schleifmühlgasse and its adjoining streets are fast filling with galleries, shops and restaurants.

Sights & Museums

Third Man Private Collection
4, Pressgasse 25 (586 4872, www.3mpc.net). U4 Kettenbrückengasse. **Open** 2-6pm Sat & by appt. **Admission** €8.50; €4.50-€6.50 reductions. **No credit cards. Map** p101 E3 **⓮**
This excellent museum houses one aficionado's extensive collection of marginalia and documentation related to *The Third Man*. Posters, lobby cards and star portraits from around the world chronicle the movie's marketing. Also displayed are an original zither played by Anton Karas and an excerpt from the film on a 1936 German Ernemann VIIb 35mm projector, the model in use when Viennese audiences shivered through the premiere in 1949.

▶ *Third Man tours (4000 3033, www.drittemann tour.at; May-Oct 10am-8pm Thur-Sun; €7; min age 12) take place through the sewers – look out for the large red square on a corner of the Girardipark at Karlsplatz, diagonally opposite the Café Museum.*

Restaurants & Coffeehouses

Café Drechsler
6, Linke Wienzelle 22 (581 2044, www.cafe drechsler.at). U4 Kettenbrückengasse. **Open** 8am-midnight Mon-Thur, Sun; 8am-2am Fri, Sat. **Map** p101 E3 **⓯ Coffeehouse**
Open since 1919, this Naschmarkt coffeehouse was given a makeover in 2007 courtesy of Terence Conran. With its pale grey walls, vaulted ceiling and marble bar, the quietly elegant interior has weathered extremely well, considering it used to open round the clock. These days, it's more of a daytime affair where you can have a drink, a coffee and a cake or a full meal.

Gergely's
5, Schlossgasse 21 (544 0767, www.schlossquadr. at). Bus 13A, 59A. **Open** 6pm-1am Tue-Sat. **Main courses** €17-€32. **Map** p100 D5 **⓰ International**
Four restaurants share one of Vienna's most well-preserved Biedermeier-era inner courtyards, shaded by horse chestnuts. For this alone it's worth visiting either Gergely's or neighbouring Silberwirt. The former serves excellent steak and fish grilled on a lava stone, as well as some pan-Oriental dishes. The latter focuses on traditional Viennese cooking. Late dining and good beers are an added bonus.

★ Motto
5, Schönbrunner Strasse 30, entrance on Rüdigergasse (587 0672, www.motto.at). U4 Pilgramgasse or bus 59A. **Open** 6pm-2am Mon-Thur, Sun; 6pm-4am Fri, Sat. **Main courses** €9-€33. **Map** p100 D4 **⓱ International**
At Motto, they camp it up well into the early hours. With low lights and a funky soundtrack, Motto is a magnet for models and media folk, since it's one of the few places to offer a reasonable meal at 3am. Despite a preponderance of beef – in the form of carpaccio, tartare and steak – the menu's increasingly Far Eastern bent at least offers vegetarians a fair choice. The gorgeous garden, swish bar and fine-looking waiters (Helmut Lang was once among them) chatting in a variety of languages more than compensate for the lack of culinary coherence.

ON Market
6, Linke Wienzeile 36 (920 9980, www.on-market. at). U4 Kettenbrückengasse. **Open** 11am-midnight Mon-Sat; 6pm-midnight Sun. **Main courses** €10.90-€23.90. **Map** p100 D3 **⓲ Chinese**
ON Market is the latest creation of Simon Xie Hong, the man responsible for upping the ante on Chinese dining in Vienna. After the success of ON and China Bar, he's poured money and effort into this splendid

high-ceilinged corner facing the Naschmarkt. On the menu are fiery Chinese/Mediterranean dishes featuring fish, seafood, offal and excellent seasonal vegetables. The cocktails are excellent too. **Other location** ON, 5, Wehrgasse 8 (585 4900, www.restaurant-on.at).

Cafés, Pubs & Bars

Café Rüdigerhof
5, Hamburgerstrasse 20 (586 3138). U4 Pilgramgasse or bus 13A, 14A. **Open** 9am-2am daily. **Map** p100 C4 ⑲
Located in a magnificent Jugendstil building, this café featured in Nic Roeg's 1980s movie *Bad Timing*. Inside it's a veritable museum of retro fittings, including some especially wacky 1950s fluorescent lamps and furnishings that previously adorned King Hussein of Jordan's Vienna home. There's a non-smoking area at the back, and a pleasant ramshackle terrace in summer. Small eats are available, but most people come for a draught Budweiser or a coffee.

Shops & Services

Flo Nostalgische Mode
4, Schleifmühlgasse 15A (586 0773, www.vintageflo.com). U1, U2, U4 Karlsplatz or bus 59A. **Open** 10am-6.30pm Mon-Fri; 10am-3.30pm Sat. **Map** p101 E3 ⑳ **Fashion & accessories**
With its carefully curated vintage clothes, Flo is popular with stylists and costume designers. It's more about stunning cocktail dresses and crocodile handbags than second-hand bargains.

gabarage_upcycling design
4, Schleifmühlgasse 6 (585 7632, www.gabarage.at). Tram 52 or bus 59A. **Open** 10am-6pm Mon-Thur; 10am-7pm Fri; 10am-3pm Sat. **Map** p101 F3 ㉑ **Homewares**
This enterprising eco-design collective uses discarded household and office items as its raw materials. Skittles might become vases, while humble wheelie bins find a new lease of life as chairs.

Der Kleine Salon
6, Linke Wienzeile 40 (676 964 1616, www.derkleinesalon.at). U4 Kettenbrückengasse. **Open** 10am-2pm Mon-Wed; 10am-6pm Thur, Fri; 10am-3pm Sat. **Map** p100 D3 ㉒ **Children's fashion**
Set up by three mothers with a flair for fashion, the Little Salon stocks some covetable kidswear brands. There are simple but chic cotton basics from Swedish label Popupshop and lovely pieces from the likes of BangBang and Mini Rodini.

Lomography Embassy Shop Vienna
4, Kettenbrückengasse 20 (890 9360, www.lomographyembassyvienna.com). **Open** 11am-7pm Mon-Fri; 10am-6pm Sat. **Map** p100 D3 ㉓ **Photography**

It was a Vienna-based team that resurrected the famous Soviet Lomo camera in the 1990s, setting off the global Lomography movement. This new store carries the full range of Lomo cameras and accessories, as well as hosting exhibitions of the world's most loved blurry photographic format.

★ Naschmarkt
4, Linke und Rechte Wienzeile(no phone). U1, U2, U4 Karlsplatz. **Open** 6am-6.30pm Mon-Fri; 6am-5pm Sat. **Map** p101 E2 ㉔ **Market**
The famed Naschmarkt, on the long esplanade by the Wien river, can be divided into sections. Approaching from Karlsplatz, the first section is taken up with fishmongers, butchers and pricey greengrocers. Further along are Chinese and Indian shops; behind is a line of stalls selling Thai, Japanese and Italian food. After the junction with Schleifmühlgasse, the flea market sets up on Saturdays.
▶ *Nearby Bananas (5, Kettenbrückengasse 15, 0664 312 9449, www.bananas.at) sells post-war design classics and bric-a-brac six days a week.*

Perlage
4, Schleifmühlgasse 1 (0676 775 8173, www.perlage.at). U1, U2, U4 Karlsplatz. **Open** 3-8pm Tue-Fri; 11am-5pm Sat. **Map** p101 F3 ㉕ **Food & drink**
This specialist shop deals exclusively in sekt, spumante and all things sparkling. More than 80 different types of champagne are stocked.

Polyklamott
6, Hofmühlgasse 6 (969 0337, www.polyklamott.at). U4 Pilgramgasse or bus 13A, 14A. **Open** noon-7.30pm Mon-Fri; 11am-6pm Sat. **Map** p100 C4 ㉖ **Fashion**
From blue cowboy boots to oversized sunglasses, 1960s A-line frocks to preppy blazers, Polyklamott's stock is always eclectic.

Rauminhalt
4, Schleifmühlgasse 13 (409 9892, www.rauminhalt.com). U1, U2, U4 Karlsplatz or tram 1, 62. **Open** noon-7pm Tue-Fri; 10am-3pm Sat. **Map** p101 E3 ㉗ **Homewares**
Offering design from the 1950s to the 1980s, the folk at Rauminhalt really know their stuff, specialising in Scandinavian pieces (though Austrian greats such as Carl Auböck are also well represented).

Record Shack
5, Reinprechtsdorfer Strasse 60 (545 77 57, www.recordshack.org). Bus 14A. **Open** noon-7pm Mon-Fri; noon-5pm Sat. **Map** p100 C6 ㉘ **Books & music**
Jörg is a 1960s and '70s soul fanatic. He started the business as a mail-order service before setting up this small, funky store. Treat yourself to some classic northern soul and vintage reggae on vinyl or CD.
▶ *Nearby Rave Up Records (6, Hofmühlgasse 1, 596 9650, www.rave-up.at) specialises in indie, reggae, electronica and hip hop.*

EXPLORE

Wein & Co

6, Getreidemarkt 1 (585 7257-13, www.weinco.at).
U1, U2, U4 Karlsplatz. **Open** 10am-midnight
Mon-Fri; 9am-midnight Sat; 11am-midnight Sun.
Map p101 E2 ㉙ **Food & drink**
Wein & Co cheekily circumvented Austria's
restrictive retail legislation by opening wine bars
and shops in one store, so you can buy bottles until
midnight. As well as wines from all over the world,
there's a smart bar serving drinks and tasty meals.
Other locations 1, Jasomirgottstrasse 3-5 (535
0916-12); 1, Dr Karl-Lueger-Ring 12 (533 85 30 12).

MARIAHILF

Vienna's 6th district, Mariahilf, rises from the
hollow of the Wien river valley via various steep
lanes and flights of steps to Mariahilfer Strasse,
the city's recently pedestrianised prime shopping
mile. Along the way you cross Gumpendorfer
Strasse, whose lower reaches house numerous
bars, shops and cafés – among them the laid-back
Phil and iconic **Café Sperl**.

Sights & Museums

Haydnhaus

6, Haydngasse 19 (596 1307, www.wienmuseum.
at). U3 Zieglergasse. **Open** 10am-1pm, 2-6pm
Tue-Sun. **Admission** €4; €3 reductions; free
under-19s & all 1st Sun of mth. **No credit cards.**
Map p100 B4 ㉚
Composer Joseph Haydn spent his last 12 years in this
small house, writing his great oratorios. Opened as a
museum in 1899, it displays letters, two pianos and
Haydn's death mask. Another room is dedicated to
Johannes Brahms, who lionised Haydn and did much
to maintain the memory of his idol. Another admirer
was Napoleon, who placed a guard of honour outside
the house as Haydn lay dying in 1809. The garden,
open to the public, was reconstructed in 2009.

Restaurants & Coffeehouses

Café Sperl

6, Gumpendorfer Strasse 11 (586 4158, www.
cafesperl.at). Bus 57A. **Open** 7am-11pm Mon-Sat;
11am-8pm Sun. **Map** p101 E2 ㉛ **Coffeehouse**
Café Sperl is the apotheosis of a Viennese *kaffeehaus,*
its faded grandeur today surprisingly cosy despite
its awesome dimensions. It has managed to retain an
atmosphere of stately silence, in part due to a ban
on mobile phones. Most Viennese have a soft spot
for the Sperl, with its grumpy tuxedoed waiters,
parquet flooring, velvet booths and expansive
windows. It also has two billiard tables.

Gastwirtschaft Steman

6, Otto-Bauer-Gasse 7 (597 8509, www.steman.at).
U3 Zieglergasse. **Open** 11am-11pm Mon-Fri. **Main**
courses €6-€16.50. **Map** p100 B3 ㊷ **Viennese**

The young crew that runs Steman zealously rejects
any contemporary touches to the original dark wood
interior of this historic *beisl*. Divided from the bar
area by a clouded glass partition, the large, spacious
dining room offers well-priced local classics such as
offal, game, wild mushrooms and the humble hog in
all its manifestations.

Ra'mien

6, Gumpendorfer Strasse 9 (585 4798, www.
ramien.at). U2 Museumsquartier. **Open** 11am-
midnight Tue-Sun. **Main courses** €11.80-€17.20.
Map p101 E2 ㉝ **Asian**
Ra'mien is a sparse, airy noodle joint that has been
pulling in the crowds since 2002. At lunchtime, the
menu features vast bowls of tasty, reasonably priced
noodles and Vietnamese phô. There are also rice
dishes and gyoza dumplings. Dinner is a costlier affair,
with great pan-Asian fish, seafood and tofu dishes,
but it can get crowded. The downstairs lounge, all
Hong Kong Phooey chintz, has karaoke on midweek
nights, and DJs spinning R&B and hip hop until 4am
at weekends. Booking is essential for dinner.

★ Zum Geschupftn Ferdl

6, Windmühlgasse 20 (966 3066 www.zum
gschupftnferdl.com). U3 Neubaugasse or bus
13A. **Open** 4pm-2am Mon-Sat. **Main courses**
from €10.80. **Map** p100 C3 ㉞ **Heuriger/organic**
This pimped-up city *heuriger* offers a modern interpretation of the traditional wine tavern. Using computer game-style graphics on its signage and menus,
the Ferdl brings a bit of swing to *heuriger* staples
such as ham and cheese platters, roast pork, goulash and speciality *krapfen* (potato dough pasties
filled with meat, cheese or black pudding). Stacks
of reasonably priced wines are on offer, including
the foxy Burgenland Uhudler, all served in vintage
green-stemmed goblets. There's outdoor seating on
Raimundhof (until 10pm), plus a charming interior.
Later on, DJs play electronica and Austro-pop.

Cafés, Pubs & Bars

Lutz

6, Mariahilfer Strasse 3 (585 3646, www.lutz-bar.
at). U2 Museumsquartier. **Open** 8am-late Mon-Fri;
9am-late Sat; 10am-late Sun. **Map** p100 D2 ㉟
As illustrated by the timeline on its homepage that
follows the passage from steaming coffee at breakfast
to zinging cocktails after dark, Lutz is all things to
all drinkers. Most of all, it provides shoppers with a
lively terrace right on Mariahilfer Strasse, and a sassy
mixed drink (pineapple-ginger mojito, perhaps) to
stand it on. There's food as well (salads and pastas)
and, if it's raining, there's a swish interior.

★ Phil

6, Gumpendorfer Strasse 10-12 (581 0489, www.
phil.info). U2 Museumsquartier. **Open** 5pm-1am
Mon; 9am-1am Tue-Sun. **Map** p101 E2 ㊱

EXPLORE

Phil feels like someone's living room transformed into an informal concept store and bar. Decked out in mix 'n' match junk-store objects and furniture, including the odd Jacobsen chair and other modern classics, it's a chilled spot to have a drink and leaf through its choice of books in English and German or listen to some good sounds.

Shops & Services

Comic-Treff Steiner
6, Barnabitengasse 12 (586 7627, www.comictreff. at). U3 Neubaugasse. **Open** 10am-7pm Mon-Fri; 10am-2pm Sat. **Map** p100 C3 ⑰ **Books & music**
This well-established comic book emporium is run by clued-up English speakers. It does a decent line in quirky US products and is good on peripheral items, from manga merchandising to *Hello Kitty*.

Lichterloh
6, Gumpendorfer Strasse 15-17 (586 0520, www.lichterloh.com). Bus 57A. **Open** 11am-6.30pm Mon-Fri; 11am-4pm Sat. **Map** p100 D2 ㊳ **Homewares**
Lichterloh is a Vienna institution, showcasing an ever-changing array of 20th-century design pieces – most of which come from house clearances. Mid-century classics feature alongside offbeat finds: an antique vaulting horse, perhaps, or a beautiful bar counter. **Other location** Glasfabrik, 16, Lorenz-Mandl-Gasse 25 (494 3490, www.glasfabrik.at).

Nachbarin
6, Gumpendorfer Strasse 17 (587 2169, www. nachbarin.co.at). Bus 57A. **Open** noon-6.30pm Mon; 11am-6.30pm Tue-Fri; 11am-4pm Sat. **Map** p100 D2 ㊴ **Fashion**
This über-cool clothing store, at the fashionable end of Gumpendorfer Strasse, stocks a cutting-edge roster of European labels: Londoners PREEN, Brighton-based shoe designer Thomas Murphy, Belgian designer Veronique Leroy and accessories hotshot Arlette Ess, who used to work at McQueen.

★ Teuchtler Alt&Neu
6, Windmühlgasse 10 (586 2133). U2 Museumsquartier. **Open** 1-6pm Mon-Fri; 10am-1pm Sat. **Map** p100 D2 ㊵ **Books & music**
An Aladdin's cave selling used and new CDs and vinyl. Jazz and classical are its strong points. Prices are the best in Vienna, although the categorisation is slightly chaotic. Featured in the film *Before Sunrise*.

Vintage in Vienna
6, Gumpendorfer Strasse 10-12 (0699 195 40444). Bus 57A. **Open** 11am-6.30pm Tue, Wed, Fri; 11am-7pm Thur; noon-4.30pm Sat. **Map** p101 E2 ㊶ **Fashion & accessories**
This boutique stocks mint-condition clothes and accessories from the 1920s to the '90s, including some wonderful dresses, shoes and purses.

RAIL REVIVAL
Otto Wagner wonders.

Architect and designer Otto Wagner (1841-1918) merged the youthful curves of Vienna's version of art nouveau, Jugendstil, with modern engineering and building techniques to create, among many other things, an urban rail network. The Stadtbahn was the only element of Wagner's far-reaching plan to modernise Vienna that actually saw the light of day. Opened at various stages either side of 1900, it was ultimately limited to five lines that followed the Wien river, the Danube canal and the Gürtel ring road. Finances dictated that the lines that should have crossed town to provide easy links across the network had to be abandoned.

Electrified after World War I, the Stadtbahn and its beautiful Jugendstil stations were severely damaged in World War II – some were never rebuilt. When plans were being made to create a U-Bahn system for the city, it was decided to integrate a number of Wagner's stations into it. Today, the elevated U6 line over the Gürtel (and a series of music venues in the archways – see p158 **Gürtel of Grunge**) and the U4 line west past Schönbrunn still stop at these renovated works of art.

The most famous of his rail buildings, though, are at Karlsplatz. One is now a museum, the **Otto Wagner Pavillon Karlsplatz** (*see p98; pictured*), dedicated to his work, and the other is a café with a fine terrace. Both were nearly demolished during the U-Bahn construction, and only a protest by students from the Technische Universität saved the day. Once located on either side of the Akademiestrasse, the buildings were disassembled and reconstructed on nearby Karlsplatz with only a few slabs of marble being replaced.

EXPLORE

Neubau

Neubau, Vienna's 7th district, is one of the most happening areas in terms of nightlife, shops and alternative lifestyles. This Green Party stronghold is full of handsome buildings housing architecture and design firms, and pleasingly quirky shops. Neubau is at its most picturesque to the east of pleasant, commercial Neubaugasse. Known as Spittelberg, this atmospheric network of cobbled streets and Biedermeier architecture is lovely for a wander. The area was once a red-light district, where Hitler reputedly had his first sight of the prostitutes that serviced the adjacent barracks. Today, homes in its narrow streets are among the most desirable in Vienna, and its numerous eateries and antiques dealers are evidence of the area's gentrification. Just east of here is the MuseumsQuartier, so top-notch culture isn't that far away either. Finally, Otto Wagner aficionados should make a pilgrimage to Neustiftgasse 40, one of his finest, most austere apartment buildings; round the corner at Döblergasse 4 is the house where he lived and worked until his death in 1918.

EXPLORE

Brickmakers Ale & Cider House

Don't Miss

1 **7tm shopping tour** Visit the indie stores of funky Neubau (p108).

2 **Westlicht** Contemporary photos and retro Leicas in a tasteful gallery (p108).

3 **Hofmobiliendepot** Mayerling furnishings, Biedermeier furniture (p108).

4 **Brickmakers Ale & Cider House** Great grub, craft beer and cider (p109).

5 **Glacis Beisl** Classic Viennese fare and an unkempt garden (p109).

EXPLORE

Brickmakers Ale & Cider House.

The three main streets of Neubau – Siebensterngasse, Neubaugasse and Lindengasse – are lined with all kinds of shops and small businesses, enough to keep the curious traveller walking and gawping. **Neubaugasse** (www. neubaugasse.at) itself has a regular flea market, when long stretches of the street become one huge bazaar and locals spend the day sipping beers outside in warm weather. On non-market days, there are so many independent shops to explore that an association was formed, **7tm**, and walking tours laid on. *See p114* **In the Know**. The area is also known for its funky bars, cafés and pubs.

From Lindengasse, take a left turn down Andreasgasse for the **Hofmobiliendepot** – an intriguing depository for the Hapsburgs' unwanted furniture. Meanwhile, following Westbahnstrasse takes you past the **Westlicht** photography gallery before finally reaching the Gürtel and impressive **Main Library** (7, Urban-Loritz-Platz 2A, www.buechereien.wien.at). Built in 2003, the building straddles the U-Bahn tracks; for far-reaching views, climb to the top and look out from the terrace or glass-fronted café.

Sights & Museums

Hofmobiliendepot

7, Andreasgasse 7 (524 3357, www.hofmobilien depot.at). U3 Zieglergasse or bus 13A. **Open** 10am-6pm Tue-Sun. **Admission** €9.50; €6-€8.50 reductions. **Map** p110 D4 ❶

Founded by Maria Theresa in 1747, this gigantic lock-up for the monarchy's unwanted furniture and fittings contains all sorts of fascinating pieces. Entire rooms have been reconstructed, but the small items are just as compelling: the pair of stuffed canaries (Bibi and Büberl) owned by Emperor Franz II, or the sumptuous ebony-and-red velvet highchair that belonged to the infant Crown Prince Rudolf. A few rooms further on are furnishings from the lodge at Mayerling, where the 30-year-old Rudolf shot himself and his lover. The museum's upper floors house a fine array of Biedermeier furniture and a series of stately, chintz-filled rooms, along with modernist pieces by Hoffmann, Loos and Wagner.

★ Westlicht

7, Westbahnstrasse 40 (522 66 36-60, www. westlicht.com). U6 Burggasse or U6 Stadthalle or U3 Zieglergasse then tram 5, 49. **Open** 2-7pm Tue, Wed, Fri; 2-9pm Thur; 11am-7pm Sat, Sun. **Admission** €7; €2-€4 reductions; free under-6s. **No credit cards. Map** p110 D3 ❷

This photography gallery displays all sorts of antique cameras, from 19th-century daguerreotype cameras to a gold-plated 1930s Leica Luxus. The permanent collection of photos is supplemented by high-profile temporary exhibitions.

Restaurants & Coffeehouses

Amerlingbeisl

7, Stiftgasse 8 (526 1660, www.amerling beisl.at). U2, U3 Volkstheater or tram 49.

Open 9am-2am daily. **Main courses** €7.20-€11.90. **Map** p111 F3 ❸ **International**

The Amerlingbeisl is Spittelberg's most iconic address. Squatted in the 1980s as part of a campaign against plans to redevelop this picturesque quarter, the building remains a focal point of political radicalism. Although the restaurant serves some fairly pedestrian brasserie grub, an hour or two in its gorgeous leafy inner courtyard is a delight.

★ Brickmakers Ale & Cider House

7, Zieglergasse 42 (1997 4414, www.brickmakers. at). Tram 49. **Open** 4pm-1am Mon-Fri; noon-1am Sat, Sun. *Kitchen* 5-10pm Mon-Fri; noon-2pm, 5-10pm Sat, Sun. **Main courses** €11.90-€27.90. **Map** p110 D3 ❹ **Gastropub**

See p115 **Going Gastro**.

Burgermacher

7, Burggasse 12 (0699 1158 9599, www. dieburgermacher.at). U2, U3 Volkstheater. **Open** 5-11pm Tue-Fri; noon-11pm Sat. **Main courses** €8.50-€11. **Map** p111 F3 ❺ **Grill**

This tiny diner (seats 20) has been at the forefront of Vienna's current obsession with burgers, and continues to attract a loyal clientele. The patties here are made with strictly organic ingredients (including the home-made ketchup and mayo). You can choose between beef and lamb, or halloumi or tofu for non-carnivores. Other variations include the very Viennese *blunznburger* with black pudding and horseradish. Sides of hand-cut fries, mixed salad and coleslaw are extra. There's a selection of 25 bottled beers in the fridge.

Café Westend

7, Mariahilfer Strasse 128 (523 3183). U3, U6 Westbahnhof. **Open** 7am-midnight daily. **Map** p110 C5 ❻ **Coffeehouse**

Set opposite the Westbahnhof, the Westend provides new arrivals in town with an authentic coffeehouse experience: slightly grubby-looking stucco, marble-topped tables, chandeliers, ceiling sunbursts, and generous portions of strudel and chocolate cake from ancient display cabinets. The coffee is very good and, in one welcome departure from tradition, the waiters are uncommonly friendly.

Gastwirtschaft Schilling

7, Burggasse 103 (524 1775, www.schilling-wirt.at). U6 Burggasse or bus 48A. **Open** 11am-1am daily. **Main courses** €7.90-€24.50. **Map** p110 C3 ❼ **Viennese**

The cosy, antiquated Schilling is *beisl* heaven on a cold winter evening. Its vintage wood-panelled and milk-glass interior, tremendous roasts and liver dishes, and powerful puddings (the *mohr im hemd* is Vienna's greatest) all induce the most wonderful sense of wellbeing.

Other location 7, Siebensterngasse 31 (523 0142).

Glacis Beisl

7, MuseumsQuartier, access from Breitegasse 4 (526 5660, www.glacisbeisl.at). U2, U3 Volkstheater. **Open** 11am-2am daily. **Main courses** €7.40-€17.80. **Map** p111 G3 ❽ **Viennese**

The Glacis Beisl was around long before the MuseumsQuartier was a twinkling in a politician's eye. After the museums opened, it returned in a stylish, contemporary form with its gorgeously unkempt garden trimmed and tamed. Since then, its repertoire of Viennese classics with a twist has been a resounding success. So much so that communication breakdowns between kitchen and staff are frequent on busy days, leading to irksome waits. Avoid weekends and public holidays.

Siebensternbräu

7, Siebensterngasse 19 (523 8697, www.7stern. at). Tram 49. **Open** 10am-midnight (food served until 11pm) daily. **Main courses** €7.20-€17.90. **Map** p111 F3 ❾ **Austrian**

A large, gregarious beer hall/microbrewery that appeals to all ages, the Siebensternbräu has an indifferent interior plagued by cooking smells. However, the garden – shaded by two large horse chestnut trees – is a lovely spot to enjoy the brewery's trademark cloudy beer and robust Austrian dishes. The hemp and chilli beers should be approached with some caution.

Wratschko

7, Neustiftgasse 51 (523 7161). Bus 13A, 48A. **Open** 5pm-1am Mon-Fri. **Main courses** €9-€22. **Map** p111 E2 ❿ **Viennese**

Wratschko's classic interior ticks all the boxes on the *beisl* authenticity scale: ancient parquet, wobbly tiling, engraved glass and cheese plants. Chef Anthony Bourdain featured the place in his *No Reservations* TV show and enthused about the lamb lasagne. Punters flock from all over Vienna for its splendid tap beer, keenly priced local wines and a menu that marries traditional dishes with a few worthwhile innovations, such as roast pork with morels. Reserve to be on the safe side – the rooms at the back are pretty sad.

▶ *There are more beisl delights nearby at Gastwirtschaft Schilling; see left.*

Cafés, Bars & Pubs

★ Espresso

7, Burggasse 57 (526 8951, www.espresso-wien.at). Bus 13A, 48A. **Open** 7.30am-1am Mon-Fri; 10am-1am Sat, Sun. **Map** p111 E3 ⓫

This lovingly renovated 1950s espresso bar is popular for coffees or cocktails. From the gleaming espresso machine to the red leather banquettes, it's a joy to behold. There's free Wi-Fi and great music in the daytime; the evenings feature occasional DJ nights that spill out on to the packed summer terrace with its retro garden furniture.

EXPLORE

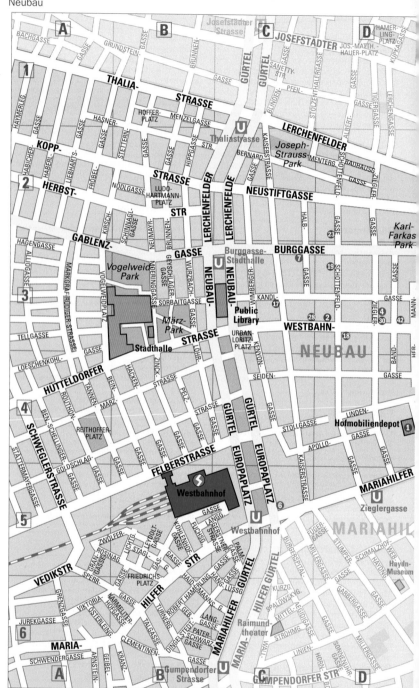

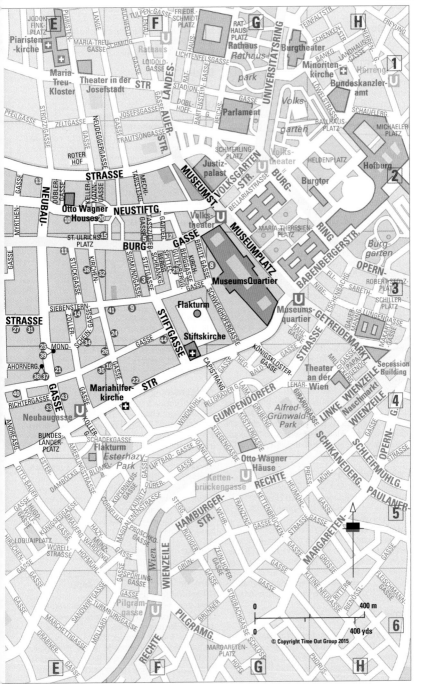

Das Möbel

7, Burggasse 10 (524 9497, www.dasmoebel.at). U2, U3 Volkstheater or bus 48A. **Open** 2pm-midnight Mon-Fri; 10am-midnight Sat, Sun. **Map** p111 F3 ⑫
Price tags dangle from the artistically mismatched tables, chairs and light fittings at this airy 7th district hangout, which doubles as a design store. It's an appealing place, with free Wi-Fi, big windows, cosy sofas and good-quality grub such as hunks of quiche with zestily dressed salad, say, or a sturdy ciabatta.

Shebeen

7, Lerchenfelderstrasse 45 (524 7900, www. shebeen.at). Tram 49. **Open** 5pm-4am Mon-Fri; 1pm-4am Sat; noon-2am Sun. **Map** p111 E2 ⑬
Calling itself the 'International Pub', this popular establishment does all the things a pub should do without having to tart itself up in faux Irish toot. Burgers, wings and chips with dips underscore the menu, while entertainment is provided by regular pub quizzes and big-screen football. Several changes of management have brought their own influence to bear, but basically this is where bar-focused individuals want to sink Kilkenny beers and Strongbow ciders till the cows come home, plus maybe a cocktail or two – encouraged by happy hours around midnight.

Shops & Services

Arnold's

7, Siebensterngasse 35 (923 1316, www.arnolds. at). U3 Neubaugasse or tram 49 or bus 13A. **Open** 11am-7pm Mon-Fri; 11am-5pm Sat. **Map** p111 E3 ⑭ **Fashion & accessories**
The likes of Edwin jeans, Carhartt, Hurley Super sunglasses (as worn by the Kills, Sienna Miller et al), and Croatian brand Sheriff & Cherry are sold at this style-conscious streetwear store, alongside local labels such as Maiko. Menswear dominates and there's a cool little 'sneaker boutique', PAAR, in the linked premises next door.

★ Burggasse 24

7, Burggasse 24 (0664 442 9598, www. facebook.com/burggasse24). **Open** 11am-10pm Mon-Fri; 11am-8pm Sat. **Map** p111 E3 ⑮ **Fashion & accessories**
Housed in a fabulously distressed space, this vintage clothing emporium is perfect for the well-travelled Viennese hipster – browse leather jackets in all hues, paisley blouses, bikinis and tearaway tanktops. Shoppers can rest their weary platforms in the café, which serves great coffee and vegetarian eats, indoors or on the cobbled terrace overlooking Ulrichskirche.

Camille Boyer

7, Lindengasse 25 (523 1449, www.camille boyer.at). U3 Neubaugasse. **Open** 1-6pm Mon-Sat. **Map** p111 F4 ⑯ **Fashion & accessories**
The eponymous owner of this small boutique has a superb eye for fashion. Dresses from Finnish label Ivana Helsinki, T-shirts from Berlin's Star Styling and unisex casualwear from hotly tipped young design duo Meshit are among her finds.

Denn's

7, Kaiserstrasse 57-59 (526 5886-18, www. denns-biomarkt.at). U6 Burggasse or tram 5. **Open** 8am-7.30pm Mon-Fri; 8am-6pm Sat. **Map** p110 C3 ⑰ **Food & drink**
Vienna's largest organic supermarket has the best and most reasonably priced fruit, veg, groceries and meat in the city. There are plenty of organic beers and wines as well, along with toiletries.

designqvist

7, Westbahnstrasse 21 (0680 504 7000, designqvist.at). U3 Neubaugasse or tram 49 or bus 13A. **Open** 1-7pm Tue-Fri; 11am-5pm Sat. **Map** p110 D3 ⑱ **Designer**
See p114 **In the Know**.

E35

7, Schottenfeldgasse 67 (956 4452, www.e35shop. com). **Open** noon-7pm Mon-Fri; 11am-4pm Sat. **Map** p110 D3 ⑲ **Fashion & accessories**
Set on resolutely non-commercial Schottenfeldgasse, E35 is worth the trudge to get your hands on brands such as Norse Projects, Nudie and Levi's Vintage. The shop is an offshoot of an Italian firm based in Modena – evident from the racks of *tifosi*-favoured Stone Island jackets. Shoes and boots by Tricker's and Red Wing round off E35's considerable appeal to solvent male fashionistas.

★ eigensinnig

7, Sankt-Ulrichs-Platz 4 (890 6637, www. eigensinnig.at). **Open** noon-7pm Tue-Fri; 10am-6pm Sat. **Map** p111 E2 ⑳ **Fashion & accessories**
The black, grey and earthy tones by designers from Germany, Denmark, Italy and Belarus – Esther Perbandt, Hannibal, Aleksandr Manamis, Sosnovska, Simona Tagliaferri, Tvscia, Leon Louis, Cinzia Araia and the like – fill the cool, vaulted premises of eigensinnig. Claiming to sell unique fashion for 'the creative, the unconventional thinkers and the visionary', this gallery-style boutique will hopefully inject some life into beautiful but sorely underused Sankt-Ulrichs-Platz.

Freitag

7, Neubaugasse 26 (523 3136, www. freitag.ch). **Open** 10am-7pm Mon-Wed, Fri; 10am-8pm Thur; 10am-6pm Sat. **Map** p111 E4 ㉑ **Fashion & accessories**
Made from recycled truck tarpaulins and seatbelts, Freitag's messenger bags have been a hipster staple in Vienna for more than ten years. The Swiss firm opened its Vienna premises in 2011 and the range has now extended to include laptop, smartphone and tablet cases, wash bags, wallets and backpacks. Everyone's got one, but fear not, each one's unique.

EXPLORE

Gerngross

*7, Mariahilfer Strasse 42-48 (52180-0, www.
gerngross.at). U3 Neubaugasse or bus 13A.* **Open**
9.30am-7pm Mon-Wed; 9am-8pm Thur, Fri; 9.30am-
6pm Sat. **Map** p111 F4 ㉒ **Department store**
Stores include electrical goods retailer Saturn, a
huge Zara and a Merkur supermarket. The rooftop
terrace has various food options and terrific views.

Glanz und Gloria

*7, Schottenfeldgasse 77 (boutique 400 6091/
hair appts 400 6089, www.glanzundgloria.at).
Tram 49.* **Open** 1-8pm Tue-Fri; 11am-6pm Sat.
Map p110 D2 ㉓ **Fashion/hairdressers**
Half of the shop is devoted to womenswear, with
clothes displayed in white-painted antique ward-
robes. The other is an effortlessly cool hairdressing
salon. Vintage hairdryers dangle from their leads like
art installations, and you'll get individual attention
from hairdresser Thomas Pavlidis. Prices are reasonable: from €30 for a cut for women, €18 for men.

Herr & Frau Klein

*7, Kirchengasse 22 (990 4394, www.herrund
frauklein.com). U3 Neubaugasse or bus 13A.*
Open 11am-6pm Mon-Sat. **Map** p111 F3
㉔ **Children's fashion**
With a strong focus on ethically produced and
traded goods, this all-rounder stocks kids' clothes,
baby accessories, toys and practical gear.

★ Ina Kent

*7, Neubaugasse 34 (0699 1954 1090, www.
inakent.com). U3 Neubaugasse. Bus 13A.*
Open 11am-7pm Mon-Fri; 11am-6pm Sat.
Map p111 E4 ㉕ **Fashion & accessories**
See p114 **In the Know.**
Other location 7, Siebensterngasse 50
(0699 14777477).

Kauf dich glücklich

*7, Kirchengasse 9 (924 7755, www.kaufdich
glueklich-shop.de). U3 Neubaugasse or bus
13A.* **Open** 10am-8pm Mon-Fri; 10am-6pm Sat.
Map p111 E4 ㉖ **Concept store**
With a concept store feel, Kdg features principally
Danish clothing brands such as Mads Norgaard,
Soulland, Han Kjobenhavn and Libertine, as well as a
selection of mid-range brands such as Ben Sherman
and Cheap Monday. Attractive home furnishings and
crockery are also available.

★ Kaufhaus Wall

*7, Westbahnstrasse 5A (524 4728, www.
kaufhauswall.com). Tram 49.* **Open** 11am-
7pm Tue-Fri; 11am-5pm Sat. **Map** p111 E3
㉗ **Fashion & accessories**
Formerly known as Be a Good Girl, this interesting
hairdresser-cum-concept store had a revamp in 2015.
Owner Andreas Wall's select choice of minimal
leisurewear sticks with regular designers such as

eigensinnig.

Barbara i Gongini, Hannes Roether and Saskia Diaz,
but with the addition of hip Berlin label Simon&Me,
and great leather bags by Swiss brand Park. There's
also a fine range of books, CDs by local heroes, accessories and beauty products.

Leica Shop

*7, Westbahnstrasse 40 (523 5659, www.leica
shop.com). Tram 49.* **Open** 10am-6pm Mon-Fri;
9am-1pm Sat. **Map** p110 C3 ㉘ **Electronics**
This shop has an astounding selection of Leicas and
other makes. It's also associated with the Westlicht
gallery in the courtyard (*see* p108). In 2012, it opened
a spectacular flagship store near the Opera.
Other location 1, Walfischgasse 1 (236 7487,
www.leicastore-wien.at).

Lena Hoschek

*7, Gutenberggasse 17 (5030 9200, www.lena
hoschek.com). U2 Museumsquartier or tram
49.* **Open** 11am-7pm Mon-Fri; 11am-5pm Sat.
Map p111 F3 ㉙ **Fashion & accessories**

After working for Vivienne Westwood, Lena Hoschek launched her own label in 2006. Inspiration comes from 1940s and '50s pin-ups such as Bettie Page, which translates to super-feminine designs with a seductively subversive edge: full-skirted dresses in vintage floral prints, tight satin pencil skirts, the odd piece of bondage-influenced gear and killer bikinis.

Market Vinyl

7, Westbahnstrasse 22 & Zieglergasse 40 (0676 376 9080, www.dasmarket.at). Tram 49. **Open** 1-8pm Tue-Fri; noon-5pm Sat. **Map** p110 D3 **30 Books & music**

This new incarnation of now-defunct cult record store Black Market is where Vienna's DJs shop for house, disco and techno.

Minimal

7, Westbahnstrasse 3 (997 1450, www.minimal wien.at). U3 Neubaugasse or tram 49 or bus 13A. **Open** 11am-6pm Tue-Fri; 11am-3pm Sat. **Map** p111 E3 **31 Children's fashion**

Opened in 2010, this über-stylish boutique is filled with chic childrenswear. Goodies include Minti's offbeat T-shirts, Luckyboysunday's alpaca knit toys and cushions, and retro prints from Bobo Choses.

Mot Mot

7, Kirchengasse 36 (924 2719, www.motmot shop.com). U3 Neubaugasse or tram 49 or bus 13A. **Open** noon-7pm Tue-Fri; noon-5pm Sat. **Map** p111 E3 **32 Fashion/gifts & souvenirs**

Behind the counter at Mot Mot is the screenprinting studio where the shop's bold, bright T-shirt designs are produced. Badges, posters, cards and design books round off the stock, along with Californian co-owner Steve's idiosyncratic comic books.

Nfive

7, Neubaugasse 5 (www.nfive.at). **Open** 10am-7pm Mon-Fri; 10am-6pm Sat. **Map** p111 E4 **33 Fashion & accessories**

IN THE KNOW DESIGN TRAIL

A combination of low rents and attractive properties attracted numerous designers to move to Neubau in the early noughties, and an association, **7tm** (www.7tm.at), was founded in 2008. It now comprises more than 50 outlets. Originally created to promote 7tm to journalists, there are now scheduled store tours and meet-the-owner walks open to the public. These vary according to theme and season, but usually involve a visit to designer-bag queen **Ina Kent** (see *p113*), the vintage Scandi homewares of **designqvist** (see *p112*) and the fetish fashion of **Tiberius** (see *p115*).

More Scandi candy for both sexes in this spacious store. Womenswear includes Swedish staple filippa K and occasionally features items from more upmarket brands such as Sonia Rykel's diffusion label Sonia. There's also cool jewellery by Danish designer Pernille Corydon and Sandqvist bags. Men's fashion is provided, most notably, by Tiger of Sweden.

Park

7, Mondscheingasse 20 (526 4414, www.park.co.at). U3 Neubaugasse or tram 49 or bus 13A. **Open** 10am-7pm Mon-Fri; 10am-6pm Sat. **Map** p111 E3 **34 Fashion & accessories**

Laid out over two gleaming white floors, Park has an impeccably cool, concept store feel. Its selection of mens- and womenswear continues to outshine the competition, with pieces from the likes of Anne Demeulemeester and Raf Simons; its owner also has a keen eye for future stars such as Natalia Brilli.

La Petite Boutique

7, Lindengasse 25 (0699 1923 9423, www.sandra gilles.com). U3 Neubaugasse. **Open** 11am-3pm Mon, Wed, Thur; 11am-6pm Tue; 11am-7pm Fri. **Map** p111 E4 **35 Fashion & accessories**

French-born Sandra Gilles specialises in beautiful night attire: from dusky pink silk camisoles to pretty, ribbon-edged pyjama bottoms. The diminutive premises also showcase Michaela Arl de Lima's jewellery; her rose gold rings, set with spherical, perfectly smooth stones, are wonderfully tactile.

Ramsch & Rosen

7, Neubaugasse 15 (586 0520, www.lichterloh.com). U3 Neubaugasse or bus 13A. **Open** noon-6.30pm Mon-Fri; 10am-2pm Sat. **Map** p111 E4 **36 Vintage**

Pieces that don't make the grade for Lichterloh or Glasfabrik are instead sold at this eccentric junk shop. Run by students, it's an endlessly intriguing jumble of fish knives, faded photographs, gilt picture frames, old medals and pretty china tea sets.

Reformhaus Buchmüller

7, Neubaugasse 17-19 (523 7297, www.reformhaus-buchmueller.at). U3 Neubaugasse or bus 13A. **Open** 9am-6.30pm Mon-Fri; 9am-5pm Sat. **Map** p111 E4 **37 Health & beauty**

This small shop sells everything from organic veg to homeopathic remedies and beauty lines. The café serves freshly squeezed juices, hunks of carrot cake and veggie mains, served with heaped salads.

Le Shop

7, Kirchengasse 40/1 (956 6633, www.le-shop.at). U3 Neubaugasse or bus 13A. **Open** 11am-7pm Mon-Fri; 11am-5pm Sat. **Map** p111 E3 **38 Accessories**

Owned by a graphic designer with a penchant for Swedish design, Le Shop opened in 2011. Stripy canvas bags and elegant laptop cases from Rib & Hull, cards by My Darling Clementine and rings that open to reveal tiny 3D landscapes are among its treasures.

★ Shu!

7, Neubaugasse 34 (523 1449, www.shu.at).
U3 Neubaugasse or bus 13A. **Open** noon-7pm
Tue-Fri; noon-5pm Sat. **Map** p111 E4 ❸❾ **Footwear**
The grown-up, quietly elegant feel of this spacious
store extends to its collections of men's and women's
footwear, running from sneakers and brogues to gorgeous heels. Understated designs by Hudson Shoes,
Chia Mihara, Officine Creative and Enrico Antinori
are beautifully displayed; prices reflect the quality.

Stil-Laden

7, Lindengasse 51 (522 3784, www.stil-laden.at).
U3 Neubaugasse. **Open** 11am-7pm Mon-Fri;
11am-5pm Sat. **Map** p111 E4 ❹⓿ **Streetwear**
Limited-edition skateboards, sneakers and clothes
are lovingly showcased at this laid-back skateshop.
You'll find Fourstar (Spike Jonze's label), cult favourite Huf and great T-shirts from Quiet Life.

Stress Deponie

7, Siebensterngasse 4 (990 4530, www.stress
deponie.at). Tram 49. **Open** 10.30am-6pm
Mon, Tue; noon-6pm Wed, Fri; noon-8pm Thur.
Map p111 F3 ❹❶ **Health & beauty**
Massage is the speciality at this calm, contemporary
establishment, running from classic Swedish techniques to hot stone, ayurvedic and reiki sessions;
prices start at around €32 for 25 minutes. Yoga and
pilates sessions are also held here.

Substance

7, Westbahnstrasse 16 (523 6757, www.substance-
store.com). U3 Neubaugasse or tram 49. **Open**
11am-7pm Mon-Fri; 11am-6pm Sat. **Map** p110 D3
❹❷ **Books & music**
Substance is run by serious aficionados – fans of
everything from John Zorn to West Coast hip hop
and indie rock. CDs predominate, but there's also
vinyl, along with some music books and DVDs.

Terra Plana

7, Neubaugasse 12-14 (890 5052, www.terra
plana.com). U3 Neubaugasse or bus 13A.
Open 10am-6.30pm Mon-Fri; 10am-6pm Sat.
Map p111 E4 ❹❸ **Footwear**
The shoes at this 7th district emporium are made
with recycled materials by Galahad Clark's eco-
friendly Terra Plana label. The shop also stocks the
Viva Barefoot line – with its ultra-thin Kevlar soles
– and shoes by United Nude, designed by a Dutch
architect with a flair for showstopping footwear.
► *If you love the designs but can't afford the prices,*
there's an outlet store two doors down.

★ Tiberius

7, Lindengasse 2 (522 0474, www.tiberius.at).
U3 Neubaugasse or tram 49. **Open** noon-
7pm Tue-Fri; 11am-6pm Sat. **Map** p111 F3
❹❹ **Fashion & accessories**
See p114 **In the Know**.

GOING GASTRO
Upscale dining and artisanal ales.

Not too long ago, Vienna barely had a pub
and bar scene to speak of. Bars were
simple affairs where locals got tipsy on
spritzers and pubs were expat places that
sold Guinness and not much else. Today,
though, that has all changed, with gastro
dining and craft beers to the fore. Leading
the charge has been **Charlie P's** (*see p123*),
near the student quarter, where owner
Brian Patton and Michelin-starred head
chef Peter Zinter have taken pub grub to
another level. Beef is 28-day-aged grass-
fed Hereford from FX Buckley's, Irish craft
butchers; and lobster is from Donegal. As
a result, in 2014 Charlie P's was the first
Irish pub in the world to be given a special
award in the Gault Millau dining guide.

Developments haven't been limited to
the kitchen. Charlie P's has a dozen or
more beers on tap, rotated on a weekly
basis, plus scores by the bottle. Many
come from small craft breweries across
Austria – Bierol in the Tyrol, for example.

Patton's latest venture, the
Brickmakers Ale & Cider House (*see*
p109) in Neubau, stocks 30 craft beers on
tap and 150 by the bottle, and was inspired
by his trip to Munich's Taphouse bar.

This success has raised the bar at the
40-plus Irish pubs across the capital. In the
3rd district, **O'Connor's Old Oak** (*see p94*)
claims to have 'some of the best food
anywhere in town'. Whether it has or not
isn't the issue – the fact is that it's selling
itself on the quality of its pork chops. Five
years ago, it wouldn't have bothered. The
Viennese, meanwhile, have focused on
craft beers. The excellent **1516 Brewing
Company** (*see p48*) near the Ringstrasse
offers its own house beer along with
seasonally chosen pale ales and fruit-
flavoured varieties. Other venues include
Siebensternbräu (*see p109*) in Neubau.

Charlie P's.

Josefstadt to Alsergrund

The genteel 8th district of Josefstadt takes its name from Josef I, during whose short reign (1705-11) this residential area was laid out. It borders Landesgerichtsstrasse directly behind the Rathaus, and the cobbled streets around Lenaugasse house some handsome examples of Biedermeier architecture. By contrast, its western border is marked by the U6 metro line, with a succession of late-opening bars and gig venues tucked away in the railway arches. Further up towards the Danube Canal, occupying a large area stretching north from Alserstrasse, is Alsergrund, Vienna's 9th district. It's home to the city's General Hospital and its university campus, as well as a decent concentration of sights. The main attraction, and one of the biggest tourist draws, is the Sigmund Freud Museum, where the renowned psychoanalyst lived and worked for 40 years.

Sigmund Freud Museum.

Don't Miss

1 Sigmund Freud Museum
Study and digs of father of psychoanalysis (p122).

2 Fernwärme Artistic attraction out of an industrial eyesore (p119).

3 Schubert Geburtshaus
The kitchen where Franz was born (p122).

4 Charlie P's Sample Vienna's new craze for craft beer (p123).

5 Museum für Volkskunde
Colourful folklore in the Palais Schönborn (p118).

JOSEFSTADT

Josefstadt has yet to acquire the fashionable buzz of adjoining Neubau. Its well-heeled residents patronise the historic **Theater in der Josefstadt** (*see p171*) and Vienna's **English Theatre** (*see p172*), read the papers in period coffeehouses such as the **Florianihof** or hang out with their children in the local parks.

Throughout the neighbourhood, plaques commemorate distinguished former residents; today, Austrian president Heinz Fischer is a high-profile inhabitant. Sights include the **Museum für Volkskunde**; the Church of the Holy Trinity at Alserstrasse no.17, where Beethoven's funeral was held in 1827; and, best of all, the Baroque excess of the **Piaristenkirche**. Otherwise, a spot of window-shopping in the streets off Josefstädter Strasse is a pleasurable pastime.

The section of the Gürtel that traces the western boundary of Josefstadt is one of the city's hippest nightlife zones, with DJ bars and gig venues built into the arches of Austrian architect Otto Wagner's Stadtbahn (*see p158* **Gürtel of Grunge**). The Gürtel is also home to peep shows and sex shops, but it's not threatening.

Sights & Museums

FREE Museum für Volkskunde

8, Laudongasse 15-19 (406 8905, www.volkskunde museum.at). U2 Rathaus or tram 5, 33, 43, 44 or bus 13A. **Open** 10am-5pm Tue-Sun. **Admission** free. **No credit cards. Map** p121 G3 ❶

Backing on to the park of the same name, Johann Lukas Von Hildebrandt's early 18th-century Palais Schönborn houses the Museum for Folklore. It deals with Austrian customs, religious rites and secular celebrations, and puts on some fine exhibitions.

FREE Piaristenkirche

8, Jodok-Fink-Platz (405 0425, www.mariatreu.at). U2 Rathaus or tram 2 or bus 13A. **Open** 9am-noon Mon-Thur; 9am-noon, 2-4.30pm Fri. **Admission** free. **Map** p121 G3 ❷

Josef I set aside land here for the Order of the Piarists to found a monastery. The Maria Treu or Piaristenkirche (1753) stands between the monastery outbuildings, flanked by two elegant towers. The original design was traced by Von Hildebrandt in 1716, but wasn't completed until the 19th century. The interior is notable for Franz Maulbertsch's ceiling frescoes and for its organ, on which Anton Brückner took his examination for the Academy.

Restaurants & Coffeehouses

Café Eiles

8, Josefstädter Strasse 2 (405 3410). U2 Rathaus or tram 2. **Open** 7am-11pm Mon-Fri; 8am-11pm Sat, Sun. **Map** p121 G3 ❸ **Coffeehouse**

A favourite haunt for lawyers and politicians, thanks to its proximity to the Parliament and Rathaus, Eiles is also a practical stop for tourists before taking on the delights of Vienna's 8th district. It serves a hearty Viennese breakfast from 8am to 11.30am.

Café Florianihof

8, Florianigasse 45 (402 4842, www.florianihof.at). Tram 2, 5. **Open** 7.30am-10.30pm Mon-Fri; 9am-7pm Sat, Sun. **Map** p121 G2 ❹ **Coffeehouse**

You won't find a more lovingly preserved turn-of-the-century *kaffeehaus* in all Vienna. With its Jugendstil cream panelling, parquet floor and curved bar, the Florianihof is a pleasure to behold.

Café Pars

8, Lerchenfelder Strasse 148 (405 8245). U6 Thaliastrasse or tram 46. **Open** 11am-midnight Mon-Sat. **Main courses** €6.90-€18.90. **Map** p121 H1 ❺ **Persian**

Headquarters of Vienna's Persian community, Café Pars cooks rice the way only Persians know. Served with butter, egg yolk and mixed fresh herbs, this would be a meal in itself, but it comes with superbly spiced chicken kebabs or strips of chargrilled beef fillet. There's also a choice of tasty appetisers and dips.

Café-Restaurant Hummel

8, Josefstädter Strasse 66 (405 5314, www.cafehummel.at). Tram 2, 5, 33. **Open** 7am-midnight Mon-Sat; 8am-midnight Sun. **Map** p121 G2 ❻ **Coffeehouse**

This bustling bar/restaurant/coffeehouse is the life and soul of the Josefstadt district. Despite an insensitive interior revamp and a rather pedestrian menu, families, students, scribblers, Powerbook posers and octogenarian card players all seem to adore the place. The waiters are gruff yet diplomatic, while the terrace is ideal for an afternoon's people-watching.

Gastwirtschaft Blauensteiner

8, Josefstädter Strasse 4 (405 1467, www.gastwirtschaft-blauensteiner.at). U2 Rathaus or tram 2. **Open** 11am-11.30pm daily. **Main courses** €7.80-€13.80. **Map** p121 G3 ❼ **Viennese**

Reopened in 2012 after lying empty for more than 20 years, Blauensteiner is a classic *beisl*, serving a competent selection of Viennese cuisine. Immortalised in Heimito von Doderer's novel of post-war Vienna, *The Strudelhof Steps*, it has a roomy interior with original fittings; the terrace on cobbled Lenaugasse is one of Vienna's best alfresco dining spots.

Hold

8, Josefstädter Strasse 50 (405 1198). Tram 2. **Open** 8am-11pm Mon-Sat. *Meals served* 11.30am-2.30pm, 6-10.30pm Mon-Sat. **Main courses** €10.50-€19.50. **Map** p121 G2 ❽ **Italian**

This small café-cum-trattoria oozes northern Italian authenticity and is a useful option if you're exploring the stately 8th district. As well as being great

EXPLORE

for a revitalising cappuccino and almond pastry, or a quick glass of chianti, it also serves reasonably priced lunches and dinners. Space is at a premium.

Konoba

8, Lerchenfelder Strasse 66-68 (929 4111, www. konoba.at). Tram 46. **Open** 5pm-midnight daily. **Main courses** €12.50-€18.90. **Map** p121 H2
❾ Croatian

In a pleasant setting, Konoba imports a refreshing taste of the Dalmatian coast with dishes such as *buzara* (mussels in a potent wine, garlic, olive oil and parsley sauce). Sea bass, bream and the occasional flatfish are grilled to perfection and served with swiss chard and boiled potatoes. Make sure you ask if you don't want garlic sauce drizzled over the fish.

★ Die Wäscherei

8, Albertgasse 49 (409 2375-11, www.die-waescherei.at). U6 Josefstädter Strasse or tram 2, 43, 44. **Open** 5pm-2am Mon-Fri; 9am-2am Sat; 9am-midnight Sun. **Main courses** €9.90-€26.90. **Map** p121 F2 **❿ International**

Almost 20 years on, the 'Laundromat' continues to pull in a young crowd with its no-longer-so-cheap yet substantial Austro-ethnic dishes and its sassy staff. Weekend €15 brunches (10am-4pm Sat, Sun) are popular and the beer is great: Trumer Pils and Die Weisse, a Salzburg wheat beer rarely seen in Vienna. The summer terrace is a great spot, as is Lavanderia, the neighbouring pizza joint at no.51.

Bars, Pubs & Cafés

Weinstube Josefstadt

8, Piaristengasse 27 (406 4628). Tram 2 or bus 13A. **Open** *Apr-Dec* 4pm-midnight daily. **Map** p121 H3 **⓫**
The entrance to this city *heuriger* is so discreet that even many Josefstadt residents are unaware of its existence. It's best enjoyed during high summer, when the ivy-clad garden becomes a shady oasis. The kitchen serves a limited selection of good-value dishes such as roast pork, black pudding, salads and dips and, unlike most *heurigen*, you can get an ice-cold Czech Budweiser. *See also p131* **Wein Wine**.

Shops & Services

Die Kräuterdrogerie

8, Kochgasse 34 (405 4522, www.kraeuter drogerie.at). Tram 43, 44 or bus 13A. **Open** 9am-6pm Mon-Fri; 9am-1pm Sat. **Map** p121 F3 **⓬ Health & beauty**
Sells healing herbs and oils, plus ayurvedic products. The food section stocks organic vegetables.

ALSERGRUND

Quiet Alsergrund, the 9th district, is Vienna's medical and university quarter, and also home to the very popular **Sigmund Freud Museum**.

The Berggasse house is where Freud lived and carried out most of his pioneering work on psychoanalysis (*see p123* **Freudian Trip**).

Directly opposite the Church of the Holy Trinity on Alserstrasse is the University Campus, housed in the former Altes Allgemeines Krankenhaus, one of Europe's oldest hospitals. It's home to the Narrenturm, an 18th-century lunatic asylum that's now the fascinating if rather gruesome **Pathologisch-anatomische Bundesmuseum** (9, Spittalgasse 2, 52177-606, www.narrenturm.at). Nearby, on Währinger Strasse, is the **Josephinum**, Josef II's academy for military surgeons – now a medical museum.

West of Berggasse, the Servitenviertel is an appealing quarter with a village feel. It's home to the only church outside the city walls to survive the Turkish siege, the late 17th-century Servitenkirche on Servitenplatz. Baroque to the marrow, it boasts a fine interior, an impressive stucco, a pulpit by Balthasar Moll (1739) and a relief showing the martyrdom of Czech saint John Nepomuk. Outside Mass times, the church must be seen through iron railings.

Nearby is the small Jewish cemetery of Seegasse. It's accessed through the old people's home at Seegasse 9-11, built on the site of the old Jewish hospital; go in and ask at the reception desk and you'll be allowed in. Like all such cemeteries in Vienna, this one bears the scars of rabid anti-semitism, with virtually every tomb desecrated. Look out for the curious mound of stones with a carved fish on top – it's not clear whether it's actually a gravestone.

Further along Seegasse you come to Rossauer Lände, which follows the canal embankment; here, various ramps and flights of steps lead to the waterside. Just over a kilometre to the north along the river is one of Vienna's most curious buildings, the **Fernwärme** rubbish incinerator.

The 9th district's most exuberant edifice, though, is Palais Liechtenstein, a wonderful Baroque garden palace built to a design by Domenico Martinelli. It remains the property of the Princes of Liechtenstein, housing the **Liechtenstein Museum** of Baroque art.

Classical music buffs may want to venture to the district's less scenic end to take in the **Schubert Geburtshaus**, the birthplace of Franz Schubert on Nussdorfer Strasse.

Sights & Museums

FREE Fernwärme

9, Spittelauer Lände 45 (313 26 20 30, www.wien energie.at). U4, U6 Spittelau or tram D. **Tours** by appt. **Admission** free. **Map** p120 A4 **⓭**
Few cities can boast a municipal rubbish incinera-tor that appears in sightseeing guides, but artist Friedensreich Hundertwasser's 1989 remodelling of a hideous industrial building is now one of Vienna's

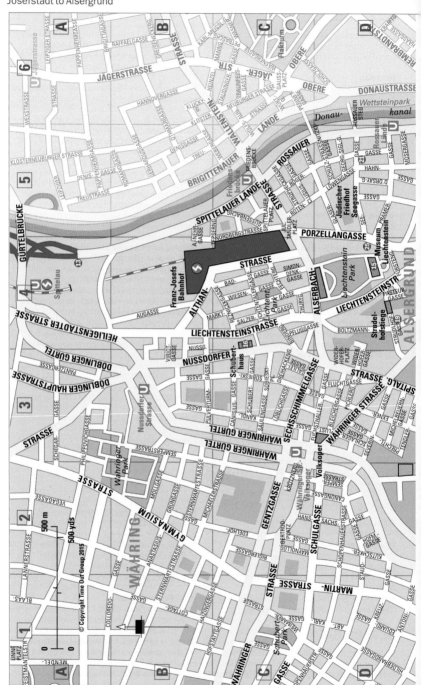

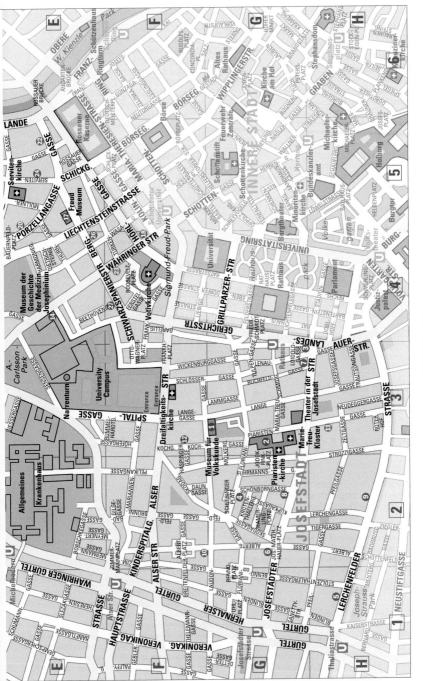

EXPLORE

great visual surprises. This is mainly due to the enormous smoke stack, wrapped in vitro-ceramic tiles and crowned with a large golden mosaic bulb.

Josephinum
9, Währinger Strasse 25 (40 160 26001, www. josephinum.ac.at). Tram 37, 38, 40, 41, 42. **Open** *History of Medicine Library* 10am-4pm Mon-Thur; 9am-noon Fri. *Exhibition* 10am-6pm Fri, Sat. **Admission** €4; €2 reductions. **No credit cards. Map** p121 E4 ⓮
The Josephinum museum of medical history occupies an 18th-century building designed by Isidore Canevale. The institution was intended as a school for military surgeons. Exhibits include a through-the-ages look at surgical instruments, but the main draw is a collection of life-size wax anatomical models made by Florentine craftsmen in 1780.

Liechtenstein Museum
9, Fürstengasse 1 (319 57 67-153, www. liechtensteinmuseum.at). Tram D. **Tours** *Garden Palace* 3pm Fri. *City Palace* 5pm Fri. **Admission** *Garden Palace tour* €20. *City Palace tour* €25. *Combined ticket* €38. **Map** p120 D4 ⓯
The Princes of Liechtenstein have been patrons of the arts for centuries, and their stupendous collection of Baroque painting now hangs in this opulent garden palace (built 1691-1711). Andrea Pozzo's monumental ceiling fresco in the Hercules Hall is probably the highlight, along with a large number of important works by Rubens, including his almost life-size *Decius Mus* cycle.

Schubert Geburtshaus
9, Nussdorfer Strasse 54 (317 3601, www.wien museum.at). Tram 37, 38. **Open** 10am-1pm, 2-6pm Tue-Sun. **Admission** €4; €3 reductions; free under-19s & all 1st Sun of mth. **No credit cards. Map** p120 C4 ⓰
Composer Franz Schubert was born in the kitchen of this two-room apartment on 31 January 1797 and lived here, along with 12 other family members, until he was four. The collection includes contemporary portraits of the composer, his trademark round spectacles and soundbites of his most important pieces.

★ Sigmund Freud Museum
9, Berggasse 19 (319 1596, www.freud-museum.at). U2 Schottentor or U2 Schottenring or tram 37, 38, 40, 41, 42, D or bus 40A. **Open** 10am-6pm daily. *Archive & Library* by appt. **Admission** €9; €4-€8 reductions; free under-12s. **Map** p121 E5 ⓱
See p123 **Freudian Trip.**

Restaurants & Coffeehouses

Café Français
9, Währinger Strasse 6-8 (319 0903, www.cafe francais.at). U2 Schottentor. **Open** 9am-midnight Mon-Sat. **Map** p121 F4 ⓲ **Coffeehouse**

Alsergrund is home to many things French, including the Lycée, so it's no surprise that Café Français has been a rousing success since it opened in 2013. Its ironically named breakfasts are a big hit, though it's doubtful that many order the Jacques Cousteau – an espresso, a glass of water and a Fisherman's Friend. If you're hankering after a quiche, a croque-monsieur, a ration of snails or a bowl of onion soup, this is the place to head.

Flein
9, Boltzmanngasse 2 (319 7689). Tram 37, 38, 40, 41, 42. **Open** 11.30am-3pm, 5.30-11.30pm Mon-Fri. **Main courses** €8.80-€19.50. **Map** p120 D4 ⓳ **Austrian/French**
Tucked away in the gardens of the now-defunct Alliance Française, Flein's charming interior has some fine old fittings. But the place really comes into its own in summer, when you can eat outside. On the menu is a selection of substantial Franco-Austrian dishes, including slow-cooked roasts accompanied by great gratins and ratatouilles. To drink, there are some good, reasonably priced Austrian wines and superb Schremser beer.

Gasthaus Wickerl
9, Porzellangasse 24A (317 7489, www.wickerl.at). Tram D. **Open** 9am-midnight Mon-Fri; 10am-midnight Sat; 11am-11pm Sun. **Main courses** €9.80-€18.90. **Map** p121 E5 ⓴ **Viennese**
Gasthaus Wickerl is a wood-panelled *beisl* that's popular with students. The city's top chefs can also often be spotted here, wolfing down the excellent dumplings and other classic Viennese dishes. Football fans will appreciate the big-screen TV in the back room and the three beers on tap (including Czech Budweiser).

Stomach
9, Seegasse 26 (310 2099). Tram D. **Open** 4pm-midnight Wed-Sat; 10am-10pm Sun. **Main courses** €14-€26. **Map** p120 D5 ㉑ **Austrian**
Much frequented by theatre folk, Stomach concentrates on Styrian beef dishes such as divine marinated *tafelspitz* with boiled egg, chives and drizzled pumpkin seed oil. Game abounds in winter in the form of wild boar and venison; there's tasty lake trout too. Reliable wines, Murauer beer and great schnapps complete the picture.

★ Zum Roten Bären
9, Berggasse 39 (317 6150) U2 Schottenring or tram 1, 2. **Open** 9am-11pm Mon-Fri; 5pm-midnight Sat. **Main courses** €7-€20. **Map** p121 E5 ㉒ **Austrian**
The Red Bear is a great, reasonably priced lunch spot. Formerly a policemen's drinking den known as the Brown Bear (it's next door to the district cop shop), it was taken over in 2014 by a young crew who renamed it the bear, and turned it into a hipster *beisl*. The €8-€9 midday menu, served until 3pm, has three options, one of which is always vegetarian. In the evening, joints of roast beef and pork are the

FREUDIAN TRIP
See where the great man lived and worked.

Nearly a century after the 1917 English-language publication of *The History of the Psychoanalytic Movement* in New York, the world's fascination with Sigmund Freud continues unabated. But it took his adopted city of Vienna several decades to honour one of the most influential men of the modern world.

Opened in 1971, the **Sigmund Freud Museum** (*see p122*) is set in the first-floor apartment where the founder of psychoanalysis lived and worked from 1898 to 1938; he died in exile in London a year later. The cramped lodgings and study that Freud was forced to abandon by the Nazis was purchased by the Austrian state and filled with scores of letters, documents, photographs and artefacts, not to mention the ethnic bric-a-brac Freud so assiduously collected.

Only the entrance hall, displaying his tartan travelling rug, cane and pocket flask for the Sunday walks he so loved, plus the cabin trunk he used for the last time in 1938, is in its original state. The rest is guesswork and period furniture. But such is the extent of the authentic material on view that even the lay visitor can't fail to be fascinated.

The museum doesn't beat around the bush when it comes to showing Freud's penchant for cocaine. 'I have had,' Freud is quoted as saying, 'broad experience with the regular use of cocaine over long periods and have taken the drug myself for some months without perceiving or experiencing any condition similar to morphism or any desire for the continued use of cocaine'. On display is a pack he would have ordered from the Merck company in Darmstadt. The remaining exhibits describe the story of a boy who grew up in Pribor, Moravia, went to school in Leopoldstadt, Vienna ('moral conduct: exemplary; general natural history: laudable', says his report) then began his medical career at Vienna General Hospital. Freud's work in cerebral anatomy, then nervous disorders, then his move into psychoanalysis and beyond can be followed as you move from room to room.

The museum also screens examples of film noir with Freudian undertones – Hitchcock's are a popular choice.

speciality of the house, washed down with a smooth draught Czech beer and some great whites from the border with Slovenia.

Bars, Pubs & Cafés

★ Charlie P's
9, Währinger Strasse 3 (409 7923, www.charlie ps.at). U2 Schottentor. **Open** 5pm-2am Mon-Thur; 5pm-3am Fri, Sat; 2pm-1am Sun. **Map** p121 F4 ㉓
See p115 **Going Gastro**.

Shops & Services

Backhausen
9, Servitengasse 6 (2852 502-314, www. backhausen.com). U4 Rossauer Lände or tram D. **Open** 10am-4pm Tue, Thur. **Map** p121 E5 ㉔ **Homewares**
Textile manufacturers Backhausen & Sons worked closely with the Wiener Werkstätte and maintain an archive of their Japanese-influenced fabric designs in a small basement museum. The shop sells home furnishings, glassware, rugs and knick-knacks.

Catrinette
9, Porzellangasse 28 (0699 11206725, www.catrinette.at). **Open** 11am-7pm Tue-Fri; 10am-3pm Sat. **Map** p120 D4 ㉕ **Homewares**
This charming vintage store has a living-room vibe and is great for small items of furniture, crockery, lamps and an ever-changing selection of curiosities.

Löwenherz Bookshop
9, Berggasse 8 (317 2982-1, www.loewenherz.at). Tram 37, 38, 40, 41, 42. **Open** 10am-7pm Mon-Thur; 10am-8pm Fri; 10am-6pm Sat. **Map** p121 E4 ㉖ **Books & music**
Connected to Café Berg (*see p144*), this friendly gay bookstore is a welcoming place for a browse.

Weltladen
9, Schwarzspanier Strasse 15 (405 4434, www.suedwind-buchwelt.at). Tram 43, 44. **Open** 10am-6pm Mon-Fri; 10am-1pm Sat. **Map** p121 F4 ㉗ **Books & music**
This fair-trade chain has stores across Vienna. This branch specialises in books and music, but also stocks coffee, tea and cocoa.
Other locations throughout the city.

EXPLORE

Further Afield

Vienna's verdant fringes are home to some unmissable attractions. To the west of the city is the vast Schönbrunn Palace and its gardens, as well as the world's oldest zoo. A little further out, Otto Wagner's Kirche am Steinhof is an absolute must-see for architecture lovers, along with the modernist and Biedermeier villas of leafy Hietzing. Nearer to the city centre, just the other side of the Gürtel, the 16th district is a Balkan/Turkish quarter centrepieced by the city's largest street market, Brunnenmarkt. Here, cutting-edge restaurants now line increasingly trendy Yppenplatz. The attractions of the southern suburbs run from the illustrious graves of the Zentralfriedhof to the Jugendstil Amalienbad baths and sleek Therme Wien spa. To the north lie more bucolic pleasures: vineyards, *heuriger* wine taverns and the Vienna Woods.

Tiergarten.

Don't Miss

1 Schönbrunn Habsburg residence in all its historic finery (p126).

2 Tiergarten The world's oldest zoo (p127).

3 Zentralfriedhof Vienna's vast cemetery, where Beethoven, Brahms and Strausses reside (p129).

4 Heurigen Traditional wine taverns in bucolic surroundings (p131).

5 Brunnenmarkt The city's biggest street market (p129).

Western Vienna

The western side of Vienna is home to the city's biggest tourist draw: the Habsburgs' summer palace of **Schönbrunn**, and its gardens and parkland. Locals flock here, too, to jog around the park and visit the zoo and botanical gardens.

The neighbouring district of Hietzing is a treat for architecture aficionados: Otto Wagner, Adolf Loos and later Viennese modernists all built in this prosperous suburb. And for those with a particular interest in Otto Wagner and Jugendstil, a trip to the 14th district is a must. It's home to two of his villas and the **Kirche am Steinhof** – Wagner's only stab at ecclesiastical architecture.

Closer to the city centre, a newly fashionable area is springing up around **Brunnenmarkt**, the city's largest street market. Nearby Yppenmarkt and Yppenplatz are now overrun with hip eateries.

Sights & Museums

Kirche am Steinhof

14, Baumgartner Höhe 1 (91060 11007).
U2, U3 Volkstheater or U3 Ottakring or
bus 48A. **Open** 4-5pm Sat; noon-4pm Sun.
Admission €2. **No credit cards.**
Otto Wagner's church is in the grounds of Steinhof (now the Otto Wagner Hospital), originally a pioneering experiment in the care of the mentally ill but later the scene of some of the greatest horrors of Nazi 'psychiatry'. Standing on a hillside amid beautiful parkland, the church was built in the early 1900s for use by patients and staff. Inside, the surfaces are light and clean, with no sharp edges, and sunlight pours in through Kolo Moser's magnificent stained-glass windows. Steinhof is haunted by its two-fold part in the Nazis' euthanasia policy, documented in an exhibition in Pavillion V. Firstly, its patients were murdered in their thousands between August 1940 and August 1941, when they were transported to the gas chambers of Hartheim Castle in Upper Austria. Secondly, at the clinic called the Spiegelgrund, which was set up in 1940, outrageous experiments were carried out on children suffering from rickets, hydrocephalus and tuberculosis. In all, 789 died. Although the director was sentenced to death in 1946, his assistant Heinrich Gross only received two years for manslaughter, later rescinded, and went on to enjoy a prestigious career in neurology. The exhibition and its website (www.gedenkstaettesteinhof.at) recount the tragic events.

Otto Wagner Villas

14, Hüttelbergstrasse 26, 28 (914 8575, www.ernst fuchs-zentrum.com). U4 Hütteldorf then bus 52A, 52B. **Open** 10am-4pm Tue-Sat. **Admission** €11; €6 reductions.
The villa at no.26 is the only one of the two open to the public, since it's home to the Ernst-Fuchs Museum – a lamentable piece of egomania by the magical realist painter of the same name, who filled the house and garden with his gaudy oeuvre. Still, some credit must be given to Fuchs and his contemporary Hundertwasser, who in 1968 squatted the house in order to save it from a demolition order. Fuchs purchased no.26 in 1972 and set about its restoration and transformation. An early work of Wagner's, completed in 1888, it's reminiscent of his Ringstrasse buildings, with ionic pillars and a touch of the palladian. The cube-like villa at no.28 is more rooted in his familiar functionalist tradition.

SCHÖNBRUNN

Schönbrunn is easily accessible via the U4 line. Alternatively, travel a stop further to Hietzing and enter the park through the Hietzinger Tor. This enables you to take a quick look at Otto Wagner's **Hofpavillon Hietzing** (www.wienmuseum.at), Franz Josef's private U-Bahn station.

Schönbrunn's connection to the Habsburgs dates back to 1569, when Maximilian II acquired the land to build a hunting lodge. It stood near what is today Meidlinger Tor, where the natural spring was discovered that gives Schönbrunn ('beautiful spring') its name. After the Turkish siege of 1683, Leopold I commissioned Fischer von Erlach to build a summer palace for his son, the future Josef I. He had originally envisaged a palace on the scale of Versailles, but plans had to be altered due to financial constraints. Although work began in 1696, it was much delayed by the War of the Spanish Succession (1701-14).

The present form of the palace owes much to Empress Maria Theresa's passion for the place. In order to house her expanding brood (she had 16 children, ten of whom lived to adulthood), her architect Nikolaus Pacassi added another floor to the two wings. She also supervised work on the rococo interiors and the layout of the gardens.

Alas, her son Josef II inherited rather more of Maria Theresa's thrift than her love for Schönbrunn, and had vast uninhabited sections of the palace boarded up. Josef did oversee the completion of the gardens, resulting in a network of avenues that intersect at two central points either side of the broad parterre. In the distance, on the brow of the hill, rises the majestic Gloriette, commissioned by Josef II to commemorate the 1775 victory over the Prussians at Kolin, which returned Prague to Habsburg rule. Today it's a rather snooty café, but has the best view of the palace and gardens. To the east of the fountain lie most of the park's follies, amid encroaching woodland: Von Hohenberg's superb Roman Ruins (1778) and his Obelisk Fountain (1777) are among them. To the west lies Schönbrunn Zoo.

Napoleon occupied Schönbrunn in 1805 and 1809, and his son, the Duc de Reichstadt, spent most of his short life within its confines. Franz Josef was born and died in Schönbrunn, but his wife Elisabeth had no fondness for the place, probably because she spent her wedding night there, reputedly staving off her husband's advances for all of two nights.

What was actually consummated in the Blue Chinese Salon at Schönbrunn was the dissolution of the Austro-Hungarian Empire in November 1918, when Karl I signed away any chance of the monarchy's survival. During the four-power occupation of Vienna after 1945, Schönbrunn was first HQ to the Russians and then to the British before it was returned to the Austrian state in 1947. In 1961, it briefly assumed centre stage when Kennedy and Khrushchev met for the first time there.

Sights & Museums

★ Schloss Schönbrunn

13, Schönbrunner Schlossstrasse (811 13-239, www.schoenbrunn.at). U4 Schönbrunn, Hietzing or tram 10, 58 or bus 10A. **Open** *Palace* Nov-Mar 8.30am-5pm daily. Apr-June, Sept, Oct 8.30am-5.30pm daily. July, Aug 8.30am-6.30pm daily. *Gardens* 6.30am-dusk daily. **Admission** *Grand Tour* €15.90-€18.90; €10.50-€14.60 reductions. *Imperial Tour* €12.90; €9.50-€11.90 reductions. *Parks & gardens* €5; €2.90-€3.90 reductions.

This vast, yellow-painted palace is the focal point of an expanse of parkland larger than the Principality of Monaco. Architecturally speaking, Schönbrunn isn't particularly distinguished, although the Great

Schloss Schönbrunn.

Court is a sight to behold. For those determined to go inside, the Grand Tour, covering 40 rooms (out of a total of 1,441), is the best option; the 22-room Imperial Tour doesn't include access to Maria Theresa's west wing, which is the most impressive section. Tickets include an audio-guide with commentary in English.

At the top of the Blaue Stiege (Blue Staircase) are Elisabeth and Franz Josef's nine private rooms, as dowdy as those at the Hofburg. After the Billiard Room and Audience Chamber comes the Emperor's Study and Bedroom, containing the simple iron bed where he died; a sombre painting by Makart recreates his demise. After the joyless bedroom, things pick up a little with the Maria Antoinette Room and the Nursery, with decor from Maria Theresa's time, and the Breakfast Room, with its lovely views.

Here the state apartments begin with the Spiegelsaal (Hall of Mirrors); as a child, Mozart played a duet here with his sister Nannerl for Maria Theresa and her daughters. In the Blue Chinese Room to the west, Maria Theresa held secret meetings with her adviser Prince Kaunitz. Beyond the Great Gallery is the Carousel Room, then the Ceremonial Hall, with Van Meytens' paintings of Joseph II's wedding to Isabella of Parma in 1760. Here those who opted for the Imperial Tour are ushered out.

Only included in the Grand Tour, the audience rooms are undoubtedly the most worthwhile. After the airy chinoiserie of the Blue Chinese Room, where Karl I abdicated in 1918, you pass into the Vieux-Lacque Room, whose black lacquered panelling was designed by Canevale in around 1770. Here, too, is Batoni's portrait of Maria Theresa's husband Franz I. The walnut-panelled Napoleon Room is where the diminutive Corsican is thought to have slept. No expense was spared in the Millions Room, where Maria Theresa reputedly spent a million silver florins on rosewood panelling; it also features priceless Persian and Indian miniatures, cut up and assembled into collages by the imperial family.

After the Gobelin Salon, with its 18th-century Brussels tapestries, comes the Memorial Room dedicated to 'L'Aiglon' (the Little Eagle), the Duc de Reichstadt – Napoleon's son by Archduchess Marie Louise. The Duc was virtually kept prisoner in Schönbrunn after his father's fall from grace in 1815 until his untimely death at the age of 21.

Tiergarten & Palmenhaus

Tiergarten *13, Maxingstrasse 13B (877 9294-0, www.zoovienna.at). U4 Hietzing.* **Open** *Jan, Nov, Dec* 9am-4.30pm daily. *Feb* 9am-5pm daily. *Mar, Apr, Oct* 9am-5.30pm daily. *May-Sept* 9am-6.30pm daily. **Admission** €16.50; €8 reductions; free under-6s. **Palmenhaus** *13, Hietzinger Tor (877 5087 406, www.bundesgaerten.at). U4 Hietzing.* **Open** *May-Sept* 9.30am-6pm daily. *Oct-Apr* 9.30am-5pm daily. **Admission** €4; €2-€3.50 reductions.

Built on the site of Franz Stefan's royal menagerie (1752), on the western side of the gardens, the Tiergarten is the world's oldest zoo. The cages are

EXPLORE

laid out around the 18th-century central octagonal pavilion (once the imperial family's breakfast room), while many of the original Baroque buildings and cages are still in use, alongside more modern enclosures. Attractions include a polarium and rainforest house, but the giant pandas are the stars of the show.

The soaring, jungly Palmenhaus (Palm House) is situated near the Hietzinger Tor entrance, beside the botanical gardens. Maria Theresa's husband, Emperor Franz, was a keen botanist and gardener, financing expeditions to Africa and the West Indies to collect rare species and bring them back to Vienna. This magnificent iron-and-glass structure has three climatic zones and dates from 1882.

HIETZING

Thanks to the presence of the imperial family at nearby Schönbrunn, the process of gentrification began early in neighbouring Hietzing. Even today, along with the 19th district around Grinzing, this remains one of the city's poshest areas.

Hietzing's rapid rail link to the city centre, and the lure of a vast area of the Wienerwald on its doorstep, attracted both the 19th-century business elite and successful bohemians such as Egon Schiele. From 1912, Schiele's studio was at Hietzinger Hauptstrasse 101. These days, this main street isn't particularly charming, but the sidestreets contain some magnificent modernist and Biedermeier villas, and retain a leafy gentility.

Palmenhaus. *See p127.*

Hietzing institutions include **Café Dommayer**, where Johann Strauss gave his first public concert in 1844. Round the corner is the Parkhotel Schönbrunn (1907), where the emperor's guests were accommodated. Other residential streets contain houses by Josef Hoffmann, Friedrich Ohmann and Adolf Loos; unfortunately, none are open to the public. The villas are widely dispersed, but there's a concentration along Gloriettegasse, west of the Schlosspark.

Werkbundsiedlung is a wedge-shaped housing project of 70 homes. It was built between 1930 and 1932 by a group of modernist architects that included Loos, Hoffmann and Richard Neutra, under the direction of Josef Frank. In the house Frank designed at Woinovichgasse 32 is an information centre (www.werkbundsiedlung.at).

Sights & Museums

FREE Hietzinger Friedhof

13, Maxingstrasse 15 (877 31 07 13). U4 Hietzing, then 10mins walk or Bus 56B, 58B, 156B. **Open** *Mar, Apr, Sept, Oct* 8am-5pm daily. *May-Aug* 8am-6pm daily. *Nov-Feb* 9am-4pm daily. **Admission** free.
The graves of many illustrious Viennese reside in this picturesque cemetery. Tomb highlights include those of Gustav Klimt and Otto Wagner, though the latter's is regrettably pompous. Also buried here are dramatist Franz Grillparzer, composer Alban Berg, leader of the Austro-Fascists Engelbert Dollfuss, and Klimt and Wagner's collaborator Kolo Moser.

Restaurants & Coffeehouses

10er Marie

16, Ottakringer Strasse 222-224 (489 4647, www.fuhrgassl-huber.at/10er-marie). Tram 2, 46. **Open** 3pm-midnight Mon-Sat. **Main courses** €5-€9.60. Heuriger
See p131 **Wien Wine**.

★ AnDo-Fisch

16, Yppenplatz, Stand 40 (308 7576, www. andofisch.at). U6 Josefstädter Strasse. **Open** 11am-midnight Mon-Sat. **Main courses** €14.90-€23.90. Seafood
The folks at Do-An in the Naschmarkt set up this fish restaurant on up-and-coming Yppenplatz. The joint is at its best when the summer terrace is open and you can take in the action on the square.

Café Dommayer

13, Auhofstrasse 2 (877 5465, www.dommayer.at). U4 Hietzing. **Open** 7am-10pm daily. Coffeehouse
Café Dommayer is one of the city's best-known traditional *kaffeehäuser*, and is just a stone's throw from the Schönbrunn Palace. Johann Strauss Jr made his debut here in 1844, but the café is now part of the Oberlaa chain of pâtisseries and no longer hosts concerts. The capacious garden remains, however.

Café Kent

16, Brunnengasse 67 (405 9173, www.kent restaurant.at). U6 Josefstädter Strasse. **Open** 6am-2am daily. **Main courses** €6-€11. Turkish
Summer at Vienna's best-loved kebab house means long evenings in its wonderful garden. Its huge popularity with locals is unsurprising: excellent meze platters and grilled meats retail at knock-down prices, with plenty of aubergine and courgette concoctions too. Located in the Brunnenmarkt, Café Kent attracts shoppers, slackers and stallholders with its long hours.

Wetter

16, Payergasse 67 (406 0775, www.wettercucina.at). U6 Josefstädter Strasse. **Open** 6-10.30pm Tue-Fri; 10am-10.30pm Sat. **Main courses** €10.50-€19.50. Austro-Italian
In his understated new premises on Payergasse, Raetus Wetter cooks an Austro-Italian mix that could mean excellent ravioli, wild boar or horse steaks, rich tiramisu and wines from both sides.

Cafés, Bars & Pubs

Café Club International

16, Payergasse 14 (403 1827, www.ci.or.at). U6 Josefstädter Strasse. **Open** 8am-2am Mon-Sat; 10am-2am Sun. **Map** p246 A6.
Part of a local initiative to help integrate Ottakring's immigrant communities through housing advice and language courses, Club International also runs a cheerful café with the sunniest terrace on Yppenplatz. Visit on a Saturday, when the nearby Brunnenmarkt is joined by an excellent farmers' market.

Shops & Services

★ Brunnenmarkt

16, Brunnengasse (no phone). U6 Josefstädter Strasse. **Open** 6am-7.30pm Mon-Fri; 6am-5pm Sat. Market
Brunnenmarkt is a colourful market with a Balkan/Turkish flavour. Stretched out along Brunnengasse, its myriad stalls and shops offer fruit and vegetables, halal meat and sticky Turkish pastries. Saturday, when a farmers' market sets up on neighbouring Yppenplatz, is the best day to go.

Southern Vienna

The southern districts of Vienna contain a few sights, most notably **Zentralfriedhof**, Vienna's main cemetery, where tombs outnumber the city's present population. A newer attraction in the 11th district is the architecturally impressive **Gasometer** complex, fashioned from four huge, circular gas tanks. It can be rather disappointing to visit, though, as visitors are generally restricted to the uninspired lower-floor shopping centre.

Vienna's 10th district, Favoriten, is its largest, with a population of around 170,000. It was the focus of emigration for Czechs in the 19th century, and a Favoritner today is something like the Viennese equivalent of a cockney, with Reumannplatz as the Bow Bells of Vienna. Named after labour leader and Socialist politician Jacob Reumann, it's a lively square with a market on nearby pedestrianised Favoritenstrasse and Vienna's best-loved ice-cream salon, Tichy. There's a fast link to the city centre via the U1.

Right on the square is **Amalienbad** (*see p138*), built in 1926 and Vienna's largest public baths. The main pool has an arched glass roof that can be opened, and facilities are decorated throughout with colourful mosaics in Jugendstil designs. This district is also home to **Therme Wien** (*see p138*) – a swanky spa complex that opened in 2010.

Sights & Museums

Gasometer

11, Guglgasse 6 (www.wiener-gasometer.at). U3 Gasometer.
These 19th-century behemoths briefly served as rave venues before the council stumped up almost €200 million to convert them into a housing complex. Gasometer A, beside the complex's purpose-built U-Bahn station, was designed by Jean Nouvel. He created nine towers inside his tank, building huge windows into the walls and cladding the exterior with a shimmery metallic finish. Gasometers C and D, designed by Austrian architects Manfred Wehdorn and Wilhelm Holzbauer respectively, both opted for communal gardens in the interior and are probably the most liveable. After the impressive exteriors, the ground-floor mall comes as a disappointment, and you can't explore the residential or office parts of the complex. For a more insightful visit, book a guided tour through the website.

★ FREE Zentralfriedhof

11, Simmeringer Hauptstrasse 234 (53469-28405). U3 Enkplatz, then tram 71. **Open** *Mar, Apr, Sept, Oct* 7am-6pm daily. *May-Aug* 7am-7pm daily. *Nov-Feb* 8am-5pm daily. **Admission** free.
Opened in 1870, the Central Cemetery's 2.5 million tombs and memorials cover an area larger than the Innere Stadt. As you'll see from the tram, one side of the Simmeringer Hauptstrasse is taken up with undertakers and stonemasons; there are none on the city's high streets. The next tram stop is at the main entrance, followed by a third by the entrance to the Protestant and new Jewish sections. From the main entrance, the path heads straight to the Ehrengräber (tombs of honour). Follow the main avenue past the semicircular line of tombs encrusted into arches – don't miss the memorial to mining baron August Zang, resembling the entrance to a mine, guarded by lamp-wielding dwarfs – and in sector 32A you'll find some of Austria's great composers. Brahms, Hugo

EXPLORE

Wolf and most of the Strauss clan repose here, as do Beethoven and Schubert, whose remains were moved here from the Währing cemetery in 1899. Across the avenue are the tombs of Ringstrasse architect Hansen and the painter Makart, while in section 33C Arnold Schönberg lies under an extraordinary cube-like form by sculptor Fritz Wotruba, buried nearby.

At the centre of the cemetery is Dr-Karl-Lueger-Kirche, dedicated to Vienna's populist mayor (and anti-semite extraordinaire) Karl Lueger. Behind the church there are fascinating sections given over to the Soviet soldiers who died during the 1945 liberation of Vienna, the graves of 7,000 Austrians who died fighting the Nazis (sector 97) and those of Austrian International Brigade members from the Spanish Civil War (section 28). But it's the old Jewish section to the north near the first gate that's the most moving. Overgrown and desecrated, the sheer size of it (over 60,000 graves) and the virulence of the vandalism that overwhelmed it emphasise the tragic fate of Vienna's pre-war Jewish community. Among those buried here are members of the Rothschild family and playwright Arthur Schnitzler.

Restaurants & Coffeehouses

Gasthaus Quell

15, Reindorfgasse 19 (893 2407, www. gasthausquell.at). U6 Gumpendorfer Strasse. **Open** 11am-midnight Mon-Fri. **Main courses** €4.90-€14.80. **Viennese**

This classic *beisl* has an atmospheric wood-panelled interior, a cracked old ceramic stove and an affable landlord. The menu offers a range of meaty Viennese staples, plus a good number of meat-free options. A further attraction is the pleasant summer terrace.

Northern Vienna

The hills of the northern part of the Wienerwald are visible from various points along the western side of the Ringstrasse. This range, ending abruptly at the Danube, is the continuation of the foothills of the Alps away to the south-west. Half an hour by tram from Schottentor, you can explore the four wine-growing villages that nestle below the Vienna Woods on the city's urban edge. Nussdorf, Grinzing, Sievering and Neustift am Walde became wealthy by supplying the Viennese with the tart white wine they so relish. With olde-worlde architecture surrounded by vines and forests, and views across Vienna, the villages soon became home to the city's wealthier residents.

Despite a peppering of significant sights – the Beethoven memorials, the exhibition on Red Vienna (www.dasrotewien-waschsalon.at) at the Socialist-era **Karl-Marx-Hof** (19, Heiligenstädter Strasse) of the 1920s, the Jugendstil villas of Hohe Warte – the chief attraction here are the *heurigen* wine taverns (*see p131* **Wien Wine**).

NUSSDORF & LEOPOLDSBERG

The nearest of the wine villages to the Danube, Nussdorf lies in the shadow of Leopoldsberg (425m/1,395ft) – the second-highest point of the Wienerwald. The summit can be reached by bus 38A from Heiligenstadt U-Bahn, along cobbled Höhenstrasse. Walkers can choose between a trek from Nussdorf or the shorter, more intense zigzag footpath that begins in Kahlenbergerdorf. At the top are the 17th-century Leopoldskirche, home to a display exploring the Turkish siege, and the ramparts of an 11th-century fortress. Nearby is a shady courtyard where you can have a drink.

Numerous *heurigen* dot Kahlenberger Strasse. Eroicagasse, on the south side of Kahlenberger Strasse, takes you to Mayer am Pfarrplatz, more a restaurant than a *heuriger*, located in a fine Biedermeier house where Beethoven lived for a time. Close by is the Heiligenstädter-Testament-Haus (19, Probusgasse 6), where he wrote his famous 'testament' to his brothers, in which he spoke frankly of his oncoming deafness and wrote his Second Symphony. The museum here contains a replica of the testament, plus Beethoven's death mask and a lock of his hair.

The area bristles with Ludwig memorabilia, including a Beethoven Monument (1910) in Heiligenstädter Park on the south side of Grinzinger Strasse. On this street, at no.64, is the house that Beethoven shared in 1808 with dramatist Franz Grillparzer.

Those who have the energy could attempt the Kahlenberg, the highest point of this section of the Wienerwald at 484m (1,588ft).

GRINZING & KAHLENBERG

Grinzing, the most famous of Vienna's wine villages, is the epitome of Viennese rural kitsch, ably manipulated by local inn-keepers and restaurateurs to keep the cash registers ringing. The combination of villagey atmosphere and lovely countryside makes Grinzing, like the lesser-known nearby villages, a popular choice with the diplomatic community and the wealthy.

Grinzinger Friedhof (Mannagettagasse, off Strassergasse) contains the austere Jugendstil tomb of Gustav Mahler, designed by Josef Hoffmann. Other famous residents include Ringstrasse architect Ferstel and art groupie Alma Mahler. The daughter she had by Walter Gropius, Manon, is also buried here.

Bus 38A follows one of the most spectacular routes in Vienna, along Höhenstrasse, taking in fine views of forest and city. The first stop is the lookout point of Am Cobenzl, where a bar and restaurant has views of Grinzing's vineyards. From there, it's a ten-minute walk west to Bellevuewiese, a gorgeous rolling meadow with the best panorama of the city and a plaque marking the spot where the 'secret of dreams was revealed to Sigmund Freud'.

Further along the 38A route, get off at Krapfenwaldgasse for a dip at **Krapfenwaldbad** (*see p139*), the city's poshest (but nevertheless municipal) swimming baths.

Restaurants & Coffeehouses

★ Bamkraxler

19, Kahlenberger Strasse 17 (318 8800, www.bamkraxler.at). Tram D. **Open** 4pm-midnight Tue-Sat; 11am-midnight Sun. **Main courses** €7.50-€16.50. **Austrian**
Bamkraxler is one of Vienna's most child-friendly locations, with a well-equipped playground, plus toys and drawing materials for rainy days. There's an acceptable choice of Austrian dishes and the excellent Augustiner, a cloudy beer from Salzburg.

Cafés, Bars & Pubs

Hirt

19, Eisernenhandgasse 165 (318 9641, www.zurschildkrot.com). S-Bahn from Franz-Josefsbahnhof to Kahlenberger Dorf. **Open** *Apr-Oct* 3-11pm Wed-Fri; noon-11pm Sat, Sun. *Nov-Mar* noon-11pm Fri-Sun. **Heuriger**
See right **Wien Wine**.

★ Schreiberhaus

19, Rathstrasse 54 (440 3844, www.das schreiberhaus.at). Bus 35A. **Open** 11am-1am daily. **Heuriger**
See right **Wien Wine**.

★ Sirbu

19, Kahlenberger Strasse 210 (320 5928). Bus 38A, then 15mins walk. **Open** *Apr-mid Oct* 4pm-midnight Mon-Sat. **Heuriger**
See right **Wien Wine**.

Weingut am Reisenberg

19, Oberer Reisenbergweg 15 (320 9393, www.weingutamreisenberg.at). Tram 38, then bus 38A. **Open** *Apr-Oct* 5pm-midnight Mon-Fri; 1pm-midnight Sat, Sun. *Nov-Dec* 6pm-midnight daily. **Heuriger**
See right **Wien Wine**.

Zawodsky

19, Reinischgasse 3 (320 7978, www.zawodsky.at). Tram 38. **Open** *Apr-Dec* 5pm-midnight Mon-Fri; 2pm-midnight Sat, Sun. **Heuriger**
See right **Wien Wine**.

Zimmermann

19, Mitterwurzergasse 20 (440 1207, www.weinhof-zimmermann.at). Bus 35A. **Open** *Mid Mar-mid Dec* 3pm-midnight Mon-Sat; 1-10pm Sun. **Heuriger**
See right **Wien Wine**.

WIEN WINE
Eat, drink and be merry.

The seven square kilometres (three square miles) of vineyards within its boundaries make Vienna the world's largest wine-growing capital city. The largest area is in the 16th to 19th districts, but the finest vines lie over the Danube in the 21st.

Open on balmy summer evenings, rustic wine taverns, *heurigen*, dot the vineyards that skirt the Vienna Woods. The website www.heurigenkalender.at is a useful resource in English with up-to-date hours for venues in Vienna and beyond. The *heuriger* has, of course, been corrupted over the years – the villages of Neustift, Nussdorf and Grinzing are now awash with places serving full meals in full rural kitsch. And more and more *heurigen*, such as **10er Marie** (see p128) – dating back to 1740 – have been overtaken by urban sprawl.

The further you go, the higher the chance of finding authenticity and stunning views. **Sirbu** (see left) overlooks the Danube from its terrace and specialises in pork, such as the superlative *kümmelbraten* (roast pork belly with caraway seeds). From there, a path runs downhill towards the flowing river and the twin-terraced **Hirt** (see left), with views of the Danube and Leopoldsberg.

For more upscale fare, **Zimmerman** (see left) attracts families with its petting zoo and lovely outdoor seating under fruit trees. By contrast, **Zawodsky** (see left) is a lesser-known *heuriger*, with tremendous views from an unkempt garden full of apple trees. **Schreiberhaus** (see left) offers great food and above-average wines in a spot low on the usual *heuriger* kitsch. Finally, the steep walk from the edge of Grinzing to **Weingut am Reisenberg** (see left) is rewarded with a panoramic vista and quality *heuriger* fare.

EXPLORE

Schreiberhaus.

Arts & Entertainment

Children

Family-friendly Vienna has plenty of parks and places of entertainment. Your first port of call – mobbed at weekends – should be the Prater park, with its age-old funfair and contemporary attractions such as Laserspy and the Darkride Insider laser show. There's a new Amazon Jungle Passage at the excellent if expensive Haus des Meeres aquarium, the world's oldest zoo at Schönbrunn, a planetarium and an observatory. While younger visitors may not appreciate an overload of museums, the MuseumsQuartier has plenty of space to run around and recliners to lounge on. After a couple of hours in the ZOOM Kindermuseum there, head across town to conduct your own orchestra at the Haus der Musik or push, pull and slide down things at the vast Technisches Museum Wien. Even the wonderfully old-school Naturhistorisches Museum has wheels you can turn to predict the end of the world. Almost all the big museums offer guided tours and workshops for children – most are in German, though. In summer, lovely outdoor bathing spots are easily accessed by public transport.

PRACTICALITIES

Public transport is free for children up to the age of 15 on Sundays, public holidays and during the school holidays (bring ID); at other times, children up to six go free while tickets are discounted for those aged seven to 15. The city is easy to get around, even with a pushchair. On U-Bahn trains, buses (middle door) and the newer trams you just roll on and park in the space allocated, and there are lifts to U-Bahn platforms. Older trams have steps and are more tricky; use the front entrance and another passenger or the driver will usually help. For weary feet or would-be princesses, you could embrace the ultimate in tourist kitsch and choose a pricey ride in a horse-drawn carriage, a Fiaker. It's a sneaky way to keep kids entertained while seeing the sights; there are stands on Heldenplatz, Stephansplatz and Albertinaplatz. Many cafés and eateries provide baby facilities, and there's a relaxed attitude to breastfeeding.

WienXtra-kinderinfo

7, MuseumsQuartier/Hof 2, Museumsplatz 1 (4000-84 400, www.kinderinfowien.at). U2 MuseumsQuartier or U2, U3 Volkstheater or tram 46, 49 or bus 2A. **Open** *2-6pm Tue-Fri; 10am-5pm Sat, Sun.* **Map** *p250 D7.*

This friendly information centre offers updates on what's going on in Vienna for children of all ages, along with lists of free museums and child-friendly restaurants. There's a great indoor play area with an aerial scrambling net, walkway and slide to keep small fry occupied while parents get the lowdown. The website has tips and information in English.

SIGHTS & ATTRACTIONS
Innere Stadt & around

The **Austrian Theatre Museum** (*see p56*) inside the Baroque Lobkowitz Palace has a small collection for children – accessible via a steep slide from the main museum. You can see magical stage sets and marionettes, and play in a mini-theatre, but you have to ring ahead to book.

In front of the City Hall, Rathausplatz is a year-round hive of activity, usually of interest to children. In January and February there's an ice-skating rink, while on summer evenings, operas and classical concerts are shown on a large screen, with food from around the world. December's Christmas market has tacky stalls, but the trees are beautifully decorated and there are pony and train rides, plus a baking and modelling workshop for three- to 16-year-olds inside the City Hall.

The **Haydn English Cinema** and **Artis** (for both, *see p141*) show English-language films.

Haus der Musik
For listing, see p46.
The Sound Museum here is terrific fun for children, who embrace its interactive sound and music displays, from beating on drums to playing super-sized instruments. The chance to virtually conduct the Vienna Philharmonic Orchestra is a highlight.

★ Haus des Meeres
6, Esterhazy Park, Fritz-Grünbaumplatz 1 (587 1417, www.haus-des-meeres.at). U3 Neubaugasse or bus 13a, 14a, 57a. **Open** 9am-6pm Mon-Wed, Fri-Sun; 9am-9pm Thur. **Admission** €15.80; €11.90 reductions; €7.30 6-15s; €4.90 3-5s; free under-3s. **Map** p246 C8.
See p139 **Sea World**.

Schmetterlinghaus
1, Burggarten, beside Palmenhaus (533 8570, www.schmetterlinghaus.at). U1, U2, U4 Karlsplatz or tram 1, 2, D. **Open** Nov-Mar 10am-3.45pm daily. Apr-Oct 10am-4.45pm Mon-Fri; 10am-6.15pm Sat, Sun. **Admission** €5.50; €3-€4.50 reductions. **Map** p250 E7.
The west wing of the Palmenhaus was converted into a butterfly house in the late 1990s. Now it's home to around 40 colourful species, none rare or endangered

but certainly bright and impressive. Several hundred butterflies flutter freely around your head amid a steamy, humid jungle of vegetation, tall trees and a waterfall. You'll see them up close feeding on a plate of fruit or they may land on your arm. Outside, the Burggarten is a pleasant park. *Photos p137.*
▶ *Next door, the airy Palmenhaus café is equipped with nappy-changing facilities; see p75.*

Urania Sternwarte
1, Uraniastrasse 1, entrance on Turmstiege (8917 4150-000, www.planetarium-wien.at). U1, U4 Schwedenplatz or tram 1, 2, O. **Open** Ticket office 15min before each show. Show times vary. **Admission** €7; €5 under-14s. **Map** p251 F6.
This old-school observatory, run under the same umbrella as the Zeiss Planetarium (*see p136*) in the Prater, is steeped in Viennese history. Opened by Franz Josef I in 1910, it was where legendary local football club Austria Vienna were founded a year later. It continues to present instructive journeys through space, for children six years old and over; commentaries in German. Show times vary.
▶ *Other location: Kuffner Sternwarte (16, Johann Staud-Strasse 10, same phone and website).*

MuseumsQuartier

The **MuseumsQuartier** (*see pp72-75*) is a relaxed place to hang out, with seating outside in summer and a scattering of cafés; it's also home to the family-focused **WienXtra-kinderinfo** information office. Just across the main road is the venerable **Naturhistorisches Museum** (*see p72*), where exhibits can be somewhat old-fashioned but tricky scientific concepts are explained well in English and German; the dinosaur section is always a favourite.

Dschungel Wien
7, Museumsplatz 1 (522 0720-20, www.dschungel wien.at). U2 Museumsquartier. **Open** Ticket office Sept-May 2.30-6.30pm Mon-Fri; 4.30-6.30pm

ARTS & ENTERTAINMENT

ZOOM Kindermuseum. See p136.

Sat, Sun and 1hr before shows start. *June-Aug* 10am-2pm Mon-Fri. **Admission** €14; €8.50-€9 reductions. **Map** p250 D7.

Established in 2004, Dschungel Wien puts on professional theatre and dance for children and teenagers, featuring local and international performers, plus workshops. Most performances are in German, but some (dance, mime, puppetry, shows for toddlers) transcend the language barrier.

★ ZOOM Kindermuseum

7, MuseumsQuartier, Museumsplatz 1 (524 7908, www.kindermuseum.at). U2 Museumsquartier or U2, U3 Volkstheater or tram 46, 49 or bus 2A. **Open** 8.30am-4pm Tue-Fri; 9.45am-4pm Sat, Sun. **Admission** €4; children free; €14 family (2 adults & 3 children). *Atelier* €6 children (1 adult free), €4 each extra adult. *Trickfilmstudio* €6 children, accompanying adults free. *Ozean* €4 children (1 adult free), €4 each extra adult. **Map** p250 D7.

Learning through play is the aim at ZOOM, and it's skilfully done. For under-sixes, Ozean is a great play and discovery area, while the Studio (three- to 12-year-olds) focuses on creative activities. There are guided, interactive exhibitions for over-fives, and an animation studio where eight- to 14-year-olds can make their own cartoons and pop songs. Numbers are limited and there are fixed starting times, so you need to check the schedule on the website and book in advance. Guides and instructors speak English. *Photos p135.*

Prater

With its famous funfair and giant Ferris wheel (*see p85*), the Prater is a must. The funfair – the **Wurstelprater** – is free to enter and runs from mid March to the end of October. Rides are charged individually.

Beyond stretches the park itself with long straight paths ideal for cycling, and several playgrounds. These include the fenced-in baby playground near the Café Restaurant Meierei at Hauptallee 3, and two larger ones on Jesuitenwiese. Just behind the funfair is a narrow-gauge railway, the Liliputbahn (www.liliputbahn.com) that runs in a loop parallel to the main path of Hauptallee, also from mid March to the end of October. Tickets are €4 for adults, €2.50 for under-14s.

Finally, two other attractions close to the funfair are the **Zeiss Planetarium Wien** and **Madame Tussauds** (*see p85*).

Wurstelprater

2, Prater 7/3 (729 2000, www.praterwien.com). U1, U2 Praterstern or tram 5, O. **Open** *mid Mar-Oct* 10am-midnight daily. **Admission** free. *Rides* vary. **No credit cards. Map** p244 H5.

The rollercoasters, ghost trains and carousels have been zooming, whizzing and whirring for generations at this revered funfair. Rides suitable for younger children include retro contraptions that range from a 19th-century carousel pulled by real ponies to 1950s racing car rides. Recent introductions include Aqua Gaudi, comprising three downhill flumes through a mock Mayan city.

Zeiss Planetarium Wien

2, Oswald Thomas Platz 1 (8917 4150-000, www. planetarium-wien.at). U1, U2 Praterstern or tram 5, O. **Open** *Tickets* 45mins before shows. *Shows* vary. **Admission** €8; €6 children. **Map** p244 H5.

The Zeiss offers several types of interstellar travel according to age group. There are a number of showings each day using computer animation and a laser image projector. Commentary in German.

Schönbrunn & around

For children, the Tiergarten is more of an attraction than the **palace at Schönbrunn** (*see p127*). That said, the palace does have a special children's museum, the Kindermuseum Schloss Schönbrunn (www.kaiserkinder.at), with dressing up, games, and plenty of trivia on how the young Habsburgs lived. In the grounds, the maze, labyrinth and Labyrinthikon playground are open from March until early November.

Marionettentheater Schloss Schönbrunn

13, Hofratstrakt, Schloss Schönbrunn (817 3247, www.marionettentheater.at). U4 Schönbrunn. **Admission** (kids' shows) €11-€13; €9-€10 under-14s.

The theatre at Schönbrunn stages exquisite but pricey puppet performances of the *Magic Flute*, *Aladdin* and *Eine Kleine Nachtmusik*, relying on music and costume rather than language to keep the audience's attention. The cheaper performances specifically for children last about an hour.

★ Technisches Museum Wien

14, Mariahilferstrasse 212 (899 98-0, www. tmw.at). U4 Schönbrunn or tram 10, 52, 58. **Open** 9am-6pm Mon-Fri; 10am-6pm Sat, Sun. **Admission** €12; €10 reductions; free under-19s.

There are all sorts of buttons to press, games to play and experiments to undertake at Vienna's massive science and technology museum. Transport-fixated kids will enjoy the locomotives, perilously flimsy-looking biplanes, model boats and impressive car collection, running from historic bone-shakers to a sleek 1950s Mercedes raced by Stirling Moss. The first-floor Mini-TMW is a terrific play area for kids aged two to six – you can time yourself racing down a slide. Almost every aspect of modern life is covered, from flushing toilets to the postal service.

Tiergarten

For listing, see p127.

Highlights at the world's oldest zoo include the Rhino Park, the giant pandas, the Aquarium and Terrarium House, the Rainforest House (complete

Schmetterlinghaus. *See p135.*

with tropical storms) and the Insect House. There's also an Alpine Farmhouse from Tyrol as well as a large children's playground, while the sea lions' feeding time is guaranteed to entertain.

SPORT & ACTIVITIES

Boating

The Alte Donau is a popular site for sailing; pedal boats and other craft can also be rented there, and on the Neue Donau.

Sailing School Hofbauer

22, An der oberen Alten Donau 191 (204 3435-0, www.hofbauer.at). U1 Kagran. **Open** *Apr-Oct* 9am-dusk daily. **Rates** phone for details.
No credit cards. Map p245 M2.
Sailing classes in English are available. Bring photo ID if you want to hire something like a rowing boat, pedalo or windsurfer.

Bowling

Ocean Park

2, Millennium City, Bauteil 2, 1.UG, Handelskai 94-96 (334 2211, oceanpark.at). U6 or S45 Handelskai. **Open** 10am-12.30am Mon-Thur; 10am-1.30am Fri; 10am-2.30am Sat; 9.30am-12.30am Sun. **Rates** per game from €1. Per lane (max 8 people) from €9/hr. Shoe rental €2.20. Deposit €10. **Map** p244 G1.

This expansive family entertainment centre comprises dozens of ten-pin bowling lanes, 23 pool and snooker tables, table tennis and other indoor games.

Climbing

Out in the 22nd district, **Kletterhalle Wien** (Erzherzog-Karl-Strasse 108, 890 46 66-0, www. kletterhallewien.at; open 9am-11pm daily) is the largest climbing wall in Austria. You can also scale a World War II-era flak tower, the **Kletteranlage Flakturm** (585 4748, www. flakturm.at; open mid Apr-early Oct 2pm-dusk daily) in Esterhazy Park. If bouldering's your thing, try **Edelweiss Centre** (1, Walfischgasse 12, 513 85 00-21, www.edelweiss-center.at; open 9am-10pm Mon-Fri; 11am-9pm Sat, Sun).

Cycling

With bike paths all over the city and beyond, Vienna is superb for cyclists. Popular spots for a ride include the Prater, along the Donaukanal and around the Alte and Neue Donau, and on the Donauinsel; you can also circle the Ring on a bike path. For out-of-town cycling, head west along the Danube, or go mountain biking in the **Vienna Woods** (*see p176*).

    Citybike (www.citybikewien.at) is a public rental scheme. Register online (€1 fee), or at one of the 120 docking stations, by using a credit card; €20 will be temporarily set aside from your card

IN THE KNOW WATER COURSE

Between the Neue and Alte Donau, a new artificial stretch of wild water has been created, 250 metres long and lined with adjustable obstacles at different heights and intervals. La Ola canoe school (www. laolakanuschule.at) and Vienna City Rafting (www.viennawatersports.at) have set up at 12, Steinspornbrücke, to provide instruction and a watery workout for the over-12s.

the first time you take a bike out, as a security against charges you might incur. If you return the bike to another docking station within an hour, the ride is free; after that, a small charge applies.

Bikes can be taken on U-Bahn and local S-Bahn trains (9am-3pm & after 6.30pm weekdays, after 9am Sat, all day Sun & hols). Bikes must go in carriages with a bike symbol and require a half-price ticket. They can also be taken on trains marked with a bicycle symbol on the timetable.

Fahrradverleih Skaterverleih Copa Cagrana

22, near the Reichsbrücke bridge, on the east side of the Neue Donau in the Copa Cagrana (263 5242, 0664 345 8585, www.fahrradverleih.at). U1 Donauinsel. **Open** *Mar, Oct* 9am-6pm daily; *Apr, Sept* 9am-8pm daily; *May-Aug* 9am-9pm daily. **Rates** from €4/hr for children, €25/day adults. **No credit cards. Map** p244 J3.

This place is centrally located for Donauinsel and river rides. All sorts of bikes are available for hire, including tandems, rickshaws and bikes for people with disabilities. There are inline skates too. Photo ID and a deposit are required.

Pedal Power Radverleih

2, Ausstellungsstrasse 3 (729 7234, www.pedal power.at). U1, U2 Praterstern. **Open** *Apr-Oct* 9am-7pm daily. **Rates** from €5/hr, €3/hr children; €27/day, €19/day children. **Map** p244 H5.

Bikes come with locks and a map, and staff can advise on routes. The store can drop off and pick up bikes from hotels; it also lays on tours by bike and Segway.

Ice skating

Vienna's outdoor rinks include the Wiener Eislaufverein at the Stadtpark and the rink at Rathausplatz (www.wienereistraum.com, late Jan-early Mar). For something closer to nature, head to the Old Danube for a skate on the river (U1 Alte Donau); you'll need your own skates.

Wiener Eislaufverein

3, Lothringerstrasse 22 (713 6353, www.wev.or.at). U4 Stadtpark. **Open** *Late Oct-early Mar* 9am-8pm

Mon, Sat, Sun; 9am-9pm Tue-Fri. **Admission** €7-€8; €3-€6.50 reductions. Skate rental €6.50 adults, €3 children. **Map** p251 E/F8.

This centrally located open-air rink has been going since 1867. There's a bar for an after-skate drink.

Playgrounds

There are plenty of well-equipped playgrounds around the city: try the park in front of the **Rathaus** (*see p68*), the **Stadtpark** (*see p75*) and the Resselpark in front of **Karlskirche** (*see p98*), not to mention the **Prater**. Full lists are available at **WienXtra-kinderinfo**.

Bogi Park

23, Gutheil-Schoder-Gasse 17 (230 0000, www.bogi park.at). Badner Bahn Gutheil-Schoder-Gasse. **Open** 10am-7pm daily. **Admission** *Daytime ticket* €4 adults, €3 reductions; €9.50 under-16s; €4 under-3s; free under-1s. *Evening ticket* €3 adults; €2 reductions; €5 under-16s; €2.50 under-3s; free under-1s.

A huge indoor playground, where kids can climb, bounce, slide and run riot to their hearts' content.

Skateboarding

Skate Area 23

3, Perfektastrasse 86 (0650 490 3550, www. skatearea23.at). U6 Perfektastrasse. **Open** *Jan-June, Sept-Dec* 2-8pm Thur, Fri; 10am-10pm Sat; 10am-9pm Sun. *July, Aug* 10am-5pm Thur-Sun. **Admission** €2. **No credit cards**.

Indoor skate area with workshops and shows.

Swimming

The banks of the Danube, either side of the Neue Donau channel, are the nearest Vienna gets to a beach. Take the U1 to Donauinsel and walk until you find a suitable spot; nude areas are marked FKK on maps. Two stops further along the U1, the Alte Donau has paying beach clubs such as the sprawling **Gänsehäufel** (269 9016, www. gaensehaeufel.at); take the U1 to Kaisermühlen-VIC, then bus 90A, 91A or 92A to Schüttauplatz.

The city also has plenty of pools. These include the 1920s Jugendstil Amalienbad, the summer-only open-air Krapfenwaldbad with superb views and the lido-like Strandbad Alte Donau. The vast Therme Wien (www.thermewien.at) appeals to adults with its renovated spa and sauna facilities, but also has its slides, rides and wave machines.

★ Amalienbad

10, Reumannplatz 23 (607 4747). U1 Reumannplatz. **Open** 9am-6pm Tue; 9am-9.30pm Wed, Fri; 7am-9.30pm Thur; 7am-8pm Sat; 7am-6pm Sun. *Outdoor pool (May-mid Sept)* 9am-6pm Tue-Sun. **Admission** (full day) €5.50, €4.10 reductions; from €1.80 children. **No credit cards**.

SEA WORLD

There are plenty of scary new guests at the Haus des Meeres.

The **Haus des Meeres** aquarium (*see p135*), or Aqua Terra Zoo as it now also brands itself, occupies a former World War II flak tower and features a 300,000-litre water tank with various sharks (bamboo, blacktip, whitetip), as well as a sea turtle called Puppi. More recent additions to the building include a smaller tank with hammerhead sharks; the Amazon Jungle Passage with plants, lizards and more than a thousand fish native to South America; and a panoramic roof terrace café (only open to ticket-holders).

From the top, work your way down past the assorted marine life, snakes and reptiles. Other highlights include the two triangular glass extensions that stick out from the sides of the tower: the warm and whiffy tropical house, and the crocodile park where gorgeously plumed birds fly past open walkways and free-roaming marmosets steal the show. Finally, there's a Mediterranean section complete with sea urchins, snakes and starfish. As you're exploring, take a closer look at the clear plastic handrails – and if you come on a Wednesday, look out for the snake-stroking sessions and shark feeding. Finish it all off afterwards by heading to the children's playground at Esterhazy Park.

This gorgeous indoor baths offers a solarium, steam room and saunas, plus an outdoor pool in summer.

Diana-Erlebnisbad

2, Lilienbrunngasse 7-9 (219 8181-10, www. dianabad-wien.at). U1, U4 Schwedenplatz or tram 1, 2. **Open** *Jan-June, Sept-Dec* 10am-10pm Mon-Tue, Fri-Sat; 1.30-10pm Wed-Thur; 10am-8pm Sun; *July, Aug* 10am-8pm daily. **Admission** varies. **Map** p251 F6.

This indoor adventure pool features a fun slide, waves, pirate ship and baby pool.

★ Krapfenwaldbad

19, Krapfenwaldgasse 65-73 (320 15 01). Bus 38A. **Open** *1st 2 weeks May, 1st 3 weeks Sept* 9am-7pm Mon-Fri; 8am-7pm Sat, Sun. *Mid May-end Aug* 9am-8pm Mon-Fri; 8am-7pm Sat, Sun. **Admission** (full day) €5.50, €4.10 reductions; from €1.80 children. **No credit cards**.

This open-air venue has a magnificent setting above Grinzing, with stupendous city views. Run by the council since 1923, it has period changing rooms, wooden loungers and two pools. A hit with the smart set, it's packed on summer weekends.

Schönbrunnerbad

Schönnbrunner Schlosspark (817 5353, www. schoenbrunnerbad.at). U4 Schönbrunn. **Open** *Apr, May, Sept* 8.30am-7pm daily. *June, July, 1st 2wks Aug* 8.30am-10pm daily. *2nd 2 weeks Aug* 8.30am-8pm daily. **Admission** (full day) €12; €10 from 1.30pm; €7 from 5pm. Under-18s €9; €8 from 1.30pm; €6 from 5pm. Under-6s €4; €3.50 after 1.30pm; €3 after 5pm. **No credit cards**.

The pool in the gardens of Schönbrunn palace is a stiff but agreeable walk through the woods. Late opening hours make it popular with young singles; small children can paddle safely in their own area.

★ Strandbad Alte Donau

22, Arbeiterstrandbadstrasse 91 (263 6538). U1 Alte Donau. **Open** *1st 2 weeks May, 1st 3 weeks Sept* 9am-7pm Mon-Fri; 8am-7pm Sat, Sun. *Mid May-end Aug* 9am-8pm Mon-Fri; 8am-8pm Sat, Sun. **Admission** (full day) €5.50, €4.10 reductions; from €1.80 children. **No credit cards**. **Map** p245 K1.

This bathing spot on the old Danube is a favourite with yummy mummies and their offspring. The poplar trees give shade in summer and there's a gorgeous 1950s pavilion selling ice-cream and hotdogs.

Film

Vienna looks like one enormous film set. The picturesque thoroughfares of the Innere Stadt and the great buildings on the Ringstrasse are ravishing reminders of Richard Linklater's love story *Before Sunrise*, while the giant Ferris wheel and ruined post-war streets famously appeared in Carol Reed's *The Third Man*, a film noir classic that's now the subject of a museum and walking tours. Austria's own contribution to film history is undisputed: Fritz Lang, Billy Wilder and Otto Preminger were all linked with Vienna and share an ironic detachment that rejects the use of facile sentimentality and soothing clichés to manipulate audience emotions. In more recent times, Austrian Michael Haneke has twice won the Cannes Palme d'Or: for *The White Ribbon* in 2009 and *Amour* in 2012 – one a disquieting World War I tale, the other about the struggles of an elderly couple. *Amour* also gained Haneke an Oscar for Best Foreign Film, while Vienna-born Stefan Ruzowitzky scooped the same prize in 2008 for *The Counterfeiters*.

INFORMATION AND TICKETS

Films are listed in all newspapers but for the best coverage of foreign-language movies try *Der Standard* (daily) or *Falter* (weekly) – the latter better, with its A-Z listing by film title. Film details are abbreviated as follows: OF or OV are original version; OmU is original version with German subtitles; OmenglU or OmeU are original version with English subtitles. Plenty of films are screened in their original language. Note also that the **Haydn English Cinema** has been showing films in English for more than a century, in recent years without any distracting subtitles.

Admission prices are reasonable, around €7-€9, often with slightly cheaper rates at the start of the week and for seats in the first three rows. Quite a few venues still don't accept credit cards.

FESTIVALS AND SEASONS

In summer, some arthouse cinemas drop their regular programming to screen classic and cult films in the **Sommerkino** season. Vienna also has a number of seasonal open-air showings, such as the popular **Cinema Under the Stars** venture (www.kinountersternen.at), with movies screened for free on Karlsplatz.

From the third week of October, the renowned, two-week **Viennale** film festival (*see p30*) features Austrian premières, retrospectives and international feature films, documentaries and shorts. Awards include the FIPRESCI, voted by the International Film Critics' Association, and the Vienna Film Prize, bestowed by the city.

CINEMAS

Admiral

7, Burggasse 119 (523 3759, www.admiral kino.at). U6 Burggasse or tram 5 or bus 48A.
No credit cards. Map p246 B/C7.
The Admiral is a cosy old neighbourhood cinema, first opened back in 1912; its only drawback is the drone of passing traffic. A sympathetic renovation in 2008 kept the lovely foyer as it was. Programming features less commercial films, shown in the original version with German subtitles.

Artis

1, Schultergasse 5 (535 6570, www.cineplexx.at/center/artis-international). U1, U3 Stephansplatz or U3 Herrengasse. Map p251 E6.
Now part of the vast Cineplexx chain, Artis shows mainstream Hollywood fare, without subtitles (OV). There are six screens to choose from.

★ Bellaria

7, Museumstrasse 3 (523 7591, www.film.at/bellaria_kino). U2, U3 Volkstheater or tram 46, 49 or bus 48A. No credit cards. Map p250 D7.
Those with a weakness for time travel will adore the Bellaria. The foyer features the original bar and box office, as well as fading portraits of the stars of Heimat and German films. The afternoon sessions include films from this era. Later in the day, expect reruns of recent arthouse productions.

Breitenseer Lichtspiele

14, Breitenseerstrasse 21 (982 2173, www.bsl-wien.at). U3 Hütteldorfer Strasse or tram 10, 49. No credit cards.
Nostalgics will adore Vienna's oldest operational cinema, which has occupied its Jugendstil premises since 1909. In 2005, the wooden seats, appliqué wall lighting and neon sign were renovated, and a piano installed to accompany silent films. It normally screens retrospectives, with films in subtitled original versions.

Burgkino

1, Opernring 19 (587 8406, www.burgkino.at). U1, U2, U4 Karlsplatz or tram 1, 2, D. No credit cards. Map p250 E7.

With two screening rooms, the Burg has been showing *The Third Man* regularly since the early 1980s. The larger hall is a poorly conceived affair that generally schedules the latest in thinking-man's Hollywood; the smaller is for reruns and classics – Stanley Kubrick's *Dr Strangelove* is another favourite.

★ Filmcasino

5, Margaretenstrasse 78 (587 9062, www.filmcasino.at). U4 Pilgramgasse or bus 13A, 14A. No credit cards. Map p247 D9.
It's worth a trip just to see the Filmcasino's magnificent neon sign and well-preserved 1950s decor. The spacious auditorium – ask for row five – premières the best in European and American cinema as well as new Asian films, with German subtitles.

Gartenbaukino

1, Parkring 12 (512 2354, www.gartenbaukino.at). U3 Stubentor, U4 Stadtpark or tram 2. No credit cards. Map p251 F7.
Saved from becoming a multiplex by the Viennale film festival, this place is great for glamorous premières but a tad too large to engender much intimacy – it has the largest cinema hall in Austria.

Haydn English Cinema

6, Mariahilfer Strasse 57 (587 2262, www.haydnkino.at). U3 Neubaugasse or bus 13A, 14A. Map p246 C8.
This four-screen cinema has been a family business since 1912, and has shown exclusively English-language films without German subtitles for more than two decades. Popular with school groups.

Metro Kino. *See p142.*

ARTS & ENTERTAINMENT

ARTS & ENTERTAINMENT

IN THE KNOW
SCREENS APLENTY

Cineplexx (www.cineplexx.at), the largest cinema chain in Austria, has eight venues in Vienna. These range from the historic Apollo in the 6th district to the high-design, 3,000-seater Cineplexx Donau Plex in the shiny business quarter over the river. Tickets are currently set at an across-the-board €8.10 (€6.20 Mon-Wed). On the banks of the Danube, **UGI Kinowelt Millennium City** (Am Handelskai, 33760, www.uci-kinowelt.at) is the most modern multiplex in Austria, with its largest screen, 21 halls and some 3,500 seats. Tickets are €9.90 (€6.90 Mon-Wed).

Lugner Kino City
15, Gablenzgasse 1-3 (985 2600, www.lugnerkino city.at). U6 Burggasse or bus 48A. **Map** p246 A7.
This modern multiplex shows Hollywood fodder, mostly in German but occasionally in English. Apart from the roomy seats, the main draw is the Lugner Lounge, where you can watch a movie in VIP comfort.

★ Metro Kino
1, Johannesgasse 4 (512 1803, www.filmarchiv.at). U1, U2, U4 Karlsplatz or tram 1, 2, D. **No credit cards. Map** p251 F7.
The lovely, belle époque Metro shows retrospectives selected by Film Archiv, the body that polices Austria's film heritage. With a stock of over 60,000 films, Film Archiv also holds summer screenings in a marquee beside its offices (Obere Augartenstrasse 1, 216 1300, same website). *Photo p141.*

Österreichisches Filmmuseum
1, Augustinerstrasse 1 (533 7054, www. filmmuseum.at). U1, U2, U4 Karlsplatz or tram 1, 2, D. **Map** p250 E7.
Not a museum but a revered national cinematheque in the same building as the Albertina. It was founded in 1964 to preserve film as a medium and make it publicly accessible. The Filmmuseum does a great job of exhuming forgotten classics and showcasing new talent from the world over. The bar is great too.

★ Schikaneder
4, Margaretenstrasse 24 (585 2867, www. schikaneder.at). U1, U2, U4 Karlsplatz or U4 Kettenbrückengasse or bus 59A. **No credit cards. Map** p247 D9.
A hip, alternative cinema that shows about ten films a week, mostly original subtitled versions. The bar pulls in the arty crowd with DJs and poetry slams.

Stadtkino
3, Schwarzenbergplatz 7 (712 6276, www. stadtkinowien.at). U1, U2, U4 Karlsplatz or tram 71, D. **No credit cards. Map** p251 E/F8.
This austere, municipally funded cinema screens original versions, with German subtitles. It's run by film buffs who publish leaflets on each film shown.

★ Votiv-Kino
9, Währinger Strasse 12 (317 3571, www. votivkino.at). U2 Schottentor or tram 37, 38, 40, 41, 42. **Map** p250 D5.
This is one of the best cinemas in the city, with a real 1960s feel. It shows films in German-subtitled original versions on its three screens, and holds film breakfasts on Sundays from September to June.
▶ *The Votiv team also runs the De France cinema (1, Schottenring 5, 317 5236, same website).*

Österreichisches Filmmuseum.

ESSENTIAL VIENNESE FILMS
The Austrian capital on celluloid.

Woman in Gold.

ARTS & ENTERTAINMENT

THE THIRD MAN CAROL REED (1949)
Starring Orson Welles and his buddy Joseph Cotten, and written by Graham Greene, this classic film noir is set in, around and below the rubble of the Austrian capital right after World War II. Its memorable score by Anton Karas helps to inspire a devoted following who still flock to the museum here and take themed tours.

THE NIGHT PORTER LILIANA CAVANI (1974)
Dirk Bogarde at his very best, as a former SS officer working at a Vienna hotel who rekindles his sado-masochistic relationship with a former concentration camp inmate, played by Charlotte Rampling. Underpinning the Nazi intrigue is Vienna's little-chronicled continuity from the Hitler era to post-war capital.

BAD TIMING NICOLAS ROEG (1980)
A dark, dark story of sexual obsession set amid the paranoia of Cold War Vienna, this controversial work by Roeg even manages to trump his previous *Don't Look Now* for X-rated action. Art Garfunkel (of all people) and Theresa Russell, who became Roeg's wife after the film was made, star in this disturbing drama.

AMADEUS MILOŠ FORMAN (1984)
Inundated with prestigious awards, this period drama recounts the story of Mozart and Salieri, as seen through the eyes of the older, inferior composer. Mozart, played here by American actor Tom Hulce, is depicted as petulant and rude, his irritating laugh even used as a cinematic full stop at the movie's conclusion.

BEFORE SUNRISE RICHARD LINKLATER (1995)
Popular romantic drama starring Ethan Hawke and Julie Delpy, strangers on a train who decide to spend the night wandering around Vienna. Partly sponsored by the city's tourist office, it features Vienna's classic sights as the backdrop to a burgeoning romance, later expanded in Paris and Greece in two sequels.

WOMAN IN GOLD SIMON CURTIS (2015)
The true story of an elderly Jewish refugee, played by Helen Mirren, and her struggle to reclaim a picture of her aunt painted by Gustav Klimt from the Austrian government. Flashbacks depict Nazi-era Vienna, when *Portrait of Adele Bloch-Bauer I* was stolen. It later sold for a then record $135 million.

Gay & Lesbian

In spring 2015, Vienna was promoting itself as the world's most tolerant city. With rainbow flags fluttering from every tram, and likenesses of same-sex couples blinking from every pedestrian signal, the Austrian capital hosted the Eurovision Song Contest. The previous winner, of course – and poster figure for LGBT rights – was Conchita Wurst, the bearded drag queen from Gmunden. An instant superstar after her victory, Conchita became an LGBT icon, performing around Europe (including Vienna's UN headquarters) and openly challenging disparaging politicians such as Vladimir Putin. The city couldn't have wished for a better marketing tool. As well as plastering Conchita all over its main information office at Albertina, the local tourist board also started encouraging gay holidaymakers to visit, issuing mini-guides to Gay Vienna alongside those themed around Mozart or *The Third Man*.

INTRODUCING THE SCENE

Although Vienna's gay scene can't compete with the likes of Berlin or Barcelona, it's still in great shape. It's at its most glitzy and self-confident in May, as the flamboyant, fabulous Life Ball AIDS fundraiser comes to town (*see p146* **You Shall Go to the Ball**). June is another prime time to visit, as the Regenbogen Parade sashays through the streets, and the biennial Identities Film Festival brings queer culture to the fore.

For the rest of the year it's a somewhat quieter affair, with most of the action centred on the 'queer quarter': Districts 4 and 6 on either side of the Naschmarkt. There's less going on for lesbians, but there are still a couple of venues and special events.

Discriminatory violence or police harassment are extremely rare. Same-sex civil partnerships were legalised in 2010, and rights have been broadened ever since. Joint adoption by same-sex couples is expected in early 2016.

Information & resources

Vienna's tourist board has long since courted the pink euro. Its website (www.wien.info/en/

vienna-for/gay-lesbian) lists bars and saunas, and hails the gayness of historic figures such as Prince Eugène of Savoy and the architects who built the Opera House. The *Vienna Gay Guide* (www.gayguide.me) is a free city map featuring hotels, restaurants, bars, clubs, saunas, shops and cruising areas. Also distributed free, the German-language *Xtra* (www.xtra-news.at) is the most well-established of Vienna's gay publications, with events, classified ads, columns, bar listings and more politics than its competitors. For details of gay community and support groups, *see p226*.

CAFÉS, BARS & RESTAURANTS

Café Berg
9, Berggasse 8 (319 5720, www.cafe-berg.at). *Tram 37, 38, 40, 41, 42.* **Open** 10am-11pm Tue-Sat; 10am-3pm Sun. **Map** p243 D/E5.
The stylish Café Berg sits slightly off the beaten track, on hilly Berggasse – just up the road from Sigmund Freud's former residence. Although diners are mixed, there's a well-stocked bookshop behind the café that's dedicated solely to gay and lesbian books and films. For more on Löwenherz bookshop, *see p123*.

★ Café Savoy

6, Linke Wienzeile 36 (586 7348, www.savoy.at).
U4 Kettenbrückengasse. **Open** noon-2am Mon-
Thur; noon-3am Fri; 9am-3am Sat; 9am-2am Sun.
No credit cards. **Map** p247 D8.
This classic café has an authentic camp interior, consisting of chandeliers, gilt statuettes and gigantic
old mirrors. Apart from Saturday afternoons, when
a mixed clientele seeps in from the Naschmarkt, it's
pretty much dominated by men of all ages.

★ Café Willendorf/Rosa Lila Villa

6, Linke Wienzeile 102 (587 1789, www.cafe-
willendorf.at). U4 Pilgramgasse. **Open** 5pm-1am
Mon-Thur; 5pm-2am Fri, Sat; 10am-3pm, 5pm-
midnight Sun. **No credit cards.** **Map** p247 D8.
What began as a squat in the 1980s is now Vienna's
most prominent gay institution. Within its pink and
purple painted walls, the Rosa Lila Villa houses a
bar/restaurant (Café Willendorf) with a shady, ivy-
clad courtyard, plus facilities for discussions and
counselling. Sunday brunch is a big hit, so reservations are recommended.

Felixx

6, Gumpendorfer Strasse 5 (www.why-not.at).
U2 Museumsquartier. **Open** 6pm-2am daily.
No credit cards. **Map** p247 D8.
A stone's throw from the MuseumsQuartier, Felixx
pulls in a dressy, thirtysomething clientele. Its decor
features 1980s-style high tables, with a magnificent
antique chandelier providing low lighting. Check out
the website for drinks specials and music nights.

Frauen Café

8, Lange Gasse 11 (406 3754, www.frauencafe.
com). Tram 2, 46. **Open** 6pm-midnight Thur, Fri.
No credit cards. **Map** p246 C6/7.
Founded in 1977, this grande dame of Vienna's lesbian scene is small, cosy and open to straight women
too. It offers reasonably priced drinks, friendly service
and a feminist agenda. Opening hours are limited.

Frauenzentrum Bar

9, Währinger Strasse 59, entrance in Prechtlgasse,
(402 8754, www.frauenlesbenzentrum-wien.at/
FZBar.html). U6 Volksoper or tram 40, 41, 42.
Open 7pm-midnight Thur, Fri. **No credit cards.**
Map p242 C4.
Known as the FZ, the women-only Frauenzentrum
plays host to various events, ranging from political
happenings to club nights. Expect stripped-down
surrounds and nothing too fancy.

Mango Bar

6, Laimgrubengasse 3 (www.why-not.at).
U4 Kettenbrückengasse or bus 57A. **Open**
9pm-4am daily. **No credit cards.** **Map** p247 D8.
This cruisey, crowded bar is under the same owner-
ship as Why Not?, Felixx and Village, and is geared
towards a young gay crowd.

Marea Alta

6, Gumpendorferstrasse 28 (0699 19 20 41 94,
http://mareaalta.bplaced.net). Bus 57A. **Open**
7pm-2am Mon-Thur; 7pm-4am Fri, Sat. **No credit**
cards. **Map** p250 D8.

Café Willendorf.

ARTS & ENTERTAINMENT

YOU SHALL GO TO THE BALL

Sweet charity at Vienna's LGBT party of the year.

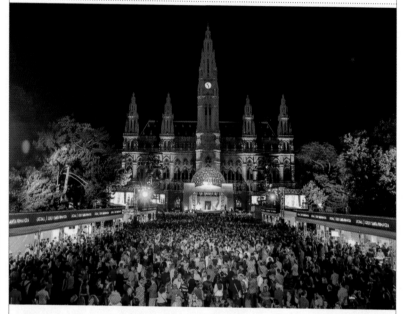

Approaching its 25th anniversary, the **Life Ball** (www.lifeball.org) in late May is the biggest charity event in Europe. It was set up by Torgom Petrosian and Gery Keszler to raise funds and awareness for their organisation, AIDS LIFE, that supports groups dedicated to people who are HIV-positive or who have AIDS.

The opening ceremony sets the scene. It fills the square in front of Vienna's City Hall with spectacular costumes, before a major figure – in previous years Bill Clinton, Sharon Stone and Elton John – gives the curtain-raising speech. Then follows live performances, generally of pop and operetta, a fashion show involving a world-famous name (think Jean Paul Gaultier, Calvin Klein and Roberto Cavalli), and all manner of glitzy hobnobbing. Which is fine if you can get in.

Covered by more than 60 TV stations worldwide, the Life Ball limits ticket sales to 3,780. These are sold over two days and usually some 60,000 people apply.

Guests can dress up according to that year's theme ('Love Is Infinite' and 'Four Elements – Fire' are recent examples)

and have the opportunity to sashay down the red carpet, thus helping to put even more spectacle into the spectacular opener (and qualify them for a cheaper ticket price). The theme is laid out every year in the 20-page, elaborate *Style Bible* (www.stylebible.org), created in English and German.

Throw in a number of high-rollers spending up to €5,000 per head for the Life Ball Package (flight, hotel, table bookings and all) and the total money raised can hit the roof. In 2015, it was €2.3 million.

So what if you're one of the 56,220 who can't get in? There are plenty of surrounding events. The Hofburg hosts the AIDS Solidarity Gala, the Burgtheater has the Red Ribbon Celebration Concert and there's a Ladies Luncheon at the Belvedere. In short, it's as if every regal landmark in the former Habsburg capital has been taken over by fashion-mad LGBT partygoers. And, of course, it's a huge weekend in the bars and clubs of Vienna, with non-stop revelry and DJ sessions. Don't forget to book your hotel room early – even if you just need it for a costume change.

A friendly, fashionable lesbian, gay, bisexual and transgender crowd frequents this hip but welcoming District 6 bar. Head down to the basement for an eclectic array of nights, from drag contests to indie-electro soirées.

SIXTA

5, Schönbrunner Strasse 21 (www.sixta-restaurant. at). U4 Kettenbrückengasse. **Open** 6pm-midnight daily. **Map** p247 D9.

Since it opened in 2013, this gay-owned and -operated restaurant has been serving delicious Austrian fare; a popular place for a good meal before a night out on the town.

Village Bar

6, Stiegengasse 8 (www.why-not.at). U4 Kettenbrückengasse. **Open** 8pm-3am daily. **No credit cards. Map** p247 D8.

This easy-going gay bar attracts customers of all ages with good cocktails, cheap shots and themed nights. It gets very crowded at weekends.

CLUBS

Although **Why Not?** remains Vienna's only exclusively gay dance joint, various nights are held at other venues across town (*see below* **Club Nights & Parties**).

★ Why Not?

1, Tiefer Graben 22 (www.why-not.at). U2 Schottentor or U3 Herrengasse. **Open** 10pm-4am Fri, Sat. **No credit cards. Map** p250 E6.

This long-running, enduringly popular bar-disco is generally patronised by younger guys (and women too). There's a subterranean dancefloor and three bars, with a lounge area with lots of red plush. The music leans towards chart, disco and cheese. Admission is free before midnight. *Photo p148.*

Club nights & parties

Check German-language site www.gayboy.at for the latest gay-driven club nights. In addition to those listed below, look out for: Ballcancan, a memorable night hosted by the Queer Balkan Society at Club Ost (www.ost-klub.at); and Up! Club, which takes over the decks at **Lutz – der Club** (www.lutz-club.at) on Mariahilfer Strasse.

★ Circus

www.circusclub.eu.

Billed as Vienna's biggest gay party, the Circus comes to town a couple of times a year to appropriately big venues such as the Ottakringer Brauerei or the open-air Arena. Local and international DJs play an entire weekend of pre- and post-party events. Smaller and more frequent offshoots include Cage and its pop cousin, Ken Club (www.kenclub.at), which take over the Club Auslage or the Säulenhalle.

G.Spot

www.gspot.at.

Held on the first Friday of the month, G.Spot draws a lesbian and gay crowd. Upstairs is techno, house and electro; downstairs is more chilled-out, with indie, pop and '80s tunes.

Heaven

www.heaven.at.

Under the watchful, extravagantly lashed eye of hostess Miss Candy, Heaven is Vienna's longest-running club event, held sporadically and at different locations. Expect electro-house, disco and garage.

Malefiz

Offering some welcome variety to the clubbing scene, Malefiz has a queer artsy crowd and takes over the performance space known as brut at the Künstlerhaus (*see p98*) once every other month. For more details, search for Malefiz on Facebook.

Meat Market

Meat Market hosts club nights and parties at hip venues such as Grelle Forelle and Das Werk. Their latest is vinyl-only event Mutter which currently takes place at the SASS Music Club (www.sassvienna. com). The crowd is mixed, though techno-loving men predominate on the dancefloor. For more details, search for Meat Market Vienna on Facebook.

★ OMG

One of the most popular parties in Vienna is hosted monthly by the OMG Society at the Chaya Fuera club (www.chayafuera.com). With cutting-edge sound and lighting on two floors, the location would rival the best in Berlin or New York. The party may be a gay favourite, but it's also straight-friendly. For more details, search for OMG Society on Facebook.

Pitbull

www.pitbull-clubbing.at.

Pitbull hosts monthly 'Bear & Butch' nights at the Club Titanic (www.titanic.at). It's a big and popular party for leather-wearers, bears in plaid shirts, cubs, hairies, chubbies and everyone in between.

Queer:Beat

www.queerbeat.at.

Queer:Beat events, tagged as pop parties for gays and friends, are generally once a month at one of five venues. The crowd is young and music is Top 40.

SAUNAS & CRUISING BARS

Apollo City Sauna

7, Wimbergergasse 34 (0660 673 6133, www.apollosauna.at). U6 Thaliastrasse. **Open** 2pm-2am daily. **Map** p246 B7.

With two floors and a small swimming pool, Apollo City Sauna has been a gay favourite for nearly three decades. It caters specifically to butches and bears.

ARTS & ENTERTAINMENT

Why Not?. See p147.

Club-Losch

*15, Fünfhausgasse 1 (895 9979, www.club-losch.
at). U6 Gumpendorfer Strasse.* **Open** 10pm-2am
Fri, Sat. **No credit cards. Map** p246 A9.

This men-only leather and fetish bar was one of the
first in Vienna. Although HardON (*see below*) may
get more traffic these days, business continues as
usual at Losch. Note that strict dress codes apply.

Eagle

*6, Blümelgasse 1 (587 2661, www.eagle-vienna.
com). U3 Neubaugasse.* **Open** 9pm-4am daily.
No credit cards. Map p246 C8.

You'll need to buzz to get into this men-only leather-
and-jeans bar. It has videos, an active darkroom with
cabins and a shop with poppers, toys and condoms.

HardON

*5, Hamburgerstrasse 4 (0681 108 55 105,
www.lmc-vienna.at). U4 Kettenbrückengasse.*
Open 8pm-2am Thur; 10pm-5am Fri, Sat.
No credit cards. Map p247 D9.

Run by Vienna's Leather and Motorbike Community
(LMC), HardON lives up to its name. In addition to an
array of theme nights, HardON also hosts events such
as Wien in Schwarz, Vienna Fetish Spring and the Mr
Leather Austria competition. Strict dress codes apply.

★ Kaiserbründl

*1, Weihburggasse 18-20 (513 3293, www.
kaiserbruendl.at). U1, U3 Stephansplatz.*
Open 2pm-midnight daily. **Map** p251 E7.

These Moorish-style baths must be among the most
beautiful bathhouses for gay men in the world. Gay
artist Stefan Riedl has added some splendid erotic
wall paintings alongside the intricate mosaics. You'll
find steam rooms, a Finnish sauna, massage, a solarium and a restaurant; check online for special events.

Sling

*4, Kettenbrückengasse 4 (586 2362, www.sling.at).
U4 Kettenbrückengasse.* **Open** 3pm-4am daily.
No credit cards. Map p247 D9.

This hi-tech cruising bar has various facilities,
including darkrooms, glory holes and a 'piss cinema'
('a very important part of the human body can be
seen without showing the face of its owner'). There's
also a good bar with free lube and condoms; a free
breakfast is served at 2am to revive flagging spirits.

Sport Sauna

*8, Lange Gasse 10 (406 7156, www.why-not.at).
Tram 2, 46.* **Open** 3pm-midnight Mon-Thur;
3pm Fri-1am Mon non-stop. **No credit cards.**
Map p246 C7.

Popular with the younger crowd, this sauna has a
solarium, Finnish sauna, bar, movie rooms and cabins.

CRUISING AREAS

Cruising is mostly safe and police seem to turn a blind
eye. The **Rathauspark** – on the left-hand side as you
face the Rathaus, past the fountain – is the most popular turf in spring and summer. Summer is also best
for the **Donauinsel**: some serious cruising goes on at
the Toter Grund nude area beside Steinspornbrücke,
a trek down the river along the Neue Donau. Take the
U1 to VIC, then bus 91A to the Roter Hiasl stop, or rent
a bike. Otherwise, the **Wiscot Center** on the Gürtel
and **Spartacus** on Mariahilferstrasse have plenty of
cabins and cinema rooms.

EVENTS

For more on the **Life Ball, Rainbow Parade** and
Identities Queer Film Festival, *see pp26-31.*
The Vienna ball season wouldn't be replete without
its colourful **Regenbogenball** (Rainbow Ball) at
the end of January, the **Rosenball** (Rose Ball) in mid
February or the **Diversity Ball** in mid April. Not to
be missed in April and May are queer cabaret artists,
comics and drag stars presented by kulturbanane.at
– performances take place at the Stadtsaal and the
Metropol. The gay fetish scene gets steamy at the
beginning of June for the **Vienna Fetish Spring**
and at the end of October during Vienna in Black.

Nightlife

Vienna's ever-improving bar, club and music scene is concentrated around several hubs within relatively easy reach of each other. After a hard day's sightseeing or shopping, you won't go thirsty in the Innere Stadt, but the city centre best excels in cocktail bars. For serious fun after midnight, you'll have to go beyond the Ringstrasse. Plenty of places stay open until dawn, and if you fancy a change of scene the U-Bahn runs through the night on Fridays and Saturdays. Music-wise, techno and minimal sounds still dominate, though newer clubs and promoters are exploring wider horizons. Vienna is also a regular stopping-off point for touring British and American bands – and as venues here tend to be on the small side, you can often see big names in intimate surroundings. As for clubs, entrance and bar prices are relatively reasonable. Audiences are enthusiastic – especially in the grungy enclave of venues free to crank up the noise below the rails of U-Bahn line U6 along the Gürtel ring road.

PLACES AND FACES

Drum 'n' bass and hip hop both have fervent scenes – rapper Nazar's gritty tales of growing up in the Favoriten hood have made a splash in the German-speaking world. Local promoters Beat the Fish, who stage shows at **Grelle Forelle** (*see p156*) and sundry festivals, have been responsible for bringing over big-name US artists such as Snoop Dogg and Kendrick Lamar.

At the weirder end of the spectrum, reflecting the Austrian love for all things niche and specialist, the current shining lights of the IDM/broken beat scene championed by Gilles Peterson are Dorian Concept, CID Rim and The cloniOUs. Though hometown appearances are quite rare, their crunchy beats can be picked up on at **Café Leopold** (*see p151*) and **Das Werk** (*see p157*). Independent **Affine Records** (www.affine records.com) has a strong roster of acts, including the aforementioned CID Rim. Label-mate Dorian Concept is creating an international stir with his complex electronic hip hop beats.

Luv Shack (www.facebook.com/luvshackrecords) regularly charts with its excellent house releases, while experimental record label and art project **Editions Mego** (www.editionsmego.com) has been relentless in its release of ambient, techno and noise records with little local fanfare but a lot of international attention. **Siluh Records** (www.siluh.com) produces plenty of rock but is known for its electronic one-offs, on coloured vinyl, found at outlets such as **Das Market** (7, Zieglergasse 40, 0676 376 9080), **Tongues** (www.tongues.at), **Rave Up** (www.rave-up.at) and **Substance** (www.substance-store.com). These record shops also act as meeting points and noticeboards for the local scene.

The stalwarts of Vienna's dance and electronica scene have diversified since the peak years of the late 1990s. Both Richard Dorfmeister, of Kruder & Dorfmeister fame, and producer Patrick Pulsinger have branched out into film soundtracks. Pulsinger has been working with acclaimed producer and musician Wolfram, now

IN THE KNOW IT'S A LOCK-IN

The inner-city waterway of the Danube Canal (Donaukanal) is now a busy nightlife hub, with bars doubling up as lidos, and boats providing pools and late-night drinks. This is nothing new – there's just much more of it these days. The long-established Badeschiff, once a nightlife staple, remains moored by Schwedenplatz but now just hosts the **Prostmahlzeit** bar-restaurant, open until 1am (www.prostmahlzeit.wien). In summer, folks sun themselves, eat, drink and swim. In peak season, it's €5 entry, which gives access to the pool or a rebate on your tab. Opposite, a handful of annual pop-ups offer street food and DJs.

on DFA Records and various other labels, with his polished, classic dance music. Also under Pulsinger's tutelage, Viennese trio Electro Guzzi produce live techno-krautrock jams.

At St Pölten, half an hour from Vienna, the **Beat Patrol** (www.beatpatrol.at) festival attracts the biggest names in the business. In Vienna itself, the **Waves Festival** (www.wavesvienna.com) has combined with a similar event in nearby Bratislava to form **Waves Central Europe** (www.wavescentraleurope.com).

BEAT ROUTE

Away from the 1st district, the city's nightlife is focused on five main areas. Just beyond the Ringstrasse lie Karlsplatz and the Naschmarkt, where venues such as **Sass** (*see p155*), **Club U** (*see p153*), **Kiosk** (*see p154*) and **Roxy** (*see p154*) can be relied upon to provide a party. From there, you're a step away from the 6th and 7th districts – home to gay hotspots (*see pp144-148*), laid-back hangouts, late-night clubs and sleek bars.

The third major cluster is concentrated along the busy Gürtel ring road, in the arches beneath the U6 U-Bahn line, between Thalia Strasse and Alser Strasse stations. There's indie here, with touring bands playing at **B72**, **rhiz** or **Chelsea** (*see p158* **Gürtel of Grunge**). DJs at Chelsea can be a little jaded, though; expect to see a haggard man in a pork pie hat still playing the Libertines.

The fourth area is along the Danube Canal, home to several boat venues. **Motto am Fluss** (www.motto.at/mottoamfluss) is a sleek mooring station for the liner service to Bratislava and a chic late-opening bar-restaurant. Just over the even narrower Vienna river, nearby **Strandbar Herrmann** (*see p153*) provides sand, deckchairs and, crucially, quality cocktails. In the other direction, near Schottenring, **Flex** (*see right*)

has long been throwing shapes by the water, its bar blessed with a riverside terrace. Further up the canal, **Summerstage** (*see p157*) offers waterside relaxation five months of the year.

Finally, beyond the canal lies the 2nd district and the Prater, worth a detour for **Pratersauna** (*see p153*) and **Fluc** (*see p152*). For the latest listings, check out German-language *Falter* (www.falter.at). Average admission for clubs is around €5-€10 unless there's a big-name act on.

BARS & CLUBS

Innere Stadt

Café Bendl

1, Landesgerichtsstrasse 6 (890 4105, www.bendl.wordpress.com). U2 Rathaus or tram 2. **Open** 8am-2am Mon-Thur; 8pm-4am Fri, Sat; 6pm-2am Sun. **No credit cards. Map** p250 C/D6.
A classic, grubby late-night hangout, with a sterling jukebox and a time-honoured (if unusual) tradition of beermat throwing. All sorts drink at Bendl, from sozzled students to politicians from the nearby Rathaus. Beware the Koksi cocktail: a potent blend of 80% rum mixed with crushed coffee beans and sugar.

First Floor

1, Seitenstettengasse 5 (532 1165, www.firstfloorbar.at). U1, U4 Schwedenplatz. **Open** 8pm-4am daily. **Map** p251 F6.
First Floor is one of Vienna's great bars. Designed by the fêted Eichinger oder Knechtl design team, using original fittings and panelling from the 1930s Mounier Bar, it's a seductive nook with minimal lighting emanating from a fishless aquarium behind the bar. The staff mix great cocktails and the piano occasionally gets tinkled for jazz standards.

Flex

1, Donaukanal & Augartenbrücke (533 7525, www.flex.at). U2, U4 Schottenring. **Open** 8pm-4am daily. **No credit cards. Map** p243 E5.
Set on the southern bank of the Donaukanal, this is the most revered club in Vienna – although the arrival of Pratersauna and smaller, more niche venues have challenged its supremacy. It has a top-notch sound system and a diverse programme of DJs spinning anything from techno to house, which tend to be better than the indie nights. Gigs often sell out, while the added Flex bar and outdoor canalside seating area are mobbed in summer.

Kix

1, Bäckerstrasse 4 (0676 603 8229, www.kixbar.at). U1, U4 Schwedenplatz or U1, U3 Stephansplatz. **Open** 5pm-1am Tue-Thur; 5pm-2am Fri; 7pm-2am Sat. **Map** p251 F6.
Fixing decent cocktails since 1986, when the father of current barman Valentin had this once-basic bar overhauled in minimalist fashion, Kix offers an

ARTS & ENTERTAINMENT

Roberto American Bar.

unpretentious, lively spot to socialise right in the heart of Innere Stadt. Craft beers, decent tunes and a silent TV backdrop of classic cartoons complete the picture.
▶ *In the same family, Italian-style L'Ombra (1, Lugeck 7, same website) is the ideal spot for post-work aperitivi.*

Planter's Club

1, Zelinkagasse 4 (533 33 9315, www.livingstone.at). U2, U4 Schottenring or tram 1, 2. **Open** 5pm-2am Mon-Wed, Sun; 5pm-4am Thur-Sat. **Map** p250 E5.
Leather armchairs and potted palms give Planter's, set in a former textiles warehouse, the air of a British colonial club – in the same style as the adjoining Livingstone restaurant. An encyclopaedic menu of 300-plus drinks, the 'holy book' devised by head barman Zoran Petrović, features any number of cocktails based on Broker's gin and almost every kind of whisky known to man. The clientele is dominated by thirtysomething suits.

★ Roberto American Bar

1, Bauernmarkt 11-13 (no phone, www.robertos bar.com). U1, U3 Stephansplatz. **Open** 2pm-late daily. **Map** p251 E6.
The Roberto in question is Roberto Pavlović; for years he was the mixology maestro at the most famous cocktail bar in town, Loos American Bar. Branching out on his own, he set up this smart, intimate spot in 2014. At first, Roberto's feels slightly cliquey, everyone seems to know each other and men without ties feel out of place. But once you settle in – over one of the finest martinis in Vienna – ties loosen,

tongues wag and a chatty atmosphere ensues, aided by excellent, friendly bar staff.

Santo Spirito

1, Kumpfgasse 7 (512 99 98, www.santo spirito.at). U1, U3 Stephansplatz. **Open** 6pm-2am daily. **No credit cards. Map** p251 F7.
This endearingly eccentric bar-restaurant is famous for playing classical music and projecting concerts on its walls; as the evening wears on, the volume steadily rises. It has a devoted gay following, but all sorts of people come here – including classical musicians and the glitterati of the Viennese theatre and opera scenes.

Ringstrasse & Around

Café Leopold

7, Museumplatz 1 (523 6732, www.cafe-leopold.at). U2 Museumsquartier. **Open** 10am-2am Mon-Wed, Sun; 10am-4am Thur-Sat. **Map** p250 D7.
Built into the Leopold Museum, home to one of Austria's most important modern art collections, this place remains a buzzy venue in the MuseumsQuartier. It's plushly appointed and draws a fashionable crowd, but the sometimes chippy bar staff and crowds can be a bit of a downer.

Passage

1, Burgring, corner Babenbergasse (961 6677-0 Tue-Fri, 0664 549 3944 Sat, www.club-passage.at). Tram 1, 2, D. **Open** 8pm-4am Tue, Wed; 9pm-4am Thur; 10pm-6am Fri, Sat. **Map** p247 D7.

With its long queues, sniffy doormen and pricey admission – and drinks – Passage is the nearest Vienna gets to a big-city clubbing vibe. Located in a former underground walkway beneath the Ringstrasse, it's a fairly bare space that mutates via all manner of lighting effects. Electro house and mainstream clubbing are the order of the day – if you like your tunes big and brash, from R&B to EDM, here's where to come.

Pavillon im Volksgarten

1, Burgring (532 0907, www.volksgarten-pavillon. at). U2, U3 Volkstheater. **Open** *Apr-mid Sept* 11am-2am Mon-Thur, Sun; 11am-4am Fri, Sat. **No credit cards. Map** p250 D7.

Fluc.

This beautiful 1950s folly is a delight on a summer evening. You can enjoy a fine view of the city to an aural backdrop of laid-back tunes, or drink on the terrace. Admission is usually free before 10pm, but entrance is charged for the oversubscribed Techno Café on Tuesdays. This is one of the busiest weekday nights in Vienna, with local and international DJs expanding the remit to spin disco, classic house – and even some good old-fashioned techno. A reasonably priced barbecue is fired up every evening, except Sunday, from 6pm.

Volksgarten

1, Burgring 1 (532 4241, www.volksgarten.at). U2, U3 Volkstheater or tram 1, 2, D. **Open** 9.30pm-late Mon-Wed; 11pm-late Thur-Sat. **Map** p251 D7.
Parts of these magnificent premises date to the mid 19th century, providing a wonderful setting for a night out. Following a €1 million revamp in 2011, the venue is divided into the Winter Garden, the Discothec and the Column Hall. Contemporary light installations illuminate a gorgeous interior, though the Volksgarten is let down by its somewhat unadventurous music policy of pedestrian techno and house, offset by the occasional exciting theme party. Drinks prices are quite steep too.

Leopoldstadt & the Danube

Bricks

2, Taborstrasse 38 (216 3701, 0699 180 0018, www.bricks.co.at). U2 Taborstrasse or tram 2. **Open** 8pm-4am Mon-Thur, Sun; 8am-5am Fri, Sat. **No credit cards. Map** p243 F4.
This dimly lit, arched basement bar has been a late-night stalwart for years, generally attracting a young crowd. In the delightfully kitsch, leopard-print interior, knowledgeable spinners such as DJ Elk delve into rock's rich tapestry from the 1960s and 1970s during the week. Electro, hip hop and pop attract the Saturday night crowds.

Fluc

2, Praterstern 5 (no phone, www.fluc.at). U1, U2 Praterstern. **Open** 6pm-2am daily. **No credit cards. Map** p244 G5.

ARTS & ENTERTAINMENT

Fluc has been trumped by new additions to the scene but its upstairs bar continues to host interesting techno, goth and indie nights, which are usually free. Downstairs, in the club space, it's anything from mental drum 'n' bass to dub, techno and even gabba. An occasional touring band might also fetch up. Set on the edge of the Prater fairground, Fluc usually attracts a messy crowd.

hammond

2, Taborstrasse 33 & Grosse Pfarrgasse (968 9215, www.hammondbar.at). U2 Taborstrasse or tram 2. **Open** 5pm-late Mon-Fri; 7pm-late Sat, Sun. **No credit cards. Map** p251 F5.

Tucked away beside a chain bakery, cool, urban hammond serves some of the best cocktails in town thanks to Vienna's finest mixologist, Sigi Ehm. More unusual drinks such as liquid sachertorte or foamy daiquiri on fire complement superior versions of the standard range, sipped by discerning regulars who chatter round the bar.

Prater Dome

2, Riesenradplatz 7 (0908 11 92 900, www.prater dome.at). U1, U2 Praterstern. **Open** 10pm-6am Thur-Sat. **No credit cards. Map** p244 H5.

The self-titled 'Most Important Club in Town' (it's Austria's largest disco, apparently) is as mainstream as it comes, tucked away behind the funfair. In fact, this is the disco equivalent of a funfair, with a flashy laser show, a warren of halls and rooms where you can run wild – plus the kind of house and techno you might hear next time you're on a waltzer.

★ Pratersauna

2, Waldsteingartenstrasse 135 (729 1927, www. pratersauna.tv). U2 Messe Prater or tram 1. **Open** *Apr-Sept* 9pm-6am Wed-Sun. *Oct-Mar* 11pm-6am Thur-Sat. **No credit cards. Map** p248 J6.

Electronic music, techno, minimal, tech-house and deep house dominate at this converted 1960s sauna. Look out for local promoter Enix's nights for disco and acid house classics and some terrific guests, including Oni Ayhun (one half of The Knife), Felix da Housecat and Jacques Renault. Support sets from Wolfram and Felix are also worth checking out. Pratersauna has scaled back its programming due to heavy pressure from competitors, but it's still the best in Vienna. On certain nights they open the still functioning sauna rooms, and in summer they sometimes open the pool and clubbers lounge on the grass. Brilliant lighting, a great sound system and arty toilets complete the picture. *Photos p154.*

Vie i Pee

2, Waldsteingartenstrasse 135 (720 2999, www. vieipee.com). U2 Messe Prater or tram 1. **Open** 10pm-late Wed-Sat. **No credit cards. Map** p248 J6.

Connected by a corridor to the long-established Pratersauna, Vie i Pee is Vienna's first nightspot dedicated to hip hop – plus a little rap, soul, R&B

and funk. Opened in March 2015, it has yet to find a hardcore customer base, and its bizarre policy of not advertising its acts (whether a US star on a European tour or a local rapper just starting out) means it doesn't attract hordes of new punters from the other side of town. Scheduling so far sees Mixwoch on Wednesdays, Hug Club on Thursdays, Total Chaos on Fridays and Mikki Maus Klub on Saturdays. There's a sleek 500-capacity interior and a large garden, and the club is looking to share major events with its illustrious neighbour.

Landstrasse & Belvedere

★ Strandbar Herrmann

3, Herrmannpark (beside Urania) (0650 718 04 01, www.strandbarherrmann.at). U1, U4 Schwedenplatz (exit Urania). **Open** *Apr-Sept* 10am-2am daily. **Map** p251 G6.

The Herrmann gets its name from its location in the canal-side Herrmannpark, which commemorates Emanuel Herrmann, the inventor of the picture post-card. And it's a bit like being beside the seaside here, as the promontory where the Wien river enters the Danube Canal is covered with sand and strewn with deckchairs. There's no swimming, but plenty of sun-bathing, eating and chilling to great sounds until 2am. The cocktails are terrific – get here for 6pm to take advantage of happy hour.

Karlsplatz to Mariahilfer Strasse

Aux Gazelles

6, Rahlgasse 5 (585 6645, www.auxgazelles.at/ club). U2 Museumsquartier. **Open** 10pm-4am Fri, Sat. **Map** p250 D8.

With its restaurants, bars, tea lounges and Moroccan steam bath, this Moorish labyrinth always seemed a bit ambitious. Nonetheless, it pulls in a global crowd with Balkan beats and Oriental dance music. It's a classy joint, but expect to drop a lot of cash: playboys and gold-diggers will be in their element.

Celeste

5, Hamburgerstrasse 18 (586 5314, www.celeste. co.at). U4 Kettenbrückengasse. **Open** 7pm-3am Mon-Thur; 7pm-5am Fri, Sat. **Map** p247 D9.

Comprising a garden, two clubs and two bars, Celeste has the feel of an old mansion, created with a lot of care. Jazz sessions have been going in the cellar since the 1990s, but now an updated club space upstairs attracts interesting DJs and live acts to a small stage. The sound could be better, but the garden is a real delight and the Czech Kozel beer goes down a treat on a balmy night. Highly recommended.

Club U

1, Otto Wagner Pavillon, Karlsplatz (505 9904, www.club-u.at). U1, U2, U4 Karlsplatz. **Open** *Club* 10pm-4am daily. **No credit cards. Map** p250 E8.

ARTS & ENTERTAINMENT

Pratersauna. *See p153.*

Under one of Otto Wagner's railway pavilions, Club U moves effortlessly from daytime coffee house and alfresco bar to arty club (downstairs and on an upper terrace). The music runs from disco to pop trash – top nights include Everybody's Darling (retro sounds with international guests) and Rhinoplasty (gay and mixed crowd, serious trannies, mad DJs spinning happy hardcore and Abba). On its night, this is one of the wildest venues in town.

Futuregarden

6, Schadekgasse 6 (no phone, www.facebook.com/ futuregarden). U3 Neubaugasse. **Open** 6pm-2am Mon-Thur; 6pm-4am Fri, Sat; 7pm-2am Sun. **No credit cards. Map** p246 C8.

The soundtrack at this leftfield bar ventures beyond the usual techno and attracts an interesting crowd. The layout is intimate, drinks are reasonably priced and the DJs are wildly eclectic, mixing 1990s pop, indie and house with panache. Admission is free.

Kiosk

4, Schleifmühlgasse 7 (no phone, www.facebook. com/KioskVienna). U4 Kettenbrückengasse or Karlsplatz. **Open** 6pm-1am Mon-Thur; 6pm-4am Fri, Sat. **Map** p247 E8.

This likeable bar is populated by media types, students and art scenesters; at the weekends, it's packed.

Puff die Bar

6, Girardigasse 10 (no phone, www.puff-bar.at). U1, U2, U4 Karlsplatz. **Open** 5pm-1am Tue, Wed; 7pm-2am Thur; 7pm-4am Fri, Sat. **No credit cards. Map** p250 D8.

A steep climb up from the Naschmarkt, on a street corner, Puff is off the beaten track but worth the effort. Illuminated pouffes dangle from the ceiling, but the bar's name refers to its previous life as a brothel. It does indeed feel like a speakeasy, though a garden opens up in summer. DJs spin all year round. Play it safe with a superior cosmopolitan or see how the barman does with an old fashioned made with Zacapa – pretty well, as it goes.

▶ *Also recommended, a ten-minute stroll away, is Eberts cocktail bar (6, Gumpendorfer Strasse 51, 586 5465, www.eberts.at).*

Roxy

4, Operngasse & Faulmanngasse 2 (0681 2030 7088, www.roxyclub.org). U1, U2, U4 Karlsplatz or tram 1, 2, D. **Open** 10pm-4am daily. **No credit cards. Map** p250 E8.

This central late-nighter, which dates from the 1960s, sports a plush interior and tiny dancefloor. Sadly, the lovely little Roxy struggles to attract good promoters, though it manages to put on hip hop, R&B and some drum 'n' bass.

Sass Music Club

1, Karlsplatz 1 (0676 411 6116, www.sassvienna. com). U1, U2, U4 Karlsplatz or tram 1, 2, D. **Open** 11pm-5am Thur-Sat; 6am-11am Sun. **No credit cards. Map** p250 E8.

Given its Karlsplatz address, near the city's main shopping quarter, it's no wonder the Sass has emerged from a recent renovation with gold leaf on the walls and a crystal chandelier. To its credit, though, Sass eschews the concept of a VIP area, has invested in a quality sound system and makes genuinely decent cocktails. It's still not quite sure if it wants to be commercial and mainsteam, or edgy and underground. Time will tell.

Tanzcafe Jenseits

6, Nelkengasse 3 (587 1233, www.tanzcafe-jenseits.com). U3 Neubaugasse. **Open** 8pm-4am Tue-Sat. **No credit cards. Map** p246 C8.

The chintz and velvet interior appears to confirm the legend that Tanzcafe Jenseits ('the beyond') was once a brothel. It remains a wonderfully retro spot for a few drinks and the odd waltz round the tiny dancefloor. The music is an appealing blend of vintage soul and funk, lounge and chanson. It can feel like a bit of a pick-up joint, but it's still pretty good fun; the fug in the smoking area has to be inhaled to be believed.

Neubau

Donau

7, Karl Schweighofergasse 10 (523 8105, www.donautechno.com). U2, U3 Volkstheater or tram 49. **Open** 8pm-4am Mon-Thur; 8pm-6am Fri, Sat; 8pm-2am Sun. **No credit cards. Map** p247 D7.

The neoclassical arches of the Donau have long been a favourite spot on the Vienna club scene. Now trading almost exclusively in electro, minimal techno and clicky pop, the lighting by Doctor Flash puts the fine interior to good use. Local DJs often play extended sets, and it's a good place to start your night out on the town.

Die Dondrine

7, Kitchengasse 20 (no phone, www.diedondrine. at). U3 Neubaugasse or tram 49. **Open** 6pm-4am Mon-Sat. **No credit cards. Map** p250 C8.

Tucked between two other bars – one quite snobby and French, the other very snobby and Viennese – Die Dondrine is a punky alternative spot, currently stretching its happy hour to three. It's not the €2.50 beer you've come for, although that helps. It's the ska tunes and the general understanding that you're here to get completely wasted and that it's going to be a lot of fun. After a while, the draught Kozel or Murauer has taken hold and you're ready to take on anything the 7th district can throw at you.

Rote Bar

7, Neustiftgasse 1 (521 11 218, table reservations 0699 1501 5013, www.volkstheater.at/spielstaette/rote-bar). U2, U3 Volkstheater. **Open** end of show-1am daily. **No credit cards. Map** p250 D7.
The interior of the Volkstheater's 'Red Bar' is a glorious panoply of crystal chandeliers and heavy velvet curtains over a marble floor. It hosts concerts, DJs and readings. Some events attract a charge, others are free. You can eat here too.

★ Ungar Grill

7, Burggasse 97 (522 4169, www.ungargrill.at). U6 Burggasse-Stadthalle or tram 49. **Open** 5pm-2am Tue-Fri; 10am-2am Sat; 10am-10pm Sun. **No credit cards. Map** p246 B7.
Formerly a Hungarian restaurant (it's still done up in kitsch Magyar livery and bears the original name), the Ungar Grill was recently taken over by the charming Darija Kasalo from Vukovar, further down the Danube in Croatia. Where fiddlers once fiddled and goulash was guzzled, she has set up a funky, alternative spot decked out with original art, a single Kodak snap of her home town and somewhat rude adaptations of toy dolls – all complemented by underground sounds, Schremser beer and affordable snacks. A spacious beer garden is a boon in summer.

Josefstadt to Alsergrund

For **B72**, **Chelsea**, **Café Carina** and **rhiz**, *see p158* **Gürtel of Grunge**. Also on the Gürtel, the **Loft** (16, Lerchenfelder Gürtel 37, www.theloft.at) puts on electronic music nights in its basement – there's a café on the ground floor and a bar upstairs. **WUK** also has some terrific nights, *see p160*.

Grande Bar

8, Josefstädter Strasse 56 (0676 499 8177, www.grande.at). U6 Josefstädter Strasse or tram 2. **Open** 6pm-2am Mon-Thur; 6pm-4am Fri, Sat. **Map** p246 B6.
With its eccentric theatrical decor (think lots of swag curtains) and expertly mixed cocktails, this place is one of a kind. The crowd is as eclectic as the decor, and although smoking is allowed, it's reasonably airy and has a no-smoking area.

Grelle Forelle

9, Spittelauer Lände 12 (no phone, www.grelleforelle.com). U4, U6 Spittelau. **Open** 11pm-6am Fri, Sat. **Map** p243 D2.
Follow the bright fish symbols along the Danube Canal to find the 'Flashy Trout', a new sleek temple to techno looking out over the canal. This addition to Vienna's club scene has dropped its pretensions to challenge Berlin, but keeps entry and drinks prices high, and admission to over-21s. Long queues at

Das Torberg.

the door and gruff security staff might put you off, although once inside you'll be impressed by the cavernous, two-storey space, imaginative lighting by Neon Golden and great sound; DJs play house, techno and minimal. Stay the course and you might see dawn peeking through the glass.

Summerstage

9, Rossauer Lände (315 5202, www.summerstage. co.at). U4 Rossauer Lände. **Open** *May-Sept 5pm-1am Mon-Sat; 3pm-1am Sun.* **No credit cards. Map** p243 E4.

A loose grouping of various restaurants sets up shop along this stretch of the Danube Canal in summer, where you can eat and drink alfresco until 1am. Why the organisers bother arranging a programme of jazz, boules and art to pull in punters is a mystery – the waterside location is a sufficient draw. Booking is strongly advised.

Das Torberg

8, Strozzigasse 47 (0664 220 3757, www. dastorberg.at). U2 Rathaus. **Open** *5pm-2am Mon-Sat.* **No credit cards. Map** p246 C6.

Renovated in 2015, the homely Torberg offers Vienna's most varied selection of gin (306 in all). But this is no exclusive cocktail bar or Victorian gin palace – amiable rockers and hard-drinking regulars gather round the well-worn bar counter, where an office worker with loosened tie is happy to shoot

the breeze with a spiky-haired punk in an Exploited T-shirt. The music is brilliant (classic Brill Building interspersed with remixed New Order) and the beer flows like it was available free in public fountains. Arrive late afternoon and you might not be staggering out until midnight, or worse.

Tür 7

8, Buchfeldgasse 7 (0664 546 3717, www.tuer7.at). U2 Rathaus. **Open** *7pm-4am Mon-Sat.* **Map** p250 C6.

Unveiled in early 2015, the unmarked Tür 7 has a friendly barman who opens the door to strangers and regulars, ushering you in and gesturing to a row of slippers. The parlour game extends to the bar's design and the bathtub in the WC. Cocktails are where Gerhard Kozbach-Tsai and his experienced little team take things seriously – and to another level. Playing on another theme (the number seven, following on from the street address, bar name and opening time), Tür 7 operates from a select menu seven drinks long, changed every seven weeks. Sure, you can ask for a Martini and get a damn good one, but where's the fun in that? The idea is to show the customer seven different directions – sour, sweet, fruity and more – and see how the night takes its course. Tür 7 is finding its feet but feels most comfortable in the slippers provided.

U4

12, Schonbrünner Strasse 222 (817 1192-0, www. u-4.at). U4 Meidlinger Hauptstrasse. **Open** *10pm-late Tue-Sat.* **No credit cards. Map** p246 B10.

U4 has been a cornerstone of Viennese nightlife for more than two decades. Kurt and Courtney once showed up, Prince played an aftershow gig, and Falco namechecked it. These days, though, it tries to attract the very broadest of audiences.

★ Das Werk

9, Stadtbahnbogen 331-333, Rossauer Lände 12 (0677 614 576 23, www.daswerk.org). U4, U6 Spittelau. **Open** *varies.* **No credit cards. Map** p243 D2.

Part of an underground cultural venture, and only recently moved to this suitably industrial space, Das Werk stages electronic music nights most weekends, mainly featuring local underground DJs. The contrast with the brazen commercialism of nearby Grelle Forelle couldn't be more pronounced – this is very much DIY, with techno pushed to the forefront. Events here include films, readings and exhibitions.

ROCK & ROOTS

Being at the heart of Europe means it's easy to find a wide spectrum of live music here: Balkan, indie, metal, Turkish, you name it. Vienna is also a regular stopping-off point for touring British and American bands who tend to play at smaller, more intimate venues than elsewhere. Ticket and bar prices are relatively reasonable, and audiences

GÜRTEL OF GRUNGE
Vienna's strip of alt sounds stretches below the U6 metro line.

Like many big-city railway stations, the area around Westbahnhof was long a red-light district. Then, in the mid 1990s, something began to change. Led by Britpunk haunt **Chelsea** (*see p159*) – stage for the Buzzcocks, the Wedding Present and I Am Kloot – music venues began opening below the elevated railway line along what is known as the Gürtel.

This beltway not only carries the U6 U-Bahn line, it also glides over the elegant former Stadtbahn stations by famed Jugendstil architect Otto Wagner. Their viaducts were not only atmospheric, they were also rattled by noisy trains every few minutes. As a result, you could safely lock intolerable racket merchants such as the UK Subs in a dark room around here and let them do anything they wanted.

The Gürtel also divides central Vienna from the suburbs. A short hop from Westbahnhof, it enabled young provincial music lovers to head into the capital, pop back on the last train at night or first in the morning, and still make it in time for college the next day.

As more venues opened – popular, compact, split-level **B72** (*see p159*); louche **Café Carina** (*see p159*), where Pete Doherty once strummed for cash – a late-night infrastructure developed under the arches including, most notably, a plethora of all-night fast food vans. The Gürtel has retained its somewhat seedy appearance, its hardier strip joints defiantly still in business, but it has become popular with every rocker and

night-owl in Austria. If you want a falling-down, what-the-hell-happened-last-night session, this is where to come.

Specifically, the hub is the section from Thaliastrasse to Josefstädter Strasse and just beyond, with occasional venues around Nussdorfer Strasse. If the band at the excellent **rhiz** (*see p159*) – known for experimental rock, electronica and quality DJs at weekends – doesn't cut it, then just hop on the U6 (all night at weekends) towards Nussdorfer Strasse. Alternatively, if you're tired of the crush around the stage – Chelsea was the first venue to bring big rock artists to a small club and it's a habit that sticks – then wander over to the dear old **Café Concerto** (*see p161*) for a DJ in the intimate upstairs bar or some folk, world or Americana downstairs.

Certain acts at Chelsea and rhiz involve an admission fee of around €5-€10; big-name acts sell out fast. Club nights at Chelsea are generally free, though, while some friendly person will pass the hat round at Carina.

Further alternatives in the same orbit as Chelsea and Carina are the **Loft** (www.theloft. at), offering three floors of music and decent cocktails, and **Fania** (www.fania-bar.com; *pictured*), a late-opening Latin newcomer that gets frantic at weekends.

Finally, you can take in all kinds of alternative bands and venues as part of the **Gürtel Night Walk** (www.guertelnightwalk.at), an annual stroll along Vienna's music mile in August, with free shows and open-air stages.

enthusiastic. Expect to pay top whack for big names, but you can easily make new discoveries within your budget – quite often for free. Given venue sizes, however, many gigs do sell out – so plan ahead. Wednesday's weekly *Falter* (www.falter.at) carries music listings, both by day and by artist. Garish posters for upcoming events cover every available surface around town, while bars and record shops creak under the weight of flyers for independent shows. The people at **Rave Up Records** (www.rave-up.at) are particularly in the know.

Festivals tend to be more basic affairs than in the UK, but the upside is decent value for money when it comes to ticket prices and drinks. The **Frequency Festival** (www.frequency.at) in St Pölten is known for indie and rock; **Nova Rock** (www.novarock.at) in Burgenland focuses on metal; and just over the border in Slovakia, the excellent **Pohoda Festival** (www.pohodafestival.sk) presents more arty fare – Björk and Manu Chao featured in 2015.

For details of **Rock In Vienna**, **Balkan Fever** and the **Donau Festival** in Krems, *see pp26-31* **Diary**.

Venues

Some venues act as bars as well, with a separate area for concerts, hence the opening hours in the listings below. Admission is often free for low-key nights or little-known acts, €5-€10 for better-known ones and €15-€20 or more for big names. Credit card payment is more a rarity than the norm.

Arena
3, Baumgasse 80 (798 85 95, www.arena.co.at). U3 Erdberg. **Open** *Winter* 4pm-late daily. *Summer* 2pm-late daily. **No credit cards. Map** p248 H8.
This former slaughterhouse has evolved from a squat into a centre for alternative film and music, and a favourite hangout of the punk, drum 'n' bass and techno crowds. Iggy Pop and Patti Smith were recent visitors, while nights such as Roadtrip to Outta Space are popular for freaky heavy rock, Iceberg for NDW and rock. In summer, indie films are shown and open-air performances take place in the courtyard. Easily one of the best venues in Vienna.

★ B72
8, Hernalser Gürtel, Stadtbahnbögen 72 (409 2128, www.b72.at). U6 Alser Strasse or tram 43. **Open** 8pm-4am daily. **No credit cards. Map** p246 B6.
See p158 **Gürtel of Grunge**.

Café Carina
U-Bahn building, 8, Josefstädter Strasse 84 (406 4322, www.cafe-carina.at). U6 Josefstädter Strasse or tram 2, 33. **Open** 6pm-2am Mon-Thur; 6pm-6am Fri, Sat. **No credit cards. Map** p246 B6.
See p158 **Gürtel of Grunge**.

Chelsea
8, Lerchenfelder Gürtel U-Stadtbahnbögen 29-32 (407 9309, www.chelsea.co.at). U6 Josefstädter Strasse or tram 2, 33. **Open** 6pm-4am Mon-Sat; 6pm-3am Sun (earlier if screening TV football). **No credit cards. Map** p246 B7.
See p158 **Gürtel of Grunge**.

Derwisch
16, Lerchenfelder Gürtel 29 (956 3677, 0699 1067 6508, www.cafederwisch.com). U6 Thaliastrasse or tram 46. **Open** 2pm-2am Mon-Thur, Sun; 2pm-4am Fri, Sat. **No credit cards. Map** p246 B7.
Completely unmarked and hidden away in the courtyard of a dilapidated Gürtel tenement, the cellar of this Turkish restaurant offers rousing live Balkan music on Fridays and occasional gigs during the rest of the week. If the vibe's right, you can expect lots of sweaty table-top dancing. Recently, cool crossover nights have seen electronic artists using Turkish folk elements. Excellent food served during the day.

Gasometer/Bank Austria Halle
11, Guglgasse 8 (0720 511 922, www.wienergasometer.at). U3 Gasometer. **Map** p249 K10.
Located in the Gasometer complex, this 3,000-capacity hall is the best venue to catch mid-ranking acts from the UK and USA on tour. The acoustics, views and atmosphere are all above average for this type of venue.

★ rhiz
8, Lerchenfelder Gürtel, Stadtbahnbögen 37 (409 2505, www.rhiz.org). U6 Josefstädter Strasse. **Open** 6pm-4am Mon-Sat; 6pm-2am Sun. **No credit cards. Map** p246 B6/7.
See p158 **Gürtel of Grunge**.

Schwarzberg
4, Schwarzenbergplatz 10 (no phone, www.ost-klub.at). Tram D. **Open** varies. **No credit cards. Map** p251 F8.
The former Ost Klub closed its doors as a Russian disco and Balkan party in 2014. Now renamed and rebranded, Schwarzberg has expanded its musical remit beyond southern and eastern Europe. Indeed, it chose a festival of Americana as its inaugural event.

Shelter
20, Wallensteinplatz 8 (0676 687 7750, www.shelter.at). U6 Jägerstrasse or U4 Friedensbrücke or tram 5, 33. **Open** 8pm-2am Tue-Thur; 8am-4am Fri, Sat. **No credit cards. Map** p243 E3.
This popular indie dive comprises a frequently rammed front bar and a low-ceilinged, garishly painted back room where bands play or DJs spin. Entry is often free and there's Guinness on draught, plus table football and pinball machines. The long-running Bravo Hits party is fun if you like a messy alternative night with cheesy pop thrown in.

ARTS & ENTERTAINMENT

★ ((szene)) Wien

11, Hauffgasse 26 (332 4641-25, http://de-de.
facebook.com/szenewien). U3 Zippererstrasse.
No credit cards.
With a fine sound system and solid reputation, the
Szene attracts some top-notch UK and US artists
– Anna Calvi, say, or the Coral – interspersed with
interesting oddities and heavy rock acts such as
Trivium and Cannibal Corpse. The auditorium is
box-like, but the acoustics are great. The two front
bars serve reliable food, and there's a large, unkempt
garden out the back.

Wiener Stadthalle

15, Roland Rainer Platz 1 (981 000, www.
stadthalle.com). U6 Burggasse-Stadthalle
or U3 Schweglerstrasse or tram 6, 18, 49.
Map p246 A7.
The Stadthalle is the place where big names play
when they come to Vienna – think Diana Krall, the
Foo Fighters and the like. Two separate halls, the
romantically named Hall D and Hall F, dispense the
usual bland trappings of *Stadion-Rock*.

★ WUK

9, Währinger Strasse 59 (401 21-0, www.wuk.at).
U6 Währinger Strasse or tram 40, 41, 42. **Open**
Office 9am-8pm Mon-Fri; 3-8pm Sat, Sun. *Bar*
11am-2am Mon-Fri; 5pm-2am Sat, Sun. **No credit**
cards. Map p242 C4.
The WUK cultural centre has been making waves
since 1981. It's based in a 19th-century, brick-built
former factory complex, with its workshops and

exhibition space arranged around a gorgeous ivy-
clad courtyard. Music is high on the agenda, with
local bands rehearsing in the basement, gigs by cult
names and club nights in the main hall.

JAZZ, BLUES & COUNTRY

Vienna has swung to the pulse of jazz since the
early years of the last century. **Porgy & Bess**
continues to shine, booking avant-garde and high-
quality modern performers. **Material Records**
(www.materialrecords.com), an active jazz label
founded by highly acclaimed guitarist Wolfgang
Muthspiel, is still going strong. For **Jazz Fest**
Wien, *see pp26-31.*

The city also has a vibrant country music
and Americana scene (see www.musikvonhier.
blogspot.co.at). The annual **Americana Fest**
Wien (http://americanafestwien.blogspot.hu)
in 2015 involved 25 shows and 40 artists.

Venues

Blue Tomato

15, Wurmsergasse 21 (985 5960, www.blue
tomato.cc). U3 Johnstraße. **Open** 7pm-1.30am
Tue-Thur; 7pm-3am Fri, Sat. **No credit cards.**
This tiny, informal jazz and improv club occupies
the back room of a friendly bar. The programme
mostly features accomplished local musicians of
the modern variety, but occasionally a legend such
as sax maestro Peter Brötzmann turns up to shake
the walls.

Porgy & Bess.

Café Concerto

16, Lerchenfelder Gürtel 53 (406 4795,
www.cafeconcerto.at). U6 Josefstädter Strasse.
Open 7pm-2am Tue-Thur; 7pm-4am Fri, Sat.
No credit cards. Map p246 B7.
See p158 **Gürtel of Grunge**.

Jazzland

1, Franz-Josefs-Kai 29 (533 2575, www.jazzland.
at). U1, U4 Schwedenplatz or tram 1, 2. **Open**
from 7pm Mon-Sat. *Shows* 9pm. **No credit cards.**
Map p251 F6.
This small cellar club is located under Vienna's oldest church, the Ruprechtskirche, and has been going
for around 40 years. The programming is similarly
venerable, with swing and traditional jazz by local
and American musicians. Jazzland doesn't take reservations, so arrive early for popular shows.

Miles Smiles

8, Lange Gasse 51 (405 9517, www.miles-smiles.
at). U2 Rathaus or tram 2. **Open** 8pm-2am Mon-
Thur, Sun; 8pm-4am Fri, Sat. **No credit cards.**
Map p250 C6.
This is a typically laid-back Viennese venue. The
name betrays the owner's weakness for jazz;
occasionally live soloists or duos appear, especially
during Jazz Fest Wien. Admission is free.

★ Porgy & Bess

1, Riemergasse 11 (503 7009, tickets 512 88 11,
www.porgy.at). U3 Stubentor or tram 1, 2.
Open 7.30pm-late daily. **Map** p251 F7.

Arguably the finest live music venue in Vienna, Porgy
& Bess is the best place to hear modern jazz, blues and
world. Its handsome split-level interior and friendly
vibe make an immediate and favourable impression,
while the programming is second to none.

Reigen

14, Hadikgasse 62 (894 0094, www.reigen.at).
U4 Hietzing. **Open** 6pm-2am Tue-Thur; 6pm-
4am Fri, Sat. **No credit cards.**
Another venue specialising in jazz and blues (though
chanson, latin, reggae and avant-garde might also
feature), Reigen is located on a thunderous main road.
Once inside, though, the performance space is cosy.

Sargfabrik

14, Goldschlagstrasse 169 (988 98 111, www.
sargfabrik.at). Tram 49, 52. **No credit cards.**
Slightly awkward to get to by public transport,
Sargfabrik is worth the effort – a housing cooperative
with a theatre and café attached. The theatre has regular world and jazz gigs, as well as acoustic Mondays,
cabaret, performance art and children's events.

Tunnel

8, Florianigasse 39 (990 4400, www.tunnel-
vienna-live.at). U2 Rathaus or tram 2. **Open**
9am-2am Mon-Sat; 9am-midnight Sun.
No credit cards. Map p246 B6.
This pleasant, studenty cellar bar with cosy booths
was revamped in 2015. Live rock and jazz are on the
syllabus most evenings, but the music tends to take a
back seat to drinking and socialising.

Performing Arts

Vienna has an unrivalled musical tradition, with Beethoven, Mahler, Mozart and Schubert among past residents. There are reminders of this extraordinary heritage everywhere you look – from the Mozart ticket touts in frock coats and frilled cuffs who lurk by Stephansdom to the packed programme of musical events at the city's many concert halls, churches and theatres. Theatre itself remains an integral part of city life. Most shows are in German – the legendary Burgtheater is one of the most important in the German-speaking world – although Vienna's English Theatre, founded in 1963, is the oldest of its kind in continental Europe. The many stars who have performed there include Benedict Cumberbatch, Dame Judi Dench and Anthony Quinn. The dance scene centres on the Tanzquartier Wien (TQW) in the MuseumsQuartier.

Classical & Opera

Music-lovers are spoiled for choice. If you prefer orchestral work, the **Wiener Philharmoniker** or **Wiener Symphoniker** are likely to be performing, and if you're interested in early and Baroque music, the **Concentus Musicus**, conducted by Nikolaus Harnoncourt, is at your service. Although the Alban Berg Quartet chamber ensemble is no more, newer world-class outfits such as **Ensemble Wien-Berlin** and **Ensemble Wiener Collage** give members of Vienna's top orchestras a chance to showcase their chamber skills. Contemporary music comes from the formidable **Klangforum Wien**.

Not every performance is a gem. The downside to the historical awe accorded Vienna and its music is a certain complacency. This can manifest itself in many ways: from a lacklustre performance 'good enough for the punters', to an attitude emanating from cloakroom staff that 'you should just be grateful for the experience'. Perhaps we should.

TICKETS & INFORMATION

Concert information is available from tourist offices (*see p230*), in listings magazines such as *Falter* and on information columns scattered all over the city. Advance tickets are available from the outlets mentioned below. At some major venues, tickets and prices are divided into five categories. In descending order of expense, these are: G (Gala), P (Première), A, B and C. Vienna also hosts festivals with classical music and opera throughout the year (*see pp26-31*).

Another useful agency is the **Vienna Ticket Office** (513 1111, www.viennaticketoffice.com).

Österreichische Bundestheaterkassen

1, Operngasse 2 (514 44 7880, www.bundestheater. at). U1, U2, U4 Karlsplatz or tram 1, 2, D. **Open** 8am-6pm Mon-Fri; 9am-noon Sat, Sun. **Map** p250 E7.
The State Theatre Booking Office has tickets for the Staatsoper, Volksoper, Akademietheater, Kasino am Schwarzenberplatz, Vestibül and Burgtheater. Staatsoper tickets are sold two months before the performance; at the Volksoper, they're released on the first day of the month for performances that month and the next. The rest release tickets a month in advance. During Advent (late November to Christmas) box office hours are extended until 5pm on Saturdays.

Vienna Classic Online

www.viennaclassic.com.
This online agency sells tickets for opera, concerts, theatre, musicals and more.

Wiener Staatsoper

*1, Opernring 2 (514 44-2250, 7880, www.
wiener-staatsoper.at). U1, U2, U4 Karlsplatz or
tram 1, 2, D.* **Open** *Ticket office 9am-2hrs before
performance Mon-Fri; 9am-noon Sat.* **Map** p250 E7.
Tickets for the Staatsoper can also be purchased
at the information office in the arcades at the
Staatsoper (9am-1hr before performance, 9am-5pm
Sat). They're also sold at the evening box office from
an hour before the show. Many of the costumed
ticket sellers on the square tout tickets to sold-out or
otherwise hard-to-see performances, but be warned
that they usually come at a hefty price.

Wien Ticket/Pavillon bei der Staatsoper

*1, Herbert von Karajan Platz (58 885, www.wien-
ticket.at). U1, U2, U4 Karlsplatz.* **Open** *10am-7pm
daily. By phone 8am-8pm daily.* **Map** p250 E7.
This ticket booth to the side of the Staatsoper sells
tickets for all venues.

MAIN VENUES

Orchestral, opera & operetta

Kammeroper

*1, Fleischmarkt 24 (512 0100-77, www.wiener
kammeroper.at). U1, U4 Schwedenplatz or tram 1,
2.* **Open** *Box office noon-6pm Mon-Fri; from 4pm
Sat (only on performance days).* **Map** p251 F6.
The Kammeroper has been dedicated to smaller-
scale opera productions since 1953. In 2012, its management was taken over by Theater an der Wien,

which draws from its carefully selected young
ensemble to cast six or seven operas each year.
Though artistic direction has changed hands, the
Kammeroper still makes its home in a tiny Jugendstil
theatre on the Fleischmarkt, which brings the action
up close and personal. Its focus is on rarities and
works that aren't likely to be included in the repertoire of the bigger houses, such as Handel's *Rinaldo*
and Ravel's *L'heure espagnole*.

★ Konzerthaus

*1, Lothringerstrasse 20 (box office 242 002,
information 242 00-100, www.konzerthaus.at).
U4 Stadtpark or tram 2, D.* **Open** *Box office
9am-7.45pm Mon-Fri; 9am-1pm Sat & 45mins
before performance.* **Tickets** *vary.* **Map** p251 F8.
The Konzerthaus is a formidable complex that
hosts around 750 world-class performances each
season. Its main spaces, which architecturally
combine historicist, secessionist and art nouveau
styles, comprise the Grosser Saal, Mozartsaal and
Schubertsaal. The Berio Hall was added in 2001, and
its modern design provides a compatible setting for
contemporary and chamber music offerings.

The venue also contains three further rooms, as
well as a much-lauded restaurant. Less conservative in its programming than the Musikverein, it
often ventures into jazz, world music, and even pop
and rock. The Wiener Symphoniker and Wiener
Philharmoniker both play here, along with numerous other orchestras and ensembles, while contemporary classical music takes centre stage for four
weeks in autumn (usually November), when the
Konzerthaus shares the staging of Wien Modern,

Konzerthaus.

Vienna's premier festival of new music. It's dedicated to promoting post-1945 compositions, and each year shines the spotlight on world-renowned contemporary composers and performers such as Péter Eötvös or the Arditti Quartet. Look out, too, for the Rising Stars concert series, which showcases young European talent.

★ Musikverein

1, Bösendorferstrasse 12 (505 8190, www. musikverein.at). U1, U2, U4 Karlsplatz or tram 1, 2, D. **Open** *Box office* Late July-Aug 10am-1pm daily. Sept-June 9.30am-3.30pm daily & 1hr before performance. **Map** p251 E8.

If you've ever joined the millions worldwide who watch the New Year's Day concert on TV, you've already seen the Vienna Philharmonic's unofficial main home, the opulent Musikverein. The magnificent, golden main hall is more than just a beautiful space, it's also an acoustic miracle. The ceiling above its 1,750 seats isn't joined to the walls, but hangs freely to allow for better vibration; there's also an entire room underneath that polished wooden floor for the same reason. The smaller 660-seat Brahms-Saal is no less ornate, and is used for chamber concerts and recitals. Four further halls, prosaically named after the materials used in their construction, were built beneath the building in 2001-2004 to designs by Austrian architect Wilhelm Holzbauer. The Gläserner Saal sometimes hosts more modern concerts – as well as performances by the accomplished students of the University of Music and Performing Arts Vienna.

Tickets to Vienna Philharmonic concerts here are among the hottest in town. For the three famous end-of-year concerts, demand is such that the opportunity to buy tickets is drawn by lot at the beginning of the year. Register on the website in January and February; if you're successful, you'll be notified by email by the end of March.

Radiokulturhaus

4, Argentinierstrasse 30A (box office 501 70-377, café 503 74 04, backstage tour 877 99 99, http:// radiokulturhaus.orf.at). U1 Taubstummengasse. **Open** *Box office* 4-7pm Mon-Fri & 1hr before performance. *Café* 9am-midnight Mon-Fri; subject to performance times Sat, Sun. **Map** p247 E9.

Part of a radio broadcasting complex, the Radiokulturhaus has a wonderfully eclectic programme. Performance spaces include the Grosser Sendesaal, home to the Vienna Radio Symphony Orchestra; the Klangtheater Ganzohr ('all ears'), now used mostly for radio plays; and the Radio Café. The Grosser Sendesaal hosts everything from classical, jazz and modern music to cabaret, exhibitions and spoken theatre. The Radio Café is poorly designed, but offers a varied mixture of evening entertainment in a laid-back atmosphere, including a small outdoor dining area in the courtyard.

Schlosstheater Schönbrunn

13, Schloss Schönbrunn, Schönbrunner Schlossstrasse (0664 111 1600, www.musik-theater-schoenbrunn.at). U4 Schönbrunn. **Open** *Box office* from 1hr before performance.

Staatsoper.

ARTS & ENTERTAINMENT

Opened in 1749 to entertain the court of Maria Theresa, this is the oldest working theatre in Vienna, and the closest you'll come to the inside of a gilded music box. Both Haydn and Mozart conducted their own works here, and Napoleon caught a couple of performances in 1809 while in town doing a bit of conquering. Nowadays, it's rented out to a variety of ensembles and interested parties, including the nearby University of Music and Performing Arts, who put on three to four operas per year.

★ Staatsoper

1, Herbert von Karajan Platz 1 (51 444-2250, tours 51 444-2606, www.wiener-staatsoper.at). U1, U2, U4 Karlsplatz or tram 1, 2, D. **Open** *Box office* from 1hr before performance. **Map** p250 E7.
Many men have overseen this pinnacle of musical and operatic achievement over the years – including great conductors such as Richard Strauss, Karl Böhm, Clemens Krauss and Herbert von Karajan. It was Gustav Mahler, director from 1897 to 1907, who left the most significant mark on the Staatsoper, simultaneously changing opera itself in ways that are now taken for granted. Among his radical innovations were dimming the audience lighting during the performance, shortening intermissions to 15-20 minutes and seating late arrivals only after the prologue or first intermission.

Designed by architects August Siccardsburg and Eduard van der Null, the Staatsoper was built in the 1860s. The neo-Renaissance-style structure initially met with ferocious criticism from the Viennese, who called it the 'sunken crate' and the 'stone turtle'.

Siccardsburg never designed again and died of a weakened heart; Van der Null killed himself. Neither lived to see the opera house officially opened, on 25 May 1869, with a performance of *Don Giovanni*. However, the citizenry eventually took the building to its heart – so much so that after 1945, when the Staatsoper had been almost completely destroyed, they painstakingly reconstructed it. During the reconstruction, the Staatsoper company took up residence in the Theater an der Wien, where the legendary Vienna Mozart Ensemble came into being.

The Staatsoper has one of the largest opera repertoires in the world, staging around 50 productions each year. It is achieved thanks to a combination of a long season (Sept-June) and a rotation system that calls for a different opera most nights of the week. This occasionally plays havoc with the quality of the performances, with limited rehearsal times and heavy physical demands on the singers. Such Wagnerian-scale pressures are rumoured to have been the among the reasons for the abrupt resignations in 2014 of the Opera's artistic director, Franz Welser-Möst, followed soon after by French conductor Bertrand de Billy, both of whom cited irreconcilable artistic differences with Dominique Meyer, the Opera's general director since 2010. Despite the mêlée, the dust seems to have settled, and under Meyer's leadership the house is mostly sticking to the tried-and-true formula that helped make previous general director Ioan Holender the longest serving in the Opera's history: a repertoire built on grand opera evergreens presented by a parade of high-profile singers and conductors.

One of the biggest names remains Russian-born star soprano Anna Netrebko, who has become a darling of the Austrian public both for her vocal prowess and for her having adopted Austrian citizenship. No matter who's singing, the Wiener Philharmoniker, under the stage name 'Das Orchester der Wiener Staatsoper', provides a luscious accompaniment from the pit.

Good seats go very quickly, and often the only way to get a ticket is by buying one from the touts. Another option, for those with strong legs, is a standing-room ticket. Tours of the building run almost daily and are available in seven languages.

★ Theater an der Wien

6, Linke Wienzeile 6 (58 830-660, tickets 588 85, www.theater-wien.at). U1, U2, U4 Karlsplatz or bus 59A. **Open** *Box office* 10am-7pm daily. **Map** p250 D8.
This 1,200-seat treasure is famous for hosting the premières of Beethoven's *Fidelio* (1805) and Strauss Jr's *Die Fledermaus* (1874) and *Wiener Blut* (1899). Beethoven actually lived here during preparations for the presentation of his only opera. Since its opening in June 1801, the theatre has also seen many performances of *The Magic Flute* (if not the première of that piece, as is often claimed). From 1983 to 2005, it was part of the Vereinigte Bühnen Wien company, which used it mainly as a venue for large-scale musicals. In 2006, the theatre returned to being a permanent opera house with an inaugural concert conducted by Plácido Domingo. It concentrates its considerable energies on staging a different première every month, followed by five or six performances of each. With a smaller space and lower public profile, it fills the gap left by the grand opera-oriented Staatsoper by focusing mainly on less-performed, smaller-scale works such as Gluck's *Iphigénie en Aulide* and Richard Strauss' *Capriccio*. It also stages a varied opera in concert cycle featuring Baroque and early classical period masterpieces. The 2015-16 season was dubbed the Jubilee to mark the venue's tenth year back in the opera business.

Volksoper

9, Währingerstrasse 78 (51 444-3318, www.volksoper.at). U6 Währingerstrasse-Volksoper or tram 40, 41, 42. **Open** *Box office* 8am-6pm Mon-Fri; 9am-noon Sat, Sun; 1hr before performance. **Map** p242 C4.
Under the directorship of Robert Meyer, the Volksoper continues to fill its traditional role as Vienna's flagship operetta house, offering a multitude of performances in that genre every year. Added to this are musicals, modern dance, children's shows and concerts by the Volksoper orchestra, as well as some operas. It certainly takes its role as 'the People's Opera House' to heart, with plenty of variety and relatively inexpensive tickets which aren't normally too hard to obtain; neither does it shy away from more populist programming whether it be *Carmen* or *The Sound of Music*. The standard here

is generally high, even if the occasional evening disappoints. The house itself has a functional exterior and a plain, almost astringent interior, somewhat relieved by the plush red decor. The acoustics are also a little dry, especially at the sides. Don't even think of sitting in the back row of a box; you'll hear little and see nothing. The 72 standing-room tickets are a bargain, and under-27s can buy unsold tickets 20 minutes before the performance for as little as €6.

Other venues

Arnold Schönberg Center

3, Palais Fanto, Zaunergasse 1-3 (712 1888, www.schoenberg.at). Tram 71, D. **Open** 10am-5pm Mon-Fri. **Map** p251 F8.
Opened in April 1998, the non-profit Schönberg Center encompasses an archive, library, concert hall, exhibition hall and seminar rooms. Its mission is to promote interest in – and knowledge of – Schönberg and the Second Viennese School of the early 20th century, and related music. The 200-seat hall is used for a plethora of events, including concerts. Performances sometimes include a free pre-lecture or discussion.

Bösendorfer-Saal im Mozarthaus

1, Domgasse 5 (504 6651-311, www.boesendorfer. com). U1, U3 Stephansplatz. **Open** *Box office* 10am-7pm daily. **Map** p251 F7.
In October 2010, the Bösendorfer concert hall moved from its previous location in the 4th district to the vaulted cellar of the Mozarthaus. Check the website for details of upcoming performances.

Odeon

2, Taborstrasse 10 (216 5127, www.odeon-theater. at). U1, U4 Schwedenplatz or tram 21. **Open** *Box office* from 6pm until start of performance. *By phone* 10am-6pm Mon-Fri. **Map** p251 F6.
Used for everything from classical concerts to theatre, the Odeon is the former 19th-century corn exchange. Although it lacks permanent seating or a stage, the voluminous space makes a big impression. The in-house Serapions Ensemble mixes physical theatre, dance and visual arts.

ENSEMBLES AND ASSOCIATIONS

Concentus Musicus Wien

This is one of the world's premier ensembles for *Alte Musik*, early to Baroque music from the 13th to the 18th centuries. It's impossible to separate the Concentus Musicus from its founder and musical guru, Nikolaus Harnoncourt (www.harnoncourt. info). Together, the man and the group have succeeded in making once dusty music come alive on original instruments. You can catch them at the **Musikverein** (*see p164*) perhaps half a dozen times during the year.

Klangforum Wien.

Jeunesses Musicales Austria
*Konzerthaus 1, Lothringerstrasse 20 (505 6356,
www.jeunesse.at). U4 Stadtpark or tram 2, D.*
Ticket office *1, Bösendorferstrasse 12,
in the Musikverein building (505 63 56).*
Open 9am-7.30pm Mon-Fri. **Map** p251 F8.
Jeunesses organises more than 600 concerts and
events throughout Austria every year. Its primary
aim is to provide music for young people, but its concert programmes, presented in Vienna at various venues including the Musikverein and the Konzerthaus,
are of such exceptional quality that music lovers of
all ages vie for tickets, which sell out quickly.

Klangforum Wien
5, Diehlgasse 51 (521 67-0, www.klangforum.at).
Since it was founded in 1985 by Swiss composer
Beat Furrer, this high-profile soloist ensemble has
become a leading force in New Music worldwide.
Klangforum Wien's democratic approach encour-
ages co-operation between interpreters, conductors
and composers, a policy mirrored in the stylistic
variety of its eclectic repertoire. This ranges from
modern classical music to works by up-and-coming
young composers, with space for experimental jazz
and free improvisation.

ORF Radio-Symphonieorchester Wien (RSO)
*Radiokulturhaus, 4, Argentinier Strasse 30A
(501 01 18420, www.rso.orf.at).*
The Vienna Radio Symphony Orchestra has a
penchant for unearthing the new, the unknown or
the almost forgotten – which is both its forte and
the reason for its relative obscurity. However, the
RSO's high level of musicianship, combined with
players' awareness that 'this is being recorded',
makes for excellent performances. Though the
Wiener Symphoniker has traditionally been considered Vienna's second orchestra after the Wiener
Philharmoniker, these days that's debatable. The
RSO's more youthful ensemble, paired with dynamic
younger conductors, generate real musical electric-
ity that perhaps the more senior Symphoniker sometimes lacks. The rising star Cornelius Meister is now
at the helm, having taken over from Bertrand de Billy
as chief conductor in 2010. You'll find the RSO performing at the Musikverein, the Konzerthaus and as
resident opera orchestra at the Theater an der Wien.

Wiener Philharmoniker
*Musikverein, 1, Bösendorfer Strasse 12
(505 6525, www.wienerphilharmoniker.at).*
Founded in 1842, the 140-strong Vienna Philharmonic
Orchestra has financed and managed itself since
1908. This has allowed it the freedom to make deci-
sions uninfluenced by contemporary fashions and,
in the past, it has given up sizeable state subsidies to
retain its right to run things as it sees fit. In the 1990s
and early 2000s, the Orchestra became a source of
controversy for its apparent institutionalised sexism

ARTS & ENTERTAINMENT

Wiener Kursalon.

– there were no women among its permanent players until 1997. Since then, the gender balance has been slowly changing. As well as presenting a full season of concerts between September and mid June at the Musikverein, including the New Year's Day Concert, the Philharmonic performs each summer at the Salzburg Festival, tours widely, and is the house orchestra of the Staatsoper, under the alternative title of Orchester der Wiener Staatsoper.

▶ *The Philharmoniker's history is documented in two rooms at the Haus der Musik (see p46).*

Wiener Sängerknaben (Vienna Boys' Choir)

2, Obere Augartenstrasse 1 (216 3942, www.wsk.at). One of Vienna's most prestigious exports, these little cherubs in blue and white sailor suits are the darlings of Austria. The boys' musicianship and general professionalism are at an indisputably high level, but at times they seem a bit jaded. It's scarcely any wonder, with their schedule. Since 2012, the choir has made its home in the Muth (short for Musik und Theater), located in Vienna's Augarten. In addition to regular shows there, you can hear their dulcet tones at the Burgkapelle (*see p54*), where the ensemble provides the music for the chapel's Sunday services from mid September to the end of June.

Wiener Symphoniker

6, Lehárgasse 11 (589 7951, www.wiener-symphoniker.at). The Wiener Symphoniker might be in the shadow of the Philharmoniker in an international sense, but it has a long and impressive history. It presents some 200 concerts a year, mostly in the Konzerthaus and the Musikverein. Dividing his time between the Symphoniker and the Opéra National de Paris, music director Philippe Jordan serves as the principal conductor, sharing the podium with numerous high-profile guests.

INDEPENDENT OPERA

None of the *Freigruppen*, or independent companies, has a permanent home. Here are the two most prominent and easily accessible.

NetZZeit

6, Sandwirtgasse 16 (224 33 68590, www.netzzeit.at). Founded in 1984, NetZZeit ('Network Time') is dedicated to promoting and presenting contemporary works. Its biennial festival, Out of Control, takes place in January and February.

Neue Oper Wien

2, Herminengasse 10/23 (218 2567, www.neueoperwien.at). Artistic director Walter Kobéra runs a tight ship at New Opera Vienna. It puts on fine, full-scale productions of modern pieces, often working in tandem with more established groups.

MUSICAL THEATRE

Raimund Theater

6, Wallgasse 18-20 (tickets 58885, www.musical vienna.at). U6 Gumpendorfer Strasse. **Open** *Box office* 2-6pm daily & 1hr before show. **Map** p246 B9.

The Raimund opened in 1893 as a theatre for the middle classes in what was then an outer suburb of Vienna. Only spoken drama was presented until 1908 when director Wilhelm Karczag introduced opera and operetta, but now the Raimund Theater is known for its Broadway-style musicals. Its sister venue is the Ronacher (Seilerstätte 9, www.musical vienna.at), home to German-language stagings of shows such as *Evita*, *The Producers* and *Phantom of the Opera*.

SACRED MUSIC

Sunday Mass is an excellent way to combine music and sightseeing; several of the city's churches host performances and recitals. As well as the **Burgkapelle**, **Augustinerkirche**, **Michaelerkirche**, **Minoritenkirche**, **Peterskirche**, **Ruprechtskirche** and **Stephansdom** are all worth a visit.

A newer addition to Vienna's musical landscape are the concerts presented under the dome of the impressive Baroque **Karlskirche** at the southern end of Karlsplatz. Just a stone's throw from where Mozart died, the church provides an appropriately lofty setting for the composer's dramatic swansong, his *Requiem*, which is performed on period instruments every Saturday evening, mid March to early December.

The church of the University of Music and Performing Arts, **St Ursula**, also has an event at least once a week, with liturgical music, organ performances and choral concerts run by the university's department of church music.

Burgkapelle
1, Schweizerhof (533 9927, www.hofmusik kapelle.gv.at). U3 Herrengasse or tram 1, 2, D. **Open** *Box office* 11am-3pm Mon-Thur; 11am-1pm, 3-5pm Fri; 8-8.30am Sun. **Map** p250 D8.
The Wiener Sängerknaben (Vienna Boys' Choir) performs here every Sunday and on religious holidays at 9.15am (except late June to mid September). Tickets must be booked in advance.

TRADITIONAL VIENNA

Hofburg: Festsaal, Zeremoniensaal & Redoutensaal
Festsaal & Zeremoniensaal *1, Heldenplatz.* **Redoutensaal** *1, Josefsplatz.* **All** *587 2552, www.hofburgorchester.at. U3 Herrengasse.* **Performances** *May-Oct* 8.30pm Tue, Thur, Sat. **Map** p250 D7.
Artists drawn from Vienna's major orchestras and opera companies perform in the historic rooms of the Habsburgs' imperial palace, producing by far the best music at these venues. There are two box offices (one for each Platz), which open an hour before each concert, but it's best to book online or by phone. None of the halls has numbered seating, so get there early.

Wiener Kursalon
1, Johannesgasse 33 (512 5790, www. soundofvienna.at). **Open** 8.30am-8.30pm daily. **Performances** 8.15pm daily. **Map** p251 E7.
The Wiener Kursalon once hosted the famous promenade concerts of the Strauss dynasty. The Salonorchester Alt Wien performs a Strauss and

Mozart programme here, which includes ballet and operetta, daily from late March to the end of February. The building itself is also worth a look.

Theatre

The **Burgtheater**, **Akademietheater** and **Kasino am Schwarzenbergplatz** are all under the management of the venerable Burgtheater. Tickets can be bought at its ticket office, and also through the **Österreichische Bundestheaterkassen** (*see p162*).

The Viennese are generally disdainful of spectacle, so global blockbuster touring troupes are generally confined to peripheral venues. At the core of the scene is reliable, well-crafted theatre, ranging from classical to experimental.

Every month, the tourist information office puts out a programme of cultural events (www. events.wien.info), but the most comprehensive listings and reviews are in weekly paper *Falter*.

Most of the city's theatres close in July and August. The **Wiener Festwochen** (*see p28*), from mid May through June, is the highlight of the calendar: an outstanding selection of international premières and contemporary productions of new and classic works.

For English-language theatre, check out the improvisations by the English Lovers group (www.english-lovers.com) at **Theater in der Drachengasse** and **Ensembletheater**. There's also a large enough expat audience to have supported the **English Theatre** since 1963. The International Theatre, though, closed in 2012.

MAIN VENUES

Akademietheater

3, Lisztstrasse 1 (info 51444-4140, tickets 51444-4740, www.burgtheater.at). U4 Stadtpark or tram 71, D. **Box office** *Burgtheater (see below).* **Map** p251 F8.

The 500-seat Akademietheater was taken over by the Burgtheater in 1922 to stage chamber works. Visitors to the city often overlook the Akademietheater in favour of the more famous Burgtheater, but visually and acoustically it's a thrilling venue for drama, albeit without the pomp of the big house. It tends to stage more contemporary and interesting works, with a programme that often includes German-language premières of plays by a global array of talent.

★ Burgtheater

1, Universitätsring 2 (info 51444-4145, tickets 51444-4440, www.burgtheater.at). U2, U3 Volkstheater or U2 Schottentor or tram 1, 2, D. **Box office** 8am-6pm Mon-Fri; 9am-noon Sat, Sun; from 1hr before performance. **Map** p250 D6.

The great standard bearer of classical theatre in the German-speaking world since its creation in 1741, *Die Burg* moved to the Ring in 1888. Like many Ringstrasse edifices, the building itself was blighted by functional defects and had to be remodelled shortly after completion to improve its appalling acoustics and poor visibility. A joke at the time claimed, 'In parliament you can't hear anything, in the Rathaus you can't see anything and in the Burgtheater you can neither see nor hear anything.' It also had to be completely rebuilt after a bombing raid in March 1945, followed by a fire a month later.

The theatre's outstanding ensemble is a magnet for innovative directors whose reinterpretations of classic works, and treatments of the latest plays by Austrian heavyweights such as Peter Handke and Elfriede Jelinek, make for compelling drama. Its main hall accommodates more than 1,000 spectators, while the 60-seater Vestibül space in one of the wings is a launching pad for young directorial talent.

▶ *No regular performances are held in July and August, but guided tours are available in English and German at 3pm. The rest of the year, English-language tours take place Friday to Sunday, with German-language tours and English summaries during the rest of the week, always at 3pm.*

Kasino am Schwarzenbergplatz

1, Schwarzenbergplatz 1 (51444-4830). Tram 1, 2, D. **Box office** *Burgtheater (see p170).* **Map** p251 F8.

Many young directors have launched their careers in this most extravagant of small theatre spaces; the marble-clad Kasino am Schwarzenbergplatz was originally the residence of Franz Josef's depraved brother, Archduke Ludwig Viktor. With seating for a maximum of 200, it has been used by the Burgtheater since the 1970s for experimental work.

★ Schauspielhaus

9, Porzellangasse 19 (317 0101, www. schauspielhaus.at). U4 Rossauer Lände or tram D or bus 40A. **Box office** 4-6pm Mon-Sat & from 2hrs before performance. **Map** p243 D4.

Since taking over from Barrie Kosky and Airan Berg in 2007, former Burgtheater dramaturge Andreas Beck has created quite a buzz around the Schauspielhaus.

The focus is on new works by up-and-coming talents, performed by an eight-strong ensemble of resident actors, joined by the occasional guest.

Theater in der Josefstadt

8, Josefstädter Strasse 26 (42 700-300, www. josefstadt.org). U2 Rathaus. **Box office** 10am-performance Mon-Fri; 1pm-performance Sat, Sun. **Map** p246 C6.

Built in 1788 and subject to a neoclassical flourish by Josef Kornhäusel in 1822, this is one of Vienna's oldest theatres. It was immortalised in a scene from *The Third Man* where Joseph Cotten dozes off while watching Harry Lime's girlfriend perform in an operetta. This reputation for boredom has lingered, despite the efforts of artistic director Herbert Föttinger. The raising of the ornate chandeliers as the lights dim is impressive, while programming runs from classic Chekhov to Strindberg. The theatre's second space is the Kammerspiele (Rotenturmstrasse 20) which puts on musicals such as *Ladies Night*, an adaptation of *The Full Monty*.

Volkstheater

7, Neustiftgasse 1 (information 52111-0, tickets 52111-400, 422, www.volkstheater.at). U2, U3 Volkstheater or tram 49 or bus 48A. **Box office** 10am-start of performance Mon-Sat. **Map** p250 D7.

When the Volkstheater was built in 1889, its brief was to present German dramatists to a wider public than the Burgtheater. Today's repertoire mixes Austrian and German classics with West End-type productions and works in translation such as *Harold and Maude* and *Misery*. The venue was renamed the 'Strength Through Joy Theatre' by the Nazis, and

Burgtheater.

current director Michael Schottenberg incurred the wrath of the heritage authorities when he dismantled the so-called Hitlerzimmer, a reception room prepared for the Führer (although he never actually set foot in it). It's now used for discussions, monologues and chamber pieces related to the period.

SMALLER VENUES

For details of the **Odeon**, *see p166*.

3raum – Anatomietheater

3, Beatrixgasse 11-17 (0699 192 632 27, www. 3raum.or.at). U4 Stadtpark or tram O. **Map** p248 G7.
Back in 2006, the operating theatres of the former faculty of veterinary science morphed into an atmospheric off-scene location. Masterminded by Hubsi Kramar, an influential figure on the Viennese scene, the 'three-room theatre' is a broad forum that features drama, cabaret and live music. It also rents out space to a variety of groups and performers, holds film screenings, and has an agreeable bar.

★ Brut Wien

Konzerthaus *3, Lothringer Strasse 20. U4 Stadtpark or tram D.* **Box office** 4.30-7pm Mon-Sat. **Map** p251 F8.
Künstlerhaus *1, Karlsplatz 5 . U1, U2, U4 Karlsplatz or tram 2, 2, D.* **Box office** 4.30-7pm Mon-Sat & 1hr before performance. **Map** p251 E8.
Both *587 8774 (10am-5pm Mon-Fri), www.brut-wien.at.*
The former Dietheater Wien, relaunched as Brut Wien, is run by dynamic Berliners Haiko Pfost and Thomas Frank. It operates from two small theatres at the Konzerthaus and the Künstlerhaus (capacity 80 and 200 respectively). The wide-ranging programme takes in lots of interdisciplinary shenanigans and international collaborations.

★ English Theatre

8, Josefsgasse 12 (402 12 60-0, www.english theatre.at). U2 Rathaus or tram 2. **Box office** *Performance days* 10am-7.30pm Mon-Fri; 5-7pm Sat. *Non-performance days* 10am-5pm Mon-Fri. **Map** p246 C7.
The most venerable establishment of its kind in continental Europe, the English Theatre was set up by husband-and-wife team, Austrian director Franz Schafranek and American actress Ruth Brinkmann, in 1963. After moving home several times, it settled in Josefsgasse a decade later. Over the course of half a century, it has attracted the likes of Leslie Nielsen, Joan Fontaine and the lead actors from *Dallas*. Schafranek and Brinkmann passed away in the 1990s, after earning an OBE and MBE respectively. With daughter Julia in place as artistic director since 1997, works such as *Proof* by David Auburn and Edward Albee's *The Goat* had their European premières here. In general, though, the repertoire tends to play it safe with works such as *Cat on a Hot Tin Roof*.

Tanzquartier Wien.

Rabenhof

3, Rabengasse 3 (712 82 82, www.rabenhof.at). U3 Kardinal Nagl Platz or bus 77A. **Box office** 2-6pm Tue-Fri. **Map** p248 H9.
Located in the enormous, 1920s Rabenhof ('Raven's Court'), which was renovated and reopened in 2008, this theatre hosts concerts, stand-up and popular cabaret-style performances, involving an irreverent mixture of trash, intellectualism and agit prop. The Rabenhof's programming ranges from lowbrow to highbrow in the blink of an eye – not everything works, but there's a lot to like.

★ TAG (Theater an der Gumpendorfer Strasse)

6, Gumpendorfer Strasse 67 (586 5222, www. dastag.at). U3 Neubaugasse or U4 Pilgramgasse or bus 13A, 14A, 57A. **Box office** 4pm-start of performance. **Map** p246 C8.
Now under artistic director Gernot Plass, who took over from Margit Mezgolich in 2013, this dynamic theatre can look forward to city funding at least until the end of 2017. Along with shows produced by its versatile in-house ensemble, the theatre hosts several guest productions a year. Young writers are supported; improvised theatre is another major strand.

Theater in der Drachengasse

1, Drachengasse 2 & Fleischmarkt 22 (513 1444, www.drachengasse.at). U1, U4 Schwedenplatz. **Box office** 3.30-7pm Tue-Sat. **Map** p251 F6.
This tiny space presents avant-garde chamber works in various languages. The bar also hosts some interesting events – from concerts to English-language improvised drama, courtesy of the itinerant English Lovers group who appear here regularly.

ARTS & ENTERTAINMENT

Theater der Jugend
Renaissancetheater 7, Neubaugasse 36.
U3 Neubaugasse or bus 13A. **Map** p246 C8.
Theater der Jugend 7, Neubaugasse 38.
U3 Neubaugasse or bus 13A. **Map** p246 C8.
Theater im Zentrum 1, Liliengasse 3.
U1, U3 Stephansplatz. **Map** p247 E7.
All 521 10, www.tdj.at. **Box office** (Theater der Jugend) 9am-5pm Mon-Thur; 9am-4pm Fri; 1hr before start of performance.

Vienna's Youth Theatre is in fine fettle, with two houses, one office and a packed programme of German-language plays and musicals: a terrific version of The 39 Steps, perhaps, or a musical adaptation of Kipling's Just So Stories. The Renaissancetheater generally runs productions for 6-12s, while performances at the Theater im Zentrum are for teenagers. With some 47,000 season ticket-holders, this is one of the largest ventures of its kind in Europe.

Werk X
Werk X 12, Oswaldgasse 35A (535 32 00).
U6 Tscherttegasse. **Box office** 1hr before evening performance.
Werk X-Eldorado 1, Petersplatz 1. U1, U3
Stephansplatz. **Map** p251 E6.
Both www.werk-x.at.

Formed in 2014 after the closure of GARAGE X and the Stadtlabor Kabelwerk social centre, Werk X stages a raft of innovative theatre outside the mainstream. It uses two spaces: one in Oswaldgasse, the other at Petersplatz. There's no resident company as such – directors Ali Abdullah and Harald Posch work on co-productions with guests 'from Europe and beyond'.

Dance

The epicentre of Vienna's contemporary dance scene is the multifunctional **Tanzquartier Wien** (**TQW**). Located in the **MuseumsQuartier**, it runs a densely packed, rigorous and experimental programme of performances, theoretical discussions, interdisciplinary projects and training for young professional dancers.

More traditional ballet is provided by the **Vienna State Ballet**, one of the world's top companies, which performs at the Staatsoper and Volksoper. Former Paris Opéra Ballet star dancer Manuel Legris, artistic director since 2010, puts together an ambitious programme.

An active fringe scene of local companies keeps dance on the programme of smaller venues. **Brut Wien** (see p172) hosts the fine Imagetanz festival of small contemporary dance works every March, while **ImPulsTanz** (mid July to mid August, see p29) is a wide-ranging international dance festival.

Tanzquartier Wien
7, Museumsplatz 1 (581 3591, www.tqw.at).
U2 Museumsquartier or U2, U3 Volkstheater or tram 49. **Box office** 9am-8pm Mon-Fri; 10am-8pm Sat & 1-2hrs before performance.
Map p250 D7.

Vienna's first facility dedicated to dance organises ambitious local and international experimental performance. It usually runs from Thursday to Saturday, changing almost every week. Performances take place in Halle G, in the Kunsthalle building next to the MUMOK. Dance workshops and symposia are held in the TQW studio spaces near the Leopold Museum.

Escapes & Excursions

Escapes & Excursions

It's not difficult to leave the Austrian capital behind – within an hour or less, you can be enjoying some breathtaking stretches of countryside. Closest of all are the Vienna Woods, the Wienerwald, which provide a green belt for the city and some welcome respite for its inhabitants. North-west, the Danube Valley makes for a glorious escape with its fortresses, monasteries and terraced vineyards. The stretch running between the towns of Krems and Melk, known as the Wachau, is particularly bucolic – a designated UNESCO World Heritage Site. For a more rugged landscape, the last flourish of the Alps is an outdoor paradise. Semmering is a popular destination, thanks to its historic and spectacular railway, cross-country trails, grand hotels and skiing for all levels and ages. There's a steam engine at nearby Schneeberg and you'll find floodlit pistes, panoramic gondolas and mountain huts serving alpine treats all close to hand.

GETTING STARTED

Many of the destinations described in this chapter are easily accessible via Austria's excellent public transport system, or even by bike. For an overview of possible excursions, consult the Austrian National Tourist Office (www.austria.info). Detailed information about specific areas is available from the regional tourist offices listed in this chapter.

For those interested in venturing further afield, the Czech Republic, Hungary, Slovakia and Slovenia are all within striking distance. In summer, one very pleasant option is to take a boat from Vienna to Bratislava or Budapest – or to the Wachau. Bicycles are allowed, but passengers should state their intention to bring them aboard when booking a ticket.

For more on seasonal boat services, public transport and driving in Austria, *see pp223-224* **Getting Around**.

Vienna Woods & Around

The Vienna Woods – the Wienerwald – inspired the likes of Schubert, Beethoven, Mozart, Strauss and Schönberg. They still make Viennese hearts sing, the capital's citizens enjoying the luxury of protected natural reserves so close. Declared a UNESCO Biosphere in 2005, the woods cover an enormous area of forests, hills and wilderness – 1,250 square kilometres (483 square miles) in total – and form a verdant horseshoe running west from the Danube round to the city's southern reaches.

Along with the Prater and the Danube Island, the Wienerwald is a Viennese playground for hiking, mountain biking, picnicking and wine-fuelled *heurigen* outings: **Grinzing**, in the 19th district on the edge of the woods, is one of the best-known vine-lined villages.

Throughout the Wienerwald there are numerous hiking trails, along with more than 40 well-signed mountain biking paths (the woods are plastered with informative signposts). For details of hiking and cycling trails, and other outdoor activities such as horse-riding, consult the Vienna Woods tourist office.

The only downside of the surroundings is the presence of ticks carrying Lyme disease and central European encephalitis (*see p228*).

Getting there

The northern section of the woods is accessible by trams 38, 43 and D from the city centre.

Tourist information

Vienna Woods Tourist Office
Hauptplatz 11, Purkersdorf (02231 621 76, www.wienerwald.info). **Open** 9am-5pm Mon-Fri.

BADEN BEI WIEN

On the eastern edge of the Wienerwald, Baden was once the Empire's most fashionable spa resort. Today, it's a genteel provincial town, full of pastel-coloured Biedermeier and neoclassical buildings and fussy parks, bathed in the smell of its sulphurous waters. Illustrious residents included Beethoven, who composed his *Ninth Symphony* at Rathausgasse 10, and – an artist of rather different stripe – one Leopold von Sacher-Masoch, whose *Venus in Furs* is set in Baden.

Baden's small Hauptplatz is home to many of the town's historic monuments: the early 17th-century plague column, Kornhäusel's neoclassical Rathaus, and the Kaiserhaus which is the former summer residence of Franz II. North of Hauptplatz is the Kurpark, the old spa complex and gardens; its main bathhouse is now Austria's largest, most grandiose casino. This and Baden's hot thermal baths are the town's main attractions. Sample the waters at the splendidly updated **Römerthermebad** (Brusattiplatz 4, 02252 45 030, www.roemertherme.at), where the thermal bath is covered by a vast glass roof.

Baden is an ideal starting point for touring the southern and western Vienna Woods, but its hotels and restaurants can be rather pompous. Beethoven's favourite was the magnificent Grand Hotel Sauerhof, which had lost its allure long before it went bankrupt in 2014. For a modern, elegant four-star, try the **Hotel Herzoghof** (Kaiser Franz Ring 10, 02262 872 97, www.hotel-herzoghof.at; doubles €70-€130) located in a beautiful turn-of-the-century building in a magnificent location in front of the Kurpark and the Casino. **Hotel Schloss Weikersdorf** (Schlossgasse 9-11, 02252-483010, www.gerstner-hotels.austria-hotels.at; doubles €105-€150) has a spa, tennis courts and overlooks the famous rose gardens in Doblhoffpark.

Try to take a detour to the whimsically named **Gumpoldskirchen**, a few miles outside Baden. As the most famous wine-growing village south of Vienna, it's packed with great *heurigen*, especially on Wienerstrasse and Neustiftgasse. Otherwise take the stiffish trail walk to **Veigl Hütte** (Oberer Beethoven Wanderweg, 0699 170 620 26, www.veigl-huette.at) for views of the vineyards and Vienna.

Baden Bei Wien.

ESCAPES & EXCURSIONS

Getting there

Baden is around 26 kilometres (16 miles) south of Vienna. The Badner-Bahn tram, which departs from the middle of the Ringstrasse by the Staatsoper, takes around an hour.

Tourist information

Baden Tourist Office
Brusattiplatz 3 (02252 22600-600, www. tourismus.baden.at). **Open** *Oct-Apr* 9am-5pm Mon-Fri. *May-Sept* 9am-6pm Mon-Fri; 9am-2pm Sat.

HEILIGENKREUZ & MAYERLING

Driving from Baden to Heiligenkreuz will take you through the Helenental, the valley of St Helena. One of the most beautiful in the woods, it was the inspiration for Beethoven's *Pastoral Symphony*; Napoleon thought it so lovely he wanted to end his days here, although in fact he died in a different St Helena.

A few kilometres up the valley is Mayerling. It became a household name after a 1935 film dramatised the tragedy that took place in Crown Prince Rudolf's hunting lodge. In 1889, the heir to the throne and his 17-year-old mistress, Baroness Maria Vetsera, died in a mysterious double suicide. Emperor Franz Josef converted the lodge into a Carmelite convent of atonement so there's not much to see, but it's still popular with tourists. The cloister has just been renovated and is now complemented by a visitor centre and a restored tea pavilion. The **Hanner** (2258 23 78, www.hanner.cc, doubles €214-€248), romantically set amid the woods, is a hotel with an acclaimed restaurant and glorious gardens.

A few miles north-east stands the still-active Cistercian **Heiligenkreuz Abbey** (02258 87030, www.stift-heiligenkreuz.at). While it blends elements of the Romanesque, Gothic and Baroque periods, its name ('Holy Cross') derives from the relic of the cross that Leopold V brought here. A 150-year gap between the construction of the three Romanesque naves and the Gothic presbytery makes the church very interesting, and there are sculptures by Venetian artist Giovanni Giuliani. The chapter house, a Babenberg burial place, contains Austria's oldest ducal tomb, and the tragic Maria Vetsera is buried in the village cemetery. Entry to the abbey is by guided tour only (check website) and there is a decent on-site inn.

Getting there

Car is easiest, although buses that stop at Mayerling and Heiligenkreuz run from both Mödling and Baden. For details of services and timetables, see www.wienerlinien.at.

MÖDLING

Some 14 kilometres (eight miles) south of Vienna, and easily accessible via S-Bahn, the pretty town of Mödling is an idyll in the woods. Back in 1818, its quiet elegance, spa waters and forested landscape persuaded Beethoven to spend two summers in the **Hafner House** at Hauptstrasse 79 (02236 24159, www.museum-moedling.at/beethovenhaus, by appt) where he wrote the *Diabelli Variations* and *Missa Solemnis*. The other famous composer associated with Mödling is Arnold Schönberg. Between 1919 and 1925, he lived in an elegant house at Bernhardgasse 6 (712 18 88-31, www.schoenberg.at), which now hosts a small museum (10am-4pm Thur, or by appointment). It's used for concerts organised by the **Arnold Schönberg Center** (*see p166*).

Mödling's **Stadtbad** swimming baths (Badstrasse 25, 02236 22335) were built in 1928, but the Bauhaus style is diminished by the water slides and bouncy castles. The friendly **Babenbergerhof** (Babenbergergasse 6, 02236 22246, www.babenbergerhof.com) is a reliable and reasonably priced place to eat and stay.

From Mödling there are around 85 kilometres (53 miles) of hiking trails through woodland to **Burg Liechtenstein** (0650 680 3901, www.burgliechtenstein.eu; Mar-Oct 10am-4pm, tours hourly), a castle built by Hugo von Liechtenstein in 1136 and restored in the 19th century. Beside this magical folly is the neoclassical Liechtenstein Palace dating to 1820, now a retirement home.

In neighbouring Hinterbrühl is the **Seegrotte** (Grutschgasse 2a, 02236 26364, www.seegrotte.at), a gypsum mine that was accidentally flooded in 1912 during a blasting operation and is now Europe's largest underground lake. In World War II, the Nazis pumped the grotto dry and assembled the fuselage of the world's first jet fighter on the site. The complex takes in an underground banqueting hall and chapel, while boat trips transport you across the chilly waters. In the village, **Höldrichsmühle** (Gaadnerstrasse 34, 02236 262740, www.hoeldrichsmuehle.at; doubles €99-€144) is a 44-room hotel and restaurant set in an old mill. Schubert reputedly composed *The Linden Tree* here.

Off the B11 between Hinterbrühl and Heiligenkreuz lies the **Naturpark Sparbach** (02237 76 25, www.naturpark-sparbach.at; Apr-Oct 9am-6pm daily; admission €5, €3 under-15s) that has deer, wild boar and a good adventure playground. The 364 bus runs here from the bus station on Badstrasse in Mödling.

Getting there

On the S1 S-Bahn line, it takes around 30 minutes to get from Vienna Hauptbahnhof to Mödling.

Mödling.

Tourist information

Mödling Tourist Office
Kaiserin-Elisabethstrasse 1 (02236 400 125, www. moedling.at). **Open** 9am-12.30pm, 1.30-5pm Mon-Fri.

The Danube Valley

After numerous attempts to regulate its flow and alleviate the danger of flooding, the Danube at Vienna appears straight and relentless. But 100 kilometres (62 miles) upstream, the river follows a meandering course through the narrow **Wachau Valley**, forming a stunning ensemble of steeply terraced vineyards and hills crowned with fortresses, monasteries and ruins. A designated UNESCO World Heritage Site since 2000, the Wachau was commended for its 'outstanding riverine landscape' along the 35-kilometre (22-mile) stretch between **Melk** and **Krems**.

The 550 or so castles and fortified monasteries that overlook the Danube on its passage through Lower Austria testify to the river's importance as a trade route between east and west, and to the violent disputes it provoked.

The locals capitalised on the mild climate, planting vineyards, and the peach and apricot orchards that fill the valley. Visitors flock here in spring to admire the ethereal beauty of the blossoming apricots, and throughout the year to enjoy the Wachau's fine wines and restaurants.

KLOSTERNEUBURG

A short bus or train ride upriver from Vienna lies the historic town of Klosterneuburg, with the arresting, Augustinian **Stift Klosterneuburg** dating to the 12th century. Its Baroque domes and neo-Gothic spires, sandwiched between the Danube and the Vienna Woods, mark it out as one of Austria's oldest and wealthiest monasteries. During the reign of Karl IV, a Spanish-bred Habsburg, plans were made for a large imperial palace along the lines of Madrid's El Escorial, but funds ran out and only one of the four inner courtyards was semi-completed. You can wander through most of the monastery, but to see the Verdun Altarpiece in the Leopoldskapelle, an astonishing winged work completed in 1181 by Nicolas of Verdun, a guided tour is obligatory.

Other sights in Klosterneuburg include the **Essl Museum**, a collection of contemporary art, and the **Museum Gugging** in the grounds of the Gugging Psychiatric Clinic in the nearby village of Maria Gugging. On the way to Gugging, the bus passes the village of **Kierling**. It was here, at Hauptstrasse 187, that Franz Kafka died of tuberculosis in 1924 while correcting proofs of his short story collection *A Hunger Artist*. The small memorial room (533 8159, www.franzkafka.at/

home/open-door) with its books and photos, can be visited most Saturdays and some Sundays, 11am-3pm. Check the website for details.

Essl Museum

An der Donau-Au, 1 3400 Klosterneuburg (02243 370 50 150, www.essl.museum). S4 from Franz-Josefs Bahnhof or Spittelau to Weidling-Klosterneuburg or U4 Heiligenstadt, then bus 238, 239 or Hop-on Hop-off bus from Vienna Sightseeing (green line) from the Burgtheater/Rathaus stop. **Open** 10am-6pm Tue, Thur-Sun; 10am-9pm Wed. **Admission** €9; €6 reductions; free under-19s & all 6-9pm Wed. Founded by DIY barons, the Essl was a brave attempt to establish a private contemporary art museum outside Vienna in a high-quality setting. Facing mounting debts however, the Essl family announced their intention to sell the museum and its contents. In 2014, a buyer emerged, Hans Peter Haselsteiner, owner of construction giant STRABAG, who stumped up the €100 million required. While the museum continues to operate, Haselsteiner put 44 items from the collection up for sale at Christie's in 2014. They included important works by German artist Sigmar Polke and international figures such as Cindy Sherman and Louise Bourgeois, and netted around €60 million in what was Christie's most successful ever single owner sale. Some of its most stellar exhibits may have gone but it's still worth the trip to see some great works of post-war Austrian art and a handful of international gems.

Museum Gugging/Haus der Künstler

*Am Campus 23, 3400 Maria Gugging (02243
87087, www.gugging.org). U4 Heiligenstadt
or Klosterneuburg-Kierling train station then
bus 239.* **Open** *Oct-Apr* 10am-5pm Tue-Sun;
May-Sept 10am-6pm Tue-Sun. **Admission** €7;
€2.50-€5 reductions; free under-6s.

The resident Gugging artists' community in the
village of Maria Gugging is well known in the Art
Brut movement. The first exhibition here was held
in 1970, nearly two decades after psychiatrist Leo
Navratil, director of the Gugging Sanatorium &
Care Home, encouraged his patients to paint and
draw. The acclaimed results, by the likes of Johann
Hauser and August Walla, were labelled Art Brut.
This museum and commercial gallery, situated
on a hill overlooking the Vienna Woods, opened in
2006. Gugging still operates as a residential care
centre, now called the Haus der Künstler, the House
of Artists. Many of the works by current patients,
some suffering from chronic psychiatric illnesses or
mental disabilities, are astonishing.

Stift Klosterneuburg

*Stiftsplatz 1, 02243 411-0 (www.stift-klosterneuburg.
at). S-Bahn from Franz-Josefs Bahnhof to
Klosterneuburg-Kierling; or S-Bahn from Franz-
Josefs Bahnhof or Spittelau to Klosterneuburg-
Weidling, then walk.* **Open** 9am-6pm daily.
Admission €17; €6 reductions; free under-6s.

KREMS

The historic centre of Krems, 70 kilometres (43
miles) north-west of Vienna, marks the entrance to
the Wachau. Made up of three formerly separate
settlements – Krems, Und and Stein – it became a
wealthy wine-growing town in the 13th century.
This prosperity is evident from the well-appointed,
late-medieval and late-Gothic buildings such as
Pfarrkirche and Piaristenkirche.

In the town's atmospheric medieval quarter, the
main Steiner Landstrasse is a delightful parade of
Renaissance townhouses that periodically opens
to cobbled squares with views of the Danube. The
centrepiece is the 13th-century Minoritenkirche,
the oldest church of the mendicant Minorite order
north of the Alps. It now serves as the **Kremser
Klangraum** for sound installations and music
concerts during events such as the off-kilter
Donaufestival (www.donaufestival.at).

Stein also contains the Kremser Kunstmeile
('Art Mile') that runs parallel to the Danube
from Kloster Und to Steiner Landstrasse. Here,
you'll find museums and galleries such as the
Kunsthalle Krems (Franz-Zeller Platz 3, 02732
90 80 10, www.kunsthalle.at; open 10am-6pm
Tue-Sun), and the **Karikaturmuseum** (Steiner
Landstrasse 3A, 02732 90 80 20, www.karikatur
museum.at), among other institutions dedicated
to architecture and literature.

Krems has some good dining options. **Salzstadl** (Donaulände 32, 02732 70312; doubles €57) is a fine old *gasthaus* with live jazz and simple rooms to rent. In the small alleys above Steiner Landstrasse, delightful *heurigen* such as **Erich Hamböck** (Steinerk Kellergasse 31, 02732 84568) have views of the Danube and of the distant **Stift Göttweig** (02732 855 81-0, www.stiftgoettweig.or.at), a hilltop Benedictine monastery six kilometres (four miles) south of Krems. Although a monastery has occupied the site since 1083, it burned down in 1718; the splendid Baroque complex that now stands here was designed by Johann Lucas von Hildebrandt. Its restaurant (02732 85581-225) also has fine views, and serves wine from the monastery's estate. The monastery itself is closed to visitors from mid November until mid March.

Getting there

By car, take the A22 north out of Vienna, then follow the S5 westwards along the river to Krems – or take the A12 west out of Vienna, exit St Pölten, then follow the S33 to Krems. It's around an hour's drive. The train also takes about an hour, with regular services. On selected Sundays from May to October, the **DDSG** (*see p223*) boat service from Reichsbrücke bridge in Vienna to Dürnstein calls at Krems, taking five-and-a-half hours to get there. If you want to take the boat back, the timetable only allows for three hours ashore.

Tourist information

Krems Tourist Office
Utzstrasse 1 (02732 82676, www.krems.info). **Open** *Mid Oct-late Apr* 9am-5pm Mon-Fri. *Late Apr-mid Oct* 9am-6pm Mon-Fri; 11am-6pm Sat; 11am-4pm Sun.

FROM DÜRNSTEIN TO MELK

Nine kilometres (five miles) upriver from Krems, the tiny walled town of **Dürnstein**, with its striking powder-blue and white Baroque tower, is one of the Wachau's most idyllic. However, the town owes its good fortune to the fact that Richard the Lionheart was imprisoned in its now

Stift Melk.

ruined castle by Archduke Leopold V. This and the ensuing legend of Blondel (Richard's French minstrel), who discovered his master's whereabouts by singing his way through central Europe, have given Dürnstein a steady stream of British visitors since the dawn of modern tourism. It's a favourite spot for Austrians to tie the knot.

Excellent eating and comfortable rooms are available at the charming, family-run **Gasthof Sänger Blondel** (Dürnstein 64, 02711 2530, www.saengerblondel.at, doubles €110-€125). Just outside town, **Loibnerhof** (Unterloiben 7, 02732 82890-0, www.loibnerhof.at) has tables in the orchard, house specials, and wines from the family's estate and other local producers.

Six kilometres (four miles) further along the Danube is **Weissenkirchen**. As well as a gorgeous riverside location, a backdrop of terraced vineyards and a white-painted fortified church, the town has a lovely network of cobbled streets. On the main square, the **Wachaumuseum** (02715 2268; open Apr-Oct 10am-5pm Tue-Sun) – a display of folk arts and oil paintings of the Wachau – is housed in the 16th-century Teisenhoferhof. Meanwhile **Raffelsbergerhof** (02715 2201, www.raffelsbergerhof.at, open mid Apr-Nov, doubles €122-€148) is an atmospheric hotel in an old vaulted shipmaster's residence.

The picturesque village of **Spitz an der Donau** is another 6 kilometres upstream from Weissenkirchen. At the **Schifffahrtsmuseum** in the Baroque Schloss Erlahof (02713 22 46, www.schifffahrtsmuseum-spitz.at; open mid Apr-Nov), the show of Danube sailing craft gives an idea of life in pre-tourist Wachau. Wine is the lifeblood of Spitz, and in a good year the town's 2,000 inhabitants produce 56,000 litres of it. As a result, there's no shortage of *heurigen* here – try the streets of Radlbach and In der Spitz.

The town of **Melk** cowers in the shadow of its mighty abbey, **Stift Melk** (02752 5550, www.stiftmelk.at; open Mar, Apr, Oct, Nov 9am-4.30pm daily; May-Sept 9am-5.30pm daily; admission €12, €6-€7.50 reductions), perched on a cliff over the Danube. The abbey is huge, sprawling over 17,500 square metres (188,368 square feet); its side facade is more than a kilometre (0.6 miles) long. Once the residence of the Babenberg family, it has

ESCAPES & EXCURSIONS

been a Benedictine monastery since 1089. Master builder Jakob Prandtauer built the abbey in its present form in the 18th century; inside, the Marmorsaal (marble hall) and the library, with their high, tiered ceilings, are impressive.

Eating options include the **Stiftsrestaurant** (02752 52555) or pavilion café at the monastery, while the **Hotel-Restaurant Zur Post** (Linzer Strasse 1, 02752 523 45, www.post-melk.at; doubles €110-€128) is a solid option for food or accommodation, with free bikes for guests' use.

Five kilometres (three miles) outside Melk stands the magnificent **Schloss Schallaburg** (3382 Schallaburg, 02754 63170, www. schallaburg.at). The castle is a compendium of architectural styles (Romanesque, Gothic, Renaissance and Mannerist). Outside, children make a beeline for the adventure playground.

Getting there

Melk can be reached by train in 75mins from Vienna's Westbahnhof. For Dürnstein (served by Dürnstein-Oberloiben), Weissenkirchen or Spitz, you need to take a train then a bus; for route details and a journey planner, visit www.oebb.at.

By car, take the A1 for speed, or follow the smaller roads through the Danube Valley.

To get to Dürnstein, the **DDSG** seasonal Sunday boat service from Vienna (*see p182*) is another option. Several different companies also run services between Krems and Melk. See www.donau.com for a list.

Tourist information

Danube Lower Austria Tourist Office

Schlossgasse 3, Spitz (02713 2363, www.spitz-wachau.at). **Open** *Apr* 9am-noon, 1-4pm Mon-Sat. *May-Oct* 9am-12.30pm, 1.30-6pm Mon-Thur; 9am-12.30pm, 1.30-7pm Fri, Sat.
Tourist office in old *schloss*, providing information on the Nibelungenau valley that runs up to Melk, the Wachau and Krems.

Dürnstein Tourist Office

3601 Dürnstein (02711-219, www.duernstein.at). **Open** *Apr-Oct* 8am-noon Mon, Thur, Fri; 8am-noon, 1-7pm Tue.

Southern Alpine Region

Although the Alps peter out south of Vienna, snowy peaks are within easy reach. The border between Lower Austria and Styria, the last Alpine hiccup before the land flattens towards the great Hungarian plain, lies only 90 kilometres (60 miles) south of the city. The area is the source of

Vienna's top-notch drinking water and a magnificent outdoor amenity for city dwellers. The Viennese don their boots and lederhosen and set off early in the day to catch some rays on the slopes of **Rax**, **Schneeberg** and **Semmering**.

These three mountains are perfect for a spot of *wandern*. All three have trains, gondolas or ski lifts working year-round that will take you a fair way up the mountainside, while adventurous hikers and climbers can follow signposted trails. For alpine skiing, Semmering is equipped for day trippers. Schneeberg and Rax also have extensive cross-country trails.

SEMMERING

Until 1854, Semmering was an undisturbed mountain pass. Then Carl Ritter von Ghega's Semmering Railway succeeded in connecting this Alpine wilderness to Vienna. Never before had it been so easy to reach the mountains. Now, direct trains leave frequently from Hauptbahnhof. The first railway to become a UNESCO World Heritage site, the Semmering stretch is admired as a feat of engineering and for its functional beauty. The train meanders along a series of 31 viaducts and tunnels amid Alpine beauty.

In the years after the railway was constructed, Semmering – with its mild weather and stunning views of the mountains Schneeberg and Rax – gained in popularity. In 1882, the first villas were built on the edge of the mountain, and in 1889 the original 44-room Panhans was opened. By 1900, the Panhans had become a massive grand hotel. Those living it up here included Emperor Franz Josef, Austro-Hungarian aristocracy, plus writers, artists, actors and intellectuals from Europe and America. There's even a photograph of Josephine Baker riding a sled outside the hotel.

Requisitioned by the Nazis during World War II, the Panhans became popular with Rommel and Göring. After the war, Semmering never regained its place in society, and the hotel closed in 1969. However, in 1994 the **Panhans Grand Hotel** (Hochstrasse 32, 02664 8181, www.panhans.at; doubles €102-€220) relaunched, having been refurbished to something approaching its former glory. Since then, Semmering has blossomed. Thousands of well-marked walks start from both the Panhans and the **Panoramahotel Wagner** (Hochstrasse 62, 02664 2512, www.panorama hotel-wagner.at; doubles €106-€200). Smaller than the Panhans, the Wagner has wonderful views, Swedish-designed rooms and a top restaurant.

In winter, people descend on sedate Semmering for downhill and cross-country skiing at one of two ski areas. The 1,318-metre (4,326-foot) **Hirschenkogel** is within walking distance of all Semmering's hotels and has artificial snow and a floodlit piste, along with welcoming mountain huts. There's also a gentle children's slope.

The **Zauberberg** ('magic mountain') cable car takes you up the peak. In summer, there's a bike park, along with various hiking trails.

In Spital am Semmering, ten kilometres (six miles) further on, the less crowded **Stuhleck** (www.stuhleck.com) has over 20 kilometres (12 miles) of pistes and a floodlit run. The pistes are good for beginners. Cross-country ski routes can be obtained from the tourist office.

Semmering-Hirschenkogel

Semmering (02664 8038, snowline 02664 2575, www.zauberberg.at). **Open** *Pistes* 8.30am-4pm Mon-Fri; 8am-4pm Sat, Sun. Special evening sessions, see website. **Day pass** €12-€35; €6-€31.50 reductions; free under-5s.

Facilities include an eight-person gondola and a four-seater chairlift. Prices vary according to low or high season, weekday or weekend visit, with discounts on some days if you buy your day pass between 8am and 9am. See website for details.

MOUNT RAX

Mount Rax, at 2,007 metres (6,585 feet), is a great place to experience the Alps without having to travel too far from Vienna. It's well signposted and has an unusually large, 34-kilometre (21-mile) plateau, dotted with eight mountain huts.

You can get most of the way up Rax with little effort. Following the signs to the Rax-Seilbahn in Hirschwang, you reach the **Rax Gondola** (Reichenau-Hirschwang, 02666 52497, www.raxseilbahn.at), which climbs 1,547 metres (5,075 feet) in eight minutes. A 30-minute walk takes you to the **Ottohaus** at 1,644 metres (5,394 feet) for refreshment. For a more vigorous hike, drive beyond the Rax Gondola to Preiner Gscheid, where you can park and take the trail for a few hours towards **Karl Ludwighaus**, 1,804 metres (5,919 feet), then to the top of Mount Rax.

From Payerbach, you can travel the five kilometres (three miles) to Hirschwang on the **Höllentalbahn** (02666 524 2312, www.lokal bahnen.at/hoellentalbahn), one of the world's oldest functioning narrow-gauge railways.

Just above Payerbach is the chalet that architect Adolf Loos built in 1929 for Viennese industrialist Paul Khuner. Today, the **Looshaus** is a hotel and restaurant (02666 52911, www. looshaus.at; from €46.50-€52.50 per person B&B in a double room; single supplement €8).

SCHNEEBERG

Schneeberg is Vienna's 'local' mountain and, at 2,076 metres (6,811 feet), the highest peak in Lower Austria. As a result of its accessibility, Schneeberg tends to be more crowded than Rax. A railway line compounds its popularity; a steam engine and the green- and yellow-dappled

Semmering Railway.

Salamander train (02636 3661, www. schneebergbahn.at) leave from Puchberg am Schneeberg to carry visitors nine kilometres (six miles) to Hochschneeberg at 1,795m (5,889 feet) near the summit. Trains run from late April until early December; full ascents take 50 minutes (Salamander) or 80 minutes (steam train).

Getting there

Direct trains (90mins) run between Vienna Hauptbahnhof and Semmering. If you're driving, the A2, a toll road, goes to Semmering. Travelling further afield to Rax or Schneeberg is easiest by car.

Tourist information

Reichenau/Rax Tourist Office

Hauptstrasse 63, 2651 Reichenau/Rax (02666 52865, www.reichenau.at). **Open** 8am-noon Mon, Wed, Fri; 8am-noon, 2-4pm Tue, Thur.

Wiener Alpen in Niederösterreich Tourist Office

Schlossstrasse 1, Katzelsdorf (02622 78960, toll-free within Austria 0800-808 117, www. wieneralpen.at). **Open** 8.30am-4pm Mon-Fri.

In Context

History

Austria's ages of empire.

TEXT: GERAINT WILLIAMS

Vienna was an insignificant Roman military camp later abandoned to the Germanic tribes. Its advantageous position was to prove the making of the city, however, set between the rolling north-eastern foothills of the Alps, on the trading route of the Danube. This made it a prized possession for the dynasties that would dominate its history: first the Babenburgs, who ruled for almost three centuries, and then, of course, the empire-hungry Habsburgs – in power for 640 years. In 1914, the assassination of the Habsburg heir presumptive, Archduke Franz Ferdinand, plunged Europe into World War I. Emperor Franz Josef died before it ended, his successor Karl I abdicated, and post-1918 Austria became a republic. The people were keen for a union with Germany, which came with the annexation into Hitler's Third Reich, the Anschluss of 1938. After 1945, Vienna slowly rebuilt, first as a divided city, then as capital of a state with a nasty Nazi past.

ROMANS AND MAGYARS

Early in the first century AD, the settlement of Vindobona was a subsidiary outpost of Carnuntum, the capital of the Roman province of Pannonia Superior; both were part of a Roman defensive line along the Danube, known as the *Limes*. But from the end of the third century, the Romans' failure to subdue the Germanic barbarians made Vindobona's situation increasingly precarious. Around AD 395, a fire destroyed the military camp and the legion withdrew. Roman influence lingered on however, until the Eastern Emperor Theodosius II formally ceded Pannonia to the Huns in 433.

When the Romans departed, the Romanised inhabitants they left behind were at the mercy of repeated waves of invaders. Nonetheless, some organised administration endured; from at least the eighth century, a governor dispensed justice from the Berghof, at the western end of the Hoher Markt. Vienna's earliest recorded church, Ruprechtskirche, was built just to the east, probably in the ninth century, and dedicated to the patron saint of salt miners. The eastward spread of Christianity also brought Bavarian settlers, ancestors of the German-Austrians who would form the region's core population.

By the ninth century, the city's modern name – which appeared as Wenia in the Salzburg annals of 881 – had become current. It's said to derive from the Illyro-Celtic word *Vedunja*, meaning woodland stream. Wenia sat at the eastern edge of the Carolingian Empire, in a buffer zone periodically overrun by the Magyars from the east. Although it was under Magyar control for several decades, a decisive victory by the German king Otto the Great in 955 was a turning point. The Magyars would later be pushed back to the River Leitha, now in Austria's Burgenland province, which became the permanent frontier.

This hotly disputed border territory between 'West' and 'East' (a role to which it reverted in the Cold War) came to be known as Austria – a name that first occurs as 'Ostarrichi' ('Eastern Realm') in a document of 996. Even before then, in 976, Emperor Otto II had awarded the territory between Enns and Traisen to the Bavarian Counts of Babenberg. This ambitious dynasty, whose members combined shrewd diplomacy with ostentatious piety, would dominate the expanding territories of 'Austria' for almost 300 years.

Leopold III of Babenberg.

TRADE AND BOOM

When Leopold I of Babenberg (976-94) took charge of his new possessions, his seat of power was Melk on the Danube. He managed to extend his lands to the east, probably as far as the Wienerwald, but Wenia itself remained in Magyar hands. The Magyars were finally forced back to the River Leitha by Adalbert 'the Victorious' (1018-55), but the Babenbergs still had to impose their authority over the powerful local lords, reinforcing their territorial claims by astute marriages into rival dynasties. Their ambitions generally projected eastwards, and the Babenberg seat moved along the Danube from Melk, via Klosterneuburg, to Vienna.

A man of piety, Leopold III of Babenberg (1095-1136) was canonised as Austria's patron saint in 1485. Refusing the German crown, he devoted himself to founding abbeys and churches. The most significant Babenberg for the history of Vienna, however, was Heinrich II 'Jasomirgott' (1141-77), so called because of his favourite oath ('So help me God!'). Although he was prevailed upon to renounce the dukedom of Bavaria, he was handsomely rewarded by the upgrading of Austria itself in 1156 to an independent dukedom; previously it had been a margraviate. Equally important was his decision to move his court to Vienna, to the area still known as Am Hof ('At the Court').

The town's economic expansion continued under Heinrich's successor, Leopold V (1177-94), who benefited from two windfalls: he inherited much of Styria and Upper Austria in 1192 when their ruler died childless, and received much of the huge ransom paid for the release of Richard the Lionheart. (In 1192, the crusading king of England was making his way home overland after being shipwrecked on the Adriatic. Recognised in Vienna, he was imprisoned at Dürnstein until March 1193.)

Late 12th-century Vienna was booming economically and culturally. Under Leopold VI 'the Glorious' (1198-1230), troubadours, or *Minnesänger*, were prominent at court, singing the praises of noble ladies and celebrating the duke's glory. Leopold also encouraged trade, awarding Vienna its 'staple right' in 1221. This obliged foreign merchants trading on the Danube to sell their goods to local traders within two months of landing, guaranteeing the lion's share of the downstream trade to the Viennese. The reign of the last Babenberg, Friedrich II 'the Warlike' (1230-46), saw a decline in the fortunes of the city. After Friedrich was killed fighting the Hungarians, leaving no male heirs, the resulting power vacuum was filled by the ambitious Ottokar II of Bohemia – who reinforced his claim by marrying Friedrich II's widow in 1252.

PLAGUE AND PERSECUTION

Ottokar cultivated the Viennese burghers – and executed a few who tried to oppose him – and most of the town swung behind him. He gave generously for the rebuilding of Stephansdom and other edifices after a fire in 1258, and founded a hospital for lepers as well as the Wiener Bürgerspital almshouse. He also initiated the building of the Hofburg, Vienna's future imperial palace, originally as a fairly simple fortress.

Ottokar's ambiguous position was made precarious, however, by a failed attempt to become King of Germany. He was further undermined when Rudolf of Habsburg was chosen as king in his place, in 1273. Rudolf, whose original small domain was in modern Switzerland, was initially seen as a harmless compromise candidate, but soon proved otherwise. He set out to challenge Ottokar's

power, and by 1276 had occupied Vienna. They made peace, but in 1278 Ottokar was killed in the battle of Dürnkrut. His embalmed body was displayed in the Minorite monastery, a reminder to the people that those who aspire to climb highest also fall furthest. With Rudolf's arrival began 640 years of virtually unbroken Habsburg rule in Austria.

From 1283, Rudolf left the government of Austria in the hands of his son Albrecht, who made himself unpopular by challenging some burgher privileges, and had to put down a rebellion in the city in 1287-88. In 1298, though, Albrecht I became the first Habsburg to add the title of German king to that of Holy Roman Emperor. Vienna would become virtually synonymous with the dynasty.

Problems beset the Habsburgs in the first half of the 14th century. In 1310, there was an uprising against Friedrich 'the Handsome' with two major consequences: one of the properties confiscated from conspirators became the first City Hall, and the city's rights were codified for the first time in the Eisenbuch (1320). During the reign of Albrecht II 'the Lame' (1330-58), plagues of locusts ravaged the Vienna Basin; hardly had they disappeared than Vienna was hit by the Black Death, then by a terrible fire.

Vienna's Christians blamed the Jews for the plague (they were said to have poisoned the wells), and Albrecht had to struggle to prevent major violence. The Jewish community, established in Vienna since Babenberg times, was concentrated near Am Hof, around today's Judenplatz. Jews traditionally enjoyed the ruler's protection; even this, though, was not always enough to spare them from persecution in times of crisis.

LINES OF COMMAND

Duke Albrecht II achieved a shrewd dynastic alliance in 1353, when his son, the future Rudolf IV, married the daughter of Karl IV of Bohemia who was then Holy Roman Emperor. Advantageous marriage was thereafter the principal pillar of Habsburg expansionism, aphoristically described in a 16th-century adaptation of a line from Ovid: 'Others make war; you, fortunate Austria, marry!' The magnificence of the Prague ruled by his father-in-law spurred Rudolf's ambitions: masons who had worked on the great cathedral of Saint Vitus were summoned to work on Stephansdom. Rudolf also founded a university in Vienna in 1365, inspired by Karl's foundation of the Prague Carolinum.

In the same year, Rudolf died in Milan, aged 26. He had reigned for just seven years, but his ingenious policies ranged from social reform to the promotion of urban renewal through rent reform. Not for nothing was he known as 'the Founder' (and, equally aptly, 'the Cunning'). His attempts to advance the claims of the dynasty over the title Holy Roman Emperor, though, were embarrassingly ill-judged. A diligently produced forgery known as the Privilegium Maius invented a picturesque lineage and titles for earlier Habsburgs. It was magisterially rubbished by Petrarch, whom the emperor had asked to verify its authenticity. Even more disastrous was Rudolf's institution of a power-sharing system among male Habsburg heirs. It resulted in a Habsburg equivalent of the English Wars of the Roses between the 'Albertine' and 'Leopoldine' lines (named after Rudolf's two quarrelling brothers and joint heirs), which lasted intermittently for four generations.

In 1411, Albrecht V, of the Albertine line, came of age and entered a Vienna that was under threat from Moravian knights and the Protestant Hussites of Bohemia. Bad harvests and the loss of the wine trade to German merchants contributed to a rancid atmosphere. Once again, the Jews were scapegoats. This time the ruler himself was the instigator of a horrifying pogrom, the *Wiener Geserah*. In 1420-21, Albrecht stripped Vienna's poorer Jews of their belongings and dispatched them on a raft down the Danube. Richer members of the community were tortured until they revealed where their wealth was hidden, then burned alive on the Erdberg. Others opted for mass suicide to escape torture, and the centuries-old ghetto by Am Hof was demolished. Albrecht's actions have never been fully explained: they represented a break in the rulers' long tradition of protecting local Jews, and also removed an important source of ducal finance.

In foreign policy, however, Albrecht showed the usual Habsburg adroitness. He married the daughter of Emperor Sigismund and, on the latter's death, inherited the Hungarian crown. In the same year, 1438, he was elected Holy Roman Emperor. Excluding a three-year lapse in the 18th century, the Habsburgs

retained this title (protected by bribing the other electors) until Napoleon forced its abolition in 1806.

A year later, Albrecht died while fighting the Turks in Hungary. His heir, born after his father's death, was known as Ladislas Posthumous (1440-57). Ladislas's guardian was Friedrich III, of the Leopoldine line, plunging the dynasty back into its inheritance disputes. Friedrich was crowned Holy Roman Emperor in 1452, but his position at home was weak. Furious at what they saw as his favouring of other towns, Viennese merchants pledged their loyalty to Ladislas. When poor Ladislas died, aged just 17, in 1457, fighting continued between Friedrich and his own brother, Albrecht, the latter supported by the Viennese. It culminated in a seven-week siege of the Hofburg in 1462, when Friedrich was holed up inside with his three-year-old son, the future Maximilian I. He was rescued by the intervention of the Hussite Bohemian king, Jiríz Podebrad, but had to agree to share power with Albrecht. Only when Albrecht died in 1463 did Friedrich regain control of Vienna.

The city also increased in importance when it was granted its own diocese in 1468, at the expense of the previously powerful Passau. For the first four decades, bishops from outside were chosen as administrators, until the appointment of Georg von Slatkonia in 1513. In 1498 he created what would later become the Vienna Boys' Choir.

Friedrich III's ultimate triumph – he effectively ruled for 53 years – is often attributed to the fact that he outlived all of his rivals, including the much younger Hungarian king Matthias Corvinus, who occupied Vienna from 1485 to 1490. The emperor's survival, the extinction of the Albertine line and the removal of the Hungarian threat cleared the way for a real expansion of Habsburg power. Friedrich's son, Maximilian, took up his inheritance at a time of expanding wealth and power, amid the pan-European blossoming of the Renaissance.

BENELUX, SPAIN AND THE NEW WORLD
Nicknamed 'the Last Knight', Maximilian was known for his feats as a hunter, soldier and athlete. Inspired by the Renaissance spirit, he encouraged new learning at Innsbruck and Vienna; the study of pure science, medicine and cartography flourished – although

disproportionate attention was dedicated to Habsburg genealogy, which was traced back to Noah.

Maximilian brought Habsburg marriage diplomacy to its zenith. Through his first wife, Maria of Burgundy, one of the richest territories in Europe (including the modern-day Benelux) came under Habsburg control. His son, Philip 'the Fair', married Joanna 'the Mad', daughter of Ferdinand and Isabella of Spain, thus acquiring Castile, Aragón, southern Italy and all the Spanish possessions in the New World for the dynasty. In 1515, Maximilian also stood proxy for the marriage of his two young grandchildren to the male and female heirs of the joint throne of Bohemia and Hungary.

Philip the Fair died before Maximilian, who was thus succeeded by his grandson Karl V, better known in English as Emperor Charles V. On his accession to the imperial throne in 1519, he ruled over a Holy Roman Empire 'on which the sun never set' – much too large for one man to direct, and already beset by problems. The Ottoman advance in south-east Europe seemed unstoppable; equally ominous, after 1517, was the gathering momentum of the Reformation.

Vienna saw nothing of Karl, who ceded his Austrian archdukedom to his brother Ferdinand in 1521. The latter was immediately faced with the rapid success of Lutheranism, coupled with Vienna's demands for more self-government. Ferdinand solved this last difficulty by executing Mayor Siebenbürger and six councillors in 1522, and subjecting the Viennese to absolutist control. He was less successful against the Lutherans and Anabaptists, despite the punishments meted out to leading Protestants (men were burned at the stake, their wives drowned in the Danube). The increasingly Protestant nobility began to make religious freedom a condition of military assistance against the advancing Turkish threat.

Having overrun Hungary, by 1529 the Ottomans were at the gates of Vienna. The morale of its religiously divided population had been lowered by Ferdinand's vicious rule and a major fire in 1525; only the heroism of Vienna's defender, Count Salm, and the early onset of winter, saved the city. Lessons were learned from the siege though, and the city's fortifications were rebuilt in 1531-66, using the Italian model of star-shaped bastions.

WITH COUNTER-REFORMATION COMES BAROQUE

From 1551, when Ferdinand summoned the Jesuits to the city, Vienna became a testing ground for the Counter-Reformation. Evangelisation was led by scholars and preachers such as Peter Canisius, who compiled the catechisms of the Roman Catholic faith to be used in the struggle for hearts and minds in a Vienna that was still 80 per cent Protestant. This struggle was characterised by dogma and paranoia; the Jewish community was again a target, suffering prohibitions on property owning and trade, and obliged to wear an identifying yellow ring on clothes. The oppressive atmosphere relaxed a little under Maximilian II (1564-76), who stuck to the letter of the Peace of Augsburg of 1555, which recognised both the Catholic and Lutheran faiths in the empire, provided that subjects followed the faith of their princes. Still, as the screw of the Counter-Reformation tightened under Rudolf II (1576-1612) and his brother Matthias, many migrated to more sympathetic parts of Europe. The dominant figure of the Counter-Reformation in Vienna was Cardinal Khlesl, who purged the university of Protestantism, and whose *Klosteroffensive* ('monastery offensive') led to the second great wave of Roman Catholic foundations in the city, 1603-38.

Protestantism was by no means dead among the nobility however and as late as 1619 a group forced their way into the Hofburg and delivered a list of demands to Ferdinand II (1619-37). The following year saw the defeat of the Bohemian Protestants at the Battle of the White Mountain, the first major engagement of the Thirty Years War (1618-48). This war, and the triumph of Catholicism in southern Germany and Austria, would mean the end for Lutheranism in Vienna, even though a Swedish Protestant army threatened the city as late as 1645. In the course of the war, the Jesuits gained control of the university in 1622, and in 1629 Ferdinand issued his Edict of Restitution, restoring to the Catholic Church 1,555 properties under Protestant control since 1552. In Vienna, Protestant laymen were also effectively expropriated by an ingenious catch-22 – only Catholics could become burghers, and only burghers could own property. This was Habsburg religiosity at

IN CONTEXT

its most ruthless, with cynical greed and oppression cloaked by a fig leaf of piety.

The Counter-Reformation also produced a flourishing of the visual arts, architecture, music, drama and literature in the 17th and 18th centuries. Leopold I (1657-1705) spent lavishly on huge operas and ballets, and the gifted could usually expect patronage. Italians long held sway, with Italian-trained local architects such as Fischer von Erlach and Hildebrandt coming to the fore a generation later. Similarly, the music preferred at court was for two centuries Italian-influenced, dominated by a series of Italian composers and librettists, from Cesti through Caldara and Metastasio to Mozart's rival, Antonio Salieri.

Leopold was not an attractive figure; the Turkish traveller Evliya Celebi describes his 'bottle-shaped head', with a nose 'the size of an aubergine from the Morea', displaying 'nostrils into which three fingers could be stuck'. His character was hardly more appealing, even if his deviousness was sometimes dictated by the need to fight wars on two fronts, against the French and the Turks. Educated by bigots, he married an even more bigoted Spanish woman, Margarita Teresa, who blamed her miscarriages on the Jews. In 1669, egged on by Christian Viennese burghers, Leopold ordered a renewed expulsion of the Jews from their settlement on the Unteren Werd. The area was renamed Leopoldstadt, and Jewish property was given to Christians. This so weakened the imperial and city finances, however, that in 1675 the richer Jews had to be invited back. Troubles multiplied with an outbreak of plague in 1679, whereupon the emperor and nobility promptly scurried off to Prague.

1683 AND ALL THAT

After the plague came the Turks, who besieged Vienna for the second time in 1683. Before this long-planned assault, the Ottomans had promised the city to the Hungarians if they joined the anti-Habsburg offensive. Though the Turkish army was mobilized in 1682, they didn't want to risk a winter campaign. In the meantime, Leopold created a crucial alliance with Poland and Venice. The following spring, Ottoman forces under Kara Mustafa Pasha joined with their Transylvanian and Hungarian allies and headed for Vienna. Immediately, Leopold fled.

The Turks reached a poorly defended Vienna in mid July 1683. Instead of bombarding the city, Kara Mustafa decided to starve it into submission. On its last legs by early September, Vienna was about to surrender when the Poles under Jan Sobieski III arrived to save the day. Though outnumbered two to one, Sobieski's hussars broke Ottoman lines, just as Turkish sappers were preparing to blow up Vienna's walls. Aided by Austrians, Bavarians and Saxons, Sobieski's men undertook the largest cavalry charge in history, causing the Turks to withdraw – but not before Kara Mustafa had executed 30,000 Christian hostages.

With Vienna and Christianity saved, the Polish army looted the Ottoman camp, finding camels, weapons and… coffee (see p202 **Behind Enemy Lines**). On Christmas Day 1683 in Belgrade, Kara Mustafa was executed by strangulation with a silken cord, a punishment ordered by Ottoman sultan Mehmed IV for the failure at Vienna. Charles of Lorraine, who had led the Habsburg forces, went on to defeat the Turks in Buda, and bring southern Hungary, Transylvania and Slavonia under Habsburg control. Prince Eugene of Savoy, only 19 when he had earned his spurs at Vienna, became known as one of the leading military commanders in European history as the Turks were beaten further and further east.

Leopold, meanwhile, returned to his *Residenz* to give his public, if grudging, acknowledgement to his saviours, and court artists got to work on bombastic depictions of 'Leopold, victor over the Turks'. His duplicitous treatment of the 'liberated' Magyars managed to provoke a Hungarian war of independence (1704-11) led by Prince Ferenc Rákóczi, whose troops devastated Vienna's outskirts in 1704. Prince Eugene advised the erection of a new defensive line, the *Linienwall*, where the Gürtel now runs. Vienna began to assume the profile it has today, with outlying villages (*Vororte*) beyond the Gürtel, suburbs (*Vorstadt*) between the Gürtel and the bastions (replaced by the Ringstrasse in the 19th century), and finally the city's medieval core.

After the Hungarian threat had receded, the reign of Karl VI (1711-40) saw a building boom. Existing churches were Baroque-ised (all 30 Gothic altars of Stephansdom were replaced) and new Baroque churches built, notably Hildebrandt's Peterskirche and Fischer von Erlach's Karlskirche. The nobility built magnificent winter and summer palaces – the greatest of which was Hildebrandt's Belvedere, for Prince Eugene. It was a time of bombast and conspicuous consumption by the ruling class and Church, not balanced by job creation for the rest – although Eugene re-employed his war veterans as labourers and gardeners.

As soon as Karl died, to rejoicing in Vienna, the empire was attacked by Friedrich II of Prussia, whose invasion of Silesia began the War of the Austrian Succession. Encouraged by Friedrich's initial success, Karl Albert of Bavaria then invaded Bohemia. In the chaos, Karl's eldest daughter, Maria Theresa, assumed the Habsburg throne in 1740. She so impressed the Hungarian nobles when she sought their support in 1741 that they offered their 'life and blood' for their 'King'; constitutionally she could officially be neither 'Queen' of Hungary, nor 'Empress'.

MARIA THERESA AND MOZART

Maria Theresa chose wise advisers and able administrators who reformed key elements in the ramshackle machinery of imperial government; in ten years she doubled the state revenue. This approach was labelled 'enlightened absolutism' – although some parts were more enlightened than others. Maria Theresa wouldn't tolerate Jews, unless they converted, and was only with great difficulty persuaded that torturing suspects did not contribute to law and order. She also introduced a risible Chastity Commission in 1751, cracking down on errant noblemen and Vienna's multitude of prostitutes. Great philanderers such as her husband, Franz Stephan, the grandson of

Jan Sobieski III defeats the Turks and frees Vienna in 1683.

IN CONTEXT

Charles of Lorraine, and Venetian lothario Casanova, were forced to tread carefully.

Maria Theresa also abandoned the stiff Spanish protocol of her forebears and lived relatively informally in the great Schönbrunn Palace. Her support of local manufacturing, the creation of a postal service and even the introduction of house numbering (originally to aid recruiting) were all signs of new thinking. After the death of her husband Franz Stephan in 1765, she ruled jointly with her son, Josef II (1765-90), who was to take enlightened reforms much further when he ruled alone after Maria Theresa's death in 1780.

Josef had travelled widely and fallen under the influence of the French Enlightenment and Masonic ideas. His most lasting achievement was his Tolerance Patent of 1781, granting religious freedom to Protestant and Orthodox Christians, followed in 1782 by a more limited Patent for the Jews. He founded the city's General Hospital in 1784, and opened the imperial picture gallery and parks to public view.

The age of absolutism had seen the last flourishing of the Baroque style, and the transition to a classicism preoccupied with purity of form. In architecture this didn't really emerge until the following century, but a

Maria Theresa.

musical change of direction was already evident in Gluck's groundbreaking 1762 opera *Orfeo* – the first to subordinate its music to the requirements of the drama, in place of the florid Baroque operas of the Italians. Gluck was followed by the great names of the *Wiener Klassik* – Haydn (1732-1809) and Mozart (1756-91), who lived in Vienna for the last ten years of his life. Ludwig van Beethoven, resident in Vienna from 1792 to his death in 1827, was influenced by both, and in turn had a huge impact on Franz Schubert (1797-1828). This unbroken line of genius – nurtured by the patronage of Austrian aristocrats, the dynasty and the Church, and encouraged by the musical enthusiasm of the Viennese – has not been equalled by any other European city.

EXIT NAPOLEON, ENTER BIEDERMEIER

Soon after Josef II came the narrow-minded Franz II. Franz's reactionary views were fuelled by events in France, where his aunt, Marie Antoinette, was executed in 1793. The rise of Napoleon brought further humiliations, including two occupations of Vienna by French troops, the enforced marriage of Franz II's daughter to the upstart French emperor and the bankruptcy of the state. While the French behaved quite graciously as conquerors (a guard of honour was placed outside Haydn's house as he lay dying), these setbacks caused the Habsburgs to lose their aura.

Franz had been Archduke of Austria and Holy Roman Emperor from 1792, among his other titles, but he styled himself as Emperor of Austria from 1804. This guaranteed some continuing imperial sparkle for the Habsburgs; in 1806, a herald on the balcony of the Kirche am Hof announced that the title of Holy Roman Emperor, founded by Charlemagne in 800, no longer existed – mainly thanks to Napoleon.

The Corsican was defeated in 1814, and the Habsburg capital became the venue for the Congress of Vienna, in which the allied powers – Austria, Britain, Prussia and Russia among them – thrashed out the frontiers of post-Napoleonic Europe. Napoleon's last stand at Waterloo in 1815 was a bloody coda. The shrewd diplomacy of Franz's chancellor, Prince Metternich, and the advantage of being hosts, meant Austria emerged with dignity intact and a generous territorial settlement.

On the other hand, it now required the repressive apparatus of Metternich's police state to keep the lid on aspirations unleashed in the wake of the French Revolution. Strict censorship meant that even Franz Grillparzer (1791-1872), Austria's greatest dramatist and a Habsburg loyalist to the core, could get into trouble; disrespect for the authorities could be voiced only indirectly, as in the brilliant ad-libbing of comic genius Johann Nestroy (1801-62). Denied any political voice, Viennese burghers retreated into a world of domesticity, and the Biedermeier culture, named after the satirical figure of a solid, middle-class citizen portrayed in a Munich magazine, predominated from 1814 to 1848.

Painters such as Friedrich von Amerling evoked the idealised family life of the bourgeoisie, Ferdinand Raimund conjured an escapist fairytale world on stage and Adalbert Stifter cultivated a quietist philosophy of resignation in his novel *Indian Summer*. In architecture, Josef Kornhäusel designed neoclassical buildings with an unobtrusive elegance. In music, the revolutionary fervour of Beethoven's *Fidelio* and *Ninth Symphony* gave way to the melodious romanticism of Schubert's introspective *Lieder*.

Meanwhile, the city's working-class population was at the mercy of the industrial revolution. Overcrowding, unemployment and disease were rife. A cholera epidemic in 1831-32 led to some remedial measures, but not before typhoid fever from infected water had killed Schubert in 1828. Vienna's population had exploded by 40 per cent between 1800 and 1835, to reach 330,000; many of the new migrants were peasants who had been driven off the land and were searching for work.

The desperation of the famine-stricken working class and frustrations of the politically impotent middle class erupted in the revolution of March 1848. At first, it seemed the old order was doomed; almost the whole empire was in revolt, the hated Metternich had to flee Vienna and the simple-minded Ferdinand I, who had succeeded Franz in 1835, was forced to concede a new constitution and lift censorship. In Vienna, a provisional city council was set up, freeing the burghers from noble control, as well as a Civil Guard recruited from local citizens.

As elsewhere in Europe, in this year of revolutions, it was the army that put an end to the uprisings. Not all of the revolution's changes could be rescinded though. Serfdom was abolished throughout the empire, and the

mere existence of liberal constitutions, however briefly they had existed, supplied a new theoretical basis for discussion.

NEW METROPOLIS AND TWIN CAPITAL

Ferdinand abdicated and was succeeded by his 18-year-old nephew Franz Josef I (1848-1916). He began his reign with the executions and repression of former revolutionaries, yet by the end of his 68-year rule, had presided over a gradual emancipation of his people. In 1867 – with Austria weak from defeat by Prussia and under pressure from his Hungarophile wife, Elisabeth ('Sissi') – Franz Josef approved the *Ausgleich*, or 'Compromise', with Hungary, giving it equal rights in the new Dual Monarchy of Austria-Hungary. Universal adult male suffrage was introduced in 1907. What couldn't be controlled were the forces of nationalism, which eventually tore the multi-ethnic empire apart, plunging Europe into war.

In 1857, Franz Josef approved the demolition of Vienna's old city bastions, and the construction of the Ringstrasse. A symbol of burgeoning civil society, it was to be lined with imposing public buildings, taking shape over some 26 years. With its city hall, museums, opera, stock exchange and theatres, the Ring transformed Vienna into a modern metropolis. Once separate communities outside the Innere Stadt, such as Mariahilf, Neubau and Wieden, had already been incorporated into the city in 1850.

Much of the financing came from the high bourgeoisie, whose tastes in the arts were conservative. The most lavish patronage was given to Hans Makart's overblown historical canvases, while statues of Habsburg rulers and generals peppered Vienna. The burghers' preference for the now-entrenched musical tradition of the late *Wiener Klassik* was satisfied by Johannes Brahms, who lived in Vienna from 1878 until his death in 1897. In contrast, Anton Bruckner was subjected to abuse and even ridicule.

The decades from 1860 to 1900 make up the so-called *Gründerzeit*, or 'Founders' Period' and saw the construction of a modern economy, society and state. The administration of Vienna was dominated from 1861 by the liberal bourgeoisie, with money made in banking, industry and property speculation. The city council followed its own interests, but for a while these coincided with those of most

IN CONTEXT

The Ringtheater burns down in 1881, killing 386 people.

IN CONTEXT

citizens. Huge investment resulted in an improved water supply, new bridges across the Danube and the channelling of the river itself. In 1870, Vienna acquired its first trams.

Unbridled capitalism had its downside, though. In 1873 the stock market crashed and many financiers were ruined; some committed suicide. The death toll among businesses was equally dramatic, as 60 companies, 48 banks and eight insurance societies went bust. Vienna's World Exhibition of that year was a financial disaster, worsened by an outbreak of cholera. The catastrophe of 1881, when the Ringtheater burned down killing 386 people, was almost the final straw.

FROM KARL LUEGER TO 1914

Turn-of-the-century Vienna has become almost a cliché of sensuality, eroticism and overripe aestheticism. It generated some of the most contrasting movements of the era, including militant anti-semitism, Zionism, psychoanalysis and several of the greatest masters of early modernism.

A new star rose in city politics in the 1880s, a renegade liberal called Karl Lueger, who founded his own Christian Social party and consolidated a power base by exposing corruption and stirring up anti-semitism in a vicious scapegoating of the city's Jews. Many of the wealthy liberal magnates were Jewish – unable to own property in the Innere Stadt, they

had built palaces along the new Ringstrasse. Lueger focused popular resentment on them.

His support was boosted by the extension of the franchise to taxpayers at the lower end of the earnings scale in 1885 and the incorporation of the peripheral settlements into the city in 1892. Vienna more than tripled its area and increased its population by over half a million, to 1,364,000. Immigrants poured into the city (especially Czechs, and Jews from the east), helping to create a climate beneficial to Lueger's politics; 'Handsome Karl' understood how to turn the envy and discontent of Vienna's petit bourgeoisie to his advantage. The young Adolf Hitler, living in Viennese doss-houses in the early 1900s, greatly admired him; Emperor Franz Josef, though, did not. Lueger's faction won a majority on the city council in 1895, but his election as mayor was vetoed three times by the emperor who, among other things, feared a flight of Jewish capital. Franz Josef relented in 1897, and Lueger remained in office until 1910.

As mayor he was supported by the lesser Catholic clergy, although the more senior churchmen denounced his radical and anti-semitic views in 1895. Pope Leo XIII, however, upheld Lueger's claim that he was merely adhering to the social doctrines of the Church, and that his objections to Jews were doctrinal, not racial. Papal support was decisive, and the Viennese hierarchy gradually backed him.

Just as the Christian Social majority was being established in the city, Budapest-born Viennese journalist Theodor Herzl published the first Zionist book, *Der Judenstaat* (1896), arguing that the persistence of anti-semitism in central Europe showed that Jews, however assimilated, couldn't be safe without their own state. It was received with incomprehension and even anger by Vienna's highly assimilated Jewish establishment, but began the process that eventually led to the foundation of Israel.

In the arts meanwhile, the passion of the pleasure-loving Viennese for theatre and music facilitated the meteoric rise of composers such as Josef Lanner and the Strauss dynasty, while the waltz became emblematic of hedonistic escapism. Its critics said the Viennese were too busy waltzing to heed the news of the catastrophic defeat of the Habsburg army by the Prussians in 1866 that marked the beginning of the end for their empire. Even more censorious comments greeted the craze for operetta, which began with Franz von Suppé's *Das Pensionat* (1860) and continued well into the 20th century.

In the 1890s, the city's peculiar atmosphere generated several new trends. From the Secession movement came architect Otto Wagner, who departed from the ponderous historicism of his youth to create early-modernist buildings of great functional integrity. A trenchant critic of Wagner, Adolf Loos rejected Secessionist ornamentation and carried the idea of functionalism still further. Gustav Klimt broke taboos to produce masterpieces of sensual eroticism, combined with an emphasis on the inevitability of death – a preoccupation he shared with the next generation of expressionists, such as Egon Schiele. Gustav Mahler took over the Imperial Opera and swept away generations of shibboleths he described as *Schlamperei* ('sloppiness'), while playwright Arthur Schnitzler's bleak depictions of sexual exploitation, societal ills and personal trauma were admired by Sigmund Freud.

Freud's own *Interpretation of Dreams* appeared in 1900, causing not a ripple. His novel treatment for 'hysteria' and newfangled technique of hypnosis were viewed with indifference or suspicion by the establishment. Kraus edited the journal *Die Fackel* ('The Torch'), which became an effective counterblast to the belligerent

Karl Lueger.

mood that overtook the city after the empire slithered into war in 1914. Other modernist writers, such as Hermann Bahr, the self-publicising leader of the *Jung Wien* literary circle, became ranting war propagandists.

POLARISED NEW REPUBLIC

The assassination of the heir presumptive, Archduke Franz Ferdinand, lit the fuse that led to World War I. With the death in 1916 of the old emperor, Franz Josef, his inexperienced great-nephew Karl I took the throne. Defeat in 1918, and political turmoil, saw him effectively resign as head of state and he went into exile the following year.

World War I also killed off the coffeehouse milieu of turn-of-the-century Vienna. The brilliant feuilletons perused over coffee, the interminable feuds, the head waiters who acted as unpaid secretaries, the unpaid bills: the whole Bohemian existence seemed anachronistic after Austria and her allies lost the war and everything fell apart in 1918-19.

In the capital, the situation was desperate. Its European empire of over 50 million people became an Austrian state of three million overnight. A third of the population was in Vienna, including thousands of bureaucrats whose jobs no longer existed, unemployed refugees and ex-soldiers. A 'Republic of German Austria' (Deutschösterreich) was proclaimed on 12 November 1918. The name

IN CONTEXT

reflected the desire of most Austrians – of all political parties – for an Anschluss, union with Germany. The proposal was rejected by the Allies, who hadn't fought a war so that Germany could increase in size. Thus the First Austrian Republic began its peculiarly unwanted existence.

In 1919, the Social Democrats swept to power in the Vienna city council. The party had been founded in 1889 by Viktor Adler, a Jewish doctor with a strong social conscience, and rapidly gained support among workers living in horrific conditions.

By 1900, the Socialists were able to win 43 per cent of the votes in local elections, but gained only two seats on the city council. After the war, though, their moment came. *Rotes Wien* ('Red Vienna') became the first city in the world administered by Socialists, and the Social Democrats embarked on one of the most intensive programmes of housing, welfare and culture ever seen in Europe.

Their measures and uncompromising struggle with the Church polarised socialist Austria (principally Vienna) and conservative Catholic Austria (much of the countryside). For most of the 1920s, power was held at national level by a Christian Social government, and differences between right and left widened inexorably. Both sides had their own militias (the conservative *Heimwehr* and socialist *Schutzbund*). In 1927 a conservative jury acquitted *Heimwehr* soldiers who had shot members of the *Schutzbund*; a mob burned down the Palace of Justice. Matters worsened as the world economic crisis deepened after 1929 and unemployment rose.

Tensions climaxed in a brief civil war in 1934, in which the relatively well armed forces of the right easily overcame socialist militias. During the fighting, the huge Karl-Marx-Hof housing block, a bastion of red support, was shelled into submission. Authoritarian rule was then imposed on Austria, and Vienna's administrative independence was terminated by the regime of Engelbert Dollfuss, a peculiar mix of extreme reactionary catholicism and home-grown fascism.

LIFE DURING WARTIME – AND BEYOND

Hitler came to power in Germany in 1933, and soon began a drive to increase his influence in the land of his birth, Austria. The Nazis attempted a coup d'état in Vienna, killing Chancellor Dollfuss; though an extreme right-winger, he had not been ready to follow Hitler's orders. Dollfuss's successor, Kurt Schuschnigg, soon found himself under pressure from Hitler and local Nazis to accept the Anschluss, creating the Greater Germany most Austrians had wanted at the end of World War I. Schuschnigg tried to rally support by calling a referendum on Austrian independence for 13 March 1938. To pre-empt this, as it would almost certainly have endorsed independence, German troops crossed the border at dawn on 12 March.

In Vienna, Hitler was ecstatically received when he addressed a crowd of 200,000 in Heldenplatz. The Church hastened to accommodate him; Cardinal-Archbishop Innitzer gave a Nazi salute on his way to meet the Führer, and urged the faithful to vote for the Anschluss in the subsequent Nazi plebiscite. When he later had second thoughts, Nazi thugs trashed his residence. Jews throughout the Reich were terrorised in the *Reichskristallnacht* of 9 November 1938; in Vienna it lasted several days, with mobs attacking Jews, stealing their property, and burning down 42 synagogues. Austrian-born Adolf Eichmann opened an office on Prinz Eugen Strasse where Jews were 'processed'. Those with sufficient resources could buy their freedom but the rest were sent to the camps. Some 120,000 Jews emigrated, while 60,000 were either executed or died through forced labour. Non-Jewish opponents of the Nazis were also sent to the camps; on 1 April 1938, the first batch of prominent Austrian politicians left for Dachau. Over 30 concentration camps were built in Austria – including the notorious Mauthausen.

As the catastrophe of World War II unfolded, a kernel of resistance appeared in Vienna, partly spurred by the Allied 1943 Moscow declaration that Austria's status at the end of the war would depend on her willingness to rebel. This was the origin of the notion of Austria as 'Hitler's first victim', rather than an equal participant in Nazism – one that remains valid for many Austrians even today.

A lot of war industry was moved to Vienna, which proved fateful after 7 March 1944, when Allied bombers could reach the city from Italy. In one air raid, over 400 people died in the cellars of an apartment block behind the Opera. They were never exhumed; in 1988, a memorial monument was erected on the

Hitler addresses the crowds in Vienna's Heldenplatz.

site. In spring 1945, the Soviet army took the already devastated city after fierce fighting: 8,769 deaths were caused by Allied bombing and 2,226 from fighting on the ground; 1,184 resistance fighters had been executed, 9,687 died in Gestapo prisons; 36,851 apartments had been destroyed. Over 50,000 Viennese Jews had been slaughtered, and a quarter of a million Austrians had died in German uniform.

While some of these statistics might fuel the idea of Austrian 'victimhood', the notion was also politically convenient for the occupying powers as they tried to detach Austria from Germany. The Soviets initially refused to accept Austrian independence until the German question had been tackled. Like Berlin, Vienna was divided into four zones, with a central one shared by the four Allied powers in rotation. But unlike Berlin, here there was no barbed wire and no blockade.

After Stalin's death, agreement was reached with the signing of the Austrian State Treaty in 1955. Based on the principle of permanent Austrian neutrality, and covertly on the 'victim' thesis, the treaty ensured that 'de-nazification' in Austria only stigmatised the most prominent Nazis, allowing huge numbers of passive, opportunistic or enthusiastic participants in Hitler's regime to present themselves as mere patriots. This failure to address the reality of the Nazi era created an identity crisis that would return to haunt post-war Austrian politics.

REBUILDING AND REBRANDING

Austria became the only European country occupied by the Soviets to regain full independence after 1945. The *Staatsvertrag* restored Austrian sovereignty by papering over internal political differences, in response to a widespread desire for post-war stability. It was achieved by the establishment of the *Proporz* system: political power was effectively shared out by the two main parties – the conservative People's Party (ÖVP) and the Socialists (SPÖ) – and the various interest groups that were represented by the corresponding Chamber of Commerce and Chamber of Labour.

Supported by UN aid and the Marshall Plan, Austrians displayed huge resourcefulness in rebuilding their shattered country. In Vienna, the burned-out Stephansdom was complete by 1952, and by 1955 the Burgtheater and the Staatsoper reopened. With cultural renewal, self-irony occasionally reared its head, notably Helmut Qualtinger's brilliant satirical portrait of the typical Viennese petit-bourgeois opportunist, 'Herr Karl', who joined the Nazis for the free sandwiches and beer. Conspicuously absent were the leading lights of pre-war Viennese drama, literature and music – most of whom had been Jews.

Vienna voted consistently for Social Democrat mayors, and in 1970 the national government became Socialist under the charismatic if imprudent Bruno Kreisky, chancellor until 1983; it was his achievement

BEHIND ENEMY LINES

*A hero of the Siege of Vienna in 1683, Jerzy Kulczycki
also brought a strange new custom to the capital.*

Just behind Hauptbahnhof, at an otherwise nondescript street corner, you may see a tourist bus stop and a gaggle of gawping, snapping sightseers crowd around, necks craned. Just as you're trying to figure out what the attraction is, you notice, carved into the stonework halfway up the corner building, a small statue of a strange figure in an Ottoman hat and attire, serving coffee from a tray.

It's not an advert for another coffee shop chain and the strange figure isn't Ottoman. He's Jerzy Kulczycki – or Georg Kolschitzky to the Viennese who named this street, off Favoritenstrasse, after him. And those parked tourist buses have Polish number plates, for Kulczycki was from Kulczyce, then part of Poland-Lithuania, now in western Ukraine.

If there were to be a branded chain café below his statue, it could trace its origins directly back to the moustached figure in the Aladdin shoes. Jerzy Kulczycki was an expert linguist who worked in Belgrade, for the Austrian Oriental Company, after earlier adventures that saw him suffer capture by Turks and being traded to Serbians who needed a translator. Suspected of being a spy, he skipped out of Serbia and came to Vienna to set up his own business.

Fast forward five years, and Kulczycki is trapped in the Siege of Vienna of 1683, with the starving city about to surrender to the Ottomans. Not only would Vienna fall but his former captors would then march on further west, into Germany. With history in the balance, Kulczycki decides to dress up. Disguised in Turkish clothes, he passes himself off as an Ottoman and slips through enemy lines. He reaches Charles of Lorraine, whose forces are cut off from Vienna but who has word of the imminent arrival of a Christian army under Polish king Jan Sobieski III. Kulczycki sneaks back through Turkish ranks to re-enter the trapped city and persuade the local authorities that help is at hand. Within days, Sobieski duly routs the Turks, who flee, leaving behind all manner of weapons, exotic clothing and sacks of beans.

The grateful Sobieski, now being hailed as the saviour of Christendom, gave Kulczycki the sacks of beans – Vienna's city council had already bestowed the savvy Pole with a house in Leopoldstadt. With his Balkan experience, Kulczycki knew that these beans were coffee. He gets another idea – to open a coffeehouse near Stephansdom, named *Hof zur Blauen Flasche*, and serve this drink to the public. Acting the part, and playing on a sense of euphoria with the end of the Ottoman threat, he again dons Turkish clothes as he concocts this strange brew, which he serves with milk; more palatable to local tastes.

Thus was born the coffeehouse and, slowly, the social mores that went with it. After Kulczycki's death in 1694, the café owners of Vienna continued to honour the great Kulczycki – or Kolschitzky – by displaying his portrait. Two hundred years after the Siege of Vienna, a statue was unveiled on the street also named after this resourceful hero.

that Vienna became a third seat of the United Nations. In the 1980s, Vienna gradually shed its dour *Ostbloc* aura. Credit for the renovation of façades, the sprouting of pavement cafés and a rejuvenation of cultural life was due to the election of new-broom mayor Helmut Zilk in 1984. However, with the election of Kurt Waldheim as president in 1986, the first cracks appeared in Austria's cosy post-war political cohabitation. Waldheim's impeccable international profile was dynamited by revelations that he had omitted details of his Wehrmacht service in the Balkans and Salonika. With the world's media on his trail, Waldheim denied knowledge of Nazi atrocities and deportations, claiming he had been on leave. Austrian voters refused to be swayed by international pressure and duly voted him president. The affair rekindled debate on the Nazi period in Austria and reached fever pitch with the arrival of maverick German theatre director Claus Peymann at the Burgtheater in 1986. His feisty productions of plays by Thomas Bernhard scandalised audiences with their taboo-breaking emphasis on Austrian complicity during World War II.

Long-awaited gestures of reconciliation with Vienna's Jewish community emerged with the opening of the Jewish Museum in 1993, although important issues relating to the restitution of Jewish property were not addressed until 2002, when the findings of the Historians' Commission were published.

CURRENT CONTROVERSIES

The fall of the Iron Curtain in 1989 and Austria's entry into the EU in 1995 brought new challenges. Fears of foreign meddling were exploited by the Freedom Party (FPÖ) of right-wing populist Jörg Haider, which in 1999 polled an astonishing 27.2 per cent of the vote after a virulently xenophobic campaign. When ÖVP leader Wolfgang Schüssel announced a coalition with Haider, it led to massive protests and much international condemnation, culminating in an EU boycott of the new government. Constant in-fighting led to early elections in 2002 and the FPÖ vote sank to ten per cent, provoking Haider's retreat into regional politics. The coalition resumed but, following the formation of a new party by the Haider wing of the FPÖ, the Alliance for the Future of Austria (BZÖ), the government was in the unprecedented

position of having ministers that belonged to a party that had never been formally elected.

In October 2006, the Social Democrat Party (SPÖ) achieved a surprising victory – though the FPÖ, narrowly pushed into fourth position by the Greens, proved there was still an audience for xenophobic demagogy. After long negotiations, the habitual SPÖ-ÖVP grand coalition was revived, with Social Democrat Alfred Gusenbauer as chancellor. It collapsed in 2008, and early elections were held. The SPÖ-ÖVP held on to coalition power. Jörg Haider promptly died in a car crash that many on the far right considered a plot; he had long maintained cordial relations with Saddam Hussein and Muammar al Gaddafi, both of whom are alleged to have contributed generously to him and his party. The truth appears more banal: Haider was more than three times over the limit and driving at 142km/h on a winding country road.

Without Haider, the BZÖ failed to achieve representation at the 2013 general elections and today barely operates outside Carinthia. These elections gave rise to yet another SPÖ-ÖVP coalition, with the two parties polling just under 50 per cent of the vote, while the FPÖ stormed in third with 20.5 per cent. Although the previous coalition rode the worst of the financial crisis of 2012-13, the new edition, again led by the anodyne SPÖ chairman Werner Faymann, is facing serious problems, above all in the banking sector. Austrian banks are more exposed to eastern European risk, particularly in Russia and Ukraine, than those of other EU countries.

In 2009, the government agreed to the nationalisation of Hypo Group Alpe Adria but it wasn't until 2014 that the regulators revealed that it could cost Austrian taxpayers as much as €17 billion, causing Faymann to remark that it was comparable to the Credit Anstalt crisis of 1931. Originally based in Klagenfurt, this regional bank branched out into the Alps-Adriatic area, striking deals and financing the activities of war criminals and drug traffickers in Croatia and Serbia, and, it is alleged, the political activities of Jörg Haider.

With the worsening of the refugee crisis in Europe in 2015, the inflammatory tone of the FPÖ today reflects, and even supersedes, Haider's anti-immigration discourse of the 1990s. Austria faces a rough ride, politically and socially.

IN CONTEXT

Literary Vienna

The Literature Museum of the Austrian National Library, opened in 2015, showcases some of the most troubled writers in modern European culture. Contemporaries of Franz Kafka, born when Prague was part of the Habsburg Empire, included Joseph Roth, who died an alcoholic destitute, and Arthur Schnitzler, a hedonistic friend of Freud's. All are featured in the museum. The building itself was the former Imperial and Royal Archive, whose first director was Austrian dramatist Franz Grillparzer.

The roots of modern Austrian literature lie with Grillparzer. Born in 1791 in Bauernmarkt, old Vienna, when the city was the cultural capital of the German-speaking world, by the time he died in 1872 the Empire was in decline. Grillparzer's Shakespearean feel for tragedy was inspired not just by those turbulent times, but also by his life. His mother and youngest brother killed themselves, and he had a longstanding affair with his cousin's wife, before falling in love with a 15-year-old girl.

IN CONTEXT

UNHAPPILY EVER AFTER

Troubles have always assailed Vienna's writers, from suicides, sickness and eminently unsuitable liaisons to enforced exiles and wider traumas. From the drug-addicted Georg Trakl (poet and self-prescribing pharmacist) to the phenomenally gifted Stefan Zweig, who fled the Nazis and later committed suicide, each story is different – but all of them seem to end badly. The darkness of the war and the collective burden of guilt that many Austrians tried to ignore would continue to resonate in Austrian literature, thanks to Thomas Bernhard and Nobel Literature Laureate Elfriede Jelinek, among others.

Towards the end of the 19th century, literature fed hungrily on the atmosphere of intoxication and melancholy that was intrinsic to the final apocalyptic spurt of the Habsburg Empire. Georg Trakl (1887-1914) has the dubious honour of being one of the unhappiest poets of this time. He was a hypersensitive, alcoholic outsider, with frequent moods of 'frantic intoxication and criminal melancholy'. His training as a pharmacist offered him easy access to drugs, and the advantage he took of this was reflected in his work. A tortured sexual relationship with his sister ('the thousand devils whose thorns drive the flesh frantic') didn't help. He died of a cocaine overdose in 1914. His sister shot herself a few years later. Trakl is notoriously difficult to translate, but was greatly admired by his contemporaries, such as philosopher Ludwig Wittgenstein (1889-1951), who supported him for a time and hailed him as a genius.

Another colourful Viennese character was the precocious Hugo von Hofmannsthal (1874-1929), already feted in Viennese intellectual circles at the age of 16. He gave up poetry following a premature midlife crisis, and ended up writing libretti for Richard Strauss.

Hofmannsthal died suddenly of a heart attack just before the funeral of his son, who had committed suicide. Another later writer who suffered an equally miserable life was journalist and novelist Joseph Roth (1894-1939). Although he was born on the eastern edge of the Habsburg Empire, today part of Ukraine, his work is closely associated with Vienna. Roth's father disappeared before he was born and died in a lunatic asylum, World War I curtailed his education, his wife went mad, and he himself survived on menial jobs and journalism before he died, exiled, alcoholic and destitute in Paris, the setting of his now-famous *The Legend of the Holy Drinker*. During the 1920s and '30s, Roth somehow managed to write the finest chronicles of the death throes of the Empire, *Radetzky March* and *The Emperor's Tomb*, as well as memorable accounts of the Soviet experiment and Mussolini's Italy.

Alongside alcoholism, the literary '-isms' of the turn of the century were symbolism, impressionism and naturalism. Hermann Bahr (1863-1934) decided he was an expressionist, and became the leading spirit of the Jungwien, a literary circle formed by the likes of Arthur Schnitzler and Hofmannsthal that convened at Café Griensteidl on Michaelerplatz and later at nearby Café Central. There in the corner you will still see a dummy of poet and regular Peter Altenberg (1859-1919).

PROFESSIONAL JEALOUSIES

The increasing influence of psychological themes in general and psychoanalysis in particular on the writing in these years is most clearly illustrated by Arthur Schnitzler (1862-1931). He became a friend of Freud, though Freud had first avoided meeting him 'from a kind of reluctance to meet my double'. Schnitzler's 1926 *Dream Story*, filmed rather loosely as *Eyes Wide Shut* by Stanley Kubrick, depends heavily on dream psychology, explores the subconscious and was, for its time, a great taboo-breaker. Despite its date, it's set firmly in fin-de-siècle Vienna, and conveys a strange atmosphere of hedonism, bourgeois hypocrisy, and the sexual and psychological frustrations peculiar to that time. Schnitzler's other internationally renowned work is the 1900 play *Reigen*, best known in English by its French title *La Ronde*, thanks to Max Ophuls' classic 1950 film.

Characteristically pessimistic, the play portrays a circle of sexual encounters through every class of end-of-the-century Vienna. Schnitzler, a Jew who, unlike many at that time, denied his Jewishness, also documented the anti-semitism of pre-World War II Vienna in his novel *The Road to the Open*.

The use of aphorisms was another trademark of Austrian writing at this time, practised to great effect by Jewish satirist Karl Kraus (1874-1936). He penned the phrase 'If I must choose the lesser of two evils, I will choose neither', which became a motto for a whole generation of Viennese. Founder of the satirical revue *Die Fackel* ('The Torch'), Kraus is best known for his anti-war drama *The Last Days of Mankind* and has returned to the spotlight with the publication of Jonathan Franzen's *The Kraus Project* (2013) in which Franzen employs Kraus' fury at the world of Viennese journalism as a means of expressing his own misgivings about modern media.

Robert Musil (1880-1942) said of Kraus that 'there are two things which one can't fight because they are too long, too fat and have neither head nor foot: Karl Kraus and psychoanalysis'. Professional jealousy aside, Musil was a celebrated essayist, and wrote a beautiful if unusual short story, 'The Temptation of Quiet Veronica', about a psychotic woman who appears to have been buggered by a dog, and, more famously, his unfinished three-volume novel *The Man Without Qualities*. Written after World War I, it dealt entirely with the last years of the Empire before 1914. Like many writers, Musil left Austria after the Anschluss, and died penniless and anonymous abroad.

Yet another casualty of the curse that seems to hover over literary Vienna and, like the Furies, follow its sons abroad was Ödön von Horváth (1901-38), a friend of Joseph Roth who fled to Paris to escape the Nazis and was killed by a falling branch on the Champs-Elysées during a freak storm. Von Horváth has recently enjoyed a reappraisal, with British director Simon Stephens rewriting his 1932 play *Kasimir and Karolina*, a tale of a relationship destroyed by poverty and desperation, as a parable of austerity Britain. Meanwhile, the 'almost over-gifted' Jewish writer Stefan Zweig (1881-1942) fled from the Nazis to South America, to kill himself with his wife in Brazil. Utterly cultured, a speaker and

IN CONTEXT

Thomas Bernhard.

Daniel Kehlmann.

translator of several languages, he was a respected figure in European literary circles, and for a time in the 1920s his hugely popular biographies and historical books made him the world's most widely translated author. Reading his autobiography, *The World of Yesterday*, it's easy to see how, as the social and political climate changed, the disillusionment that led to his suicide set in. As he himself put it, 'After one's 60th year, unusual powers are needed in order to make another wholly new beginning. Those that I possess have been exhausted by long years of homeless wandering'.

STYLISTIC FIREWORKS

If Austria's post-war politicians embraced the notion of victimhood, its most celebrated writers begged to differ. For Thomas Bernhard (1931-89), Peter Handke (born 1942) and Elfriede Jelinek (born 1946), the country that emerged from the war is a crass fiction, what Bernhard described as a *Geschäftshaus*, an emporium retailing a schmaltzy blend of Alpine scenery and imperial myths, inhabited by 'six-and-a-half million idiots'. For Jelinek 'internal exile' is the only option: 'Austria is a nation of criminals. This country has a criminal past.' Such vitriol earned them the epithet *Nestbeschmutzer* or 'nest foulers'. Whatever the truth of their statements, they point to

an insurmountable breach between a nation and the representatives of its literature.

Haunted by illegitimacy, maternal rejection, and a series of life-threatening illnesses, Bernhard was an irascible figure, a self-confessed troublemaker whose plays and novels eschew any utopian political activism for meandering repetition and scabrous humour. At home, he is remembered for his play *Heldenplatz*, a merciless dissection of the myths surrounding Hitler's annexation of Austria. For a glimpse into his world, call in at Café Bräunerhof (1, Stallburggasse 2), where his meetings with Paul Wittgenstein, the philosopher's clinically insane nephew, led to his most readable work, *Wittgenstein's Nephew*.

Like Bernhard's, Elfriede Jelinek's work depends heavily on stylistic fireworks that often sit uncomfortably in translation. When she was awarded the 2004 Nobel Prize for Literature, the world responded with a resounding: 'Who?'. There was even stony silence in Austria. Her name probably registered among those who had read the credits for Michael Haneke's film version of her novel *Die Klavierspielerin* ('The Piano Teacher'). This fearful portrait of Erika, a frustrated middle-aged piano teacher whose masochistic demands alienate the student she desires as a lover, savagely juxtaposes the Vienna Conservatoire with the Gürtel's

Literature Museum. See p204.

peep shows to attack another Austrian sacred cow: the male-dominated world of classical music. Jelinek alleged a 'social phobia' to avoid the Nobel ceremony, lamenting that Bernhard had been overlooked in his lifetime. However, by singling out 'her musical flow of voices and counter-voices in novels and plays that with extraordinary linguistic zeal reveal the absurdity of society's clichés and their subjugating power', the Swedes may well have had Bernhard in mind.

THE HERE AND NOW

Since the heady days of Bernhard and Jelinek, the public profile of Austrian fiction has been more discreet. Nevertheless, to judge from the number of young contemporary writers lauded in the rest of the German-speaking world, and whose work has been translated into English in recent years, Austrian literature is in relatively good shape. It even produced a true international bestseller: *Measuring the World* by Daniel Kehlmann (born 1975), the engrossing re-imagination of the lives of two German giants, the mathematician Carl Friedrich Gauss and geographer Alexander von Humboldt. Since its publication in 2005, it has sold more than a million copies. Born in Germany and resident in Vienna from the age of six, Kehlmann's previous novel, *Me and Kaminski*, an occasionally hilarious account

of a mediocre journalist attempting to revive his career by writing the biography of a reclusive painter, was also well received in the international press.

Since the turn of the millennium, the work of a trickle of young Viennese, or Vienna-based, writers has appeared in English translation. *Vienna*, an enjoyable Jewish family saga by novelist and journalist Eva Menasse (born 1970) was enthusiastically praised, while *Pull Yourself Together* by Thomas Glavinic (born 1972), a coming-of-age tale about an overweight young Viennese chancer, was compared, perhaps generously, to JK Toole's comic classic *A Confederacy of Dunces*. Glavinic's earlier novel, *Night Work*, a dystopian saga of a man who wakes up to find he's the only living being in Vienna, was awarded Germany's most prestigious crime-writing prize. However, the nearest Vienna has come to a Scandi-style thriller writer is Wolf Haas (born 1960), creator of the former cop and disenchanted detective Simon Brenner. *Brenner and God*, the latest of the four to be translated into English, sees Brenner taking some downtime working as a chauffeur for a wealthy couple, only to get mixed up in the kidnapping of their daughter. Like Glavinic, Haas is a former advertising copywriter, a fact that probably contributes to his protagonist's world-weary disposition.

Essential Information

Hotels

Visitors to Vienna are spoilt for choice in a city that now racks up around 13 million overnight stays each year. Pick yourself a hotel with history, a plush palace where princes retain rooms, a family-run pension or stripped-down designer digs. Many of these come with quintessential Viennese features such as fishbone parquet floors, double doors and ceilings so high that even the smallest box room appears palatial. While there are few real bargains, bedding down here needn't break the bank. Like the majority of Vienna's sights, most accommodation is found in the Innere Stadt, the city's historic centre. If you venture out into districts 2-9, you can often make great savings without skimping on quality, and still only be a short walk from the attractions. Recent additions at either end of the price scale include the Park Hyatt Vienna, the Palais Hansen Kempinski and, unique to the city, Magdas Hotel, staffed mainly by refugees.

STAYING IN VIENNA

The city is currently enjoying a boom in visitor numbers and hotel openings, especially in the luxury category. Since 2011, the Ritz-Carlton, the Palais Hansen Kempinski and the Park Hyatt Vienna have all opened their doors in prime locations, not to mention more boutique establishments such as the Guesthouse Vienna and Sans Souci. In the budget bracket, low-cost German chain Motel One now has four branches here, including prominent spots by the Opera House and two main railway stations. Mid-range oldies, such as the Mailberger Hof and Hotel Pension Suzanne, have the luxury of solid, year-round return custom.

Given that everyone's reserving rooms or organising city breaks via online agencies, hotels are keen to encourage potential customers to book direct – Sans Souci even throws in a spa session and bottle of champagne. Many also offer attractive advance rates.

Breakfast is a way of life in Vienna and even the lowliest pension will put on a decent spread. If *frühstück* isn't included in your deal, you'll be looking at upwards of €20 a head to pay for it separately. Unless you just need a coffee in the morning, it may be worth going for the all-in rate, setting yourself up for the day.

Vienna is busy 12 months of the year, but stays at Christmas, New Year and for the Life Ball in late May are especially popular.

CATEGORIES & PRICES

Hotels are classified according to their location, then by price category for a standard double room: deluxe (€300 or over), expensive (€200-€299), moderate (€100-€199) and budget (€99 or under). At weekends, you can often find a double in a four- or even five-star for less than €125, but these are not standard rates. A nightly city tax of 3.2 per cent is added to your final bill, usually paid in cash if you've booked online.

INNERE STADT

Deluxe

★ Do&Co Hotel

1, Stephansplatz 12 (24 188, www.docohotel.com). U1, U3 Stephansplatz. **Rooms** *43.* **Map** *p251 E7.*

Occupying architect Hans Hollein's cylindrical Haas Haus, Do&Co stands directly opposite Stephansdom, with jaw-dropping views. Dutch design duo FG Stijl slotted in the rooms like slices of *torte*, cladding them in sophisticated teak, stone and suede. Bang & Olufsen flatscreens, torrential glassed-off overhead showers with Etro toiletries, and large, inviting beds are thrown in for good measure. Staff are exceptionally helpful – a minor miracle considering that the reception and other communal areas are woefully cramped. This is exacerbated by the popularity of the restaurant and bar, adored by the city's movers and shakers. Breakfast is an excellent but pricey affair; there's plenty of choice nearby.

Hotel Residenz Palais Coburg

1, Coburgbastei 4 (51818-0, www.palais-coburg.com).
U3 Stubenring or tram 2. **Suites** 31. **Map** p251 F7.
Built in 1857 for Ferdinand Saxe-Coburg-Gotha (Queen Victoria's uncle), this late neoclassical palace is now a 31-suite hotel. Its entrance is a spectacular sight, hewn out of one of the few remaining chunks of Vienna's city walls, and the public rooms are breathtaking. Named after various regal blood relations of the Saxe-Coburgs, the huge suites are wonderfully well appointed, featuring fully equipped kitchens, seating areas and balconies. Interiors vary from imperial opulent (antique desks, crystal chandeliers) to modern minimal with lots of high-tech toys, and there are views of the Stadtpark or over the rooftops of old Vienna. The rooftop pool, spa and sun terrace are never crowded, while service is supremely discreet and attentive. Prices start at €1,150 per night for the smallest City Suite; the hotel runs the motto 'You only live once' above its price list.

Park Hyatt Vienna

1, Am Hof 2 (22740-1234, www.hyatt.com).
U3 Herrengasse. **Rooms** 143. **Map** p251 E7.
The city's newest big hitter, opened in 2014, is set in what was a bank in the Habsburg days, deep in the historic centre. The Park Hyatt will also form the core of the Golden Quarter, an exclusive retail hub being fashioned around the only Louis Vuitton outlet in central Europe, plus Prada, Armani and so on. Occupying a whole side of the pretty, enclosed square of Am Hof, with its regular antiques fair and seasonal Christmas market, the Park Hyatt has the primest of prime locations. And what a high-end hotel: walk-in rain showers in every room, whirlpool tubs and Illy espresso makers. As for the communal attractions, apart from the top-notch Arany spa, there's a whisky-and-cigar bar, a terrace café and an impressive restaurant, Bank, serving regional European cuisine. Oh, and there's also a gold-tiled swimming pool in what was the vault.

Sacher.

Sacher

1, Philharmonikerstrasse 4 (514 560,
www.sacher.com). *U1, U2, U4 Karlsplatz*
or tram 1, 2, D. **Rooms** 162. **Map** p250 E7.

IN THE KNOW FEEL THE LOVE

Although Japan may lay claim to the dubious honour of inventing the modern-day love hotel, Habsburg Vienna also appreciated people's short-term needs for privacy. The legendary **Orient** (1, Tiefer Graben 30, 533 7307, www.hotelorient.at) was originally a tavern for Danube boatmen, and has functioned as a hotel since 1896. Today, it's Vienna's classiest love hotel, with suites sold in three-hour slots, and by the night on Saturday and Sunday. Decked out in over-the-top fashion, and overseen with great discretion, the suites sport suggestive names such as *1001 Nights*. There are rooms, too, such as *Black Tulip*, a snip at €63 for a 180-minute… um… session. Former guests such as Orson Welles and Kenneth Anger contribute to the Orient's mythical status in the city.

Guesthouse Vienna.

As befits a hotel of its standing, the Sacher is awash with history: spiritual home of the celebrated *sachertorte*; patronised by Emperor Franz Josef (after his austere banquets at Hofburg, the aristocracy would repair to the Sacher restaurant); and virtually synonymous with the Staatsoper since 1876, it also played a prominent role in Carol Reed's *The Third Man*, as it was commandeered as British HQ during the four-power occupation. Rooms are a vision of stately elegance, dotted with antiques, while three new panoramic penthouse suites were opened on the seventh floor in 2012. The superb location, legendary service and magnificent Blaue Bar appeal to lovers of bygone days, but the hotel's fame means that its cafés and *sachertorte* outlet are often packed. There's also a tranquil spa and a fitness centre.

Expensive

Amadeus

1, Wildpretmarkt 5 (533 8738, www.hotel-amadeus.at). U1, U3 Stephansplatz or bus 1A, 3A. **Rooms** 32. **Map** p251 E6.
This intimate hotel is wonderfully central, set on a quiet side street close to Stephansdom. Rooms are furnished in period style, mainly in white and dark red, while the bathrooms are pristine white. The smallest singles are compact, the doubles smallish but comfortable; outside high season, weekend packages offer double rooms at the single rate. Staff are friendly and helpful, and the continental breakfast should set you up for the day.

Ambassador

1, Kärntnerstrasse 22 & Neuer Markt 5 (961 610, www.ambassador.at). U1, U2, U4 Karlsplatz or U1, U3 Stephansplatz. **Rooms** 85. **Map** p251 E7.

In keeping with the general trend of Kärntner Strasse, the Ambassador must be the only five-star hotel with a branch of Mango inside. Nevertheless, this grand old establishment has welcomed everyone from Josephine Baker to Mark Twain in its day. The rooms are large and plush, with parquet floors and velvet curtains. They're also air-conditioned, which is useful in summer when downtown revellers tend to whoop it up a bit. If noise bothers you, ask for a room on the Neuer Markt side; it's quieter and the view is better.

Guesthouse Vienna

1, Fürichgasse 10 (512 320, www.theguesthouse.at). U1, U2, U4 Karlsplatz or tram 1, 2, D. **Rooms** 39. **Map** p250 E7.
Designed by Sir Terence Conran, this cosy yet contemporary spot is in a prime location by the Albertina. Each room, not to mention the suites, feels like a flat all of its own, with couch, coffee table and separate areas for sleeping and relaxing. Large tubs, heated floors and Lederhaas soaps enhance bath time, and you can even pour yourself a glass of wine from the in-room fridge. Room service is 24/7, while the Brasserie & Bakery restaurant serves up Viennese treats. All in all, a home from home less than seven minutes' walk from the Opera House.

★ Hollmann Beletage

1, Köllnerhofgasse 6 (961 1960, www.hollmann-beletage.at). U1, U4 Schwedenplatz. **Rooms** 26. **Map** p251 F6.
Spread over several floors of a 19th-century apartment building, this place is renowned for its epicurean breakfasts, featuring smoothies, fruit salad, pastries, cold meats, eggs cooked to order and plenty more besides. Such gluttony aside, the rest of the

hotel is charming. It centres on an airy living room with a high-tech log fire, books, an honesty bar and an electric piano (equipped with headphones, so other guests aren't disturbed); other facilities include a garden terrace, stylish little sauna and eight-seater cinema. Rooms are elegantly minimalist, with bathrooms and flatscreen TVs often hidden away behind pale wood panels. Bathrobes, iPod docks, CD players and free Wi-Fi are present and correct, while larger rooms might also feature stand-alone baths, writing desks and sofas. Reception is unmanned at night, so out-of-hours guests are given an entry code.

Hotel am Stephansplatz

1, Stephansplatz 9 (53 405-0, www.hotelam stephansplatz.at). U1, U3 Stephansplatz. **Rooms** 56. **Map** p250 E6.
You can't get a much more central location than this: right on Stephansplatz, 56 steps from the cathedral according to the hotel brochure. The decor in the rooms and suites is inoffensively modern, with light wood furniture, warm hues and acacia parquet flooring; happily, in light of the crowds that throng the square outside, there's good soundproofing as well. The hotel's green initiatives are also commendable, from its environmentally friendly construction and materials to the organic breakfasts on offer. Specify when booking to make sure you get that all-important view.

Kaiserin Elisabeth

1, Weihburggasse 3 (515 26-0, www.kaiserin elisabeth.at). U1, U3 Stephansplatz. **Rooms** 63. **Map** p251 E7.
The red velvet and gilt lobby at the Kaiserin exudes a suitably imperial atmosphere, with a portrait of Empress Elisabeth in pride of place. It's well located,

just off Kärntnerstrasse, and many of the 63 rooms have soaring ceilings, parquet floors and elegant oriental rugs. The front desk is a decided plus point, with well-informed, welcoming staff.

König von Ungarn

1, Schulerstrasse 10 (515 84-0, www.kvu.at). U1, U3 Stephansplatz. **Rooms** 44. **Map** p251 F7.
Standing in the shadow of the cathedral, the 'King of Hungary' occupies a 16th-century house. Mozart once lived next door. Conversion into a hotel turned the central courtyard into a delightful atrium lobby and lounge, with a tree at its centre. The 33 classic rooms are accessed via galleried hallways, and feature Biedermeier-style chairs, country antiques and traditional fabrics. In 2009, ten further rooms and a penthouse suite were added, with more modern styling and bold colours.

Mailberger Hof

1, Annagasse 7 (512 0641, www.mailbergerhof.at). U1, U2, U4 Karlsplatz or U1, U3 Stephansplatz. **Rooms** 40. **Map** p251 E7.
Tucked away in two Baroque houses on a pedestrian side street off Kärntner Strasse, this family-run hotel is a favourite with opera stars and other regulars who welcome its discreet location. The rooms are old-fashioned in style – some teetering on twee and looking rather dated, others in elegantly restrained period decor – and there are also small apartments with kitchenettes. The cheapest rooms can come in at under €150.

Radisson Blu Style Hotel

1, Herrengasse 12 (22 7800, www.radissonblu.com/ stylehotel-vienna). U3 Herrengasse. **Rooms** 78. **Map** p250 E6.

The Style Hotel is set on palatial Herrengasse, two doors from Café Central and a short stroll down to the Hofburg. Traces of its past life as a bank remain, with the sauna and fitness area in the old strongroom, a transparent-walled wine cellar in the cashier's kiosk, and a grand oval lobby with a spectacular, backlit glass floor. Rooms and suites are all decorated in warm reds, creams and browns, with vast double beds and spacious marble- and mosaic-tiled bathrooms; flatscreen TVs, complimentary mini-bars (think fruit juices, snacks and a beer rather than a fridge crammed with booze), CD/DVD players and free Wi-Fi are among the thoughtful extras. The Sapori restaurant serves Austrian dishes with a modern twist, and there's a stylishly appointed bar. Note: breakfast isn't included for standard rooms.

Starlight Suiten

1, Salzgries 12 (535 9222, www.starlighthotels. com). U2, U4 Schottenring or tram 1, 2. **Suites** 50. **Map** p251 E6.
Of this chain's three Vienna outposts, choose the Salzgries address to be close to the bar action of the Innere Stadt. Set in thoroughly renovated former apartment buildings, the suites are airy and functional, each with a separate living room that incorporates a working area with Wi-Fi. The substantial buffet breakfast is €18, but in-room Wi-Fi is free.
Other locations 1, Renngasse 13 (533 9989); 3, Saliesianergasse 2 (710 7808).

Moderate

Hotel Lamée

1, Rotenturmstrasse 15 (532 2240, www.hotel lamee.com). U1, U3 Stephansplatz. **Rooms** 32. **Map** p251 E6.
See p216 **The High Life.**
Other location Hotel Topazz (1, Lichtensteg 3, 532 2250).

Hotel Pension Suzanne

1, Walfischgasse 4 (513 2507, www.pension-suzanne.at). U1, U2, U4 Karlsplatz or tram 1, 2, D or bus 3A. **Rooms** 25. **Map** p251 E7.
The family-managed Suzanne attracts a host of loyal regulars, so book early. Most of the rooms in the building, accessed by a single, old-school lift, were originally small apartments. Some have kitchenettes; a few even sport small outside terraces. All are comfortable and come with compact bathrooms; those on the courtyard or in the back building are the quietest. The Suzanne plays up its historical credentials, having once housed a ladies' hat shop in Habsburg days, but the real attraction here is the central location by the Opera and mid-range prices.

Kärntnerhof

1, Grashofgasse 4A (512 1923, www.karntnerhof. com). U1, U4 Schwedenplatz or tram 1, 2, 21 or bus 2A. **Rooms** 44. **Map** p251 F6.

Hotel Lamée.

Reopened in 2013 after a revamp, the Kärntnerhof is now on the expensive side of moderate, but it's still a charming little hotel. Hidden in a small cul-de-sac leading into the delightful Heiligenkreuzerhof, its discreet entrance sports a splendid 1950s neon sign. The hotel has 44 modernised yet slightly kitsch rooms (including three suites) and exceptional service; there's also a fine antique lift and an appealing roof terrace. The location is quiet, despite being close to public transport, restaurants, shopping and nightlife. Breakfast, included in the rate, is substantial.

Pension Nossek

1, Graben 17 (533 7041-0, www.pension-nossek.at).
U1, U3 Stephansplatz. **Rooms** 30. **Map** p250 E6.
Occupying three floors of a late 19th-century building, the family-owned and -managed Pension Nossek is set amid the smart shops of the pedestrianised Graben. The rooms range from compact to fairly spacious, with oriental carpets, chandeliers and period-style furnishings. Single rooms, some with separate facilities, are a bargain given the location.

Pertschy Palais Hotel

1, Habsburgergasse 5 (534 49, www.pertschy.com).
U1, U3 Stephansplatz. **Rooms** 55. **Map** p250 E7.
In a side street off the Graben, this former pension, now a four-star hotel, is set in the old Cavriani Palace, looking on to a gorgeous inner courtyard (sadly used as a car park). The interior is full of period touches, including an elegant stairway. Most of the rooms are spacious, with comfortable beds; a couple still have their original ceramic ovens as showpieces. Those at the front, on the top floor, are elegantly decorated in rose and cream, with parquet floors and crystal chandeliers. For location, and the distant sound of *fiaker* horses, the Pertschy is an atmospheric choice.

Sacher Apartments

1, Rotenturmstrasse 1-3, 7th Floor (533 3238,
www.pension-sacher.at). U1, U3 Stephansplatz.
Apartments 9. **No credit cards.** **Map** p251 E6.
Pension Sacher comprises nine one- and two-bedroom apartments, on the seventh floor of a post-war office block in the heart of the city. Seven have views of Stephansdom, and the Innere Stadt is on your doorstep. The apartments offer compact but comfortable accommodation with antique furniture and well-equipped kitchenettes. The owners, who speak fluent English, are welcoming. Longer stays are charged at a lower rate, the smaller apartments at just over €100 a night. There's no breakfast, though.

RINGSTRASSE & AROUND

Deluxe

Hotel Bristol

1, Kärntner Ring 1 (515 160, www.bristol
vienna.com). U1, U2, U4 Karlsplatz or tram
1, 2, D. **Rooms** 150. **Map** p250 E7.

Opened in 1892, the Bristol scores highly on service, location and history. In February 1935, the Prince of Wales checked in with Wallis Simpson, while other notable guests have included Rachmaninoff, Puccini and Gershwin. Set on the Ringstrasse, across Kärntner Strasse from the Staatsoper, it offers unadulterated, old-fashioned luxury, plus state-of-the-art technology and elegant modern bathrooms. Rooms are decked out in opulent Viennese style, with some of the smaller ones a little overwhelmed by cumbersome furniture – not a problem if you're in the huge Prince of Wales suite. The Bristol bar is an intimate meeting place with velvet armchairs, while the Bristol Lounge restaurant is an art deco delight, with an open fireplace in winter. *Photo p217.*

★ Imperial

1, Kärntner Ring 16 (501 100, www.hotelimperial
vienna.com). U1, U2, U4 Karlsplatz or tram 2, D.
Rooms 134. **Map** p251 E8.
As the first sight of the Imperial's towering marble-clad lobby confirms, this place is a grande dame of the city's hotel scene and the exquisite service matches the refined decor. Built in 1863 as the Vienna residence of the Prince of Württemberg, transformed into the Hotel Imperial for the World Exhibition in 1873, this town palace remains one of the most imposing edifices on the Ringstrasse, set just around the corner from the Musikverein. The lower floors are given over to luxurious suites festooned with antiques and 19th-century paintings; from the executive junior suites upwards, each is provided with a personal butler. The rooms become progressively smaller as you go higher up, but high ceilings, swag curtains and period details dominate throughout. The Café Imperial Wien has been newly renovated, while the 1873 HalleNsalon is a wonderfully plush, red velvet affair, with piano accompaniment five days a week.

Palais Hansen Kempinski Vienna

1, Schottenring 24 (236 1000, www.kempinski.
com). U2, U4 Schottenring. **Rooms** 152.
Map p250 E5.
Another heritage overhaul, this time of a palatial Ringstrasse hotel created for the 1873 World Exhibition, the Kempinski oozes 21st-century style while honouring its historic past. The in-room iPad entertainment system allows you to order room service, check tomorrow's weather and change TV channels with three quick taps on the screen. The spa, open 12 hours a day, has been inspired by the bathing culture of the Ottomans. The cosmopolitan Edvard restaurant gained a Michelin star within a year of opening, the hotel's cigar lounge is the largest of its kind in Vienna and there's even an in-house, high-end florist.

Ritz-Carlton

1, Schubertring 5-7 (31188, www.ritzcarlton.com).
U4 Stadtpark. **Rooms** 202. **Map** p251 F7.

ESSENTIAL INFORMATION

ESSENTIAL INFORMATION

THE HIGH LIFE

Vienna discovers that good things come in tall packages.

Although the city has no shortage of luxury hotels, they tend to be in the Innere Stadt or on the Ringstrasse. Opulence and comfort they have in spades – but what they lack is perspective. True, quite a few have views, slices of cityscape even. The **Ring** (*see p217*) included a rather clever feature in its design of a porthole cut into the wall of its sauna so that you can gaze over the metropolis while sweating off those slices of *sachertorte*.

From 2010, however, a new concept came to Vienna, one more common to Dubai or the Far East: the high-design high-rise. The **Sofitel Vienna Stephansdom** (*see p218*) is nowhere near Stephansdom. It's not even in the Innere Stadt, as it stands just over the Danube Canal. But it can allow itself to be called Stephansdom and get away with it because it has design touches inspired by Vienna's best-known landmark and offers a jaw-dropping view of the spire. In fact, of the whole city.

Housed in an 18-storey glass-and-steel tower rather than a stone-built Ringstrasse palace, this was a radical departure for a city with so strong an antipathy to high-rise construction. The work of French architect Jean Nouvel, it towers above the Donaukanal. Near the base, a wedge-shaped slice appears to have been cut away, with a sloping plane of diamond-shaped panes of glass that pays subtle tribute to the tiled roof of Stephansdom. At night, the swirling video panels designed by Swiss artist Pipilotti Rist are backlit, and the monochome tower becomes a beacon. At the top is its fine dining restaurant and bar, Le Loft, an illuminated eyrie perched high above the city, with dramatic floor-to-ceiling windows.

The guest rooms are equally daring – and uncompromising. Echoing the building's sleek, monochrome facades, the rooms are decorated in all-white (north-facing) and pale grey (south-facing); on the west facade, three suites are all black. Looking towards Stephansdom and the Innere Stadt, the luxury grey rooms are also equipped with vast, geometric sliding shutters, allowing guests to frame their own views of the city. Who says shrines to high design can't have a sense of fun?

In 2013, the **Meliá Vienna** (*see p218*) raised the bar even higher. At 220 metres (722 feet) and 58 storeys high, the Donau

City Tower 1 (*pictured*) that houses the hotel is the tallest building in Austria. It's also the first entirely self-sustainable one. Designed by French architect Dominique Perrault, it soars above the other landmarks of the burgeoning Danube City business quarter on this island in the Danube, most notably the nearby United Nations building and Austria Center Vienna conference complex. It has made headlines with its 57th-floor restaurant (although the views wowed critics early on more than the somewhat confusing fare), panoramic fitness centre, 2,000sq m (21,528sq ft) sun terrace, and rooftop bar with DJ sessions at weekends.

Back in town, another newbie has poked its head up above Vienna's somewhat uniform downtown skyline. The **Hotel Lamée** (*see p214*), which opened its doors in 2012, may not be 58 floors high, but its main feature is a roof terrace set at eye level with the richly coloured roof of Stephansdom. Located only a few steps away from the iconic cathedral, the Lamée occupies a slender building typical of the era that inspires its design: the 1930s. The ten upper-floor suites all have Stephansdom views, neatly juxtaposing with the Makassar ebony panelling and honey-coloured walls of the room interiors. Dubai-style skyscapers by the Danube and design hotels shoulder by shoulder with Stephansdom. Whatever next?

Hotel Bristol. *See p215.*

Four Ringstrasse palaces have been merged into one divine hotel, overlooking the Stadtpark and a short walk from the city centre. Equipped with the most contemporary facilities – a Guerlain Spa, top-quality gym and Vienna's longest hotel pool, plus a chocolate sommelier, the Crystal Ballroom, a superb steakhouse and rooftop bar – this high-end lodging still echoes the glory days. Even the smallest rooms are 38sq m (409sq ft), with heated floors in the bathrooms, separate showers and bathtubs, and Asprey bubblies. All is elegant wood and comfortable, muted furnishings. Noon check-out is a boon, although an hour's free in-room Wi-Fi for entry-level guests seems mean considering the high rates.

Expensive

Le Méridien

1, Opernring 13 (588 90-0, www.lemeridien vienna.com). U1, U2, U4 Karlsplatz or tram 1, 2, D. **Rooms** 294. **Map** p250 E7.

Set in the shell of three Ringstrasse townhouses, with an interior designed by London's Real Studios, Le Méridien features public areas full of theatrical lighting and art installations. Music starts playing when you step through the revolving door, there are lift 'soundscapes', and the lobby and bar are positively pumping in the evening. The clutter-free rooms are much calmer, however, with light wood floors and muted colour schemes. The Ligne Roset beds feature backlit, etched-glass headboards and crisp white linen, the TVs are huge, and the bathrooms have impressive power showers (and freestanding baths in larger rooms). The fitness area takes in a hot tub and pool, while innovative extras include video cameras or scooters for hire. Note: breakfast isn't always included in the rates.

★ Ring

1, Kärntner Ring 8 (22122, www.theringhotel. com). U1, U2, U4 Karlsplatz or tram 1, 2, D. **Rooms** 68. **Map** p251 E8.

Opened in 2007 in a prime Ringstrasse location, this hotel has a boutique feel and a laid-back vibe. Touting itself as 'Vienna's casual luxury hotel', it has swiftly become a favourite among the A-list crowd, and counts Kevin Spacey and Scarlett Johansson among its former guests. Rooms are kitted out in a restrained colour palette that runs from creams and browns to sober greens and reds; Nespresso coffee machines, Molton Brown toiletries, a turn-down service and free Wi-Fi all come as standard. If you're after serious floor space of 40-50sq m (around 430-530sq ft), opt for one of the 'X-Ordinary' rooms, most of which look out over the Ringstrasse. On the top floor, there's a panoramic view across the Vienna skyline from the sauna – part of the hotel's polished day spa.

Budget

Motel One Wien-Staatsoper

1, Elisabethstrasse 5 (585 0505, www.motel-one.com). U1, U2, U4 Karlsplatz. **Rooms** 400. **Map** p250 E8.

Budget beds on the Ringsstrasse? Whatever next? Actually, this latest of four budget Motel One venues in Vienna is just off the Ring, between Karlsplatz and the Opera House. But at these rates, who's quibbling? Motel One's popular formula of attractive design and knockdown prices has swept across Germany and central Europe since 2010, with features such as 24-hour reception, convivial communal areas and classy-looking lobby bars obscuring the fact that you're paying well under €100 for your room.
Other locations Wien-Hauptbahnhof (10, Gerhard-Bronner-Strasse 11, 602 000); Wien-Prater (2, Ausstellungstrasse 40, 729 7800); Wien-Westbahnhof (15, Europaplatz 3, 5935-0).

LEOPOLDSTADT & THE DANUBE

Expensive

★ Sofitel Vienna Stephansdom

2, Praterstrasse 1 (906 160, www.sofitel.com). U1, U4 Schwedenplatz. **Rooms** 182. **Map** p251 F6.
See p216 **The High Life**.

Moderate

Meliá Vienna

2, Donau-City-Strasse 7 (90104, www.melia.com). U1 Kaisermühlen-VIC. **Rooms** 253. **Map** p244 J2.
See p216 **The High Life**.

Budget

Magdas Hotel

2, Laufbergergasse 12 (720 0288, www.magdas-hotel.at). U1, U2 Praterstern then tram O or bus 80A. **Rooms** 78. **Map** p248 H6.
See p220 **Status Symbol**.

LANDSTRASSE & BELVEDERE

Expensive

Hilton am Stadtpark

3, Am Stadtpark 1 (717 000, www.hilton.com). U3, U4 Landstrasse. **Rooms** 579. **Map** p251 F7.
This huge, 1970s high-rise is just off the Ringsstrasse, overlooking the Stadtpark, in easy reach of the CAT airport train. Rooms are comfortably appointed and geared towards a business clientele, while facilities include a fitness centre, spa and sauna. In-room Wi-Fi is extra and pets are charged at €40 a day. The Hilton Vienna Plaza is a polished 1st district alternative, while in the 2nd district the Danube Hilton is a converted river warehouse with spacious rooms.
Other locations Hilton Vienna Plaza (1, Schottenring 11, 313 900); Danube Hilton (Handelskai 269, 727 770).

InterContinental Wien

3, Johannesgasse 28 (711 220, www.vienna.intercontinental.com). U4 Stadtpark or tram 2. **Rooms** 459. **Map** p251 F8.
When it went up in the mid 1960s, the 459-room InterContinental gave Vienna its first chain hotel. Although the boxy exterior is a bit of an eyesore, the interior has worn well, from the velvet and crystal lobby to the more modern, individual style of the

Motel One Wien-Staatsoper.

rooms – go for the ones at the front with great views over the Stadtpark. For service and accommodation, the hotel remains one of InterContinental's flagships. There's a 24-hour fitness centre and a beauty centre, along with a relaxed lobby café, a bar and a restaurant. The city centre is about ten minutes' walk and the CAT airport train is also close by.

Moderate

Mercure Grand Hotel Biedermeier Wien

3, Landstrasser Hauptstrasse 28 (716 710, www.mercure.com). U3 Rochusgasse. **Rooms** 198. **Map** p251 G7.

Now one of seven Mercures in the city, including a new one at Westbahnhof, the Grand Hotel Biedermeier is a jewel of a hotel resulting from the skilful conversion of a cluster of 19th-century residential buildings. A real sense of old Vienna remains, thanks to the simple, period-style decor in its 198 rooms. Modern-day comforts have not been overlooked, though – you'll find a sauna, gym and two restaurants. Set between two U-Bahn stations, the hotel is about 20 minutes' walk from the city centre. **Other locations** throughout the city.

Budget

NH Wien Belvedere

3, Rennweg 12A (206 11, www.nh-hotels.com). S-Bahn Rennweg or tram 71. **Rooms** 114. **Map** p247 F9.

Part of the expanding Spanish hotel chain with four other branches in Vienna, the NH Belvedere is housed in a Jugendstil building that was formerly the Austrian government's printing works. Backing on to the Belvedere botanical gardens, it has 114 rooms, a fitness area and a bar. The decor may be a little lacking in character for some, but the prices are very competitive considering the location and facilities. Note: breakfast isn't always included in the cheapest deals. **Other locations** NH Wien City (7, Mariahilfer Strasse 32-34, 521 720); NH Wien Atterseehaus (7, Mariahilfer Strasse 78, 524 5600); NH Wien Airport (Einfahrtsstrasse 1-3, A-1300 Flughafen Wien, 701 510); NH Danube City (A-1220, Wagramer Strasse 21, 260 200).

Vienna Feeling

2, Volkertplatz 5 (0650 41 77 801, www. vienna-feeling.com). U2 Taborstrasse then bus 80A. **Apartments** 2. **Map** p244 G4.

Set in the heart of the old Jewish quarter, this pair of privately owned one-bedroom apartments are a delightful alternative to the city's hotels. Both have been lovingly kitted out with vintage finds, running from flower-besprigged china teacups and old books to Biedermeier writing desks and panels of art deco stained glass. The polished parquet floors and high double doors exude a stately, old-fashioned charm, as does the spread of homebaked goodies and beautifully set table that the owner leaves out on her guests' arrival. Each apartment sleeps up to four people, with lets running from a minimum of three nights to a maximum of six months; prices vary accordingly. The basic rate of €100 for two is a snip.

KARLSPLATZ & SOUTH

Moderate

★ Das Triest

4, Wiedner Hauptstrasse 12 (589 180, www. dastriest.at). U1, U3, U4 Karlsplatz. **Rooms** 72. **Map** p247 E8.

STATUS SYMBOL
Magdas is a concept hotel with a conscience.

Firstly, the name. There was nobody called Magda. In fact, the hotel isn't even called Magda's but **Magdas** (see p218), which is a German play on words (*mag das*) inviting you to like the place.

Secondly, and more importantly, the concept. This is the world's first hotel run by refugees. Opened on St Valentine's Day 2015, this former old people's home by the Prater soon had the world's press singing its praises. *The Guardian*, *Frankfurter Allgemeine*, *Berliner Zeitung* – everyone's beating a path to its somewhat institutional door down a quiet, leafy side street.

Inside is a riot of invention and colour. After Caritas Austria, the adventurous local branch of the international Catholic charity, had decided to go ahead and fund this conversion – into a workplace for asylum seekers and an attractive budget hotel – the neighbours pitched in to help.

The students of the sculpture department of the Academy of Fine Arts, whose works lie around the garden next door, have lent a significant creative touch to the communal areas and individually decorated rooms. Funky and retro – note the customised street map of Vienna in the entrance – the decor lends a youthful, bright touch, lifting the tone of the backstories of the cheery staff.

People make places and Magdas is all about those that work here. There are 20 former refugees employed in the business and each has a brave tale of escape from oppression and years of bureaucratic limbo as an asylum seeker.

For its €1.5 million (plus €60,000 raised through crowd-funding), Caritas has not only created a cool hotel with a conscience but also invested in training. Some staff even enjoyed a stint working at one of the most famous five-star hotels on the Ringstrasse, as big a step as it's possible to make from a village in Africa or war zone in the Middle East. A job coach, with experience in the hotel trade, has also been working in situ since the project began.

The garden – where breakfast is taken – and the expansive, well-stocked bar lend themselves to social and cultural events, a chance for Viennese to meet refugees and find out for themselves what underpins this venture they've read so much about.

It's hoped that word will also reach the various bureaucrats who flit into the United Nations building on the other side of the Prater, perhaps even prompting a debate on the refugee crisis this hotel is doing its bit to solve. If some well-known mandarins chose Magdas rather than an all-expenses-paid, five-star with spa, it might help bump up already buoyant occupancy rates. It's hardly a sacrifice. After all, this hotel has brilliant staff, accommodation for less than €100, Wi-Fi, rain showers, each room with a unique design, and some with balconies overlooking the whole Prater park, rotating Riesenrad and all. *Ich mag das.*

Das Triest is Vienna's original boutique hotel, designed by Terence Conran in 1995, in an old stage-coach inn on the route south to the Habsburg port of Trieste. Although a little scuffed in places, it's generally wearing well and is popular with touring pop stars. The attractively understated rooms and lobby are full of fresh flowers and designer details (Castiglione lamps, flatscreen TVs, Molton Brown toiletries), while the grassy inner courtyard is planted with olive trees and bathed in sunshine. You can enjoy good northern Italian cuisine in the chic Collio restaurant or in the courtyard in summer. The Silver Bar is one of Vienna's coolest hotel drinking spots, with precision-mixed cocktails.

Das Tyrol

6, Mariahilfer Strasse 15 (587 5415, www.das-tyrol.at). U2 MuseumsQuartier. **Rooms** 30. **Map** p250 D8.

The rooms at this cosy hotel have been cleverly fitted into unusual spaces, and have a bright, welcoming feel with warm colours and contemporary art. Features include Nespresso coffee machines, while the bathrooms are gleaming white affairs. Breakfast is hearty with a generous buffet, eggs cooked to order and a complimentary glass of prosecco. The spa comprises a steam room and sauna. Located just off Vienna's main retail artery, across the street from the MuseumsQuartier, the Tyrol is also within easy walking distance of the Innere Stadt and its attractions. Staff are charming.

Budget

Carlton Opera

4, Schikanedergasse 4 (587 5302, www.carlton.at). U1, U2, U4 Karlsplatz or U4 Kettenbrückengasse. **Rooms** 52. **Map** p247 D8.

The facade reveals the 1904 origins of this hotel; inside, many of the art nouveau touches have also been preserved. The 52 air-conditioned rooms are mostly high-ceilinged, many with parquet floors; the larger rooms have kitchenettes. Furnishings are comfortable if undistinguished, as are the white-tiled bathrooms. The Carlton is right beside the Naschmarkt and the Schleifmühlgasse gallery scene, and around 15 minutes' walk from the city centre. If you're driving, the hotel has a garage and a limited amount of cheaper street parking cards (€8/day).

★ Wombat's City Hostel the Naschmarkt

4, Rechte Wienzeile 35 (897 2336, www.wombats. at). U4 Kettenbrückengasse. **Map** 247 D8.

Launched in 2011, this branch of the Wombat's chain is set on the Naschmarkt, with a swanky lobby and a dimly-lit red and purple bar. The mezzanine-level breakfast room is light and airy, and there are kitchens for guests' use; the basement has laundry rooms and bike storage space. Dorms are neat and bright, with cream-painted wooden bunks, laminate flooring, sturdy lockers and clean, white bathrooms;

there's a pink wing exclusively for women. Some of the en-suite doubles feel more like boutique hotel rooms: number 508, with its huge windows overlooking the market, is probably the best in the house. The buffet breakfast is €4.50 extra.

Other location Wombat's City Hostel the Lounge, 15, Mariahilfer Strasse 137 (897 2336).

NEUBAU
Expensive

Sans Souci Wien

7, Burggasse 2 (522 2520, www.sansouci-wien.com). U2, U3 Volkstheater. **Rooms** 63. **Map** p250 D7.

Close to the city's main hub of culture and filled with original paintings by Allen Jones and Roy Lichtenstein, the recently opened Sans Souci complements its artistic kudos with luxurious exclusivity. The treatments in its spa match any in town, with detox massages and facials using Austrian Vinoble cosmetics, while the cocktail bar has the zip common to every new venture. A hotel in a previous life – occupied by the US Army after 1945 – even further back Sans Souci was a lively tavern where Johann Strauss once premiered a polka. Although remaining true to its holistic values (it's a member of the Healing Hotels of the World), Sans Souci hasn't lost its sense of fun. In-room design touches, a turndown service and welcoming staff make up for an ever so slight lack of space. Direct bookings are encouraged with the incentive of a free 30-minute spa session.

Moderate

25hours Hotel at MuseumsQuartier

7, Lerchenfelder Strasse 1-3 (521 510, www. 25hours-hotels.com). U2, U3 Volkstheater. **Rooms** 217. **Map** p250 C7.

The first part of this hotel opened in 2011, with 34 suites and a top-floor lounge and bar, with a splendid terrace. A further 183 rooms, a restaurant and a gym were unveiled in 2012. The design is modern and playful, with circus-inspired wall murals, splashes of vibrant colour and quirky lighting. All rooms feature flatscreen TVs, iPod docks and free Wi-Fi, and there's free bike rental too. The Dachboden loft bar is a boon, though it's often rented out for private parties. On sunny days, the Burger de Ville grill provides meat treats from an Airstream trailer alongside the ground-level terrace bar-restaurant overlooking the pretty urban greenery of Weghuberpark. With these attractions, and given the location close to the tourist sights of the Hofburg and bar vortex of the 7th district, 25hours pulls in a significant number of non-guests to dine and drink of an evening.

★ Altstadt

7, Kirchengasse 41 (522 6666, www.altstadt.at). U2, U3 Volkstheater or bus 48A. **Rooms** 45. **Map** p246 C7.

Close to Spittelberg and the MuseumsQuartier, the Altstadt is a brilliant boutique option, conceived by owner Otto E Wiesenthal in 1991 after years of globetrotting. Decor in the rooms and suites varies immensely, running from straightforward classic rooms to more exciting collaborations with different designers. For sheer opulence, it's hard to beat the creations of Italian architect and designer Matteo Thun. A fantastic synthesis of period elegance and contemporary touches, the grand chandeliers, red velvet headboards and black mosaic-tiled bathrooms feel delightfully decadent. The refurbished salon and breakfast room are boldly and beautifully appointed, and the in-house massage service is a popular feature. Staff are friendly and guests are offered a complimentary afternoon tea with homemade cake.

K+K Hotel Maria Theresia

7, Kirchberggasse 6 (521 23, www.kkhotels. com). U2, U3 Volkstheater or tram 49 or bus 2A. **Rooms** 132. **Map** p250 D7.
In the quaint Spittelberg district, the K+K is handy for the city's museums and some good shopping, and has easy transport links to the city centre, some 15 minutes' walk away. Rooms are spacious and tastefully muted, with work desks, down duvets, free Wi-Fi and quietly elegant black marble and granite bathrooms. Staff members are friendly and helpful, and there's a gym and sauna.
Other location K+K Palais Hotel (1, Rudolfsplatz 11, 533 1353).

FROM JOSEFSTADT TO ALSERGRUND

Expensive

Levante Parliament

8, Auerspergstrasse 9 (228 28-0, www.the levante.com). U2, U3 Volkstheater or tram 2, 46. **Rooms** 67. **Map** p250 C6.
This superb conversion of an early 20th-century sandstone building is one of Vienna's leading design hotels. While the glass sculptures of Romanian artist Ioan Nemtoi that adorn the restaurant and massive inner courtyard may not be to everyone's taste, the 67 rooms are elegant and uncluttered. The materials are in harmony with the building's modernist roots, and the feel is pared down and chic.

Moderate

★ Hotel Rathaus Wein & Design

8, Lange Gasse 13 (400 1122, www.hotel-rathaus-wien.at). U2, U3 Volkstheater or tram 46. **Rooms** 39. **Map** p250 C7.
The family-run Hotel Rathaus combines innovative boutique styling with a viticultural theme. All rooms are named after top Austrian vintners, and bottles of their produce sit temptingly on the wooden shelving. The creaky wrought-iron lift helps to retain a touch

of fin-de-siècle ambience, a nice contrast to the hyper-modern rooms, reception areas and bar. The last of these is naturally wine-oriented, does light lunches and will lay on a bit of cheese and even some antipasti for guests arriving late. The breakfast buffet, served in the inner courtyard or winter garden, is a feast – although it does cost an extra €17.

Hotel Zipser

8, Lange Gasse 49 (404 54-0, www.hotel-vienna. travel/en). U2 Rathaus or tram 5, 33. **Rooms** 53. **Map** p246 C6.
This former apartment block behind the town hall in the charming 8th district dates to 1904, and is now a friendly, family-run hotel. The 53 fair-sized rooms are fresh, inviting and simply appointed; the free Wi-Fi is a nice extra. Some rooms at the back also have splendid tree-shaded balconies.

Budget

Hotel-Pension Lehrerhaus

8, Lange Gasse 20 (403 2358, www.hotel-lehrerhaus.at). Tram 2, 46. **Rooms** 40. **Map** p250 C6/7.
This old-fashioned, inexpensive hotel offers high-ceilinged rooms of various sizes, all immaculate and welcomingly decorated. Rates vary depending on the facilities; rooms without en suite baths or toilets are a real bargain. Breakfast isn't served, so you'll need to repair to a café or buy supplies to store in the communal fridges found on each floor.

Pension Wild

8, Lange Gasse 10 (406 5174, www.pension-wild. com). U2, U3 Volkstheater or tram 46. **Rooms** 22. **Map** p250 C7.
Combine a relaxed family-managed environment with a convenient location, and it's not surprising that this pension is usually fully booked. The rooms are relatively plain but attractive enough, with colour-matched fabrics and light wood furniture. A buffet breakfast is offered in a cheerful front room, and the small kitchenettes on each floor are handy.

CAMPING

Aktiv Camping Neue Donau

22, Am Kleehäufel (202 4010, www.camping wien.at). U1 Kaisermühlen-VIC, then bus 91A to campsite Kleehäufel. **Open** mid Apr-Sept.
This campsite is just north of the 'New Danube' recreation area, parallel to the main Danube, and there are hiking, cycling, swimming, boating and nude bathing areas nearby. It's about 4km (2.5 miles) north-east of the city centre. Facilities include lounges, kitchens, a shop, a self-service restaurant and washing machines.
Other locations Camping Wien Süd (1230-Wien Breitenfurterstrasse 269, 867 3649, open June-Aug); Camping Wien West (1140-Wien Hüttelbergstrasse 80, 914 2314, open Jan, mid Feb-Dec).

Getting Around

ARRIVING & LEAVING

By air

Vienna International Airport
(7007 22 233, www.vienna airport.com).
Vienna's international airport is located 18km (11 miles) south-east of the city. It's linked by **CAT** airport train (www.cityairporttrain. com) and S-Bahn line 7 to central Wien Mitte station. The CAT (€11 single, €17 return, €2 surcharge on board) takes 16mins, the S-Bahn (€4.40) 25mins. Each runs every 30mins. Children up to 14 travel free. There are also various types of travel passes integrated with city transport.
Airport taxis such as **C&K** (444 44, www.ck-airportservice.at) and **Airport Driver** (228 22, www. airportdriver.at) charge a flat rate of €33 into town. The C&K stand is situated to your left as you leave the arrivals hall.

Airlines

Aer Lingus *(585 2100, www.aerlingus.com).*

Air Berlin *(0820 737 800, www.airberlin.com).*

Austrian Airlines *(05 1766 1000, international +43 5 1766 1061, www.austrian.com).*

British Airways *(7956 7567, UK office 0844 493 0787, www.britishairways.at).*

easyJet *(0820 320 950, UK office 01582 525 330, www.easyjet.com).*

germanwings *(0820 900 144, UK office 0330 365 1918, www.germanwings.com).*

Jet2 *(0810 1025 1565, UK office 0800 408 1350, www.jet2.com).*

Lufthansa *(0810 1025 8080, www.lufthansa.at).*

By rail

Austrian trains offer a comfortable, efficient service. The main operator,

ÖBB (Austrian Federal Railways), has plenty of online discounts. It also offers a useful 'Haus zu Haus' luggage service, which picks up and delivers your bags (up to three, maximum 30kg each), charging from €19.40 for one bag, €29.40 for a pair of skis or €39 for a bike.
If travelling west towards Salzburg or Tyrol, it provides a 'Panorama' compartment, a first-class car with huge windows for viewing the scenery.
In Vienna, the main station is now **Hauptbahnhof**. Opened in 2014, it replaced Südbahnhof and is still marked as 'Südtiroler Platz' on many local metro maps on the red U1 line. The new station, which forms part of a vast mall containing 90 shops and restaurants, has significantly improved the city's international connections.
Many stations still use **Westbahnhof**, which was also renovated and reopened in late 2011. **Wien Mitte** was also expanded and reopened in 2013 – it now contains a handy check-in desk for CAT passengers *(see left)* heading to Vienna International Airport. Westbahnhof has its own metro station on the U3 and U6 lines, while Wien Mitte is shown as Landstrasse (Wien Mitte) on the U3 and U4 lines.

ÖBB

Austrian Railways
05 1717, www.oebb.at.

By bus

Erdberg (798 29 00, 0900 128 712, www.eurolines.at) is the main station for all international Eurolines bus services. It has its own metro station on the U3 line.

By river

The **Twin City Liner** (588 80, www.twincityliner.com) runs daily fast boat services to and from Bratislava (€20-€35 one-way) between May and October. The terminus is the new landing station near Schwedenplatz.
DDSG Blue Danube (588 80, www.ddsg-blue-danube.at) links Vienna and Budapest between May and the end of September (from €109 one-way, €125 return), and also offers assorted day trips and cruises.

PUBLIC TRANSPORT

Vienna has an excellent public transport network comprising U- and S-Bahn lines, trams and buses. Daytime transport runs from around 5am until 11pm or midnight. Nightline bus services are marked with an N. On Fridays and Saturdays, the U-Bahn now runs all the way through the night. **Wiener Linien** (7909 100, www.wienerlinien.at) can provide a range of maps, tickets and information from its offices at selected U-Bahn stations, including **Stephansplatz, Karlsplatz, Westbahnhof, Hauptbahnhof, Landstrasse (Wien Mitte)** and **Schwedenplatz**.

Fares & tickets

Tickets can be bought from the multilingual vending machines at U-Bahn stations and at tobacconists for €2.20. They're valid for one journey on all modes of transport, for up to one hour.
Validate your ticket at the start of your journey by using the blue validation machines at the entrance to each U-Bahn line, or on board all buses and trams. U-Bahn stations are barrier-free so the system operates on trust. Plain-clothes inspectors operate, so fare dodging could mean a fine of €103. Once you validate your ticket, keep it in case you get checked.
Money-saving options include monthly (€48.20), weekly (€16.20; valid from Mondays only), 72-hour (€16.50), 48-hour (€13.30) and 24-hour (€7.60) cards, along with an eight-day card (€38.40) that doesn't have to be used on consecutive days but does need to be validated.
Another option is the **Vienna Card** (€21.90). Valid for 72 hours, it also entitles you to modest discounts at museums, galleries and restaurants.
Children up to the age of six travel free. Those up to 15 can travel free on Sundays, public holidays and Austrian school holidays – otherwise they're charged half-price.
Senior citizens of any nationality (women over 60, men over 65) can travel with a two-journey half-price ticket (€2.80), provided they have ID.

U-Bahn

The **U-Bahn** underground is quick and comfortable. The five lines are colour-coded: U1 is red, U2 purple, U3 orange, U4 green and U6 brown. U-Bahn stations display a limited number of network maps – it may be best to try and work out your journey in advance.

The extension of the U1 will be ready by 2017. The second phase of the U2 extension will begin in 2018. There are also plans to build a new U5 line from 2023.

Doors don't open automatically: pull the handle sharply or press the illuminated button.

Local trains

The **S-Bahn** and **Lokalbahn** are the local, fast railways that run in Vienna and further afield. The **Badner Bahn** connects Vienna and the town of Baden.

If you're taking an S-Bahn within Vienna you don't need another ticket, but if you travel outside zone 100, you'll need an additional ticket depending on how many zones you're travelling in. You can find this out by looking at the bull's-eye zone map posted in all stations.

Trams

Vienna's trams or *Strassenbahnen* cover the city and its outskirts. All tram stops are marked, each one with a single timetable – you may have trouble quickly finding the route and schedule if a certain tram happens to be coming in. Once on board, each stop is announced by name, with corresponding connecting lines.

Note that you need to buy a separate ticket (from €8) if you want to take the yellow-painted **Vienna Ring Tram**, which circles the Ringstrasse (10am-5.30pm daily). It offers multilingual commentary on headphones and LCD information screens. If you can live without that, you can follow the same route by catching Trams 1 and 2, using an ordinary ticket, though you'll have to change en route.

Buses

Buses go to places that trams can't. Their stops look like the tram stops and also have a single timetable displayed. Bus numbers end with an 'A' or have three-digit numbers.

Nightline

Safe, reliable Nightline buses (marked with an N) run from 12.30am to 5am on the half-hour on 22 routes. All transport tickets are valid for Nightlines.

TAXIS

Vienna's taxis are reliable and not too expensive. Hailing them on the street sometimes works, but taxi ranks are clearly marked. Phoning for a taxi often takes less than three minutes' waiting time.

Fares are metered, with a basic pick-up rate then a per-kilometre charge; on Sundays, public holidays and at night (1-6am) both rates go up. A small tip or rounding up of the fee is expected. To order a taxi, call one of the following numbers:

31 300

60 160

81 400

DRIVING

Driving is regulated and relatively safe. You're required by law to carry driving licences and luminous waistcoats. Speed limits are 30-50 km/h (18-31mph) in residential areas, 100km/h (62mph) on country roads and 130km/h (80mph) on motorways. Motorways are four to six lanes wide and fast, and their use requires a road tax sticker (*Pickerl*), which is sold at the borders and at most Trafik shops. These cost €84.40 for 12 months, €25.30 for two months and €8.70 for ten days, with different rates for motorcycles (€33.60/€25.30/€5). Drivers who don't display the appropriate sticker on the upper middle or left side of their windshield will be fined €300. Spot checks are common, as are breath tests.

Breakdown services

Austria has two 24-hour major services, both of which are free for members. Non-members can also call on their services. These charges may be reimbursed if you have insurance that covers you for Austria.

ARBÖ

24hr emergency hotline 123, office 891 210, www.arboe-wien.at.

ÖAMTC

24hr hotline 120, office 711 990, www.oeamtc.at.

Fuel stations

All major petrol stations in Austria take credit cards; local stations may not so check before filling up. The three listed below are open 24 hours a day.

BP

1, Morzinplatz 1. **Map** p251 F6.
19, Heiligenstädterstrasse 46-48. **Map** p243 D1.

Shell

22, Wagramerstrasse 14. **Map** p245 K2/3.

Parking

Parking in most of the 1st district is a nightmare, and the police are quick to ticket and tow, costing anything from €36 to €242.

Districts 1-9 and 12, 14, 15, 16, 17, 20 have blue zones (*Kurzparkzonen*), where you purchase vouchers (*Parkscheine*) at tobacconists. In the 1st district you can park for up to two hours, 9am-10pm Mon-Fri, and Saturday as marked. In other districts you can park for up to two or three hours, 9am-7pm Mon-Fri, and Saturday as marked. Look for designated spaces marked with blue lines. Vouchers come in 30-, 60- and 120-minute increments.

Vehicle hire

Renting a car is a fairly standard procedure, but do specify if you plan to drive into Eastern Europe.

Autoverleih Flott

597 3402, www.flott.at.

Avis

0800 0800 8757, www.avis.at.

Europcar

86616 11/airport 86616 10, www.europcar.at.

Hertz

512 8677, www.hertz.at.

CYCLING

Vienna offers plenty of designated bike paths; the route around the Ringstrasse is a lovely way to tour the city without getting lost. The Danube Canal bike path is another good way of crossing the city, and the ramp beside the Prater Bridge will take you to Vienna's largest car-free cycling area.

For the **City Bike Wien** scheme, see www.citybikewien.at. For more on city cycling in general, visit www.wien.gv.at/english/leisure/bike/.

WALKING

Vienna is a very walkable city. However, beware the change in normally placid Austrians when they get behind the wheel.

ESSENTIAL INFORMATION

Resources A-Z

ADDRESSES

House and building numbers, and door numbers, follow the street name (Alserbachstrasse 54/9, for example). *Strasse* (street) is often abbreviated to Str. A smaller street (usually a side street) is called a *Gasse*. Addresses in Vienna are preceded by the district number: for example, Wittgenstein-Haus is at 3, Parkgasse 18 – meaning number 18 Parkgasse, in the 3rd district.

AGE RESTRICTIONS

The legal age for drinking and smoking is 16, and for driving is 18. The age of consent for heterosexual and homosexual sex is 14.

BUSINESS

Conventions & conferences

Austria Center Vienna
22, Bruno-Kreisky-Platz 1 (260 69-0, www.acv.at). U1 Kaisermühlen-VIC.

Hofburg Congress Centre & Redoutensaele Vienna
1, Heldenplatz (5873 6660, www.hofburg.com). Tram 1, 2, 71, D. **Map** p250 D7.

Couriers

DHL
11, Bleibtreustrasse (0820 550 505, www.dhl.at). U3 Grillgasse then bus 76a to Bleibtreugasse. **Open** 8am-7pm Mon-Fri.

Office services

Regus Business Centres
1, Parkring 10 (516 33-0, www.regus.at). Tram 1, 2, D. **Map** p250 D6. **Open** 8am-5pm Mon-Fri. Regus provides office space to rent, plus related services.

UNIVERSITAS Österreichischer Übersetzer und Dolmetscherverband
19, Gymnasiumstrasse 50 (368 60 60, www.universitas.org). U6 Nussdorfer Strasse. **Map** p242 C3.

The Austrian Association of Translators and Interpreters can connect you with a suitable service.

Useful organisations

Austrian Chamber of Commerce
1, Stubenring 8-10 (514 50, www.wko.at). U3 Stubentor or tram 2. **Open** 8am-5pm Mon; 8am-4.30pm Tue-Thur; 8am-4pm Fri. **Map** p247 E10.

British Embassy
Commercial Section
3, Jauresgasse 12 (716 13 6161, www.britishembassy.at). Tram 71. **Open** 9.15am-12.30pm, 2-3.45pm Mon-Fri. **Map** p247 F8. Keeps a directory of British companies in Austria.

US Chamber of Commerce
9, Porzellangasse 39/7 (319 5751, infoline 0900 833 933, www.amcham.or.at). Tram D. **Map** p243 D4.
A directory of US firms and licencees in Austria is available for members for €120; non-members €150.

CONSUMER

If you have questions about your consumer rights, contact the **VKI** (*see below*).

Consumer Information Association (VKI)
6, Mariahilfer Strasse 81 (58 877-0, www.konsument.at). U3 Neubaugasse. **Open** 9am-6pm Mon-Thur; 9am-4pm Fri. **Map** p246 C8.

CUSTOMS

If you've purchased items in another EU state, you can bring limitless

LOCAL CLIMATE

Average temperatures and monthly rainfall in Vienna.

	High (°C/°F)	Low (°C/°F)	Rainfall (mm/in)
Jan	1 / 34	-4 / 25	39 / 1.5
Feb	3 / 37	-3 / 27	44 / 1.7
Mar	8 / 46	1 / 34	44 / 1.7
Apr	15 / 59	6 / 43	45 / 1.8
May	19 / 66	10 / 50	70 / 2.8
June	23 / 73	14 / 57	67 / 2.6
July	25 / 77	15 / 59	84 / 3.3
Aug	24 / 75	15 / 59	72 / 2.8
Sept	20 / 68	11 / 52	42 / 1.7
Oct	14 / 57	7 / 45	56 / 2.2
Nov	7 / 45	3 / 37	52 / 2.0
Dec	3 / 37	-1 / 30	45 / 1.8

ESSENTIAL INFORMATION

goods into Austria as long as they're for personal use. Guidelines are as follows: 800 cigarettes, 400 cigarillos, 200 cigars, 1kg tobacco; ten litres of spirits, 90 litres of wine (or 60 litres of sparkling wine) and 110 litres of beer. The same quantity of goods can be taken out of Austria, if you're going to another EU state.

When entering from a non-EU country or when purchasing in duty-free shops within the EU, you can bring: 200 cigarettes or 100 cigarillos or 50 cigars or 250g tobacco; four litres of wine and two litres of spirits, or two litres of champagne and 16 litres of beer; and 50g perfume and 250ml eau de toilette.

Tax refunds

Non-EU residents can claim VAT (*Mehrwertsteuer*, or MwSt) refunds on goods worth over €75 purchased in Austria. Ask to be issued with a tax-free shopping cheque (or U34 form) from the store where you bought the item/s and present it, together with the receipt, at the refund office at the airport. Allow an extra 15 minutes to queue and have your refund processed.

DISABLED

Vienna is a relatively easy city to get around, and all U-Bahn stations can be accessed via lifts or ramps. Bus drivers will bring out ramps for wheelchair users, while most trams are low enough to allow access; a flashing wheelchair symbol on the information board shows when the next accessible service will depart.

For information on accessible travel and sights, medical aid and more, check the 'Accessible Travel' section on www.wien.info.

Bizeps
2, Schönngasse 15-17/4 (523 8921, www.bizeps.or.at). Open 10am-3pm Mon-Thur; 10am-1pm Fri.
A multilingual support group run by and for people with disabilities.

Fahrtendienst Gschwindl
810 4001, 2246/27 870, www. gschwindl.at. Open 6am-6.30pm Mon-Fri.
Offers taxis that are equipped to transport wheelchairs. There's a flat rate of €30 to destinations within Vienna.

DRUGS

No drugs, either soft or hard, are allowed in Austria, and the

laws are broadly similar to those in the UK. Prescription drugs such as sleeping pills, sedatives and Prozac are considered illegal in large quantities; if you bring any of these drugs into Austria, take your prescription to avoid the risk of confiscation.

ELECTRICITY

The current used in Austria is 220V, which works fine with British 240V appliances. Plugs have two pins, so UK visitors should bring an adaptor. For US 110V gadgets, you'll need to use a transformer.

EMBASSIES & CONSULATES

Australian Embassy
4, Mattiellistrasse 2-4 (506 740, www.austria.embassy.gov.au). U1, U2, U4 Karlsplatz. **Open** 10am-noon Mon-Fri. **Map** p251 E8.

British Embassy & Consulate
3, Jaurèsgasse 10 (Embassy 716 130, Consulate 716 13-5900, www.britishembassy.at). Tram 71. **Open** *Embassy* 9am-5pm Mon-Fri. *Consulate* By appt only Mon-Fri for consular and passport enquiries. **Map** p247 F8.

Canadian Embassy
1, Laurenzerberggasse 2 (3rd floor) (531 38 3000, www.kanada.at). U1, U4 Schwedenplatz or tram 1, 2. **Open** 8.30am-12.30pm Mon-Fri. **Map** p251 F6.

Irish Embassy
1, Rotenturmstrasse 16-18 (5th floor) (715 4246, www.embassyofireland. at). U1, U3 Stephansplatz. **Open** 9.30am-12.30pm Mon-Fri. **Map** p251 F6.

US Consulate
1, Parkring 12A (313 39 7537, www. usembassy.at). U3 Stubentor or tram 1, 2. **Open** *Visas* 8-11.30am Mon-Fri. *Phone enquiries* 9.30-11.30am Mon-Fri. **Map** p251 F7.

US Embassy
9, Boltzmanngasse 16 (31 339-0, www.usembassy.at). Tram 37, 38, 40, 41, 42. **Open** 8.30am-noon, 1-4.30pm Mon-Fri. **Map** p243 D4.

EMERGENCIES

Beware: *Ambulanz* means emergency room or outpatient clinic, and *Rettung* means ambulance. *See also right* **Health**.

Ambulance
Rettung 144.

Fire
Feuerwehr 122.

Police
Polizei 133.

GAY & LESBIAN

For information on HIV and AIDS, *see p227. See also pp144-148* **Gay & Lesbian**.

Hosi Wien
4, Heumühlgasse 14/1 (216 6604, www.hosiwien.at). U4 Kettenbrückengasse. **Map** p251 G5. This leading gay and lesbian rights organisation runs various groups and initiatives, along with the annual Rainbow Parade.

Rosa Lila Tip
6, Linke Wienzeile 102 (gays 585 4343, lesbians 586 8150, www. dievilla.at). U4 Pilgramgasse. **Open** *Info evenings for lesbians* 5-8pm Mon, Wed, Fri. *Info evenings for gays* 5-8pm Mon; 8-10pm Thur or by appt. **Map** p246 C9.
Counselling, discussion groups and advice for gays and lesbians.

HEALTH

Most doctors in the Austrian Health Service (*Krankenkasse*) speak English. Hospital care is divided between general care (*allgemeine Klasse*) or private (*Sonderklasse*). Treatment is available for citizens of all countries that have reciprocal treaties with the Krankenkasse – in effect most European states. Britain has a reciprocal arrangement with Austria, so emergency hospital treatment is free when you show a UK passport.

Holders of the European Health Insurance Card (EHIC) will be treated free at any hospital listed below or with any doctor who takes patients from *Alle Kassen* (all insurance funds). The **Wiener Gebietskrankenkasse** (regional insurance fund) can inform you which doctors take the EHIC. For more on the EHIC, see www.nhs.uk/ NHSEngland/Healthcareabroad. Non-EU citizens should take out full health insurance.

Wiener Gebietskrankenkasse
10, Wienerbergstrasse 15-19 (601 22-4200, www.wgkk.at). U1 Reumannplatz, then bus 7a. **Open** 7am-2.15pm Mon-Thur; 7am-2pm Fri.

Accident & emergency

A&E hospitals (*Unfallspitäler*) are listed under hospitals (*Krankenhäuser*) in the white pages of the phone book. The following hospitals accept emergencies 24/7.

Allgemeines Krankenhaus (AKH)

9, Währinger Gürtel 18-20 (40 400-0, www.akhwien.at). U6 Michelbeuern. Map p242 B5. The AKH is affiliated with the University of Vienna. It's your best option in central Vienna.

Lorenz Böhler Unfall Krankenhaus

20, Donaueschingenstrasse 13 (059 3934-1000, www.auva.at/ukhboehler). U6 Dresdnerstrasse. Map p243 F2.

Sankt Anna Kinderspital

9, Kinderspitalgasse 6 (401 70-0, www.stanna.at). U6 Alser Strasse or tram 43, 44. Map p242 B5. This children's hospital has doctors on hand 24 hours a day to check out high fevers, rashes or worse.

Complementary medicine

The pharmacies listed below specialise in homeopathy.

Apotheke Kaiserkrone

7, Mariahilfer Strasse 110 (526 2646, www.kaiserkrone.at). U3 Zieglergasse. **Open** 8am-7pm Mon-Fri; 8am-6pm Sat. Map p246 C8. A reliable address for homeopathy.

Internationale Apotheke

1, Kärntner Ring 17 (512 2825, www.internationale-apotheke.at). U1, U2, U4 Karlsplatz or tram 1, 2, D, J. **Open** 8am-7pm Mon-Fri; 8am-6pm Sat. Map p251 E8. Specialists in all types of homeopathic treatments.

Contraception & abortion

Outpatient Clinic for Pregnancy Help

1, Fleischmarkt 26 (24hr hotline 512 9631-250, www.prowoman.at). U1, U4 Schwedenplatz or tram 1, 2. **Open** 8am-5pm Mon-Sat. Map p251 F6. Pregnancy tests, birth control advice and abortion counselling.

Dentists

Austrians have good dental care, but only some costs are covered by the state system. Many Austrians skip across the border to Hungary, where they can get the same treatment for a third of the cost. Dentists (*Zahnärtzte*) are listed in the phonebook; most speak English.

University Dental Clinic

9, Sensengasse 2A (400 70). Tram 37, 38, 40, 41, 42. **No credit cards.** Map p250 D5. The university emergency dental clinic is open weekdays, but only for a few hours. Phone for times.

Doctors

If you need an English-speaking doctor, phone 513 95 95 (24hr hotline). The British Embassy (716 130) can also provide you with a list of English-speaking doctors. Take your EHIC card or private insurance documents with you.

HIV & AIDS

AIDS-Hilfe Wien

6, Mariahilfer Gürtel 4 (599 37, www.aids.at). U6 Gumpendorfer Strasse or tram 6, 18. **Open** 9am-2pm Mon, Tue, Fri; 9am-1pm Wed; 4-8pm Thur. Map p246 B9. For tests, results and counselling.

Medicine Delivery Service

Medikamentenzustelldienst

404 14-100. For €7, this 24-hour service will pick up and deliver medicines from pharmacies.

HELPLINES

Alcoholics Anonymous

3, Barthgasse 7 (01-799 5599, www.anonyme-alkoholiker.at). U3 Schlachthofgasse. **Open** 6-9pm daily. Map p248 J9. A number of English-speaking groups meet regularly, two evenings and two days a week.

Drogenberatungstelle

6, Gumpendorfergürtel (24hr hotline 4000 53600, www.suchthilfe.at). U6 Gumpendorferstrasse. **Open** 9am-5pm Mon-Thur; 9am-2pm Fri. Map p246 C9. Gives advice and help to those with drug problems.

Viennese Children & Youth Protection

Wiener Kinder und Jugendanwaltschaft *9, Alserbachstrasse 18 (7077 700, www.kja.at). U4 Friedensbrücke or tram 5.* **Open** 9am-5pm Mon-Fri. Map p243 D4. English spoken.

Women's Emergency Centre

Frauen Notruf der Stadt Wien *71 719.* Council-funded rape crisis centre with counselling in English.

ID

There is no law obliging citizens to carry means of identification. However, if the police want to check your passport and you don't have it with you, they may insist on accompanying you to wherever you've left it.

INTERNET

Most restaurants, bars and businesses have homepages, which are generally well constructed and maintained. Wi-Fi access is widely available throughout the city, and is common in hotels and cafés.

LEFT LUGGAGE

At the airport, left luggage is in the entrance hall across from the rental cars and costs €4-€8 per day, depending on the size of luggage. All major credit cards are accepted.

In the larger train stations in Vienna, there are no longer any left-luggage offices but you are able to leave your bag in a locker (€2-€3.50).

LEGAL HELP

If you run into legal trouble, contact your insurers or your embassy or consulate (*see p226*).

LIBRARIES

Austrian National Library

1, Heldenplatz (514 1437, www.onb.ac.at). U2 Volkstheater or tram 1, 2, 71, D. **Open** 9am-9pm Mon-Sat. Map p250 E7.
Browse the catalogue, select what you want and pick the books up the next day to take to the reading room. There's a varied choice of English titles.

Städtische Büchereien

7, Urban-Loritz Platz 2A (4000-84 500, www.buechereien.wien.at). U6 Burggasseee or bus 48A or tram 6, 9, 18, 49. **Open** 11am-7pm Mon-Fri; 11am-5pm Sat. Map p246 B8. Vienna's public libraries have an excellent collection of books and CDs. This splendid central branch also has panoramic city views.

LOST PROPERTY

To trace possessions left on a tram or bus, call the **General Information Office** (790 943-500). After one week, everything is removed to the central police lost and found office. Go in person, with plenty of patience.

Zentrales Fundamt
Hotline 0900 600-200,
www.fundamt.gv.at).
Provides online access to a database of lost and found items.

MEDIA

Press

International newspapers and magazines are available from kiosks, street sellers and tobacco stores all over town. The **Austrian Times** (www.austriantimes.at) and **Austria Today** (www.austriatoday.at) have news online in English, while the **Vienna Review**, produced by the Vienna Journalism Institute, is available online or in print.

For listings, there's the weekly German-language *Falter* (www.falter.at), sold at every news kiosk.

Radio

The state-run ÖRF's station, **Österreich 1** (92.0 FM, 87.8 FM), offers a blend of classical, jazz and opera music, including concerts and other cultural programmes. **Radio Wien** (89.9 and 95.3 FM), one of ÖRF's regional stations, has pop, news, weather and traffic. **Ö3** (99.9 FM) is a slick commercial station.

For visitors, the ÖRF-run **FM4** is still the best option, broadcasting indie/dance music 24/7 (103.4 FM), in English from 1am to 2pm, with English-language news on the hour from 6am to 7pm.

Radio Austria International (6,155kHz, 5,945kHz, 13,730kHz) is ÖRF's shortwave station designed by the government to be the 'voice of Austria' abroad. It has news and information, and an English, Spanish and Russian service.

Probably the best bet for more diverse programming is **Radio Orange** (94 FM), playing soul, hip hop, jazz and African. **Superfly** is a soul-music station (98.3 FM).

Television

ATV screens re-runs, bad movies and shows such as *Die Lugners*, an *Osbournes*-inspired chronicle of a society building contractor, and *Bauer sucht Frau* (Farmers seek

Wives). Austrian TV (www.orf.at) consists of two state-run national channels, **ÖRF1** and **ÖRF2**. Other channels are available via cable or satellite.

MONEY

Compared with much of Europe, Vienna is not the most credit card-friendly of cities, so don't assume that smaller hotels and restaurants will accept cards.

ATMs

Hole-in-the-wall machines are dotted around Vienna and have a lit sign with two horizontal green and blue stripes. The specific cards that each machine takes are marked and there's a choice of languages. Note that the machines don't give receipts. There are also a few automatic currency-converting machines, stating 'Change/Wechsel' with instructions in English, that will accept foreign banknotes.

Banks

Most banks open 8am-12.30pm and 1.30-3pm during the week, staying open until 5.30pm on Thursday. A few banks, such as the main Bank Austria on Schottengasse and Die Erste at Graben 21, don't close for lunch. Some banks, generally at railway stations and airports, stay open longer.

Bureaux de change

City Air Terminal U
3, U4 Wien Mitte. **Open**
8am-12.30pm, 2-6.30pm daily.

Opera/Karlsplatz
U1, U2, U3, U4/tram 1, 2, D.
Open 8am-7pm daily.

Lost/stolen cards

If you lose your credit card, or it has been stolen, phone one of the 24-hour emergency numbers below.

American Express 0800 900 940.

Diners Club 501 3514.

MasterCard 0800 218 235.

Visa 711 11 770.

NATURAL HAZARDS

Austria's only natural hazards are Lyme disease and Central European encephalitis (CEE), or tick-borne

encephalitis. Both are transmitted by infected ticks, but the former is an easily treatable bacterial infection. CEE, however, is a viral infection of the central nervous system with no known cure. Both are highly prevalent in forested areas of Central Europe such as the Vienna Woods, particularly from April to October.

The risk of CEE should not be exaggerated as over 90% of tick bites are harmless. If infection does take place, flu-like symptoms appear one to three weeks later, normally lasting two to four days. Only around one in 250 cases actually leads to encephalitis.

OPENING HOURS

From Monday to Friday, shops in Vienna are now legally allowed to open between 6am and 7.30pm, and until 9pm on two days. In practice, these longer opening hours are only operative in commercial areas such as Mariahilfer Strasse and the 1st district. Many smaller shops still close for lunch.

On Saturday, 6pm is the latest closing time. With the exception of bakeries, all shops are closed on Sunday and public holidays, apart from those located in main railway stations.

POLICE STATIONS

The emergency number for the police is 133. The police are generally straightforward to deal with and speak English. Police stations (*Polizeiwachzimmer*) are marked with a red-and-white sign and some of the most central are: 1, Am Hof 3 (313 10-213-10); 1, Stephansplatz U-Bahn station (313 10-213-70).

Central Police HQ
1, Schottenring 7-9 (313 100).
U2 Schottenring. **Map** p250 D5.

POSTAL SERVICES

The postal service is efficient and easy to use, and most workers speak English. Postboxes are painted bright yellow and sport a two-ended horn, and are often mounted on the wall. An orange stripe denotes that the box is still emptied at weekends. For more information, call the Post Office 24-hr hotline (0810 010 100).

Look in the phone directory's white pages under P*ost- und Telegraph-enverwaltung* for locations of post offices and their opening times, or visit the website at www.post.at. The following post offices have extended opening hours:

Franz-Josefs-Bahnhof
9, Althanstrasse 10 (0577 677 1090). Tram 5, D. **Open** 7am-8pm Mon-Fri; 9am-2pm Sat, Sun. **Map** p243 D3.

Main Post Office
1, Fleischmarkt 19 (0577 677 1010). U1, U4 Schwedenplatz or tram 1, 2. **Open** 7am-8pm Mon-Fri; 9am-2pm Sat, Sun. **Map** p251 F6.

Poste restante

Poste restante facilities are available at any post office, but only the main post office (*see above*) has a 24-hour service. Letters should be addressed to the recipient 'Postlagernd, Postamt' – along with the address of the particular post office. They can be collected from the counter marked *Postlagernde Sendungen*. Take your passport along with you.

RELIGION

Because of Vienna's musical heritage, many people attend church simply to enjoy the music on offer. Look out for details of Sunday Mass at Augustinerkirche, Karlskirche, Minoritenkirche, Stephansdom and Michaelerkirche. The acclaimed Vienna Boys' Choir sings Mass at the Burgkapelle on Sundays and religious holidays at 9.15am, except from July to mid September. To hear them, you must pay both a concert fee and have a bag thrust under your nose for donations. If you can't arrange seats on the chapel floor, don't bother with the balconies – many have obstructed views.

Christ Church
3, Jaurèsgasse 17-19 (714 89 00). Tram 71. **Map** p251 F7.
This Anglican church holds Sunday services at 8am and 10am; members of Viennese choirs are often invited as guest singers.

Church of Jesus Christ & Latter Day Saints
19, Silbergasse 1 (367 5647). Tram 38 or bus 10A.
Vienna's Mormon church.

City Synagogue
1, Seitenstettengasse 4 (535 0431 412). U4 Schwedenplatz. **Map** p251 F6.
In order to be admitted, you must show your passport.

International Baptist Church
6, Mollardgasse 35 (no phone). U4 Margareten Gürtel. **Services** 11.30am, 12.30pm Sun.

St Augustin
1, Augustinerstrasse 3 (533 7099). U1, U2 Karlsplatz. **Mass** 11am, 6.30pm Sun. **Map** p250 E7.
A Roman Catholic church next to the Hofburg.

St Stephen's Cathedral
1, Stephansplatz 3 (515 52). U1, U3 Stephansplatz. **Mass** noon, 6pm daily. **Map** p251 E6.

United Methodist Church
15, Sechshauser Strasse 56 (604 53 47). Bus 57A. **Services** 11.15am Sun. **Map** p246 A10.

SAFETY & SECURITY

Vienna is one of the safest cities in Europe, and most people don't think twice about walking alone in most districts, even late at night. That said, there is some pickpocketing and petty crime in tourist locations, so take precautions in crowded areas and markets in particular. Karlsplatz station is notorious as a drugs hub, while the Prater at night is known for pickpockets.

SMOKING

Austrians are among the heaviest smokers in Western Europe. Under the current laws, smaller cafés, bars and restaurants (less than 50sq m) can choose whether they are smoking or smoke-free establishments. Larger places have to partition an area for non-smokers. A general smoking ban comes into force in 2018.

STUDY

Language classes

Berlitz
1, Graben 13 (512 8286, www.berlitz.at). U1, U3 Stephansplatz or bus 1A. **Open** 8am-8pm Mon-Fri. **No credit cards.** **Map** p250 E6.
Individual, intensive and evening courses in German.

Cultura Wien
1, Bauernmarkt 18 (533 2493, www.culturawien.at). U4 Schwedenplatz or bus 1A, 3A. **Open** 9am-6pm Mon-Thur; 9am-5pm Fri. **No credit cards.** **Map** p251 E6.
Cultura Wien offers daily intensive four-hour classes, and evening classes too.

Inlingua
1, Neuer Markt 1 (512 2225, www.inlingua.at). U1, U3 Stephansplatz. **Open** 9am-6pm Mon-Fri. **No credit cards.** **Map** p250 E7.

Intensive courses (four hours per day) are run in sessions lasting two weeks or longer. Inlingua also offers evening courses in business German twice a week. Classes are limited to three to six students.

University of Vienna
9, Universitätscampus-Altes AKH, Alser Strasse 4, Hof 1.16 (4277 24101, www.sprachzentrum.univie.ac.at). Tram 43, 44. **Open** July-Sept 8.30am-4pm Mon-Fri. Oct-June 9am-4pm Mon, Wed-Fri; 9am-6.30pm Tue. **No credit cards.** **Map** p242 C5.
Cheap nine- or 12-week courses in German for foreigners.

VHS Polycollege
5, Stöbergasse 11-15 (5466 6100, www.vhs.at/5-vhs-polycollege-margareten). Bus 12A, 14A, 59A. **Open** 8.30am-6.30pm Mon-Fri. **No credit cards.** **Map** p247 D10.
Volkshochschulen, Vienna's adult education colleges, offer a wide range of language courses, as well as many others such as cookery, photography and yoga. The Polycollege is the most dynamic of the 18 that operate in Vienna.

TELEPHONES

You can make cheap international calls from the privately run phone shops dotted across the city.

Dialling & codes

To make an international call, you need to dial the country code, city code and telephone number. A few country codes are: Australia 61, Germany 49, Hungary 36, Ireland 353, New Zealand 64, South Africa 27, UK 44, USA/Canada 1.
    All telephone numbers in Austria have prefixes, which are usually printed in parentheses. To make a call to Vienna from elsewhere in Austria, dial 01 and then the number. To phone Vienna from abroad, dial 00 43, followed by 1 and then the number. To dial an Austrian mobile phone from abroad (usually 0676, 0699, 0650 or 0664 numbers), dial 00 43, then the number without the 0.
    Many general city numbers only have four digits. Austrian telephones have direct-dial extensions that are often placed at the end of the phone number, preceded by a hyphen.

Mobile phones

As there's plenty of competition, you can get your mobile free and just pay for your calls, plus line rental.

Drei
0800 30 30 00, www.drei.at.

Mobilkom/A1
0800 664 664, www.A1net.at.

Telering
0800 650 650, www.telering.at.

T-Mobile
0676 2000, www.t-mobile.at.

Operator services

Directory enquiries 11 88 77.

International directory enquiries
0900 11 88 77.

Telekom Information
0800 100 100.

Public telephones

A local call costs a minimum of 50¢ from public telephone booths; many have internet terminals.

TIME

Austria is on Central European Time, which means that it's an hour ahead of the UK. Like Britain, Austria puts its clocks forward by an hour on the last Sunday of March and puts them back by an hour on the last Sunday of October.

TIPPING

There are no fixed rules about tipping, but in a restaurant it's customary either to give a ten per cent tip or round up the bill. Announce the total sum to the waiting staff as they take your money – they will normally pocket the tip and then return your change. Bar staff always welcome a modest rounding up of the bill – again, tell them the final sum you're looking to pay.

Taxi drivers normally receive an extra ten per cent over and above the metered fare, and €1 per bag is normal for porters and bellhops. Tipping is common in Austria, so an extra €1 or €2 for any services will never hurt.

TOURIST INFORMATION

City Hall Information

1, Friedrich-Schmidt-Platz 1 (52 550). U2 Rathaus or tram 1, 2, D. **Open** phone enquiries 8am-6pm Mon-Fri. **Map** p250 D6.
The City Hall provides a number of maps and brochures in English.

You can also phone for details of museum hours, plus opera performances and ticket sales.

Vienna Tourist Board

1, Albertinaplatz 1 (24 555, www.vienna.info). U1, U2, U4 Karlsplatz or tram 1, 2, D. **Open** 9am-7pm daily. **Map** p247 E7.

Wien Xtra-Kinderinfo

1, Babenbergerstrasse 1 (4000 84100, www.jugendinfo.at). U2 Babenbergerstrasse or tram 1, 2, D. **Open** 2-7pm Mon-Wed; 1-6pm Thur-Sat. **Map** p250 D7.
Advice for parents and families, dispensed from a family friendly office in Babenbergerstrasse.

VISAS & IMMIGRATION

Citizens of other EU countries have the right to enter Austria and remain for an indefinite period of time. However, anyone staying in Austria in a private house or apartment for more than 60 days is technically required to register with the Magistratisches Bezirksamt, although this is not enforced (*see below* **Residence permits**).

A visa is not required for US citizens for stays of up to three-months; at the end of a six-month stay you must leave the country if you don't have a residence permit.

Residence permits

If you're planning on staying in Austria for more than 60 days, you'll need to register with the Magistratisches Bezirksamt (of your district) to obtain a *Meldezettel* – a confirmation of where you live. A *Meldezettel* is requested for everything from renting a flat to applying for a library card.

Buy the forms at any tobacconist and locate the Bezirksamt in your area in the phone book under *Magistratisches Bezirksamt/ Meldeservice* or fill it in online at www.wien.gv.at/verwaltung/ma62/ ahs-info/informationenmeldeservice. html#unterkunftgeber. Bring your passport with you.

If you specify a religious affiliation in the 'Religion' section of the form you may be automatically registered as a member of that particular church and therefore be liable to church taxes. Religion is taken very seriously in Austria, so shrugging off their demands won't work. If you change address, you'll need to de-register at your current Magistratisches Bezirksamt and re-register in the new one.

WHEN TO GO

Vienna's rather mild continental climate, hot in summer and cold in winter, is growing milder and hotter by the year. Wind can often make the temperature seem lower than it really is, and can be biting. During the winter the city sometimes ices over, while rain is frequent in summer. The best times to go are May-June and September-October. Note that many museums and sub-four-star hotels don't have air-conditioning – so be prepared to swelter in the height of summer.

Public holidays

New Year's Day (1 Jan)
Epiphany (6 Jan)
Easter Monday
May Day (1 May)
Ascension Day
Whit Monday
Corpus Christi
Assumption Day (15 Aug);
Austrian National Holiday (26 Oct)
All Saints' Day (1 Nov)
Immaculate Conception (8 Dec)
Christmas Day (25 Dec)
St Stephen's Day (26 Dec).

WOMEN

American Women's Association

1, Singerstrasse 4/11 (966 29 25, www.awavienna.com). U1, U2, U4 Karlsplatz or tram 1, 2, D. **Open** 10am-4pm Mon-Thur; 10am-3pm Fri. **Map** p251 E7.
A non-profit organisation to help English-speaking women living and working in Vienna.

WORKING IN VIENNA

Citizens of the European Economic Area are exempt from the bureaucratic requirements of obtaining work permits. If you're not a citizen of the EEA, then gaining a permit is a hassle. You'll need a work permit (*Arbeitsgenehmigung*) unless you're specifically exempt according to the law governing the employment of foreigners (*Ausländerbeschäftigungsgesetz*).

If you marry an Austrian, then life becomes much easier. Even so, in order to be able to work in the country, you must have a residence permit (*Aufenhaltsbewilligung*) and a written confirmation from the regional Labour Office (*Arbeitsmarktservice*) that certifies your work permit exemption.

Vocabulary

Austrian German and Standard German are often said to be about as similar to each other as American English and British English. Fortunately, you'll find that the vast majority of locals, especially younger ones, speak good English. Below is a list with basic pronunciation, plus some useful words and phrases.

PRONUNCIATION

z pronounced *ts*
w like English *v*
v like English *f*
s like English *z*, but softer
r like a throaty French *r*
a as in father
e sometimes as in bed, sometimes as in day
i as in seek
o as in note
u as in loot
ch as in Scottish loch
ä combination of a and e, like paid or set
ö combination of o and e, as in French eu
ü combination of u and e, like true
ai like pie
au like house
ie like free
ee like hey
ei like fine
eu like coil

USEFUL PHRASES

Hello/good day *guten Tag*
Goodbye *auf Wiedersehen*
Goodbye (informal) *tschüss*
Good morning *guten Morgen*
Good evening *guten Abend*
Good night *gute Nacht*
Yes *ja*; (emphatic) *jawohl*
No *nein*
Maybe *vielleicht*
Please *bitte*
Thank you *danke*
Thank you very much
danke schön
Excuse me *entschuldigen Sie mir bitte*
Sorry! *Verzeihung!*
I'm sorry, I don't speak German *Entschuldigung, ich spreche kein Deutsch*
Do you speak English?
sprechen Sie Englisch?
Can you please speak more slowly? *können Sie bitte langsamer sprechen?*

I don't understand you
Ich verstehe Sie nicht
My name is… *ich heisse…*

AT THE SHOPS

I would like… *ich möchte…*
How much is…? *wieviel kostet…?*
Can I have a receipt? *darf ich bitte eine Quittung haben?*
Open/closed *geöffnet/geschlossen*
With/without *mit/ohne*
Cheap/expensive *billig/teuer*
Big/small *gross/klein*

TRAVEL & TRANSPORT

Entrance/exit *Eingang/Ausgang*
Arrival/departure *Ankunft/ Abfahrt*
Airport *der Flughafen*
Railway station *der Bahnhof*
Ticket *die Fahrkarte, der Fahrschein*
Airline ticket *die Flugkarte, der Flugschein*
Can you call me a cab? *können Sie bitte mir ein Taxi rufen?*
Cashier/ticket office/ box office *die Kasse*
Passport *der Reisepass*
Petrol *das Benzin*
Lead-free *bleifrei*
Traffic *der Vehrkehr*

DIRECTIONS

How do I get to…? *wie komme ich nach…?*
How far is it to…? *wie weit ist es nach…?*
Where is…? *wo ist…?*
Left *links*
Right *rechts*
Straight ahead *gerade aus*
Far *weit*
Near *nah*
Street *die Strasse*
Square *der Platz*
City map *der Stadtplan*

ILLNESS & EMERGENCY

Help! *Hilfe!*
I feel ill *ich bin krank*
Doctor *der Arzt*
Dentist *der Zahnarzt*
Pharmacy *die Apotheke*
Hospital *das Krankenhaus*
I need a doctor *ich brauche einen Arzt*
Please call an ambulance *rufen Sie bitte ein Krankenwagen*
Please call the police *rufen Sie bitte die Polizei*

NUMBERS

0 *null*
1 *eins*
2 *zwei*
3 *drei*
4 *vier*
5 *fünf*
6 *sechs*
7 *sieben*
8 *acht*
9 *neun*
10 *zehn*
11 *elf*
12 *zwölf*
13 *dreizehn*
14 *vierzehn*
15 *fünfzehn*
16 *sechszehn*
17 *siebzehn*
18 *achtzehn*
19 *neunzehn*
20 *zwanzig*
21 *einundzwanzig*
22 *zweiundzwanzig*
30 *dreissig*
40 *vierzig*
50 *fünfzig*
60 *sechszig*
70 *siebzig*
80 *achtzig*
90 *neunzig*
100 *hundert*
101 *hunderteins*
110 *hundertzehn*
200 *zweihundert*
1,000 *tausend*

DAYS & TIMES OF DAY

Monday *Montag*
Tuesday *Dienstag*
Wednesday *Mittwoch*
Thursday *Donnerstag*
Friday *Freitag*
Saturday *Samstag* or *Sonnabend*
Sunday *Sonntag*
Morning *Morgen*
Noon *Mittag*
Afternoon *Nachmittag*
Evening *Abend*
Night *Nacht*
Today *Heute*
Yesterday *Gestern*
Tomorrow *Morgen*

EATING OUT

Haben Sie einen Tisch für… Personen?
Do you have a table for (number) people?
Ich möchte einen Tisch für… Uhr bestellen

Vocabulary

I want to book a table for (time) o'clock
Ich nehme... I'll have...
Ich bin Vegetarier I'm a vegetarian
Zahlen, bitte The bill, please
Couvert/Gedeck cover charge
Menü fixed-price menu
Speisekarte menu
Tageskarte menu of the day
Weinkarte wine list
Frühstück breakfast
Vorspeise starter
Mittagessen lunch
Abendessen dinner

Basics

Bratkartoffeln roast or sauté potatoes. **Brot** bread. **Gebacken** fried. **Gebraten** roast. **Gekocht** boiled. **Ei (Spiegelei; Rührei; pochiertes/verlorenes Ei; weiches Ei; hartgekochtes Ei)** egg (fried; scrambled; poached; boiled; hard-boiled). **Essig** vinegar. **Käse** cheese. **Kernöl** pumpkin seed oil. **Knödel** dumplings. **Nockerl** gnocchi. **Pommes frites** chips. **Öl** oil. **Pfeffer** pepper. **Reis** rice. **Saft** gravy. **Salz** salt. **Serviettenknödel** sliced dumplings. **Suppe** soup. **Topfen** curd cheese. **Zucker** sugar.

Fish & seafood

Fisch fish. **Forelle** trout. **Garnelen** prawns. **Hecht** pike. **Heringsalat** pickled herring salad. **Kabeljau** cod. **Lachs** salmon. **Meeresfrüchte** seafood. **Saibling** lake trout. **Seeteufel** monkfish. **Thunfisch** tuna. **Wolfsbarsch** sea bass.

Meat

Beiried entrecôte. **Blunzn** black pudding. **Brathendl/Backhendl** fried/roast chicken. **Durch** well done. **Englisch** rare. **Ente** duck. **Gans** goose. **Hendl/Huhn** chicken. **Käsekrainer** sausage filled with melted cheese. **Kalb** veal. **Kotelett** chop. **Kutteln** tripe. **Lamm** lamb. **Leber** liver. **Leberkäse** meatloaf. **Lungenbraten** fillet steak. **Nieren** kidneys. **Rind** beef. **Rostbraten** steak. **Schinken/Speck** ham. **Schwein** pork. **Sulz** brawn. **Wurst** sausage.

Vegetables & herbs

Basilikum basil. **Bohnen** beans. **Eierschwammerln** chanterelle mushrooms. **Erbsen** peas. **Fenchel** fennel. **Fisolen** green beans. **Gemüse** vegetables. **Gemischter Salat** tomatoes, potato salad, green beans, lettuce and onions, covered in tart wine or cider vinegar. **Gurke** cucumber. **Ingwer** ginger. **Karfiol** cauliflower. **Kartoffel/Erdäpfel** potatoes. **Kichererbsen** chickpeas. **Knoblauch** garlic. **Kren** horseradish. **Kümmel** caraway seed. **Kürbis** pumpkin. **Linsen** lentils. **Lauch** leek. **Mangold** chard. **Minze** mint. **Oliven** olives. **Paprika** peppers. **Paradeiser** tomatoes. **Petersilie** parsley. **Pilzen** fungi. **Schittlauch** chives. **Spargel** asparagus. **Steinpilze** porcini mushrooms. **Thymian** thyme. **Vogerlsalat** Lamb's lettuce. **Zwiebel** onion.

Typical dishes

Bauernschmaus 'Peasants' treat', a plate of hot meats including roast and smoked pork, frankfurters and ham. **Beuschel** offal stew. **Bretteljause** a kind of ploughman's lunch available in Heuriger: cold cuts, cheeses, raw vegetables, mustard and horseradish served on a wooden board. **Eierspeise** scrambled omelette, sometimes with ham. **Erdäpfelgulasch** potato stew, often with frankfurter. **Frittatensuppe** clear beef broth with slivers of pancake. **Gebratene Bachforelle mit Petersilerdäpfel** fried brook trout with potatoes, in parsley sauce. **Griessnockerlsuppe** clear beef broth with semolina dumplings. **Käsespätzle** baby dumplings in cheese sauce. **Kraut/Schinkenfleckerl** pappardelle-type pasta with cabbage or ham. **Leberknödelsuppe** clear beef broth made with liver and small dumplings. **Rindsgulasch** beef stew spiced with paprika, served with dumplings. **Schweinsbraten** roast pork, often served with sauerkraut and sliced dumplings. **Tafelspitz mit g'röste** boiled beef with fried, grated potatoes, and apple and horseradish sauce. **Tiroler g'röstl** potato, beef and pork hash. **Wiener Eintopf** vegetables, potatoes and sausage in a clear beef broth. **Wiener Schnitzel** veal or pork escalope in breadcrumbs. **Zwiebelrostbraten** tenderloin steak in gravy, with crispy onions and gherkin.

Desserts

Die Nachspeise dessert. **Eis** ice-cream. **Mehlspeise** pâtisserie. **Schlag (obers)** whipped cream. **Schokolade** chocolate. **Torte** cake. **Germknödel** sweet dumplings, jam-filled. **Griessschmarrn** semolina pancake cut into small pieces, served with a plum compôte. **Kaiserschmarrn** thick fluffy pancake, chopped, covered in icing sugar; usually served with plum compôte. **Mohr im Hemd** Rich steamed chocolate pudding with chocolate sauce and whipped cream. **Palatschinken** thick crêpe, sweet or savoury. **Reisauflauf** rice pudding. **Topfen/Marillenknödel** curd cheese or apricot dumplings, covered in breadcrumb and fried in butter; served with hot fruit purée.

Fruit

Birne pear. **Erdbeer** strawberry. **Himbeer** raspberry. **Marillen** apricots. **Obst** fruit. **Pfirsich** peach. **Trauben** grapes. **Zitrone** lemon. **Zwetschke** plum.

Drinks

Almdudler herbal lemonade. **Apfelsaft (-gespritzt)** apple juice (mixed with soda water). **Eiswürfel** ice-cube. **Leitungswasser** tap water. **Orangensaft** orange juice. **Milch** milk. **Mineralwasser** mineral water. **Rotwein** red wine. **Tee** tea. **Wasser** water. **Weisswein** white wine. **Grosses Bier**, or **Krügel** in Viennese half litre. **Kleines Bier**, or **Seidel** in Viennese third of a litre. **Pfiff** 0.2 litre.

Further Reference

BOOKS

Non-fiction & travelogue

Ilse Barea *Vienna* Readable account of the city from the Baroque era to World War I by a Viennese émigrée.
Bill Bryson *Neither Here nor There* Includes a flippant but perspicacious account of his Vienna sojourn as a teenage backpacker in Europe.
Elias Canetti *The Tongue Set Free* The first volume of the author's autobiography explores his school days in Vienna before World War II.
George Clare *Last Waltz in Vienna* A moving account of the ominous pre-Anschluss years, as seen through the eyes of a young middle-class Jew.
Patrick Leigh Fermor *Between the Woods and the Water* Classic travelogue includes an entertaining stay in early 1930s' Vienna.
Françoise Giroud *Alma Mahler: or the Art of Being Loved* A racy defence of Alma's talents, scathing on Gustav Mahler's attempts to stifle her musical career.
Brigitte Hamann *Hitler's Vienna* Grim, fascinating and essential reading about pre-war Vienna in an unsatisfactory translation.
Ingrid Helsing Almaas *Vienna; A Guide to Recent Architecture* Pocket-sized, opinionated and well illustrated.
William M Johnston *The Austrian Mind: An Intellectual and Social History 1848-1938* A dry but thorough American work.
John Leake *The Vienna Woods Killer: A Writer's Double Life* A disturbing investigation into the life and crimes of serial killer-turned-writer Jack Unterweger.
John Lehmann and Richard Bassett *Vienna, A Travellers' Companion* Eyewitness accounts, letters and stories of Vienna.
Jan Morris *50 Years of Europe: An Album* Several illuminating pieces on Vienna show Morris's barely disguised contempt for the city.
Paul Strathern *Wittgenstein in 90 Minutes* Summary of Wittgenstein's life and philosophy ('If people did not sometimes do silly things, no intelligent would ever get done').
Edmund de Waal *The Hare with Amber Eyes: A Hidden Inheritance* This painstakingly researched, compelling family history reveals the horrors of the Anschluss for Vienna's Jewish residents.

Stefan Zweig *The World of Yesterday* A fascinating exploration of the role Jews played in the artistic development of Vienna.

Fiction & poetry

Thomas Bernhard *Cutting Timber* Portraying contemporary Viennese artistic and literary circles. It shows the author at his trademark maniacal and misanthropic best.
Thomas Glavinic *Pull Yourself Together* A coming-of-age yearn featuring an overweight Viennese slacker by one of Austria's most celebrated contemporary novelists.
Peter Handke *The Goalkeeper's Fear of the Penalty* Austria's most celebrated contemporary novelist. His work doesn't deal specifically with Vienna.
Wolf Hass Four of his series featuring the flawed but decent Viennese detective Simon Brenner have been translated into English, the latest being *Brenner and God* (2012).
Elfriede Jelinek *The Piano Teacher* Filmed by Michael Haneke, Jelinek's novel captures the stifling atmosphere of 1950s Vienna. Numerous other works by the 2004 Nobel Prize winner are available in English.
Eva Menasse *Vienna* Much acclaimed, entertaining Jewish saga by debut novelist.
Frederick Morton *A Nervous Splendour: Vienna 1888-89* and *Thunder at Twilight: Vienna 1913-14* Engrossing, dramatised accounts of the end of Habsburg Vienna. The first centres on the Mayerling affair, the latter on events prior to World War I.
Robert Musil *The Man without Qualities* Impressive in size and reputation: the kind of book you really should read, but never get round to (you could just read chapter 15, for its account of the intellectual revolution).
Christoph Ransmayr *The Dog King* A dystopian, beautifully written tale about the horrors of war, set in a fictional Alpine town.
Joseph Roth *The Radetzky March* and *The Emperor's Tomb* Roth's finest novels chronicle the decline of the Empire. Splendid translations by Michael Hofmann.
Joseph Roth *The String of Pearls* The Shah of Persia visits Vienna, demands the services of a countess, and gets a look-alike whore instead. Lots of doomed characters and scenes in coffeehouses.

Frank Tallis *The Liebermann Papers.* Six-volume series of page-turning whodunnits set in fin-de-siècle Vienna featuring psychoanalyst/sleuth Max Liebermann.
Georg Trakl *Selected Poems* For serious melancholics.
Dan Vyleta *The Quiet Twin* A deft character study and dark thriller, set in Nazi-occupied Vienna.
Stefan Zweig *The Royal Game* The influence of Freud and the early psychoanalysts is impossible to miss.

WEBSITES

www.austria.org Austrian press and information service based in Washington, DC.
www.ballesterer.at Online version of Austria's finest football publication, with intelligent features on the game both here and abroad. German only.
www.bier-guide.net/bier-lokale/wien.html Comprehensive, informative German-only resource on the city's bars, where they are and what they serve.
www.falter.at Vienna's best listings paper: in German.
www.mqw.at Full details of events at the MuseumsQuartier.
www.spaceandplace.at English-and German-language cultural community behind urban initiatives such as the debate-encouraging Coffeehouse Conversations.
www.viennaclassic.com One-stop ticket shop for classical concerts, plays and musicals.
www.vienna.info The city's official tourist information site.
www.viennareview.net English-language journal that covers culture, travel, politics and events in Vienna and Central Europe.
www.vienna-unwrapped.com One-woman travel site created by Viennese blogger Barbara Cação with tips for walks, tours and attractions.
www.viennawalks.com By theme, by district and by era.
www.viennawurstelstand.com English-language cornucopia of all things contemporary and Viennese.
www.wien.gv.at Municipal site with general info on Vienna. Excellent historical pieces too.
www.wienerlinien.at The city's public transport system.
www.wieninternational.at The latest news and cultural events in Vienna, in English and German.

Index

INDEX

INDEX

Kunstforum

Silberka

Schatzkammer

Nationalbibliothek

Maps

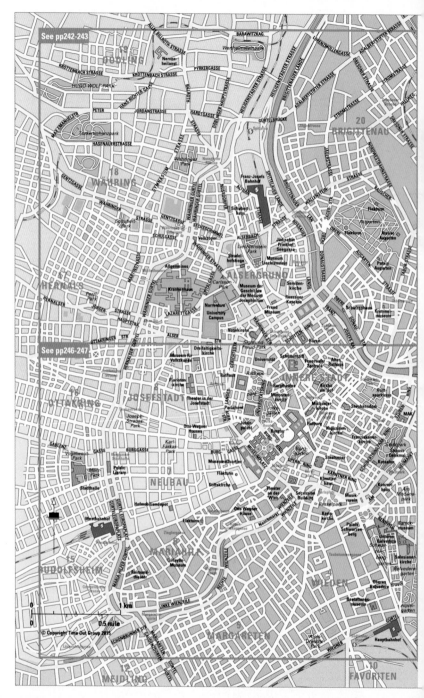

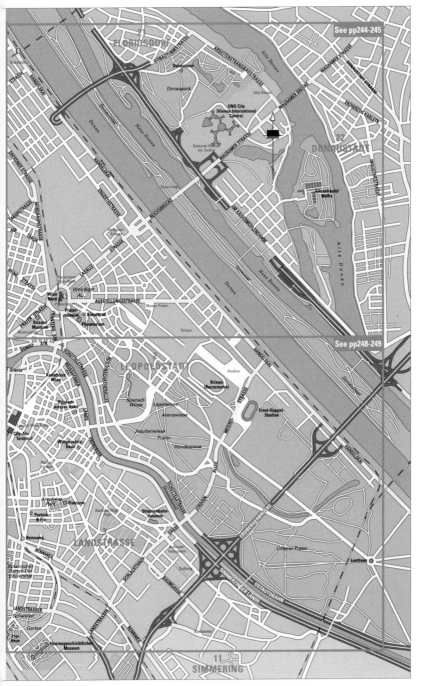

MAPS

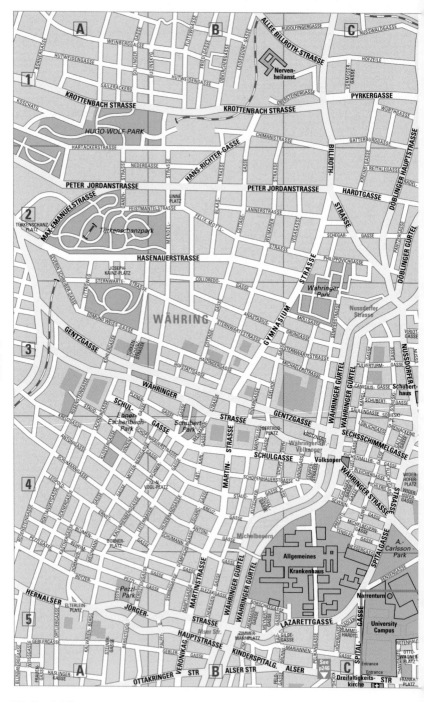

MAPS

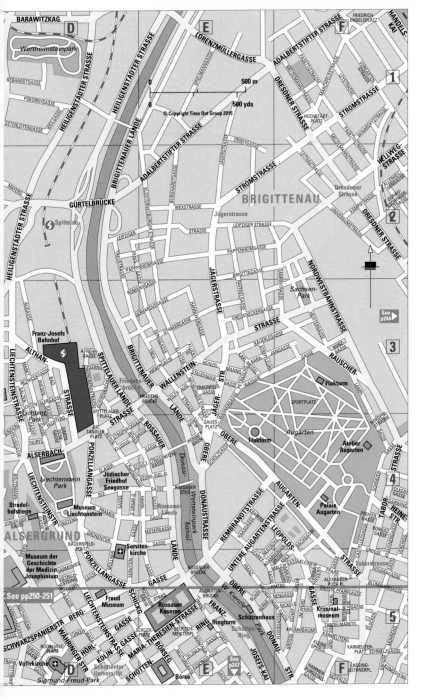

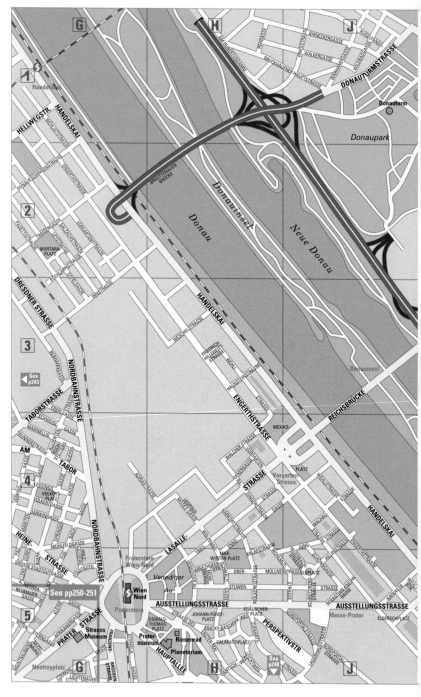

MAPS

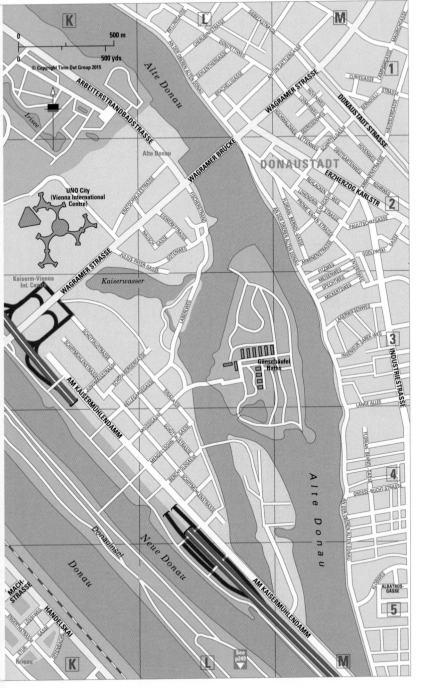

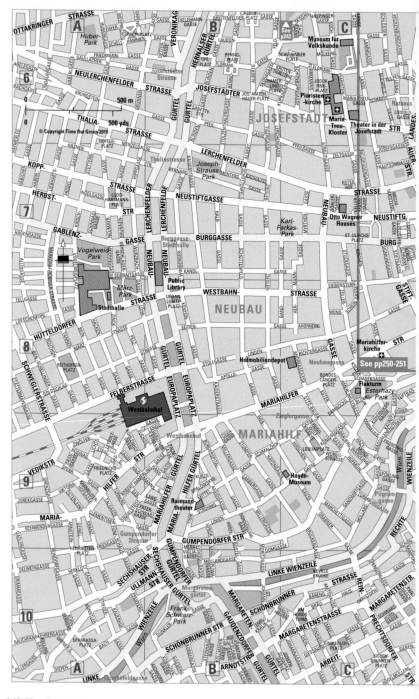

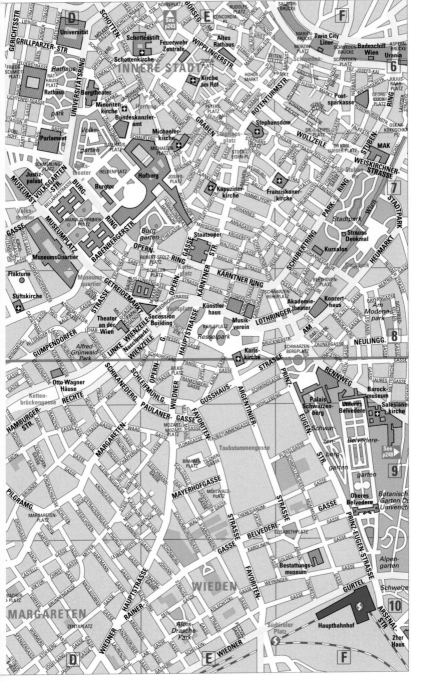

MAPS

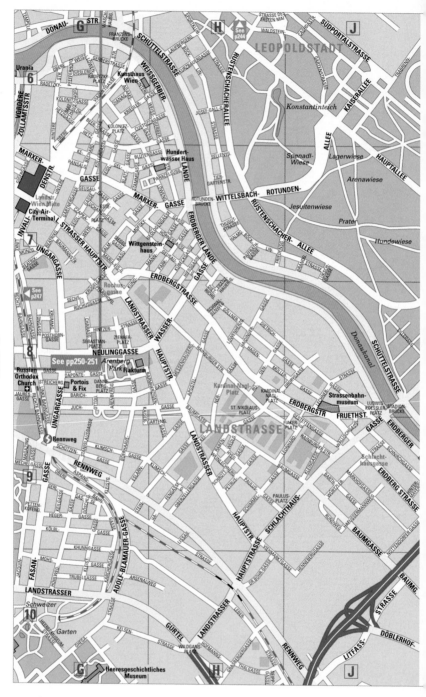

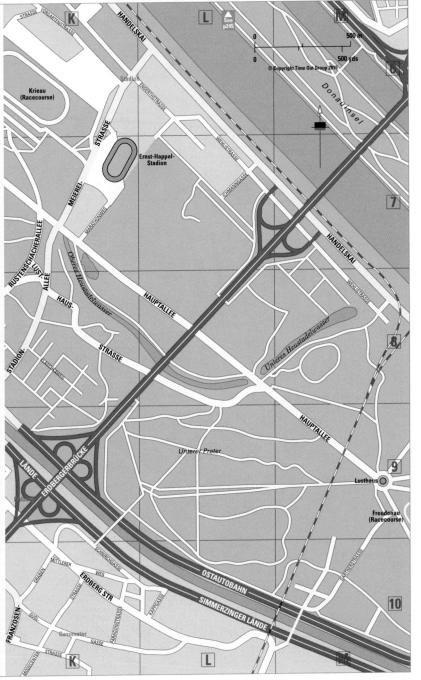

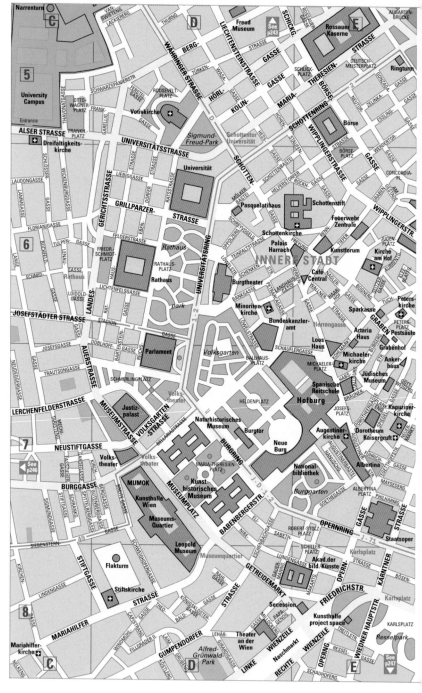

MAPS

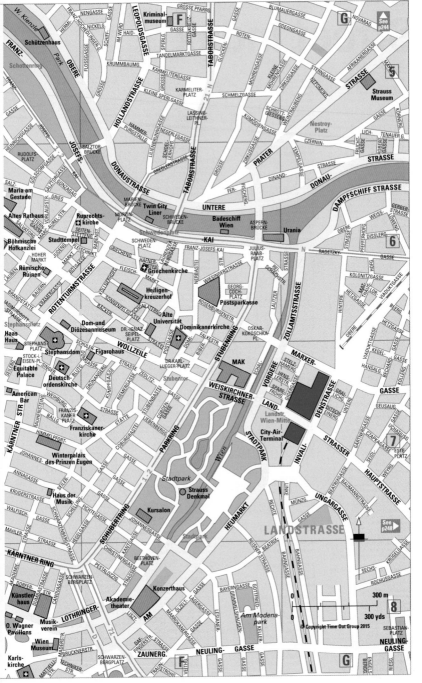

Street Index

STREET INDEX

SCHNELLVERBINDUNGEN IN WIEN

Die Stadt gehört Dir. WIENER LINIEN

MAPS